NEW SOVIET THINKING
AND U.S. NUCLEAR POLICY

NEW SOVIET
THINKING
AND
U.S. NUCLEAR
POLICY

David B. Myers

TEMPLE UNIVERSITY PRESS

PHILADELPHIA

Temple University Press, Philadelphia 19122
Copyright © 1990 by Temple University. All rights reserved
Published 1990
Printed in the United States of America

The paper used in this publication meets the minimum
requirements of American National Standard for Information
Sciences—Permanence of Paper for Printed Library Materials,
ANSI Z39.48−1984 ∞

Library of Congress Cataloging-in-Publication Data
Myers, David B., 1944–
    New Soviet thinking and U.S. nuclear policy / David B. Myers.
       p.   cm.
    Includes bibliographical references (p.
    ISBN 0-87722-710-1 (alk. paper)
    1. United States—Military policy. 2. United States—National
security. 3. Nuclear warfare. 4. Soviet Union—Defenses.
I. Title.
UA23.M95   1990
355'.033573—dc20   90-10863
                                                            CIP

For Aaron Myers and Elizabeth Myers

Contents

Acknowledgments   xi
Preface   xiii

Introduction
New Soviet Thinking and U.S. Nuclear Strategy   3
What the Soviets Declare   4
Assessing the New Doctrine   7

Chapter One
Nuclear Weapons Policy   9
The Fundamental Policy Question   9
The Components of a Nuclear Weapons Policy   12
Declaratory Versus Action Policy   15
The Undemocratic Origins of Nuclear Defense
   Policy   18
The Case for Leaving Nuclear Policy to Experts   21
The Case for Public Participation   22

Chapter Two
The Evaluation of Policy Proposals: Seven Tests   32
Instrumental Coherence   35
Moral Defensibility   37
Legal Defensibility   40

Feasibility   43
Affordability   45
Appropriateness vis-à-vis Soviet Policy   47
Disaster Avoidance   53
Summary and Conclusion   55

Chapter Three
**The Domestic Analogy: Criminal Correction
Theory and Defense Policy**   **57**
A Survey of Correction Theories   58
Application of Correction Theories to Nuclear
   Policy   62

Chapter Four
**Deterrence Policy: Security Through Mutual
Nuclear Threats**   **66**
The Requirements of Deterrence   67
Differences Between Domestic and Nuclear
   Deterrence   69
Types of Nuclear Deterrence   73
Guarding Against the Failure of Deterrence   98

Chapter Five
**Social Defense: Security Through Protection
of the Homeland**   **109**
Application of Social Defense to Nuclear Policy   110
Avoiding Destabilizing Ambiguity   113
A Unilateral Initiative and the Problem of
   Countermeasures   119
Implementation of Social Defense   122
The Problem of Fallibility   128
The ABM Treaty   130
Strategic Defense and NATO   135
The Case for a Social Defense Policy   137

Chapter Six
**Retribution Policy: Security Through Measured
Retaliation**   **140**
The Just War Tradition   141

The Rationale of Laws of War   144
Retribution as a Just War Objective   147
Culpability and Military Policy   148
Proportionality and Military Policy   161
Implications for Force Development   163
The Search for Precision Retaliatory Forces   168
Objections to a Retribution Policy   184
The Case for a Retribution Policy   188

Chapter Seven
**Rehabilitation Policy: Security Through
Nonviolent Prevention and Correction**   **191**
Globalizing the Concept of Rehabilitation   192
Three Levels of Rehabilitation   208
Rehabilitation Failure Compared with Military
    Failure   216
Implementation of Rehabilitation Policy   217
The Case for Rehabilitation   222

Chapter Eight
Hybrids   **225**
National Social Defense plus Rehabilitation   225
Existential Deterrence plus Unilateral Arms
    Reduction   227
Countervailing Strategy plus Limited Strategic
    Defense   228
Existential Deterrence plus Nonoffensive
    Retribution   229
The Exclusion of World Government   231

Conclusion   **233**

Appendix
Criticisms of the Major Policy Options   **239**
Critique of Deterrence Policies   239
Critique of National Social Defense Policy   244
Critique of Retribution Policy   247
Critique of Rehabilitation Policy   250

Glossary   253
Notes   265
Bibliography   283
Index   293

Acknowledgments

Most of the research and writing for this book was completed during a sabbatical granted by Moorhead State University in Minnesota. Earlier versions of some chapters appeared in various journals of applied philosophy, whose reviewers provided helpful criticisms. My revisions of the manuscript as a whole benefited from comments by outside reviewers for Temple University Press. On parts of the book concerned with military strategy and weapons, I received helpful criticisms and information from Lt. Col. Harvey J. Crawford, a military doctrine analyst for the Center for Aerospace Doctrine, Research, and Education at Air University, Maxwell Air Force Base, Alabama.

An earlier, much shorter draft of this book was used in classes on war and peace. I am indebted to students who indicated what they found most useful in my treatment of nuclear policy options.

I wish to thank Jane Cullen for her early enthusiasm, helpful suggestions, and general guidance throughout the revision of the manuscript. I am indebted to Jane Barry for her thorough copy-editing of the original manuscript.

I also want to thank Elizabeth Myers, my wife, for her moral support. Her encouragement made a significant difference in the completion of this project.

Preface

Given recent changes in the Soviet Union, one might be tempted to conclude that there is no longer any risk of a Soviet–American nuclear war. From all appearances, the United States no longer confronts the aggressor and empire-builder of old (at least as the USSR was perceived through Cold War lenses), but rather a nation preoccupied with overwhelming domestic problems: economic failure, ethnic violence, and secession-minded republics. The new Soviet Union no longer has any reason—if it ever did—to launch a nuclear attack against the West. Indeed, a plausible case could be made that the Soviet Union needs the West's assistance—managerial and technological know-how—in order to rebuild its shattered economy. On this view, although the Soviet Union may continue to possess a powerful nuclear arsenal, we no longer have reason to fear it.

The fact that the Soviet Union retains nuclear weapons does not by itself make it a threat to U.S. security. After all, Britain has nuclear weapons, but we do not perceive Britain as a threat. Given the announced changes in Soviet military strategy—away from offensively configured forces toward a posture of pure defense—and the actual reduction in Soviet (conventional and nuclear) forces, isn't it time to conclude that the Soviet Union's nuclear weapons are no more of a threat to U.S. security than those of Britain?

The answer to this question is *no*. There are four significant reasons for rejecting the comparison with Britain. First, regardless of changes in policy, Soviet nuclear weapons are targeted at the United States. Second, despite *our* professed peaceful intentions, the USSR cannot easily dismiss the fact that our weapons are aimed at the Soviet Union. Third, the two nuclear arsenals are so tightly coupled that, during a crisis, a false warning (of a nuclear attack) in one system could trigger preparations for retaliation that might in turn be construed by the other side as preparations for an attack—thus causing an inadvertent nuclear war. Can we rest assured that nothing will create new tensions in the future—tensions that could again make inadvertent nuclear conflict a real possibility? Although military conflict with the Soviet Union *now* seems unlikely, things may look very different in the future. This is the fourth point: given the instability of economic and political conditions in the Soviet Union, the recent changes in military policy could be reversed. Under a hard-line leadership, the Soviet Union would (even after a substantial arms-reduction agreement) still have enormous means to threaten U.S. security and to achieve aggressive objectives. Therefore, what we now require is a defense policy appropriate both to new Soviet military thinking and to unstable conditions.

But what policy? I explore competing options—including nuclear and nonnuclear strategies—for dealing with what will remain a fact of life for some time to come: a relatively unstable and thus unpredictable Soviet Union that is armed with devastating nuclear forces.

In the following pages I sketch the conceptual revolution that has occurred in Soviet foreign policy and military doctrine, lay out the components that must be ingredients of any policy response to the Soviets, provide criteria for critically evaluating the competing policy options, explain the case for four distinct policy options, and formulate hybrids of the options.

A guiding analogy in this book is the comparison between defense policy and criminal correction theory. I show that our strategic options roughly correspond to domestic-level methods for dealing with criminal threats to society: namely, deterrence, social defense, retribution, and rehabilitation. The application of this analogy does not presuppose the criminality of the Soviet Union. A criminal correction policy does not assume the criminality of any particular citizen, but rather seeks to achieve domestic security in the face of all possible criminal misconduct. The analogy is designed to illuminate the range of policy choices we have in responding to a nation that has announced a new, nonaggressive military posture while retaining a capacity to destroy the United States.

The defense-policy question central to this book is, How do we deal with the prospect that a well-armed Soviet state might one day be tempted to use its forces in an aggressive way? For example, what if a future Soviet regime decided to use its military power to reclaim part of Eastern Europe? What would the United States do if confronted with a newly aggressive and still nuclear-armed Soviet state? The point is that we cannot (to borrow the language of correction theory) rule out recidivism and must be prepared for it.

Although it may not now be rational to fear that the Soviets are planning a disarming nuclear attack against the United States, we cannot dismiss the fear that the Soviets might in the future threaten our security with their nuclear forces. The basis of the fear is—to repeat a central concern—*instability* in the Soviet Union. Extreme conservatives in this country warn that the Soviets are moving into a precarious and dangerous future in which a resort to nuclear coercion or nuclear attack by a desperate Soviet leadership cannot be foreclosed. Although we may judge this unlikely, prudence in defense policy nevertheless requires us to be cautious and to plan for all contingencies. A prudent defense policy for the next decade and beyond does not require, at this writing, that we treat the Soviet Union as an adversary, but simply the recognition that a potential for armed conflict remains.

We are entering a multipolar world in which there will probably be more serious threats than that posed by the Soviet Union. There are defense strategists, for example, who see German unification as a greater threat to the security of Western and Eastern Europe—and thus indirectly to the security of the United States. Others believe that the development by nations in the Middle East of long-range missiles capable of delivering chemical or nuclear warheads now constitutes the greatest threat to international security. Still other strategists would argue that the invasion of drugs threatens to tear American society apart—undermining U.S. security much more seriously than whatever remains of the Soviet threat. We could easily add to this list of new threats to national security.

The focus of this study is, however, the Soviet Union and U.S. nuclear strategy. It is intended to be a contribution to the search for a defense policy that will enable the United States to achieve security in a manner that takes cognizance of two facts: (1) the Soviet announcement that its military policy is now purely defensive, and (2) the existence of Soviet nuclear weapons designed to destroy the United States. These two facts do not necessarily constitute a contradiction in Soviet military strategy. The second fact can be taken as consistent with a purely defensive posture: it can be seen as a response to U.S. nuclear forces. It must be remembered that we threatened the Soviet Union with nuclear arms before they threatened us with such forces.

How should we respond to the second fact? Should we continue to conduct policy on the premise that the Soviet Union might launch a surprise nuclear attack, or is this a relic of Cold War thinking? Should the United States continue with some form of nuclear deterrence—the long-standing and still-operative policy of achieving security through a capacity for nuclear retaliation? Even if we decide that this remains the most rational policy, there is still the question of whether we need thousands of nuclear weapons to achieve deterrence. Should we retain a nuclear deterrence strategy while working toward a stable, mutual reduction in numbers? According to some strategists, a few hundred invulnerable weapons on both sides would be sufficient for the purpose of deterrence.

Or should we—on the premise that the second fact is a product of a U.S.-initiated nuclear threat—eliminate our nuclear weapons, unilaterally if need be? Is it now desirable—in light of changes in the Soviet Union—to abandon the strategy of nuclear deterrence altogether, to get rid of our nuclear weapons and start afresh? If the Soviets aim nuclear weapons at us only because we aim nuclear weapons at them, then perhaps we should not only cease aiming our forces at them, but—in order to eliminate all ambiguity and suspicion—abolish these forces altogether. Is it possible to achieve security without retaining a capacity for nuclear retaliation? There are, as the reader will see, strategists who argue that we can satisfy security needs in the face of all threats without nuclear weapons.

If we decide on nuclear abolition, should we substitute less powerful nonnuclear forces—perhaps high-tech, accurate conventional weapons—for nuclear arms? Would some form of strategic defense provide the best security for a nuclear-free United States? Or should we conclude that war is now obsolete and adopt a defense policy that is strictly nonviolent? These are the questions that an adequate nuclear defense policy must answer. In this book I explore competing policy proposals that are distinguished by the very different answers they provide to these questions.

This study combines philosophical and strategic concerns. It attempts to bridge the worlds of philosophy and strategy by engaging in an empirically informed conceptual analysis of strategic policy options. If philosophical analysis of nuclear strategy is to be useful, it must deal with the historical background of nuclear policymaking, the concrete dilemmas that plague different strategic options, and the practical problems connected with implementation of policy proposals. If strategic analysis is not to be narrowly pragmatic, it must take into consideration moral questions and moral criteria.

I attempt to show why the making of nuclear strategy is a value-charged enterprise that should not be left to a priesthood of strategists. I also try to show how ethical thinking and strategic options logically fit together. Each policy option I discuss is shown to be grounded in a specific ethical perspective.

On the other hand, I make it clear that morality alone cannot be the basis of policymaking—that such practical criteria as feasibility and affordability must be considered, in order to avoid utopian thinking. In fact, I formulate six nonethical criteria that should be weighed along with ethical considerations in choosing a defense policy.

Thus, this study is interdisciplinary, as any work in normative policy analysis must be. Philosophy serves a useful function when it clarifies policy choices, elucidates their different moral foundations, explains their justification, and formulates substantial criticisms of each. That is what I have attempted to do in this work of applied philosophy.

April 1990

NEW SOVIET THINKING
AND U.S. NUCLEAR POLICY

New Soviet Thinking and U.S. Nuclear Strategy

Is Stalinism in the Soviet Union really dead, as George Kennan has argued?[1] Has Soviet foreign policy irreversibly, and not just temporarily, changed? To what extent is a less threatening Soviet military strategy contingent upon domestic economic success? According to Kennan, regardless of internal failures or instability in the Soviet Union, the Cold War is over and we must no longer regard the USSR as our primary enemy. The following is Kennan's view of political reality:

> It appears to me that whatever reasons there may have been for regarding the Soviet Union primarily as a possible, if not probable opponent, the time for that sort of thing is clearly passed. That country should now be regarded essentially as another great power, like other great powers—one, that is, whose aspirations and policies are conditioned outstandingly by its own geographic situation, history and tradition, and are therefore not identical with our own but are also not so seriously in conflict with ours as to justify any assumption that the outstanding differences could not be adjusted by the normal means of compromise and accommodation.[2]

This is an important statement because it comes from the architect of the policy of containment. "For four decades," observes Graham Allison, a specialist on foreign policy, "the cardinal rule in our policy of containment has been to oppose virtually whatever the Soviet Union was for."[3] In a period of significant change, Allison warns, "such a rule falls into the trap Nietzsche noted when observing that the most common form of human stupidity is forgetting what one is trying to do."[4]

What has the United States been trying to do? A simple answer is the one given by Allison: "to preserve the United States as a free nation with its fundamental institutions and values intact."[5] The assumption has been that Soviet nuclear weapons, as well as Soviet conventional forces, threaten our security. This has led to a policy based not merely on the threat of nuclear retaliation, but on a threat to use nuclear weapons first—should, for example, Soviet-led conventional forces ever overrun NATO conventional forces in Western Europe. Our assumption has been that the USSR is an aggressive, expansionist power, and that Soviet forces are capable of, and designed for, offensive warfare against the West.

In the face of the announcement of a new Soviet military doctrine—one described as purely defensive, nonaggressive, and sufficient only for the purpose of retaliation against aggression—it is appropriate that we begin to rethink our defense policy vis-à-vis the Soviet Union. This study is a contribution to a reassessment of one part of that policy—its nuclear dimension. Our nuclear weapons policy has been grounded in the assumption that the Soviet Union might, if it did not have to worry about unacceptable nuclear retaliation or nuclear counterthreats, use its nuclear weapons either to attack or to coerce the West in order to achieve world domination.

It is now reasonable to ask whether there is still a Soviet nuclear threat. If we take seriously what is called the "new political thinking" in the Soviet Union, the answer is, of course, no. There is, however, another important question: To what extent should U.S. nuclear policy be contingent upon the pronouncements of those who happen to be in power in the Soviet Union? It would not be defensible either to ignore Soviet declarations of intention or to take these revolutionary pronouncements at face value. Instead, they should be examined carefully and critically with the aim of ascertaining to what degree word is matched by deed. An understanding of the so-called new Soviet thinking on foreign policy in general and nuclear policy in particular should provide an important opportunity to begin a reassessment of both the Soviet nuclear threat and U.S. nuclear strategy.

What the Soviets Declare

On the face of it, a conceptual revolution is occurring in the Soviet Union. There is clearly a revolution in *thinking*. Although thinking alone is not enough, it must be recognized that before there can be a behavioral revolution, there must first be a conceptual one.[6]

The conceptual revolution appears—to borrow from the analysis of a specialist on Soviet foreign policy, Robert Legvold—on three different but critically linked levels: basic foreign policy concepts, security concepts, and fundamental ideological assumptions.[7]

Basic Foreign Policy Concepts. The first level of change involves key notions by which Soviet leaders make sense of the opportunities and problems posed to them by the outside world.[8]

The concept of national security vis-à-vis the United States, for example, has been altered in two ways: (1) military power is declared to be insufficient for the achievement of national security, and (2) national security is now linked to common or mutual security. We are told that "the character of contemporary weapons leaves no country with any hope of safeguarding itself solely with military and technical means."[9] Connected with this is the announcement that Soviet security is dependent on the security of the United States: to the extent that the Soviet Union threatens U.S. security, it threatens its own. In a nuclear age, the Soviets now assert, security is necessarily a mutual problem. Indeed, on this view, the military forces of one nation must not even *appear* to threaten other nations. This means that political solutions, rather than military ones, must come to the forefront of policy in conflicts with the United States.[10] In practical terms this requires that concessions be made—for example, the kind of asymmetrical cuts in nuclear forces the Soviet Union made under the Intermediate Nuclear Forces (INF) Treaty, which required them to destroy several missiles for every one destroyed by the United States.

A second novel foreign policy concept is, on the face of it, Marxist heresy: namely, that the struggle between classes as a central imperative must give way to concern for the common plight of humankind.[11] The Soviets remind us that this is a world whose history can end with the turn of a nuclear key. According to the new thinking, peaceful coexistence is not merely a subtle form of class struggle: the point is that proletarian class interests and the class struggle are to be subordinated to universal human interests. In place of the conflict between capitalism and communism, there must be cooperation in defense of universal values. More specifically, the ultimate human value of peace must take priority over all the others to which different nations are attached.[12] In sum, the new thinking declares that "humankind interest" transcends class interest because commitment to the former is the only way to save the human species from destruction.[13]

The third new foreign policy concept is that third world conflict is no longer to be viewed as primarily an opportunity for militantly supporting liberation movements. Rather, such conflict is seen as a drain on the resources of developing countries and a catalyst to international tensions, making it imperative to set limits on superpower intervention in regional conflicts.[14]

Finally, according to Legvold, "the concepts by which Soviet leaders order their relations within the world of socialism—with Eastern Europe, China, and nonruling communist parties—are no less in flux."[15] Legvold wrote this prior to the upheavals in Eastern Europe. Soviet nonintervention in changes occurring in Poland, Hungary, East Germany, Czechoslovakia, Bulgaria, and Romania appears to confirm Legvold's claim that there is a revolution in foreign policy. This laissez-faire policy seems to mark the end of the Brezhnev Doctrine, which held that Moscow had the right to "save" socialist regimes in Eastern Europe and beyond.[16]

Security Concepts. In the area of military strategy, at least three new concepts have been introduced. First there is the concept of war prevention. Authoritative political and military sources now unambiguously state that preventing war is the fundamental goal of Soviet military doctrine.[17] Makhmut Gareyev, deputy chief of the General Staff of the Armed Forces of the Soviet Union, states:

> Previously military doctrine was defined as a system of views on the preparation for and conduct of war. Now military doctrine concentrates on the prevention of war. The task of precluding war has become the supreme goal of military doctrine, the main function of the state and its armed forces.[18]

A second new strategic policy concept is that of reasonable sufficiency, which Mikhail Gorbachev introduced at the Twenty-seventh Party Congress in 1986. By this, Gorbachev and other military commentators seemed to suggest that the Soviet Union will try to achieve nuclear security without imitating every new U.S. weapons program. The Soviets claim to seek only a retaliatory force capable of ensuring some essential but minimal level of deterrence. On this view, the nuclear capability of the Soviet Union must be sufficient to absorb the worst possible attack and be able to retaliate—while at the same time not so great as to threaten the security of other nations.[19] Reasonable sufficiency regards previous nuclear force requirements as based upon an exaggerated estimate of the likelihood of attack by the West and the possibility of victory in nuclear war.

A third (and related) new security concept is defensive defense—the notion that in the sphere of theater warfare (e.g., war fought in the theater of Europe), neither side should be able to launch a successful offensive attack. The Soviets assert that although their military doctrine has always been defensive, Soviet forces were configured and deployed to carry out a decidedly offensive strategy. That is, on their account, it was previously believed that the best way to defend Soviet territory was to be able to carry any conflict onto the territory of the attacker. Defensive (or nonprovocative) defense represents a departure from this doctrine, suggesting a theater capability sufficient to repel an attack, but incapable of conducting a surprise attack with massive offensive operations against the territory of the other side.[20] If taken seriously, this means that NATO does not need a policy of first use of nuclear weapons, in so far as that policy is premised on the assumption that the Soviet Union has forces capable of suddenly overwhelming Western Europe.

Fundamental Ideological Assumptions. Some basic assumptions previously thought to be fundamental to Marxism–Leninism have been called into question. First, it is no longer assumed that militarism is essential to capitalism. Capitalism, on the new view, has reached a stage that permits it to pursue its goals without resort to war. This makes peaceful coexistence possible.[21]

Second, armed struggle is no longer viewed as a necessary instrument of communism. Previously, war was viewed positively, since it was the path to liberation. Now, in Mikhail Gorbachev's words, "the use or threat of force no longer can or must be an instrument of foreign policy."[22] No war, especially nuclear war, can be considered a continuation of politics by other means. Violence, once thought central to Marxism–Leninism, is now declared to be counterproductive and, in a nuclear world, possibly self-destructive.

Assessing the New Doctrine

In evaluating Soviet pronouncements one must always keep in mind the distinction between word and deed. Those who are reluctant to reduce the U.S. nuclear arsenal or to change U.S. nuclear strategy on the basis of the "new political thinking" in the Soviet Union point out that there have been announced changes before, with no real effect on Soviet forces. Leon Gouré, a specialist on Soviet strategy, warns:

> Whether Gorbachev's enthusiasm for change will also give rise to a really new and different military doctrine and strategy remains to be seen. In this connection, it is worth recalling that the Soviet military resisted, and to a significant degree circumvented, Khrushchev's defense policies and strategic concepts in the late 1950's and early 1960's. It is not inconceivable that the same may happen to truly new Gorbachev defense policies and force structure concepts, with the military aligning themselves with the large array of opponents of Gorbachev and his *perestroyka*.[23]

The most cynical view of Soviet pronouncements is that they are a ruse designed to get the West to disarm while the Soviets remain militarily powerful. H. Joachim Maitre, in an editorial in the journal

Strategic Review, warns: "Strategic deception remains a hallowed tenet of Soviet strategy."[24] David J. Trachtenberg, senior analyst for the Committee on the Present Danger, holds that we should see developments in Soviet foreign policy as a mere tactical shift designed to dispel the adversarial image of the Soviet Union rather than as signaling real changes in strategy or goals. On the question of whether new thinking is something genuine or a ruse, Trachtenberg asserts that history places the burden of proof on those who contend the former.[25]

Even if one takes Soviet declarations seriously, there will be a significant lag between the proclamation of the new doctrine and its implementation, a period in which the Soviets will remain a significant threat to the West. Jacques Chirac, former prime minister of France, comments:

> Does the Soviet Union still constitute a threat to the West? Just as the Soviet Union will not become a democracy overnight in the true sense of that word, so it is not likely to cease being a highly militarized nation for a long time to come—even if we were to assume that the Gorbachev regime desired such a demilitarization.[26]

Regardless of Soviet declarations, the fact remains that the Soviet Union will, for some time to come, have an enormous nuclear arsenal. This arsenal constitutes a threat because thousands of Soviet nuclear weapons are aimed at the United States and its allies. The Soviet Union retains the nuclear capacity to destroy the West in a matter of minutes. A single Soviet missile can deliver a warhead whose explosive power surpasses that of the 2.2 million tons of bombs dropped on Germany in World War II. To be adequate, a nuclear weapons policy must take into consideration the enormous destructive capability of the Soviet Union as well as its peaceful declarations.

In the course of this study, it will become clear that the choice of a nuclear arms policy will turn in part on how seriously one takes Soviet declarations of intention. Obviously, in rethinking U.S. nuclear weapons policy, so-called new Soviet thinking will have to be considered. First, however, it is important to understand the components of a nuclear weapons policy, how such policy has been made in the United States, and the case for public participation in its formation. That is the task of the next chapter.

CHAPTER ONE

Nuclear Weapons Policy

Decisions about nuclear strategy have largely escaped public scrutiny. The language of the debate is so technical that most citizens are relegated to the role of outsiders who must view the arguments between different schools of nuclear strategy as something forever beyond ordinary understanding. The objective of this study is to make the issues and options of the nuclear weapons policy debate more accessible to interested citizens.

In this chapter I make a case for greater public participation in the making of nuclear weapons policy. In the course of doing this, I consider and rebut the case for leaving this area of policymaking to government officials with specialized knowledge. I also sketch the range of options from which citizens can choose in trying to decide on the best policy. These options are systematically developed in subsequent chapters.

First, however, by way of background, I explain the nature of nuclear weapons policy, give a brief history of it, and say something about current U.S. nuclear policy.

The Fundamental Policy Question

It is important to repeat a point made in the Introduction: no matter how ready one is to believe that the Soviets have changed their thinking about nuclear war and nuclear weapons, the fact remains that the Soviet Union has an enormous nuclear arsenal targeted at the West. The fundamental policy question is this: What should the United States do in the face of thousands of Soviet nuclear weapons aimed at America and its allies? To answer this question is to develop a *nuclear defense policy*—that is, a systematic plan for dealing with the Soviet nuclear threat. A nuclear defense policy, which can also be referred to as a *nuclear weapons policy*, does not necessarily require nuclear weapons, because policymakers might decide that the best counter to the Soviet nuclear threat is a nonnuclear defense strategy. The policy proposals I explore include nuclear and nonnuclear responses to the threat posed by the Soviet nuclear arsenal. Here are the fundamental questions a nuclear weapons policy must address:

- Should the United States retain nuclear weapons? If so, we should ask:
- What kinds of nuclear forces should the nation possess?
- What plans, if any, should the United States formulate for using nuclear weapons?

If it is decided that the United States should not retain nuclear weapons, then we must ask:

- What alternative forces, if any, should we have?
- Is there a nonmilitary way to defend the nation?

This study deals exclusively with the *Soviet nuclear threat*. There are, of course, other Soviet threats to Western security: chemical weapons, biological weapons, conventional forces, low-intensity warfare, and disinformation. This book touches on nonnuclear Soviet threats only to the extent that they are relevant to choosing a nuclear defense policy.

There are, in addition, *non-Soviet nuclear threats*. Examples include the existence of "minor" nuclear states, such as China, whose foreign policy objectives are at least potentially at odds with U.S. security interests; the problem of the spread of nuclear weapons or weapons production facilities to more and more countries, including friendly countries, such as Israel, whose use of nuclear weapons in a regional conflict could draw the United States into a conflict with the USSR; and the prospect of nuclear terrorism—the possibility of a Qaddafy-type leader using atomic devices for blackmail. This study does not address these other nuclear threats but concentrates on what, after all, is the biggest and most destructive nuclear threat we still face: the one that the Soviet nuclear arsenal poses for our security and that of our allies.

The nature of the Soviet nuclear threat is a matter of controversy. The very concept of a *nuclear threat* is ambiguous. It can refer to the potential destructiveness of Soviet nuclear forces, apart from Soviet intentions. Or it can refer to the real danger that the Soviet Union might deliberately launch a first strike against the United States. Whether or not one believes it is likely that the Soviets would intentionally, and without provocation, use their nuclear forces against us, there remains the possibility of inadvertent nuclear war. The fact is that each super-power relies on sophisticated detection and tracking systems to provide information at a rate that adds significantly to the pressure on the fallible humans who must interpret it. Everyone now knows that false alarms have occurred in the U.S. warning system. In a world in which Soviet and U.S. nuclear forces are kept at a high state of readiness, a false alarm in the Soviet warning system could one day accidentally trigger a Soviet nuclear attack. Whether or not a false alarm will lead to nuclear war depends on whether there is a launch-on-warning arrangement: that is, whether the retaliatory policy calls for launching missiles as soon as there is a warning of a nuclear attack. It is not known whether the United States or the Soviet Union has adopted a launch-on-warning strategy.[1]

In the course of this study, I provide an exposition of four compet-ing nuclear weapons policies—four plans for achieving security in the face of Soviet nuclear weapons. To clarify these options, I show how they are analogous to four criminal correction theories: deterrence, social defense, retribution, and rehabilitation.

The first two policy options have been thoroughly debated by the defense establishment and have been widely discussed in the popular media: the policy of *nuclear deterrence* (in its major variations) and the *strategic defense initiative* (SDI), or "Star Wars," as it is popularly called. Nuclear deterrence policy, it will be seen, embraces a variety of compet-ing strategies that have one thing in common: the aim of inhibiting Soviet nuclear aggression by threatening to retaliate with nuclear weap-ons. Although SDI has also been given different twists—including ones that incorporate it into a nuclear deterrence framework—I focus on the version whose objective is to replace security based upon a threat of nuclear destruction with security based upon assured protection from nuclear destruction.

The other two nuclear weapons policy options that I explore are less familiar and have been largely ignored by the defense establish-ment and the media: *just war defense* (retribution) and *nonmilitary defense* (rehabilitation). The former seeks to achieve nuclear security through the construction of weapon systems capable of responding to nuclear aggression in a manner that punishes only the combatants of the ag-gressor nation: it repudiates, in the name of retributive justice, all weapons of mass destruction. The even more exotic fourth nuclear defense proposal calls for a transformation of the political–economic conditions that breed armed conflict and demands the organized use of nonviolent methods to correct aggressive behavior. Mixtures of the four proposals are also explored.

The Components of a Nuclear Weapons Policy

Whatever its particular thrust, every nuclear weapons policy consists of at least three components: a primary objective, a strategy, and a force system.

Primary Objective. The fundamental objective of U.S. policy is to ensure the security of the nation against the Soviet nuclear threat. More specifically, the fundamental objective is to make our free institutions secure against this Soviet threat. This objective is grounded in a moral–political principle—namely, the government's moral obligation to preserve the institutions that embody the nation's basic political values. In the American case, these institutions include a complicated system that provides for both majority rule (as manifested in the popular election of government office holders) and the protection of individual rights (including guarantees of freedom of expression, assembly, religion, due process, and so on, as embodied in state and federal constitutions and sustained by the judiciary). Thus, the freedom that defense policy is supposed to protect is complex in the sense that it embraces both democratic and individual freedoms.

Democratic freedom refers to the right of the people to make the kind of laws and policies they choose without foreign interference. The only limit placed on this democratic power of the people is an internal one—namely, the constitutional protection of minority rights against majority tyranny, which guards *individual freedom* by guaranteeing equal rights to all citizens. Of course, individual freedom is not absolute: for example, there are "clear and present danger" qualifications of free speech; individual freedom must not be so great that it threatens to destroy or significantly harm society. The aim is to achieve a reasonable balance between the two domains of liberty: the freedom of the majority to make law and policy and the freedom of individuals to pursue their own happiness in their own way. Thus, when I speak of freedom or free institutions, I will be referring to the complicated and delicate balance that characterizes American society.

It may now seem unjustifiably Cold Warish to consider the Soviet Union's nuclear forces as still a threat to U.S. free institutions, as if the Soviets were bent upon achieving a nuclear victory over the United States. Yet, to restate a point that is becoming a refrain, no matter how one reads Soviet *intentions*, the fact that they have the nuclear *capacity* to destroy the United States gives Soviet leaders the potential to coerce and intimidate it. The important policy question is this: What do we need to dissuade the Soviet Union from *ever* using its nuclear weapons to attack or to coerce the United States? Can we, for example, prevent a nuclear attack or nuclear coercion without having nuclear weapons of our own? If the answer is yes, then we still need to explain how we could abolish nuclear weapons and satisfy the fundamental objective of defense policy.

It is important to keep in mind this fundamental objective—that is, the defense of democracy and individual rights—when considering the goal of avoiding nuclear war. A nuclear *defense* policy, in the sense in which I am using the term, is not the same as a nuclear *war-prevention* policy. It is conceivable that a policy could ensure the avoidance of nuclear war and still not qualify as a nuclear defense policy. Such a policy might, for instance, involve the abandonment of the defense of free institutions. The United States could, after all, easily prevent a nuclear conflict with the USSR simply by disarming and permitting the USSR to do whatever it desires in the world. That would surely appease the most aggressive Soviet leaders and prevent them from ever attacking us. Therefore, it must be kept in mind that the objective of U.S. defense policy is not only the prevention of nuclear attack but the preservation of free institutions as well.

Of course, there are those who argue that anything is preferable to nuclear war: that, to recall an old phrase, it is better to be red than dead. Now, with the emergence of *glasnost* (openness in terms of information and debate) and *perestroika* (restructuring of the economy), redness may look less objectionable. Still, the Soviet system remains a long way from achieving the kind of freedoms the United States has established.

Those who assert that living under any system is preferable to nuclear war are expressing a willingness to trade freedom for nuclear security: they are not uttering anything that might be developed into a nuclear *defense* policy. As Chapter Seven shows, one can be opposed to the possession of nuclear weapons and to the use of armed force—even in national self-defense—without adopting an appeasement response. A nuclear policy must seek to avert nuclear war in a manner consistent with the preservation of democracy and individual rights. That is, from the standpoint of the fundamental objective, the avoidance of a nuclear war is not an absolute good to which all else must be subordinated: in fact, we may have to risk nuclear destruction in order to preserve something more important than mere survival. In short, the fundamental objective of a nuclear defense policy is—or should be—to prevent a nuclear holocaust while defending freedom.

Beyond the aim of defending freedom in the United States, the requirements of nuclear defense policy become less clear and highly debatable. Should we defend Western Europe? Membership in NATO would seem to require this. Does American freedom require the defense of Western Europe? Even if it does not, do we nevertheless have a moral obligation to ensure its security? Do we now have a moral obligation to defend embryonic East European democracies in the event that new Soviet leaders would try to reclaim these societies? We also are currently committed to ensuring the security of Japan. What about South Korea? Is its security really crucial to our own? Does it matter if a nation whose security we guarantee has free institutions? Is the flow of oil in the Persian Gulf a vital interest of the United States and worth the risk of nuclear war?

The business of determining what constitutes a vital interest is a difficult one. Although the preservation of free institutions in the United States is a fundamental objective of the four defense policies explored in this study, defenders of the competing proposals may disagree about whether U.S. defense responsibilities should extend beyond the homeland.

Strategy. In the broadest sense, strategy refers to the art of distributing and applying (military or nonmilitary) power for the purpose of realizing the fundamental policy objective. Once we have formulated such an objective, we must figure out what organization and distribution of forces and resources will enable us to realize it. Military power may be only one element of strategy understood in this broad sense. For example, we might make use of diplomacy, economic incentives/pressure, and other nonmilitary means. Moreover, defense strategy, in the sense in which I am using the term, is not synonymous with the organization of forces for the purpose of destruction. Intelligent strategy—even when it embraces military power—calls for destructive acts only when there is no better way to achieve the policy objective. In sum, those who design strategy must always keep in mind the political end or ends it is supposed to realize, so that the strategy can be clearly seen as a rational instrument for the realization of the policy objective.

Forces. These are the physical means used to implement the strategy. After deciding on a strategy, the final step in policy formation is to determine what kind of forces the proposed strategy calls for: offensive, defensive, or some combination of both? Are the forces that the strategy requires already in existence, simply waiting for the proper organization, or do we need to design and produce them? These are some of the questions we must answer in developing an appropriate system of forces. As I am using the term, *forces* can refer to something as sophisticated and impersonal as laser beam weapons (used to incapacitate missiles in flight) or to something as simple and personal as unarmed human beings joining together in an act of organized resistance (the "power" of nonviolence). The function of forces, whether military or nonmilitary, is to permit an efficient realization of the strategy.

If defense policy were decided in a fully rational fashion, policymakers would begin with the formulation of a fundamental objective and then proceed to implement it through the development of an appropriate strategy and system of forces. This, historically, has not always been the actual sequence of policy development. Before describing the development of nuclear policy in the United States, it will be useful to discuss the ambiguity of the term *policy* as it is used in the defense community.

Declaratory Versus Action Policy

It can now be said, by way of summary, that competing nuclear weapons policies are in effect different answers to a single question: In responding to the Soviet nuclear threat, what fundamental objective, strategy, and force system should the United States adopt? In practice, U.S. policymakers appear at times to have divided this question into two distinct problems:

1. How should the United States publicly say that it will respond to a nuclear attack?
2. How should the United States actually plan to respond to a nuclear crisis or a nuclear attack?

These are obviously very different questions. Answers to them have at times produced conflicting policies within the same administration: one for public consumption and one to guide actual military operations. To answer the first question is to formulate a public policy statement that will meet with popular approval while effectively dissuading the Soviets from using their nuclear weapons. The second is concerned with working out an effective military strategy, a rational response in case deterrence fails.

The president's (or secretary of defense's) public articulation of American nuclear policy has not in fact always coincided with what the United States really planned to do in the event of a Soviet nuclear attack. Whether or not it reflects actual policy, a public declaration is crafted to fulfill three functions: (1) give Americans a sense of national security in the face of Soviet nuclear weapons; (2) reassure allies that this policy enhanced their security against the Soviet nuclear threat; and (3) dissuade the Soviets from using nuclear or conventional forces against either the United States or its allies.

The second question, by contrast, asks for a plan (or set of options) for action that will enable the United States to deal effectively with a nuclear crisis or nuclear attack. To protect national security as well as avoid public opposition, this plan of action has at times been kept secret, "secured" as an in-house document meant only for a few eyes. During the Kennedy administration, for example, mutual assured destruction (MAD, a strategy calling for indiscriminate, all-out retaliation against Soviet urban–industrial centers) was the announced U.S. policy. It is now known that the actual war plan called for giving primacy to attacks on Soviet nuclear and other military forces, with the aim of limiting the war and ending it before it was necessary to execute the part calling for attacks on cities.[2]

Thus, over the years, American policymakers may have been "guilty" of policy duplicity—of formulating two responses to the Soviet nuclear threat: a policy statement meant for public consumption and a covertly decided policy designed for practical military needs. Different answers to the first and the second questions constitute the distinction between *declaratory* and *action* policies. Paul Nitze, a man who for decades has been deeply involved in the making of nuclear defense policy, explains the difference in this way:

> The word "policy" is used in two related but different senses. In one sense, the action sense, it refers to the general guide lines which we believe should and will in fact govern our actions in various contingencies. In the other sense, the declaratory sense, it refers to policy statements which have as their aim political and psychological effects.[3]

As long as nuclear policy is under the control of a policy elite, a conflict between declaratory and action policy remains a real possibility, because the policy the administration articulates for the nation and the world may not coincide with its actual plan for responding to a nuclear crisis or attack. Policy duplicity will cease only if the declared policy is enforced—that is, only if there is a mechanism that ensures a correspondence between action policy and declaratory policy.

Even if we, in the name of democracy, repudiate the practice of policy duplicity, it is useful to recognize that such duplicity reflects two objectives of defense policy that may be in perpetual tension: (1) the goal of making the public statement that will work best in peacetime (in a climate of zero tension) to keep the peace, and (2) the goal of having a plan of action suitable for a crisis situation or for the response after an attack. The temptation to engage in policy duplicity may stem from the difficulty of harmonizing two aims of nuclear defense strategy: to prevent a nuclear attack and to prevent total destruction if preventive measures fail.

A particular strategy may satisfy one requirement and not the other. A strategy designed to deter nuclear war by making it maximally destructive may prove disastrous if—despite the odds—deterrence fails. On the other hand, a strategy that promises to limit damage in the event of a nuclear attack may prove to be profoundly destabilizing as a peacetime declaratory policy.

For example, advocates of mutual assured destruction seem to place absolute confidence in the preventive dimension of nuclear policy: that is, MAD is designed for the sole purpose of deterring nuclear war. It stakes everything on the objective of deterrence. Hence, defenders of MAD must concede that if their strategy fails, it would be disastrous for civilization. They believe, however, that the risk of having to act on the MAD threat is small enough, and its deterrent value is great enough, to justify adopting a strategy that involves no plan for terminating nuclear war and limiting nuclear destruction. MAD is an example of a policy that may be valuable as a declaratory doctrine but disastrous as an action policy. Lynn Davis, former director of the International Institute for Strategic Studies, points out: "The best way to deter a war may be very different from the best way to fight and stop it."[4]

By contrast, a nuclear strategy that would be very effective as an action policy could be destabilizing as a declaratory policy. For instance, a plan to fight a limited nuclear war (limited, that is, to attacks on the other side's nuclear forces) and quickly terminate the hostilities might substantially limit destruction to both sides if deterrence fails: that is, if nuclear war occurs, such a strategy would certainly be more useful than a strategy of all-out retaliation. But an announced policy of deterrence based upon a limited nuclear war–fighting strategy (including a force system capable of destroying the bulk of the Soviet nuclear arsenal) could be misinterpreted by the Soviet Union as a first-strike, war-winning plan. A public declaration that the United States is prepared, in the event of an attack, to fight a nuclear war could be destabilizing if it provokes distrustful Soviet leaders into an offensive posture—that is, if it disposes the Soviets, in a crisis, to launch a preemptive strike because they fear that we plan to launch a disarming first strike.

The point is that it may not be possible to find a policy that adequately fulfills both the preventive function (dissuading the Soviets from using their weapons) and the damage-limitation function (terminating aggression on favorable terms and with minimal damage to our side). Efforts to limit the damage of a Soviet–American war tend to make nuclear war more thinkable. Attempts to create an effective deterrent appear to make the failure of deterrence cataclysmic by leaving neither side with an effective way to limit damage in the event that one side attacks the other. Although the ideal solution is a policy that satisfies both objectives, this may be too much to hope for. In choosing a policy one may, unfortunately, have to decide which function should receive the most weight.

The Undemocratic Origins of Nuclear Defense Policy

As I pointed out above, U.S. nuclear policymakers have sometimes been guilty of policy concealment—of keeping actual plans for the use of nuclear weapons from the public. While, avowedly, U.S. nuclear strategy has been developed to defend American democracy, the irony is that in practice this strategy, in all its vicissitudes, has not been subject to democratic checks: by and large, strategic nuclear policy has not been a product of public debate and majority approval. One of the paradoxes is that U.S. nuclear deterrence strategy—a strategy allegedly created for the purpose of preserving open debate and democratic decision making in the face of the Soviet threat—is the result of a generally secretive and nondemocratic process. Michael Walzer observes:

> The policy of deterrence has been worked out and implemented by small groups of politically powerful or scientifically expert men and women. The most important arguments have been unpublicized, the key decisions have been made in secret or on the basis of information fully available, or fully comprehensible, only to an inner circle of scientists, soldiers, and political leaders. And what is true of past choices about policies must be all the more true about future choices about the execution of policies. If a crisis comes, there won't be time for Congressional hearings, editorials in newspapers and journals of opinion, the organization of parties and movements. Even in the inner circle, disagreements will be brief, and awareness may well come to the rest of us only in a blinding flash.[5]

At the beginning of the nuclear age, secrecy in nuclear policy was justified in the name of national security. After the United States entered World War II, secrecy was necessary to prevent the enemy (the initial focus was on Germany) from developing the bomb first. Subsequently, in order to bring the war to an end as soon as possible, secrecy concerning the existence and number of atomic bombs was said to be necessary because victory over Japan required that we exploit the psychological elements of surprise and shock.[6] For all the Japanese knew, we had enough bombs to destroy their cities indefinitely, one after another. It can be argued that the success of our strategy of atomic coercion required secrecy about the fact that we had (and could produce) only a few atomic bombs.

After World War II, it was asserted that we needed to keep knowledge about the workings of the weapon and our specific plans for its use from our new postwar enemy, the Soviet Union. In concealing from the Soviets U.S. nuclear war plans—which, as noted above, have at times included first-strike preparations[7]—officials of course kept those plans from the American public as well. Indeed, the creation of nuclear strategy was for a period the monopoly of one man, General Curtis LeMay, who did not even disclose *his* plans to the president or the Joint Chiefs of Staff.[8]

The case for keeping nuclear strategy out of the democratic sphere of public debate and collective decision making was clearly stated in once-secret documents, now declassified. In 1948 the National Security Council formulated Document No. 30 (NSC 30), which concluded that *any public discussion* of nuclear policy would threaten national security. This document further asserted that an open debate about the possibility of not using nuclear weapons might encourage the "Russians" to conclude that the United States would hesitate to retaliate—which might also destroy our allies' faith in the U.S. willingness to come to their defense. The document states: "Deliberation or decision on a subject of this significance, even if clearly in the affirmative, might have the effect of placing before the American people a moral question of vital security significance at a time when the full security impact of the problem had not become apparent."[9]

For many years, the general public was effectively shut out of the nuclear policymaking process. Decisions of great importance to citizens were not publicly discussed. Only recently have ordinary citizens demanded to be heard in this area of public policy.

This is not to say that successive policy elites have unilaterally shaped nuclear strategy and forces. It does not appear that the evolution of our nuclear arsenal is the deliberate product of a single elite or succession of elites. Decisions about nuclear weapons and nuclear strategy appear rather to be the result of a nondemocratic, nonconspiratorial, and uncoordinated pluralism: defense science, defense industry lobbying, interservice rivalry, congressional interests, intelligence reports (sometimes incorrect) on Soviet strategy and weapons, worst-case analysis, the given administration's preference, and, to a minor degree, public opinion.[10] Thus, Michael Walzer's thesis concerning the undemocratic formation of nuclear strategy is mistaken to the degree that it implies that successive policy elites have single-handedly made nuclear policy.

Perhaps one of the most powerful determinants of nuclear strategy has been emerging weapons technology, the yield of defense science and the defense industry. Even when Curtis LeMay had, for a period, disproportionate control over strategic targeting, his plans were always limited by the nature of the weapons and delivery systems under his command: gravity bombs and slow-flying strategic bombers. LeMay's strategy of atomic strategic bombing, which concentrated on area targets (such as cities), eventually gave way to a new emphasis on hitting military installations, not because of a deliberate change in objectives, but because later target planners found themselves with a greater number of warheads carried on more accurate delivery systems. The United States had more weapons than were necessary for the objective of destroying enemy cities, and weapons capable of greater discrimination. Freeman Dyson, a physicist and former consultant to the Defense Department, observes:

> As strategic weapons became more numerous and more accurate the mission of assured destruction no longer provided enough targets for available warheads. The professional targeters were compelled, whether they believed in limited nuclear war or not, to assign warheads to missions of a more limited character than assured destruction. In this fashion the concept of limited nuclear war became unofficially embodied in the targeting lists long before it was officially acknowledged as a determining factor in strategic policy.[11]

According to this account, current U.S. strategic policy—deterrence based upon a nuclear war–fighting capability, including an ability to destroy enemy nuclear forces—has been generated by the constantly changing quantity and quality of weapons. If this is true, then the idea of well-thought-out strategy preceding and determining the development of weapons is a reverse image of actual practice: instead of strategy shaping weaponry, weaponry has shaped strategic policy. This is in fact how things have worked, according to Solly Zuckerman, former scientific advisor to the British Ministry of Defense: "During the twenty years or so that I was professionally involved in these matters weapons came first and rationalizations and policies followed."[12]

This suggests a kind of technological determinism, which means, in effect, ad hoc policymaking. The thesis that weapons determine strategy appears, however, to overstate the role of weapons in the formation of policy. After all, at least some weapon systems (e.g., multiple-warhead missiles) have been *deliberately created* to solve particular strategic problems (e.g., the Soviet anti-ballistic missile program). A more balanced view is that nuclear strategy has not been the product of any single causal agent, but instead the result of a confluence of factors, with weapons development and policy elites playing roles in a process complicated by several other influences.

The Case for Leaving Nuclear Policy to Experts

To the question, who is in charge of nuclear policy? there is perhaps no one answer, no one group that can be identified and held clearly accountable. This is a fundamental problem for those who seek to democratize nuclear defense policy: how can we break the grip of the plurality of nondemocratic forces and put strategic policy under rational public control?

Critics of the policymaking process might, of course, agree that we need to introduce rationality into the process, but object that democratization of decision making will introduce chaos, not intelligent order. They might argue that a thoughtful, informed policy cannot be made by ordinary citizens after work. Crafting an adequate nuclear policy requires considerable time and substantial knowledge, neither of which is a possession of ordinary citizens.

While agreeing that nuclear policy should not be the chaotic product of competing special interests and uncontrolled weapons innovation/proliferation, such critics might instead argue that we need to turn nuclear defense policy over to highly trained and nonpartisan defense specialists: individuals who are competent to formulate the most rational plan for achieving nuclear security. It might appear that a truly rational approach would be one that creates a supreme nuclear policymaking council composed of the best strategic minds. Isn't it only reasonable to place nuclear policymaking in the hands of defense experts? They alone, it might be argued, have the competence required, an expertise that is technically beyond ordinary citizens. In other words, the complexity of the subject simply does not lend itself to public discussion or majoritarian determination. We must, on this view, recognize a simple truth: a policy shaped by the public, whose knowledge of these matters is rather limited, cannot be as informed as a policy fashioned by professional strategists who fully comprehend the complex requirements of real security.

The conclusion of this reasoning is that democracy has its limits—that this is one area where ordinary citizens must keep their distance. Is it rational to leave to amateurs the formation of a policy crucial to the security of the free world? Aren't ordinary citizens, in the end, likely to be manipulated by the most powerful of the competing interests? Wouldn't it be better to have a system in which nuclear policy is shaped by defense specialists who make judgments based on substantial knowledge rather than a system in which nuclear policy is subject to the fickle winds of public opinion?

In sum, it can be argued that it is irrational to allow ordinary citizens, who lack expertise about nuclear matters and military doctrine, to shape, or even debate, nuclear policy. No more than we would allow ordinary (lay) individuals to diagnose medical problems and prescribe treatments should we allow them to diagnose security problems and prescribe strategies. The point is that answers to numerous crucial technical questions about nuclear weapons and strategy lie outside the domain of ordinary knowledge. Competent treatment of policy questions requires information that is inaccessible to the general public either because national security requires it to be kept secret or because the data are so complex that their proper understanding and analysis are simply beyond the ability of most citizens.

Furthermore, it could be argued, if we leave policy to popular sentiment—to something resembling an opinion poll—this gives the Soviets a "strategic" advantage. After all, despite all the talk about *glasnost*, we still are not free to influence Soviet public opinion, and even if we were, it would not make much difference in a society in which all decision making remains highly centralized. Furthermore, through front groups and the like—it might be argued—the Soviets are free to manipulate American public opinion: the fact that the United States is a truly open society gives the Soviets an edge in any propaganda war. On this view, we must keep in mind the warning found in NSC 30: allowing nuclear policy to be publicly decided, or even openly debated, undercuts national security. If the Soviets work in various covert ways (within peace groups, for example) to raise public doubts about the use of nuclear weapons—and perhaps even manipulate the public into demanding that the U.S. government repudiate the use of nuclear weapons—then the Soviets will have scored an important victory. If they could significantly weaken U.S. resolve to use its nuclear forces, they might even be able to achieve their goals without firing a shot. For these reasons, it might be concluded, we ought to leave nuclear policymaking to experts.

The Case for Public Participation

Against the foregoing viewpoint, Michael Walzer maintains that despite the technicalities, the arguments about nuclear policy "must be carried on in the open" and that "ordinary citizens must listen and join in."[13] Freeman Dyson in his book *Weapons and Hope* also endorses the need for a democratic assessment of defense objectives: "The time has come for a new public debate, placing in question the fundamental objectives of military policy."[14] In his second book on the nuclear predicament, *The Abolition*, Jonathan Schell calls for public choice and a *deliberate* nuclear policy.[15]

This study is motivated by the idea that public debate and citizen input are important elements in the formation of nuclear weapons policy. This does not mean that policy should be determined by an opinion poll or that strategic planning at higher and more detailed stages should not ultimately be delegated. The public may democratically decide to leave the final shaping of strategic policy to defense specialists. Delegation of decision making is not, however, the same as a permanent alienation from decision making. Under the former, the public can recover power if it wishes; under the latter, it is disenfranchised. The point is that the public should never be completely shut out of the process and that nuclear weapons policy should always be subject to democratic constraints.

A strong case for some degree of public participation in nuclear policymaking—as opposed to a process that leaves nuclear policy formation to a nuclear priesthood—was made by Robert Dahl in his book *Controlling Nuclear Weapons: Democracy Versus Guardianship.*[16] Since it would be difficult to improve upon his arguments, much of what I say below in support of public participation in the debate on nuclear policy owes a debt to Dahl.

The case against public determination of, or even participation in, policymaking goes back to Plato, who in *The Republic* argued that only a few individuals have sufficient knowledge to make wise political decisions. Dahl calls Plato's approach *guardianship.*[17] In the area of nuclear policy, this would mean that an autonomous policymaking elite—the kind of supreme council of policymakers discussed above—would determine the U.S. response to the Soviet nuclear threat, including strategy, the kind of forces used, and the targets to be destroyed (assuming that this policy elite decides on a military strategy). This council of experts on weapons, strategy, and Soviet doctrine would have the exclusive right to decide nuclear policy.

There are at least seven reasons to reject the guardianship proposal. The first five reasons presented below are a recapitulation of Dahl's arguments, with perhaps, in the case of some points, a slightly different emphasis. The last two points are my supplement to Dahl's case.

1. Moral Considerations. In rebutting the guardianship thesis, Dahl begins by pointing out that nuclear policy decisions are not merely technical: they are also moral. Nuclear policy questions are moral in the sense that they require an adequate understanding of—in Dahl's words—"proper ends, goals, or objectives that the government should strive to reach."[18] The ends are moral ones in the sense that they are concerned with the defense of values such as justice, freedom, equality, and security.

Moreover, the selection of means to achieve these ends—the task of nuclear weapons policy—also calls for moral judgments. What are the moral judgments that nuclear policy requires us to make? Here are a few of the moral questions such a policy must answer:

- Is it morally permissible to *threaten* to use nuclear weapons against population centers? If so, how does such a threat differ from terrorism?
- Is the military *use* of nuclear weapons ever morally justifiable? If so, when are we justified in using such forces? Only when attacked with nuclear weapons? When nuclear war appears imminent? To stop Soviet conventional aggression in Western Europe? To protect the flow of oil in the Persian Gulf?
- Assuming that the use of nuclear weapons can be morally justified, what are the *morally permissible targets?* Should we aim only at military installations, or is it permissible to attack the civilian population?
- Do the laws of war morally require us to replace our nuclear forces with conventional weapons more capable of discriminating between civilian and military targets?
- Is it morally permissible to leave the U.S. homeland vulnerable to nuclear destruction, or does the U.S. government have a moral obligation to protect the U.S. population from nuclear attack?

Answering these questions requires more than a technical knowledge about how weapons work or special expertise in the area of military strategy. This, then, is the first objection to the guardianship thesis: it fails to do justice to the moral dimension of nuclear policy issues.

2. Political Wisdom. It might be assumed that the weakness described above can be corrected simply by providing nuclear strategists with instructions that will sensitize them to the moral issues and to competing moral criteria. There is, however, no reason to believe that technically trained individuals (specifically defense specialists) will, even with some kind of education in ethics, be capable of making wise decisions about the best means to realize moral ends. This is a second objection to the guardianship thesis: it assumes, without justification, that defense experts can attain political wisdom.[19] Wise policymaking, according to Dahl, requires *political competence*—the ability to bring together factual (or technical) knowledge and moral understanding.[20] There is no good reason to believe that defense specialists are capable of bringing together the worlds of strategy and morality for the purpose of making wise choices.

Does anyone seriously believe that a Robert McNamara, a James Schlesinger, a Caspar Weinberger, a Dick Cheney, or a professional strategist from the RAND Corporation possesses the wisdom of Plato's mythical philosopher–kings, who perfectly understood the workings of the world while also being perfectly attuned to the requirements of morality? We cannot assume that technical specialists (even experts with a comprehensive knowledge of Soviet doctrine, nuclear physics, and strategic theory) are capable—if they simply put their minds to the task—of achieving political wisdom. It simply does not follow that individuals capable of mastering the technical intricacies of nuclear weapons and nuclear strategy are equally capable of deciding the morally best means to realize the fundamental political objective of nuclear policy. Indeed, *political rationality*—understood as the wise integration of means and ends—may require a sensitivity to rights, values, and human suffering that has little in common with what has so far passed for *strategic rationality.*

3. Ontological Insight. If there is good reason to doubt that a professional elite of strategic guardians would have the ability to make superior moral judgments or wisely integrate means and ends, there is equally good reason to doubt that even the so-called factual judgments made by these individuals would always be based upon assumptions that are strictly technical, scientific, or empirically rigorous. Sometimes what pass for factual judgments in the area of nuclear policy reflect covert ontological judgments—that is, judgments that the world is this way and not that, that human nature is this and not that.[21] In fact, professional strategists often make judgments that are grounded in speculation about the nature of the world and human behavior, as opposed to being grounded in unequivocal facts.

For example, many professional nuclear strategists attribute to Soviet and American leaders a rationality that is a projection of their own strategic mind-set; consequently, their policy decisions may be rooted in unjustifiably optimistic assumptions about human nature and human rationality. These strategists assume that heads of state rationally calculate before they act—and that these leaders will *necessarily* choose the strategically reasonable course of action: maximize gains, minimize losses, and avoid risk.

Moreover, strategists who believe in deterrence based upon a limited nuclear war–fighting capability may have a confidence in military technology that exceeds the evidence: for example, they may assume that in the midst of nuclear conflict the U.S. leadership's communication with both its own forces and the enemy leadership can be maintained while both sides control their nuclear exchanges, thereby keeping the conflict from escalating into an all-out nuclear war.

By contrast, "ordinary" citizens may be skeptical of both the assumption that superpower leaders tend to behave rationally and the assumption that a nuclear war–fighting technology can be trusted to operate as designed. Having frequently observed U.S. and Soviet leaders engage in foolish actions, ordinary citizens may seriously question the idea that heads of state tend to avoid irrational behavior. With respect to systems designed to ensure command and control of nuclear weapons, skeptical citizens may find it more prudential to believe in Murphy's Law—the idea that if something can go wrong, it will. The common sense of ordinary citizens may lead them to doubt that the real world—including real leaders and real technology—will operate according to the nuclear strategist's idealized rules.

It would be valuable if the strategists made explicit their ontological assumptions—that is, their beliefs about human nature and the nature of technology—so that their worldview could be critically examined and compared with alternative perspectives. Professional strategists tend to be isolated from the healthy skepticism and powerful counterarguments of outsiders who do not begin with the *accepted* premises.

4. Risk Assessment. Another reason for questioning the guardianship thesis is that nuclear policy judgments reflect assessments of risks, uncertainty, and trade-offs.[22] Nuclear policy choices are risky in the sense that they require a choice between alternatives whose consequences are only probable under circumstances where a wrong choice could mean global tragedy. For example, should we allow NATO forces to adopt the policy of using nuclear weapons first in the event that they are losing a conventional war to Soviet forces, at the risk of inviting Soviet nuclear retaliation that would devastate the very nations we are trying to protect; or should we renounce the initial use of nuclear forces, at the risk of encouraging Soviet aggression against Eastern or Western Europe? Should we be willing to guarantee European security at the risk of global catastrophe? Is that a reasonable risk? Given announced changes in Soviet military doctrine—the adoption of a posture of defensive defense—is it really likely that the Soviets will direct an attack on Eastern or Western Europe?

The fundamental question is this: how can we know whether a given strategy is likely to trigger, or prevent, nuclear war, and how can we know what risks are worth taking? In the face of the need to reach decisions based upon risk assessment, it is not clear from the empirical evidence that experts perform any better than ordinary people.[23] What weakens any claim to expertise on these questions is that the probabilities are unknowable. Indeed, as Dahl points out, "the outcomes are not merely risky in a probabilistic sense: they are genuinely uncertain in the sense that we can at best only guess at the probabilities over a large, vague range."[24]

5. *Checks and Balances.* A fifth objection to the guardianship thesis is that it places too much confidence in the goodness of policy guardians. This objection differs from the second one in that it is concerned with the trustworthiness of guardians rather than with their capacity to make superior moral judgments. More specifically, it has to do with the human tendency to be corrupted by unchecked power. Dahl points out that the essential truth of Lord Acton's famous aphorism—that power corrupts and absolute power corrupts absolutely—has been repeatedly supported by historical experience.[25]

Plato's solution was to give power to altruistic "philosopher–kings," individuals who are in love with knowledge and who are reluctant to rule—that is, wise human beings incapable of being corrupted by power. In other words, Plato's solution to the problem of the abuse of power was, in effect, to empower angelic human beings, people who are constitutionally incapable of doing evil.[26] In the real world, as Alexander Hamilton warned, since human beings are not and cannot become (even with the best moral training) angels, we need ways of checking the abuse of power, of limiting and distributing political power, so that it is not concentrated in the hands of any one group.[27] That is why policymakers cannot be left to their own devices and why they must be subject to democratic checks and constraints.

6. *Coherence of Means and Ends.* This brings us to a sixth weakness of the guardianship plan, one related to the thing that distinguishes the United States from the USSR (even with *glasnost*) and that defense policy is meant to defend: namely, the right of all citizens to participate in policymaking. To the degree that citizens are shut out of a vital area of policymaking—one having to do with war and peace—the difference between the United States and the USSR is diminished, thereby generating an incoherence between the fundamental objective of nuclear policy and the means of achieving it. If public participation in and control of policymaking are significantly weakened, then questions arise about whether the defense of this society is worth great risks.

7. *Lack of Consensus.* Finally, there is no consensus among defense intellectuals about the wisest nuclear policy. Although there is a general bias in favor of a deterrence strategy, there is widespread disagreement about what form such a strategy should take. Unlike Plato's philosopher–kings, defense intellectuals cannot settle questions by reference

to a set of transcendent eternal standards. The policy formulated by a nuclear priesthood—a group of policy guardians—would depend on their peculiar values, risk assessments, ontology, and guesses.

The important point can be expressed in words borrowed from Clemenceau: nuclear weapons policy is too important, controversial, and unscientific to be left to defense professionals. Defense professionals should be heard—in all their conflicting voices—in the process of working toward a democratically sanctioned policy, and defense specialists will ultimately have to work out the details of the policy that is chosen. But somewhere in the middle of policy formation, citizens should be allowed to join in the debate. Only after a debate in which the public is allowed to evaluate policy options and express its collective judgment should policymakers fashion a strategy—one that can be understood and supported by the public.

It is not just that ordinary citizens are going to have to pay for the implementation of the policy and thus should be won over for revenue purposes (no taxation without representation), but that the public's very existence depends on a sound nuclear policy. Nuclear defense strategy does not simply raise one policy question among many: it raises one whose answer may determine whether U.S. society, as citizens now know it, will continue to exist at all. Given the new thinking in the Soviet Union, citizens may want to challenge old assumptions that still operate in U.S. policy. If we accept the principle that policies affecting the fate of all citizens ought to be widely discussed, and in some sense controlled, by the public, then issues about nuclear weapons are among those which should be openly debated.

In order, however, to open nuclear policy to free discussion and permit interested citizens to join in the policy debate, two obstacles must be overcome: *linguistic alienation*, the terminology that distances the laity from the world of nuclear policy, and *policy impoverishment*, the artificial restriction of the range of policy options that are deemed worthy of debate.

Linguistic alienation is a term I borrow from William Gay's essay "Nuclear Discourse and Linguistic Alienation,"[28] in which he argues that insiders—professional strategists, military doctrine analysts, and officials in the Pentagon—achieve special power and status through their mastery of the technical terminology of the nuclear debate. Even those in this linguistic community who are not in a policymaking position still retain an edge over the rest of society because of a specialized vocabulary that enables them to speak the "private" code language of nuclear policy. The insider language of the nuclear policy debate—containing such technical terms as *countervailing, counterforce, crisis instability, C³I, countervalue,* and MIRV—intimidates, mystifies, and alienates otherwise interested citizens. As a result, members of this special linguistic community (directly or indirectly) exercise considerable control over the nuclear debate.

Technical nuclear discourse thus functions to disenfranchise the public in a crucial area of public policy. Some officials in the top levels of the military, recognizing the need for public understanding and support for current doctrine, acknowledge the problem of linguistic alienation. General John T. Chain, Jr., USAF, commander-in-chief of the Strategic Air Command, admits in *Air Force Magazine* that

> we often use terms not commonly understood by the public (throw-weight, damage expectancy, delivery vehicles, MIRVs, and rideout) and thereby have made our task "un-understandable" to many. We make it sound so complicated that only those directly involved with the strategic nuclear mission can carry on a substantive conversation about it.[29]

For citizens to gain a mastery of this alien vocabulary is therefore an act of empowerment. By translating strategic jargon in the course of my exposition, I intend in this book to contribute to overcoming linguistic alienation. I have also included a glossary of technical terms. Interested citizens should be warned: intelligent participation in the nuclear defense debate is not for the lazy. It requires time and thought. But for those who are willing to do the necessary homework, the strategic debate can be demystified.

The second obstacle to democratic debate on nuclear policy issues cannot be completely separated from the first. What do I mean by *policy impoverishment?* Just this: those in the government who shape policy, and those professionals outside government who communicate and debate with those in power, conspire (even if unintentionally) to create a world of restricted possibilities: the technical terms these insiders coin often set limits to the debate, shaping its conceptual framework by establishing the parameters of argument. More specifically, it requires that argument be conducted within the language and framework of *nuclear deterrence*, with everything else being assigned to the realm of the impossible or the unrealistic. That is, the language and conceptual framework of nuclear deterrence define what is worth hearing and how the policy world is named.

For many years the inside debate was exclusively between advocates of nuclear deterrence based on assured destruction and advocates of deterrence based on a war–fighting capability—as if the only issue were how to decide among nuclear deterrence options.

To enrich and enlarge the defense debate, we must go beyond

nuclear deterrence options. As I stated above, it may turn out that there is no real alternative to nuclear deterrence, but that can only be concluded after the largely neglected competing alternatives have had their day in the public court. The point is that—given the changes in the Soviet Union and Eastern Europe—we need to explore alternative visions of possible futures and to develop alternative concepts of security. Only by seriously entertaining new possibilities can we replace the conceptual monopoly reflected in the present tendency to equate security with nuclear deterrence. If the changes in Soviet doctrine turn into substantial changes in Soviet forces, it may be appropriate to reassess the value of nuclear deterrence as a defense policy.

In his original 1983 proposal for research on strategic defense, Ronald Reagan did the cause of fresh thinking a useful service by daring to challenge the doctrine of deterrence—by entertaining the possibility of a radical departure from the doctrine of security based on nuclear threats. Although many scientists and defense professionals responded with shock, seeing SDI as destabilizing, unaffordable, unfeasible, and an extension of the arms race into space, the resulting debate on this proposal had democratic utility in so far as it expanded the range of options and opened up strategic policy to greater public scrutiny. After President Reagan's speech of March 1983, various members of his administration tried—in a concession to the established tradition—to assure the defense community that the proposal was not really a departure from deterrence, but only a path toward its enhancement. Still, Reagan's original SDI proposal broke new ground. As a *possible* new path to nuclear security, it still deserves consideration.

We need, of course, to be aware of the danger that in an age weary of living under the nuclear threat, the public may too hastily embrace a vision that promises to deliver us from nuclear annihilation. Tiring of the insecurity of assured destruction, people may be too quickly lulled into accepting the promise of assured survival. The problem is that a new policy initiative, such as the idea of strategic defense, can become entrenched before its merits are openly debated and before the public can intelligently assess it, especially if the proposal offers lucrative government contracts to industries and huge grants to research laboratories and universities—beneficiaries who may become its powerful lobbyists, indifferent to the proposal's real merits in terms of the needs of national defense. Just as specific weapon systems (especially ones profitable for defense contractors and certain congressional districts) have too often been developed and deployed before their feasibility or desirability was established, so there is the danger that a newly proposed strategy may be "purchased" and institutionalized before the public has been given sufficient evidence that it is the best path to U.S. nuclear security. Only later—after billions have been spent—may it become apparent that the new strategy and weapons do not advance the cause of security.

Before looking at policy options that include and go beyond nuclear deterrence, it will be worthwhile to gain a sense of how the competing options can be evaluated. The next chapter formulates seven grounds for assessing policy proposals.

CHAPTER TWO

The Evaluation of Policy Proposals: Seven Tests

My aim in writing this book is neither to defend nor to refute any nuclear policy proposal: it is to provide a clear exposition of competing proposals and criteria for making a well-informed and independent choice among them.

When confronted with the variety of policy options, citizens may wonder how they can rationally decide which one is the best response to new Soviet thinking. The range of choices and the persuasive arguments in favor of each option may leave some feeling intellectually paralyzed. What, after all, makes one option superior to another? What considerations are relevant to a choice among all the possibilities? In this chapter I provide criteria that will be useful in the critical analysis of the policy proposals to be presented in subsequent chapters.

Application of these criteria will not necessarily make one's choice any easier or provide any assurance that—having selected a policy that appears to satisfy all the criteria—one has made the indubitably correct choice. Indeed, the introduction of these criteria could make a decision more difficult because readers will be made aware of both the ambiguity of some of the criteria (i.e., the fact that criteria are open to more than one interpretation) and the necessity, in the case of a conflict among criteria, of deciding which are to be given more weight than others.

Given the complexities, the confusing variety of choices, and the uncertainties ingredient in the selection of any option, many people will gladly turn this matter over to generals and defense professionals—to an elite of defense policy guardians. That is their choice. This book was not written for them, but instead for individuals who are uneasy about turning this issue over to a national security priesthood. We are talking about the fate of the earth; choosing the wrong policy can mean global catastrophe. This policy choice is not something thoughtful citizens will want to leave to "experts."

Without repeating the critique of the guardianship thesis developed in Chapter One, I will recall one obvious weakness in the guardianship solution: defense specialists have their own biases and tend to ignore important considerations that should be included in the making of policy—for example, moral concerns and doubts about the rationality of heads of state. Nuclear weapons policy must be opened to public debate in order to get as many viewpoints as possible, both those of defense specialists concerned with strategic niceties and those of interested "lay" citizens who bring other concerns to the debate.

There has not yet been a comprehensive public debate in this country on nuclear policy in which a wide spectrum of options was explored. New Soviet thinking on defense strategy makes such a debate more urgent than ever. Competing experts should present their arguments in the open, perhaps before televised sessions of appropriate congressional committees. As Michael Walzer recommends: "It is a good thing that all sides have their experts so that what the experts say is subject to peer review—and so that peer reviews are subject to lay review."[1] The assumption of democracy, according to Walzer, is that the public brings to political debate a healthy common sense that is valuable in choosing the best course.

To subject proposals to lay review is to subject them to a democratic test. If, however, this lay review is to be sufficiently thorough, it will be helpful for citizens to keep in mind a wide range of considerations as they assess the competing policy options. Just as juries composed of ordinary citizens are charged with the burden of reaching a verdict on the basis of specific rules of evidence—using their common sense to assess various claims and counterclaims—so too ordinary citizens who participate in the debate on nuclear policy must subject the various proposals to impersonal criteria, using their common sense to interpret and apply those criteria.

But what criteria? Is there anything in the realm of defense policy comparable to rules of evidence? In this chapter I will explain seven tests that I believe should be applied to a policy option before declaring it acceptable: instrumental coherence, moral defensibility, legal defensibility, feasibility, affordability, appropriateness vis-à-vis Soviet policy, and disaster avoidance. These tests provide grounds for a comprehensive evaluation of any proposal. If we are to evaluate policy options in a thoroughgoing way, then we cannot restrict ourselves to a narrow set of requirements. For example, some advocates of nuclear deterrence limit themselves to the criterion of success (see "Disaster Avoidance" below)—the "fact" that the policy has worked to prevent a nuclear war for over forty years—leaving out the question of the moral acceptability of the policy. Such omissions have characterized the approach of many professional strategists who pride themselves on their realism and practicality.

On the other hand, a preoccupation with moral considerations—to the exclusion of, for example, economic and technical ones—has led many peace activists to embrace utopian or impractical proposals. It is easy to say that morality requires the abolition of all nuclear weapon systems. It is more difficult to say how we can do this, given the knowledge of how to make nuclear weapons, or (assuming we could eliminate them) how we can maintain security in their absence.

The mutual exclusiveness and the narrowness of the worlds of strategists and moralists inhibit communication. In *Nuclear Ethics* Joseph Nye, former deputy undersecretary of state and currently director of the Center for Science and International Affairs at Harvard University, describes the myopia on both sides:

> Humility has been notably absent in the nuclear debate. Many strategists ignore nuclear ethics, and many moral absolutists refuse not only to tolerate nuclear weapons, but even to tolerate those who do, preferring to categorize strategists and their arguments as corrupted. All too often moralists and strategists tend to talk past each other as though they live in separate cultures of warriors and victims rather than fellow citizens of a democracy. The moralists formulate fine principles that seem to the strategists about as relevant to a foreign policy as a belief in the tooth fairy is to the practice of dentistry. The strategists, on the other hand, tend to live in an esoteric world of abstract calculations and a belief in a mystical religion called deterrence, which is invoked to justify whatever is convenient. Strategists would do well to realize that there are no experts, only specialists, on the subject of nuclear war, and to listen more carefully to the moralists' criticisms. At the same time philosophers and moralists would do well to pay more heed to the strategists' arguments and to realize that they need to work with more realistic assumptions if they wish to be effective in a dialogue between ethics and strategy.[2]

The point is that we must not restrict ourselves either to the strictly principled viewpoint of the moralist or to the purely pragmatic viewpoint of the strategist. While a proposal may be appealing from the standpoint of one criterion, it may be problematic from the perspective of another. That is why it is wise to multiply perspectives so that as many viewpoints as possible can be brought to bear on the problem. We should keep in mind a broad spectrum of considerations when trying to decide among options. The more criteria that go into a policy decision— the more factors that are weighed—the more adequate will be our final choice, and the less likely it is that we will err by ignoring a significant dimension of the problem. This chapter provides seven angles from which to view policy proposals. There may be an eighth, a ninth, or more that I have overlooked; I do not claim that these criteria are exhaustive of the possible criteria of policy evaluation. The assumption is simply this: if we keep in mind *at least* the seven tests, it will help us engage in a more comprehensive—and less distorted—evaluation of the options.

Instrumental Coherence

Beyond a fundamental objective of preserving free institutions and avoiding nuclear war, a nuclear defense policy contains two instrumental components: a strategy and a force system. These components are instrumental in the sense that they are designed as means to implement the fundamental objective. For example, mutual assured destruction seeks to preserve freedom and prevent a Soviet nuclear attack through the threat of massive nuclear retaliation; that is, its instruments include a strategy of indiscriminate retaliation combined with inaccurate nuclear forces. To apply the coherence test to MAD is to attempt to determine whether its combination of strategy and forces constitutes a coherent package.

The term *coherence* is used here to refer both to consistency and to clarity. The coherence test asks whether the instruments of the policy involve any inconsistencies or significant ambiguities.

Inconsistency. An instrumentally inconsistent policy is one that is at odds with itself because there is a contradiction (1) within the strategy itself, (2) within the force system, or (3) between the strategy and the force system. Examples may be helpful in illustrating the three types of inconsistency. For instance, a strategy calling for a combination of mutual assured destruction and strategic defense would be incoherent because it would embrace incompatible strategic aims: assured vulnerability and assured survival of the population. As an illustration of a self-contradictory force system, consider a policy proposal that calls for weapons that are purely defensive while also calling for first-strike forces. Finally, an example of a policy with a strategy and force system in mutual contradiction would be one that endorses a counterforce strategy (one restricted to military targets) while settling for a force system composed of high-yield, inaccurate thermonuclear weapons.

Ambiguity. An ambiguous policy is one that fails to communicate a clear intention because: (1) the formulation of the strategy is equivocal; (2) there is no formal declaration of strategic aims; or (3) the system of forces is itself ambiguous. The first kind of ambiguity resides in the equivocal language of a nation's strategic policy declarations; for example, a nation formulates what it calls defensive strategy in language that allows for offensive action. (Soviet strategic formulations have until recently been characterized by such equivocation.) The second kind of ambiguity lies in silence about strategy: a nation makes no statement about its strategic intentions. The third type of ambiguity is reflected in the force structure itself: the forces can accommodate more than one strategic interpretation.

Ambiguity is dangerous if it creates crisis instability—that is, if the ambiguity could provoke the other side, in a time of crisis, into preemptive nuclear attack. For instance, even if nation A unequivocally declares that its strategy is purely defensive, as long as nation B can *interpret* nation A's current or planned force structure (e.g., strategic defenses) as even potentially aggressive, the criterion of coherence has not been satisfied.

Of course, there may be cases in which the cultivation of ambiguity is not destabilizing. We will see that advocates of what is called "existential deterrence" believe that the United States can best maintain nuclear peace through declaratory silence. Arguing that it is unnecessarily provocative for a nation to make nuclear threats, existentialists insist on leaving unspecified the circumstances under which nuclear weapons would be used. This intentional ambiguity is acceptable so long as it is not accompanied by forces that could be perceived as capable of a disarming first strike. In other words, as long as there is nothing threateningly ambiguous (e.g., possibly "disarming") about a nation's force structure, the ambiguity of declaratory silence is consistent with crisis stability.

In fact, advocates of existential deterrence, as we will see in Chapter Three, tend to favor a relatively modest but invulnerable retaliatory force system whose very existence speaks for itself and serves as an effective deterrent. Thus, although the nation's strategic intentions may be unclear, its possession of modest but still sufficiently punitive retaliatory forces can be both reassuring to allies and dissuasive to an adversary.

The important point is that policy ambiguity becomes serious only when the obscurity of a nation's intentions—the lack of a clearly stated or explicit policy—sends the wrong message. A wrong message might take one of two very different forms: either a nation signals preparations for a first strike against the adversary, or it communicates an unwillingness or inability to defend itself or retaliate if attacked. If a nation, as a result of policy ambiguity, makes it possible for an adversary to "read" its posture either way—as either a disposition to aggression or a disposition to appeasement/nonretaliation—the result may be crisis instability. A nation can ensure instrumental coherence and avoid unwanted ambiguity by arranging its security apparatus so that the other side cannot possibly interpret its strategic declarations, or its silence about its intentions, as concealing either a plan for a first strike or an incapacity for self-defense.

Of course, the only way adversaries can *objectively* judge each other's policies is by looking at forces and their deployment. Neither forces nor their mode of deployment should be destabilizingly ambiguous. No matter what a nation declares or how lucidly it declares it, the other side will probably weigh all statements against the adversary's force structure and mode of deployment. For example, no matter how frequently the United States repeats that its silo-threatening counterforce weapons are solely for retaliation, the Soviet Union may remain unconvinced because of the simple fact that these weapons can serve their counterforce function only if they destroy Soviet missiles in their silos—that is, in a first strike.

Thus, the clarification of policy is not always a matter of making policy declarations more lucid; it may be a matter of restructuring, altering, or reducing forces so that they "speak" in a manner that accurately conveys the message a nation wants its adversary to receive. The same, of course, applies to Soviet declarations. The United States must not rely on Soviet declarations alone: there must be evidence that the declarations cohere with Soviet forces.

Moral Defensibility

A nuclear weapons policy may be instrumentally consistent and unambiguous (or at least not ambiguously destabilizing) and yet be unacceptable because it is morally indefensible. Morality, as I am using the term, requires us to transcend self-interest, to be as impartial as possible, and to arrive at a judgment that we would be willing for everyone to apply to similar situations. These features of morality can be satisfied in different ways, according to different approaches. In contemporary ethics there is an ongoing debate between two schools of moral thought: deontological and teleological ethics.

The Deontological Viewpoint. The term *deontological* derives from the Greek word *deon*, which means duty or that which is binding. Those who adopt this perspective believe that morality is a matter of doing one's duty, regardless of consequences. A well-known formulation of this viewpoint derives from Immanuel Kant (1724–1804), who asserted that it is always our duty to respect persons as ends in themselves and to avoid treating them as mere means. On Kant's view, we should fulfill this obligation regardless of whether doing so contributes to our individual happiness or that of society as a whole. The emphasis here is on respect for all human beings (impartiality)—on the notion that every person has a right to be respected and that we, therefore, have an obligation to show respect for each person. This deontological viewpoint seeks to defend the absolute dignity of persons against attempts to justify using them as mere means to benefit other persons.

From this normative point of view, intentions as well as (deliberate) actions are important. Not only must we refrain from actually using persons as mere means; we must also avoid making threats to do so. That is, within this ethical perspective, it is immoral to *threaten* to do what it is immoral to do. The morality of an action resides in the will as well as the act—it resides as much in what one is willing to do as in what one deliberately does. Hence, if it is immoral to treat persons as mere means, then it is immoral to threaten to so treat them, in so far as the threat involves a genuine intention. The idea that it is wrong to intend to do what it is wrong to do is called the "wrongful intentions principle."

Anticipating an analogy that will be central to the exposition of competing policy options, it is important to note that the Kantian viewpoint does not rule out punishment, including the death penalty, as long as the punishment involves respect for the offender as a person, and as long as the punishment is proportional to the seriousness of the crime. A Kantian will argue that violators of the law deserve punishment in so far as they are free and responsible beings. Punishment shows respect for criminals as persons in so far as it treats them as autonomous agents who freely and rationally chose the legal consequences of crime when they chose crime. What Kantianism rules out is punishing criminals merely to maximize the well-being of noncriminals: this would involve treating them as mere instruments.

Applied to military policy, the implications of this normative viewpoint are clear: (1) we should not attack or kill (punish) *some* persons (whether civilians or combatants) within an enemy society in order to benefit a *greater number* of other persons (in our society or the world), and (2) we should not *threaten* to attack or kill innocent persons within an enemy society, even if the consequences of making such threats are beneficial to a great number of other persons. More specifically, the deontological viewpoint rules out terror bombing of cities for the purpose of breaking civilian morale and terminating the war; it also rules out the use of threats to the innocent to achieve deterrence.

Teleological Viewpoint. The term *teleological* derives from the Greek word *telos*, which means "end," "purpose," or, more loosely, "consequence." There is a popular tendency to identify morality with the deontological viewpoint—that is, with a perspective that values intentions over consequences. This is especially tempting because the major teleological theory is utilitarianism. There is also a popular tendency to associate utilitarian thinking with the kind of cold, amoral, strategic thinking that is merely concerned with finding the most efficient means to achieve an end.

In fact, utilitarianism is a moral point of view that is concerned with more than cost-effectiveness. As developed by John Stuart Mill (1806–1873), the principle of utility calls upon us to weigh the happiness of each person equally. Thus, utilitarianism also endorses a notion of equality in so far as it aims at the maximization of the good of all persons: in striving to promote happiness and reduce suffering, no person is to count more than any other. Utilitarians recognize, however, that in the real world, in which there are frequently conflicts of interest, it is not possible to make everyone equally happy or to eliminate suffering from every life. With this in mind, utilitarians argue that our goal should be to maximize happiness and minimize suffering for the greatest number. In practice we must, from time to time, sacrifice the happiness, and even the lives, of some persons in order to bring about a greater good or avoid a greater evil. It must be emphasized that, from a utilitarian perspective, the infliction of suffering on some individuals, no matter how small the number, is never seen as good: it is viewed as an evil that must always be justified. The important utilitarian point is that all suffering is evil and should be kept to a minimum.

For example, punishment, from a utilitarian viewpoint, is only justified to the extent that it benefits society and achieves the objective of deterrence while inflicting a minimal amount of suffering on offenders. The utilitarian view is that we should cause no more suffering or deprivation than is necessary to achieve the aim of deterrence. Only if punishment prevents more suffering than it causes is it justified.

Applied to military policy, utilitarianism could justify the use of armed attacks on an enemy society in order to prevent a greater evil—provided that every attempt was made to minimize the suffering inflicted on the adversary. Whether or not *innocents* should be attacked or threatened will, according to this viewpoint, turn on the probability of the overall utility or disutility of such a strategy. Unlike Kantianism, utilitarianism cannot *a priori* rule out either threats to the innocent or attacks on the innocent. Their acceptability would depend on the magnitude of benefits compared with the losses. If, for example, a ruthless adversary shelters its soldiers and weapons among unwilling civilians, and if a refusal to attack population centers means the loss of the war to this especially evil enemy (whose victory would most probably produce more suffering than one's attacks on civilians), then civilian centers may be attacked. If millions of lives can be saved by deliberately killing thousands of civilians, then such direct attacks on noncombatants may be justifiable. If, on the other hand, the likely gains from an attack on civilians are outweighed by probable losses, then the attack is not justified.

The same can be said about *threats* against the innocent. Such threats are not *a priori* evil: their moral defensibility depends on the likelihood that such threats will produce great benefits. We cannot, as in the deontological position, absolutely rule out threatening the innocent. Consider, for example, a terrorist who is threatening to blow up a stadium containing a crowd of a hundred thousand unless officials meet his demands. Let us assume that the only way we can stop him is to threaten to kill his wife and children if he does not give up. For some utilitarians this might be a case in which it is justifiable to make threats against the innocent in order to prevent a grave harm. In such cases, we have to compare two things: the negative consequences of the threat and the negative consequences of not making the threat.

Deontological and teleological theories thus provide different criteria for judging the morality of policies and actions. Some ethicists seek a synthesis of the two viewpoints by requiring us to keep both perspectives in mind as we make moral decisions. In practice, there may be cases in which both ethical viewpoints lead us to the same conclusion. Still, situations will sometimes require us to choose between them. We must keep in mind that morality—even if conceived of as an enterprise concerned with the transcendence of self-interest, the cultivation of impartiality, and the willingness to universalize one's judgments—is itself a pluralistic enterprise that requires us to choose between competing moral standards.

Legal Defensibility

To submit a policy proposal to the test of legal defensibility is to ask whether it conforms to established law, national and international.

On the national level we might inquire about the constitutionality of the policy. It could be argued that a nuclear policy that enables the president unilaterally to decide to go to war is unconstitutional, on the grounds that the power to declare war belongs to Congress. Of course, there appears to be an important constitutional exception: the case of a surprise attack on the United States. If the United States is the victim of a surprise attack, there is no time to consult Congress: in this supreme emergency it would appear that we must allow a legitimate exception to Congress's war-making powers. After warning of a surprise Soviet launch of submarine missiles off the eastern coast, for example, the president might have between ten and fifteen minutes to decide on the appropriate response: no retaliation, limited retaliation, or massive retaliation.

Congress could, of course, assert its authority by placing limits on the president's response to a nuclear attack. There are several alternatives. One possibility is to impose on the commander-in-chief a ride-out strategy—a strategy that required the United States to be capable of riding out or absorbing a nuclear attack while retaining sufficient destructive power to inflict unacceptable damage on the attacker. This would prevent immediate retaliation and thus extend the time for deliberation. In case the warning of an attack was a false one, the possibility of delayed retaliation might be important. Alternatively, Congress could impose on the president a graduated retaliatory strategy that would require that our nuclear response be proportional to the level of any Soviet attack. A third possibility is for Congress to require the development of nonnuclear weapons and a targeting strategy that allows for discriminate retaliation. Finally, Congress could instruct the president to dismantle all strategic forces (whether nuclear or nonnuclear), thereby making it impossible for the president to retaliate.

In addition, assuming that nuclear forces are retained, Congress could require that in the (unlikely) event of a Soviet conventional attack on Western Europe, the president consult with designated congressional leaders from both political parties before authorizing the use of nuclear weapons. This would prevent the president from unilaterally starting a nuclear war. As it now stands, the president, in conformity with the NATO policy of flexible response, has the power (after consultation with NATO allies) to command the first use of nuclear weapons—that is, to order their use even when the adversary is attacking our allies with only conventional forces. Legal critics of first-use policy could argue that allowing the president such unilateral power violates the spirit, if not the letter, of the Constitution. Of course, any delay in nuclear use could also be catastrophic for NATO because it would give the Soviets, while deliberations were occurring, time to destroy land-based nuclear forces and acquire more territory.

Is the attempt to keep Congress in the decision-making loop sufficiently justified by invocation of Congress's war-making powers, or is it a strategically unwise obstacle that will prevent the president from acting quickly enough to protect the free world? Assuming that our defense policy retains a nuclear posture, the question is whether the Constitution requires that Congress be kept in the chain that leads from weapons development through targeting strategy to the ultimate decision about how to respond to a Soviet attack. That is a fundamental legal question to which there is, unfortunately, no clear answer. Therefore, any attempt to apply a constitutional test to policy proposals may be problematic rather than formulaic.

On the international level, we might inquire whether a military policy proposal—including targeting and weapons strategy—conforms to war conventions to which the United States is a signatory. For example, Department of Defense Instruction 5500.15, dated 16 October 1974, requires that all Department of Defense actions concerning the acquisition and procurement of weapons and their planned use in war be consistent with U.S. international obligations, including obedience to the laws of war.[3]

The U.S. obligation to conform to the laws of war was reinforced by U.S. ratification of the 1977 Protocols to the 1949 Geneva Conventions, Article 85 of which prohibits making the civilian population or individual civilians an object of attack. It requires belligerents to distinguish between civilians and combatants and to direct operations only against military objectives. The 1977 Protocols also place restrictions on means and methods of warfare, prohibiting those which (1) cause unnecessary suffering, (2) cannot distinguish between clearly separated military and civilian objects in the same area, and (3) are intended or expected to cause widespread, long-term, and severe damage to the natural environment.[4]

Other conventions, such as Article I of the 1907 Hague Conventions, declare that the territory of neutrals is inviolable in time of war, implying that weapons that harm such territory violate the laws of war.[5] These conventions appear to rule out the use of nuclear weapons.

Advocates of nuclear deterrence have two responses. First, the United States signed the 1977 Protocols on the condition that the rules "were not intended to have any effect on and do not regulate or prohibit the use of nuclear weapons."[6] (Opponents of nuclear weapons will of course argue that this exception makes the Protocols's prohibitions on civilian targeting and indiscriminate methods of warfare practically meaningless.)

Second, at least some proponents of nuclear deterrence will argue that we must keep in mind the difference between the *existence* of these weapons and their *employment* in war. If the weapons *exist* only to deter nuclear or conventional aggression, then, it can be argued, they are *not being employed* in any way that violates international law. The objective of nuclear deterrence is, after all, to prevent the employment of nuclear weapons. Thus, an apologist for deterrence can reason as follows: until there is an international agreement that explicitly outlaws the *possession* of nuclear forces, these weapons, if viewed as instruments of deterrence, remain in conformity with the spirit as well as the letter of international law.

Critics of nuclear deterrence will not be convinced by this legal defense, because (1) it ignores the possible inadvertent or unauthorized use of these indiscriminate weapons, and (2) unless nuclear states are bluffing, they are prepared, at any moment, to violate prohibitions against the use of indiscriminate weapons.

Some will argue that where the spheres of international and national law overlap, another legal obligation is revealed—a principle that can be found in the 1977 Protocols and that might be said to be implicit in the U.S. Constitution: the government has an obligation to protect its citizens from attack.[7] Advocates of strategic defense see this as providing legal support for their position. Naturally, advocates of other strategies will argue that their proposals also, at least indirectly, satisfy this obligation. Perhaps proponents of mutual assured destruction would have to strain the hardest to make this claim plausible.

The legal questions can, of course, be multiplied, but the above discussion gives at least a sampling of the kinds of legal problems that can be raised about policy proposals.

Feasibility

A proposal may be instrumentally coherent, morally defensible, and legally justifiable, but unworkable. The fundamental question is, how likely is it that the policy can achieve what it claims? Does the policy require a technology or a strategy beyond practical reach? If the components of the policy are on the drawing board, how likely is it that the forces or techniques it calls for can actually be created and implemented, and will actually perform as required? The feasibility test can be broken down into three questions, reflecting three types of feasibility.

1. Is the proposal *scientifically* feasible? That is, is the proposed strategy and/or force system physically (or psychologically) possible? If, for example, the strategy calls for placing platforms in space for the purpose of firing particle beams through the atmosphere to destroy missiles in the boost phase, can this in fact be done? If the strategy calls for making certain behavioral demands on citizens (e.g., disciplined nonviolent resistance to violent attacks and physical provocation), does this fit in with our knowledge of human psychology? A proposal that calls for weapons or strategies inconsistent with the laws of physics or human psychology is one that fails the test of scientific feasibility.

2. Is the policy proposal *operationally* feasible? Granting that it is scientifically possible, can we actually test and put in place the system it calls for? Is there a way to make sure that it will "operate" as designed? If there is no way experimentally to test the proposal—if, for example, the only possible test is a wartime situation—then there is no way to know if it is operationally feasible. Thus, a proposed strategy (e.g., the use of nonlethal chemical weapons to temporarily paralyze the enemy) may not contradict anything science tells us, and yet be unfeasible because it is untestable.

3. Is it *technically* feasible to carry out the proposal? Granting that a proposed policy is physically possible and operationally testable, a question remains: working with available (human and technological) resources, can we construct and implement the system in a reasonable amount of time? If, for example, the completion of the proposed system will take twenty years and we need it in ten years, it is not technically feasible.

Answers to feasibility questions often require knowledge beyond that which is available to or understandable by most citizens. A great deal of the information relevant to the nuclear policy debate may simply be beyond the cognitive or educational levels of a significant portion of the electorate or, for that matter, of their representatives in the Congress and White House. How well do the president and most members of Congress understand the technical issues in the nuclear debate? How can lay citizens make rational judgments about policy feasibility, especially when there is no consensus among the experts? For example, there is disagreement among defense scientists about the feasibility of population defenses (Reagan's 1983 proposal). Do we simply count scientific heads? Should we always ignore a minority of scientists who assert, against the grain, that something is feasible? It is important to note that Einstein expressed doubts about the feasibility of atomic weapons. What now seems impossible may one day, given sufficient research and resources, prove feasible.

Perhaps the jury model would be useful in handling this problem. Just as in courtrooms experts from different sides testify before juries who must attempt to arrive at a reasonable verdict, so experts on the technical aspects of a defense policy could be asked to present their views in clear, nontechnical language in televised congressional hearings, giving the public their varying assessments of the different proposals. After hearing this testimony, citizens could then try to make a reasonable choice.

Or, commissions composed of defense specialists could be asked to assess various policy proposals and issue a report outlining in nontechnical language their conclusions about their feasibility—from strategic defenses to civilian-based (nonviolent) defense. There might have to be majority and minority reports. In addition, the commission would have to be independent of external controls, and its membership would have to be pluralistic in the sense of representing a cross-section of political orientations.

Another possibility—suggested by Robert Dahl[8]—is a "mini-populus" consisting of a representative group of interested citizens chosen at random (or by some method that would minimize the chance of ideological one-sidedness) who would be provided (for a year) with the opportunity to study the feasibility of competing proposals, reading through material on both sides, listening to and questioning experts, and engaging in debate and discussion with each other. The mini-populus would "stand in for" the general public, representing, in effect, what the public would itself prefer if members of the public were as well-informed as the minipopulation had become. As Dahl sees it, a minipopulus "would reflect public opinion at a higher level of competence."[9] At the end of the period, they would offer nonbinding recommendations to the Congress and the president. The minipopulus might also have to provide majority and minority reports.

Of course, no special commissions or citizen study groups now exist to provide the rest of us with clear, thoughtful, and objective assessments of the feasibility of strategic defense, competing nuclear deterrence strategies, civilian-based defense, or the denuclearization of all military forces. There are, however, numerous books on defense options designed for lay audiences, and many recent ones deal specifically with strategic defense. Interested citizens can find literature containing comments by technical experts on both sides of most nuclear defense questions. "Citizen–jurors" must seek out this literature, carefully searching for arguments on both sides of the feasibility question. After working through these, a more thoughtful and reasonable conclusion can be drawn about the feasibility of a specific proposal.[10]

Affordability

How much will it cost to implement the proposal? A proposal may be coherent, morally desirable, legally justifiable, and feasible, but so economically burdensome as to be impractical. The public must ask itself what it is willing to pay to implement a strategic policy.

Costs and Benefits. Heavy expenditures on a proposal may require substantial reductions of spending in other areas. Will the funding of the proposed policy mean less money for education, medical care, improvement of the environment, social welfare, and other public needs? Are the projected benefits of the proposal worth the costs—social as well as economic? In response to any proposal we reasonably ask whether we could attain the same objective with less public expenditure. How do the costs and benefits of the proposal compare with alternative proposals?

Should cost-effectiveness be the decisive factor when it comes to the protection of free institutions? Perhaps we should be willing to make considerable economic and social sacrifices in order to improve the security of this country.

Of course, we might also ask to what degree the weakening of our economy through heavy defense expenditures ultimately weakens free institutions. If we cannot provide adequate housing, education, employment opportunities, consumer goods, and medical care for citizens as a result of burdensome defense spending, then the quality of the life we are defending will significantly decline. Are individuals truly free who lack housing, employment, education, medical care, and other necessities?

Effect on the Soviet Economy. Some will also be interested in whether the policy in question will require costly countermoves by the Soviets that might severely damage the Soviet economy. In other words, we might apply the criterion of affordability to the Soviet system as well as to our own. If the high costs of countering a proposed policy would further weaken an already sick Soviet economy, wouldn't this also diminish the Soviets' ability to return to a strategy of aggression, by keeping Soviet leaders preoccupied with domestic economic crises? Assuming it did not cause serious economic dislocations in the United States, a policy that threatened to severely damage the Soviet economy might be judged by some to be desirable. (This is why some strategists favor strategic defense: they believe our technological superiority and healthier competitive economy could bury the Soviets were they to try offsetting our defenses through an increase in expenditures on offensive missiles and other countermeasures.)

Or do we want the Soviets to succeed in their new economic programs? Will the world be more or less secure if the Soviet experiment in *perestroika* fails? Is it possible that the Soviets could become more of a threat to the world if the Soviet economy completely collapsed?

Economic Conversion Considerations. If a policy proposal requires a radical transformation of the structure of U.S. forces (e.g., a transition from nuclear to nonnuclear forces), then one must consider the economic effects of the shut-down of industries that produce the components of nuclear weapon systems and the consequent unemployment. This would require economic conversion of some kind. We cannot assume, for example, that workers in nuclear-weapons plants would necessarily find work in other industries. What is to happen to the corporations that depend on government contracts for nuclear weapons or their delivery systems? What would be the general economic impact of the loss of the purchasing power of the displaced workers? Any proposal that requires a radical reduction in, or transformation of, current military forces must include a plausible economic conversion plan.

Appropriateness vis-à-vis Soviet Policy

Since a nuclear weapons policy is designed to meet the Soviet nuclear threat, it obviously must be based upon assumptions about the intentions of the USSR. That is, any U.S. policy is necessarily premised on a particular understanding of Soviet military objectives and how the Soviets plan to use their forces to achieve their objectives. Three critical questions must be asked about any policy proposal.

1. Are the policy assumptions about Soviet doctrine (understood in terms of action policy) reasonable? Is there evidence to support the assumptions? What is it? Does it derive from official public statements by Soviet leaders or from the internal writings of Soviet military strategists? U.S. strategy and forces will obviously be inappropriate if they are premised on a misunderstanding of actual Soviet intentions—that is, if they are based on a misunderstanding of the nature of actual Soviet strategy.

2. Assuming that the understanding of Soviet objectives is correct, is the policy in question the best way to deal with the Soviet threat, or does it make the threat worse? In other words, is the proposal crisis-stabilizing or crisis-destabilizing? We might correctly understand Soviet intentions and yet respond in a fashion that increases the likelihood of Soviet aggression. If, for example, the United States correctly understands Soviet policy as mainly defensive and yet persists in building offensive forces that threaten to destroy the bulk of Soviet retaliatory forces (e.g., by building counterforce weapons capable of destroying Soviet land- and submarine-based missiles as well as its small bomber force), the Soviets may feel compelled to launch a first strike against our forces in order to prevent the destruction of its retaliatory capability. If, on the other hand, one correctly understands Soviet policy as offensive while failing to ensure that one's forces can survive a first strike, such inertia may invite a disarming nuclear attack.

3. Should we merely react to Soviet forces in such a way as to match them with equivalent forces, or should we attempt to shape Soviet doctrine in a positive way, even taking some risks to reduce military competition? If, for example, current Soviet forces (not to

mention modernization plans) do not yet fit in with the announced new political thinking, should we ignore Soviet pronouncements and concentrate on matching their existing forces, or should we encourage the Soviets in their new thinking by making some unilateral moves that would support the new thinking? It may be that Western behavior will affect the viability of the new thinking. The struggle between the old and the new thinkers in the Kremlin reflects divergent perceptions of the Western threat to Soviet security. Western behavior could either undercut the new thinking or reinforce it. For example, the United States might in fact unilaterally eliminate, or stop development of, some of its strategic weapon systems as a move in the direction of reasonable sufficiency.

The answer to this question will, of course, depend on one's understanding of Soviet intentions: whether the Soviets are perceived as still bent on world domination (no matter what we do), or as oriented to a new nonaggressive policy that can be either sustained or undercut by our policy responses.

Is there any way to discover *actual* Soviet plans, as opposed to mere *theories* concerning their plans and intentions? The short answer is no. The most that citizens can do is inform themselves about competing interpretations of Soviet behavior and conflicting theories of Soviet policy as a basis for reaching an educated judgment about actual Soviet intentions. I will lay out two competing perspectives on Soviet strategy, along with supporting arguments, so that readers can draw their own conclusions.

Soviet Doctrine as a Victory Strategy. According to one hawkish view, actual Soviet plans are offensively oriented, including preparations to win a nuclear war. On this view, any Soviet talk about new political thinking is strategic deception, designed to divert attention from the Soviet objective of world domination. The following is a brief summary of the case for this viewpoint:

1. Soviet talk about defensive defense is misleading. Closer analysis will show that defensive operations are projected to play only a modest role in war. According to Stephen Meyer, an authority on Soviet strategy, defensive operations are viewed by the traditional military—as opposed to new civilian thinkers in the Kremlin—as merely a component of a larger offensive-oriented strategy. "Defensive operations," Meyer states, "hold the enemy and buy time until appropriate forces and means can be assembled for transition to the counteroffensive. . . . This defensive phase of the war would be temporary, a transitional phase, in the view of the traditional thinkers."[11]

2. An examination of Soviet officers' training manuals and military journals provides, it is argued, a clear picture of the Soviet plan to emerge from nuclear war as a viable and victorious society. Phillip

Petersen and Notra Trulock, conservative strategic specialists, conclude that although the Soviet military may have been given the mission to prevent war, "the Party has not absolved the military of the responsibility of finding victory in the event war occurs."[12] Another specialist in Soviet strategy, Leon Gouré, points out that despite Soviet officials' public insistence that nuclear wars are too destructive to be won, "the concept of 'victory' in nuclear war is by no means considered obsolete by the Soviet military."[13]

Moreover, Soviet doctrine is said to be oriented toward preemption: Gouré, citing articles in Soviet military manuals, argues that "there is persuasive evidence that the concept of preemptive action, even if Soviet forces are on the defensive (let alone on the offensive), is still very much an integral part of Soviet strategy and warfighting plans."[14] That is, Soviet strategy still relies on striking first when and if the Soviets believe a war is imminent. On this view, the Soviets are not as concerned as we are about survivable retaliatory forces, because it is not their plan to ride out a nuclear attack. There is a plausible reason for this: to achieve its defensive objective of protecting its forces and society through damage-limiting attacks on the potential enemy's (strategic) military facilities, the USSR must be the first to deliver a strike. Otherwise its nuclear weapons will land on empty missile launch silos and airfields. Thus, Soviet doctrine requires the ability to engage in a first strike that will destroy enough of the enemy's forces to make a Soviet victory possible. The important point is that Soviet military literature makes it clear that the Soviets believe victory in nuclear war is possible—but only if they get in the first blow, a preemptive strike.

3. The Soviets view nuclear deterrence doctrine, at least as conceived in the West, as an unacceptable strategy. First, deterrence in the form of mutual assured destruction violates the Soviet concern to protect the homeland—an indisputable central concern of Soviet doctrine. The Soviets simply do not accept a condition in which war means the destruction of Soviet society. Second, a deterrence strategy is unacceptable because it makes Soviet security dependent on American rationality (on the assumption that no U.S. leader would be irrational enough to start a nuclear war)—a condition too precarious for Soviet defense requirements.[15]

4. The heavy losses of the Soviet Union in World War II—20 million dead—have contributed to the Soviet objective of initiating and winning a nuclear war. This experience showed them that they could recover from substantial losses in a major war. Furthermore, they believe that a crippling first strike against U.S. retaliatory forces would improve their chances of keeping Soviet losses close to the World War II figure. In addition, the experience of World War II has convinced the Soviets that they should never again remain inert and simply lash out in

a retaliatory response. That is why they put a premium on forward "defenses"—on a strategy that demands that any future wars be fought on the adversary's territory, not their own.[16]

5. The most realistic way of determining Soviet objectives is to infer them from Soviet forces, and an examination of the Soviet arsenal reveals an offensive orientation—a steady emphasis on heavy land-based missiles, culminating in the decision taken in the 1960s to proceed with the production of SS-18 and SS-19 intercontinental ballistic missiles (ICBMs)—two major MIRVed counterforce systems with great throwweight and high accuracy. These weapons are capable of destroying U.S. missiles in their silos. Even if Soviet military doctrine denied or was silent about war-winning intentions, Soviet forces would speak for themselves: they are designed for a preemptive strategy and victory in nuclear war.[17]

Moreover, the very fact that almost three-fourths of the Soviet nuclear arsenal consists of land-based ICBMs requires that the Soviet Union be prepared to use them first if it does not wish to lose them. The bulk of Soviet nuclear weapons are useless as retaliatory forces because they are vulnerable to destruction: in sum, to have utility, Soviet ICBMs must be used as offensive forces.

6. Soviet preparations in the area of strategic defense, including massive investments in antiballistic missile research and civil defense, make it clear that they reject mutual assured destruction and are planning to survive a nuclear war. The Soviets have been doing research on active defenses for decades. Soviet civil defense, with an annual budget of one billion dollars and employing about 100,000 persons, is far more substantial than the U.S. effort. It fits in with a war-winning plan.[18]

7. Marxism–Leninism endorses a view of historical development that makes victory over capitalism inevitable: to concede that the communist system might fail to win in a war with capitalism would be a contradiction of Soviet ideology. Military force has always been an essential instrument of Marxist revolutionary success. The Soviet assumption must be that they can use their nuclear forces to defeat the West and establish communism as the dominant political system in the world. The goal of world domination remains a powerful incentive to the development of a nuclear victory strategy. Despite a bout of self-criticism, Soviets still believe that they have history on their side—that they cannot lose in a conflict with capitalism.[19] To achieve their historical destiny—victory over the capitalistic West—the Soviet Union pursues nuclear superiority while using arms control agreements (which they systematically violate) to retard U.S. force development.

Soviet Doctrine as a Defensive Strategy. An alternative perspective repudiates the aggression–victory thesis, arguing that when it comes to nuclear war, the Soviets have no illusions and reject the idea that winning is a real possibility. The evidence for this worldview consists of the following observations.

1. The Soviets have officially declared their commitment to defense—to a policy of reasonable sufficiency that will provide them with the capacity to retaliate but not to conduct offensive warfare. They have made proposals that would contribute to the implementation of this policy, including the call for mutual reductions in both conventional and nuclear forces. They have also made unilateral moves in this direction by reducing forces in Europe, with plans for further reductions.

2. The Soviets have signed the Anti-Ballistic Missile (ABM) Treaty, a document that incorporates the doctrine of mutual assured destruction. This is proof that they realize there can be no impenetrable defense against nuclear weapons and no victory in nuclear war. They have not violated the treaty in a way that threatens Western security. Although neither side is absolutely committed to the ABM Treaty, the point is that the Soviets accept one of its major premises: to wit, that nuclear war would inflict unacceptable damage on each society and that neither side's security is enhanced by trying to defend against nuclear weapons.[20]

3. Soviet leaders since Nikita Khrushchev have repeatedly repudiated the idea of a winnable nuclear war. Khrushchev asserted in 1963 that nuclear war "would result in disease, death, and would cripple the human race."[21] In an address to the Twenty-sixth Party Congress (1981), Leonid Brezhnev said: "It is dangerous madness to try to defeat each other in the arms race and to count on victory in a nuclear war."[22] "Mankind," warned Yuri Andropov in 1982, "cannot endlessly put up with the arms race and with wars unless it wants to put its future at stake."[23] And Mikhail Gorbachev called in 1986 for the elimination of all nuclear weapons by the year 2000 and, to show good faith, suspended nuclear testing unilaterally for a year and a half.[24] If there was a time when the Soviets believed in victory in nuclear war, that is now history. Michael MccGwire, formerly a British naval officer and now with the Brookings Institution, argues in *Military Objectives in Soviet Foreign Policy* that as early as December 1966, at a meeting of the Party Central Committee, Soviet leaders embraced a new military strategy that had as its central objective what he terms "avoiding the nuclear devastation of Russia."[25] According to MccGwire, senior Soviet officials and military planners came to the profound realization that nuclear deterrence was mutual and consequently that neither superpower could hope to escape catastrophic, nationwide destruction in the event of a strategic nuclear war with the other.

4. Soviet leaders prefer to achieve their objectives without a war,

whether nuclear or conventional. Given the enormous destruction nuclear war would inflict on the Soviet Union in the short and long term—as well as the devastation it would cause to valued Western territory—it is simply not in the Soviet Union's self-interest to try to gain victory through the very risky path of nuclear war. Soviet leaders have now repudiated the use of armed force as a means to achieve political objectives. This does not mean that Soviet leaders have completely repudiated Marxism–Leninism. Clearly, they still affirm the value this ideology places on the development of productive forces and natural resources—assets that would be damaged or destroyed in armed conflict. The costs of all kinds of warfare have been judged too high.

5. The fact that the Soviet Union has developed a counterforce capability does not mean that it is eager to fight a nuclear war, or that it seriously contemplates a meaningful victory. On the contrary, this capability is designed to reduce the likelihood of nuclear war. Raymond Garthoff points out that "it is not accurate . . . to counterpose Soviet military interests in a 'war fighting' and hopefully 'war winning' posture to a 'deterrent' one; the Soviets see the former capability as providing the most credible deterrent, as well as serving as a contingent resort in the event of war."[26] After all, for years U.S. strategists have been giving the same justification for our development of a war-fighting capability; if it works as a credible deterrent for us, why not for them?[27]

6. The theory of Soviet aggression and expansionism is much exaggerated. Some conservatives, for example, seem to believe that Soviet leaders are just waiting for the right opportunity to invade Western Europe. This assumption about Soviet intentions is dubious for a number of reasons. First, the Soviet Union already has too many serious internal problems to contemplate invading and occupying Western Europe. Second, it was the Soviet Union's own fear of invasion that led it to establish the Warsaw Treaty Organization and to keep control over Eastern Europe, which served as a protective buffer zone between the USSR and the NATO countries of Western Europe.[28] The Soviet Union has a long history of being invaded: it should be remembered that Western nations, including the United States, did in fact invade and occupy part of its territory shortly after the Bolshevik Revolution.

Soviet military preparations and actions have largely been defensive and preventive responses to the perceived military threats of the United States and NATO as well as the threat posed by its huge communist adversary, China. For decades it perceived itself as surrounded by hostile powers—both communist and noncommunist. Given unilateral Soviet cuts in forces in Europe and Asia, there is now evidence that Soviet leaders are reassessing external threats and are beginning to conclude that there is no longer a threat that justifies the large military forces they have hitherto maintained. In addition, economic exigencies make it difficult for them to continue heavy investment in the military.

7. The loss of 20 million citizens during World War II makes the Soviet Union less—not more—disposed to war than the United States. In fact, this experience gave them a greater appreciation for peace than is possible for citizens of the United States. The Soviets, after all, have a memory of what it is like to be attacked and suffer the devastation of war. It is not an experience that they wish to repeat, but one they want above all to avoid. To citizens of the United States, on the other hand, an attack on the homeland is an abstraction: they cannot relate to the horrors of war in the same concrete way that Soviet leaders can.[29]

8. The idea that the Soviets have superior nuclear forces, which the United States must match if it is not to fall far behind, is reminiscent of all the other gaps alarmists used in the past to justify increased military expenditures. The new gap is no more a reality than the bomber gap of the 1950s, the missile gap of the 1960s, and the ABM gap of the early 1970s—all of which turned out to be fictions. These gaps were used to prove the "growing Soviet threat." The aim was, according to Henry Trofimenko, "to frighten the public into loosening its purse strings for the sake of a new offensive arms build-up."[30] Even the Central Intelligence Agency agrees that there is a rough parity of Soviet and U.S. nuclear forces.[31]

Disaster Avoidance

The final policy test seeks to answer the following question: Which policy option promises to be least disastrous? There are two different ways of construing the notion of *least disastrous*. It can refer to the likely consequences in case of policy failure, or to the likelihood of a policy's failure.[32] What should be given more weight—the likely consequences of failure or the likelihood of failure?

The ideal, of course, is to find a policy that promises to be least disastrous in both senses. The problem arises when no proposal satisfies both concepts. In that case, we must decide whether the magnitude of disaster or the probability of disaster is more important. This choice roughly corresponds to the two aims of nuclear policy that I discussed in Chapter One: the prevention of a nuclear attack and the prevention of total destruction should a nuclear attack occur. If we focus on the latter, then we may be willing to increase the risk of nuclear attack in order to decrease the destruction that would occur if such an attack took place. If we focus on prevention of a nuclear attack, then we may be willing to risk total destruction in order to decrease the probability of a nuclear strike.

Magnitude of Disaster. One interpretation of the disaster-avoidance criterion would require that after considering the possible outcomes of each policy, we choose the one that has the best of the worst outcomes. If we follow this rule, we must choose that policy whose worst consequence is still better than the worst consequence of any alternative policy.

Of course, one must make a value judgment about what constitutes a worst outcome. For example, is all-out nuclear war (the worst consequence of a failed nuclear strategy) a worse outcome than Soviet domination (the worst outcome of a failed unilateral disarmament strategy)? Obviously proponents of unilateral disarmament are going to argue that it offers the best worst outcome because even a harsh life under Soviet domination still allows for a reorganized struggle for freedom in an undamaged world whose resources remain intact, whereas after an all-out nuclear exchange, the struggle for freedom will have almost no meaning: liberty will be an empty concept in a world of rotting corpses, mass starvation, millions of burn victims, radiation sickness, and spreading disease due to lack of medical care.

Although proponents of unilateral disarmament who support a strategy of nonviolent defense would agree with nuclear strategists that survival is not an absolute value—after all, a nonviolent defense strategy, we will see, accepts a risk of casualties—the survival of society is nonetheless a necessary condition for the enjoyment of the values we are defending. Failure under a strategy of nonviolent defense means that the loss of political values can be reversed with the passage of time. On the other hand, the extinction of the species—the worst possible outcome of a failed nuclear strategy—is irreversible.[33]

Probability of Failure. On a second interpretation of *least disastrous*, we are to focus on the *probability* of disaster—disregarding magnitude—and choose the policy with the least likelihood of failure. While the first approach is concerned with the size of potential disasters to the exclusion of their probability, the second approach is concerned with probabilities of the disasters to the exclusion of their magnitude.[34]

It is, of course, very difficult to defend claims about probabilities in this area. Still, advocates of mutual assured destruction argue that we should adopt MAD because we can be confident that the likelihood of its failure is very small. They point to decades of successful deterrence—and to the continued irrationality of nuclear attacks by either side—as evidence for their claim that threats of nuclear retaliation make war improbable. Although the magnitude of disaster would be enormous if MAD failed—perhaps greater than with any other policy—the low risk of failure, combined with a recognition of its value in preserving free institutions, is used to justify the policy. Defenders of MAD might further argue that even if one grants that failure under a strategy of nonviolence offers the best worst outcome compared with all other policies, it should still be rejected because it is the one most likely to fail; it invites Soviet aggression by granting the Soviet Union something it will exploit to the detriment of the free world: namely, a monopoly of physical force. Because a strategy of unilateral disarmament and nonviolent resistance is likely to fail, advocates of assured destruction could argue, it is really the most disastrous policy we can adopt; indeed, it invites disaster. In sum—on this view—the least disastrous option is the one whose failure is most improbable. (Of course, proponents of a limited nuclear war–fighting strategy will argue that their policy is even less likely to fail than MAD because it deters nuclear aggression at all levels.)

In the best of all possible worlds, we would not have to make a choice: we could find a policy that is both unlikely to fail and, even if it did fail, would have the best worst outcome of all the policy options. If this ideal cannot be achieved, then our judgment about which policy is the least disastrous will depend on the kind of risks we are willing to take and on the relative value we place on the nature of the consequences versus the likelihood of failure. There is no objectively correct view of *least disastrous*, only different interpretations. The point is to be clear about the particular meaning we give to the concept of disaster avoidance and why we choose that understanding over other possibilities.

Summary and Conclusion

To maximize rationality in choosing among the variety of proposals, I have formulated seven criteria that can be used for evaluating and comparing policy options. I have also indicated problems in interpreting, applying, and reconciling these criteria. For example, although affordability is an important criterion in the assessment of any proposal, ultimately we have to *decide* how much weight we will give this requirement compared with other criteria, such as moral defensibility. For years, nuclear weapons have given the United States more bang for the buck, but it is not clear that this very affordable path to security is morally the best policy.

Should morality be the overriding criterion? An advocate of a nuclear war–fighting strategy might, for example, acknowledge that while national security based on a broad range of nuclear threats, including the threat to destroy cities, may be less satisfactory from a strictly moral viewpoint than other proposals, it remains, on balance, the best choice, when judged by other criteria, especially the criterion of appropriateness vis-à-vis Soviet policy.

On the other hand, an advocate of strategic defense might argue that moral considerations should be overriding and that we ought not subordinate them to other criteria—that we must be willing to spend what is required to protect the population, that we must make our defensive system as effective as possible (even if not perfect), that we must somehow persuade the Soviets that such a policy is in their interest, and so on.

The seven criteria cannot be easily placed in a hierarchy in such a way that we can clearly see, in the case of a conflict, which criteria are to take priority over others. Value judgments are unavoidable. Moreover, where a criterion is ambiguous (e.g., disaster avoidance), there may be no obviously best interpretation. Here again, a normative judgment about the best construction is unavoidable.

Finally, there is nothing magical about the number seven. Other criteria may need to be added. The point is to bring as many different considerations as possible to the evaluation of policy proposals so that we do not ignore anything that is relevant to making the most rational choice. (In the Appendix, I use the seven criteria to criticize the major policy options.)

In the next chapter I will introduce the major policy options by conceiving of them as analogical extensions of four well-known criminal correction theories. This, I hope, will make the policy alternatives more accessible and easier to evaluate.

CHAPTER THREE

The Domestic Analogy:
Criminal Correction Theory and Defense Policy

One way to make the unfamiliar more familiar is through the device of analogy. I believe that Michael Walzer in his important study *Just and Unjust Wars*[1] has provided us with a fruitful analogy that, if developed and applied to nuclear weapons policy, could give us a way of understanding the distinct logic of, and the qualitative differences between, four policy options. Moreover, as I will show, additional or hybrid options are derivable by combining some of the four general frameworks in various ways.

According to Walzer, the "legitimate" response of a nation to the threat of armed aggression can be fitted within what he calls the *domestic analogy*. On this analogy, aggression is conceived as the international equivalent of robbery or murder. The morally justified response to the threat of aggression is conceived as requiring something analogous to such domestic concepts as crime, law enforcement, and punishment.[2] That is, the threat of aggression—an international crime—calls for the international equivalent of a correction doctrine. Of course, an important difference between the domestic and the international spheres is that the latter lacks a legitimate coercive authority—a world government with the power to police and enforce international law. This means that in facing the possibility of an armed attack, a potential victim of aggression (and/or its allies) must be prepared to perform the task that, on the domestic level, is assigned to the criminal justice system.

Despite the imperfect nature of the analogy, I believe that the debate on nuclear weapons policy can be illuminated by conceiving the national security decision we face in dealing with the Soviet nuclear threat as analogous to the domestic security decision we confront in

57

dealing with criminal threats to society. *Prima facie* what makes a criminal correction theory the appropriate analogue for defense policy is that the former tries to provide a practical and morally justifiable response to violent threats to the social order. In both the domestic and the international domain, the problem is how best to deal with threats to society. The difference is that in the former the threat is internal; in the latter, external. The preservation of the given social order—including the freedom, lives, and property of citizens—is the concern of both criminal correction theory and defense policy.

Within the framework of the domestic analogy, the Soviet Union is to be viewed as at least a potential offender. Regardless of its public declarations of peaceful intentions, it has in fact a record of international crime (Hungary, Czechoslovakia, Afghanistan), and it remains capable of inflicting great harm on the United States and its allies. The question is, which theory of correction is the most appropriate response to the existing Soviet state?

A Survey of Correction Theories

In domestic society, deterrence is only one of four possible responses to the threat that crime poses to society. The other major correction options are social defense, retribution, and rehabilitation.[3] I believe that these four alternatives provide us with an idea of the range of options we have for dealing with the threat of nuclear aggression, which might be described as the ultimate international crime. Before I show how these theories of correction apply to nuclear policy, however, it will be necessary to sketch the primary strategy, the requirements, and the ethical foundation of each theory. In practice, of course, most criminal justice systems involve a combination (sometimes incoherent) of these correction responses. For the purpose of analysis—in order to show what is distinctive about each doctrine—I will treat these correction perspectives as ideal types, giving an exposition of each in isolation from the others. That is, I will consider each in its pure form, uncontaminated, as it is in the real world, by elements from the other types.

Deterrence

A criminal correction system based on deterrence adopts the strategy of using punitive threats to inhibit criminal behavior. The aim is to convey the message that crime does not pay. To do this successfully, three conditions must be satisfied: (1) the message must be clearly communicated; (2) the subjects to whom it is communicated must find the threat of punishment credible; and (3) these subjects must be capable of rationally weighing the consequences of their actions and must perceive the threatened punishment as outweighing the rewards of crime, concluding that the possible gains are not worth the possible losses. Punishment under a deterrence system is not designed to satisfy abstract justice; the point is to reduce crime.

Traditionally, deterrence has been grounded in the principle of utility. That is, the overall beneficial effects of punitive threats and acts of punishment are viewed as justifying the suffering that this correction system inflicts on a minority of the population—the criminal agents. From a utilitarian viewpoint, the infliction of suffering—even on the guilty—must always be justified and, in so far as possible, minimized. No more suffering must be inflicted on offenders than is necessary to achieve the desired end: deterrence.

A standard objection to utilitarianism is that it allows us to justify the punishment of the innocent, provided that the expected consequences of such punishment look sufficiently beneficial. Although in practice one will be hard pressed to find a supporter of domestic deterrence who is in favor of the punishment of the innocent, the theoretical possibility of justifying such action cannot be *a priori* ruled out so long as one's moral judgments are based upon utility. Indeed, nuclear deterrence in one of its variants (MAD) justifies a threat to kill millions of innocents on the basis of the good consequences of such a threat.

Is it always wrong to threaten to kill the innocent? Is it always wrong to punish the innocent? An examination of the application of deterrence theory to nuclear policy will reveal some important differences between deterrence on the domestic and international levels.

Social Defense

The primary aim of the correction theory of social defense is the protection of society from dangerous individuals. The strategy is to find ways of incapacitating dangerous individuals, whether by imprisonment, exile, or execution.

In this doctrine, there is (1) no assumption that people are essentially rational or that potential offenders are affected by threats and (2) no concern to punish wrongdoers either to make them examples or to make them pay for their crime. The defense of society is the sole function of correction procedures. No deterrent, retributive, or rehabilitative claims need be made to justify social defense measures. The only requirement is that the procedures prevent individuals who have been judged to be dangerous to society from harming law-abiding citizens.

The normative foundation of social defense is a combination of utility and moral rights. Such a system can be seen as providing social benefits that outweigh any negative consequences, such as the suffering of the offender who is deprived of freedom or life. The good consequences of incapacitation are viewed as sufficiently good to justify any losses imposed on individuals.

There is, in addition, an important deontological reason for supporting social defense: it is designed to protect the rights of the innocent to security in their person, liberty, and property. If all law-abiding citizens have an equal right to such security, the government is said to have a duty to render dangerous individuals incapable of harming society. This governmental obligation should not depend on the cost-effectiveness of incapacitation procedures—or whether the tax burden these measures impose on the majority (in order, for example, to guarantee security even for a minority in poor communities) can be justified in utilitarian terms. If there is truly an equal right to protection, then it is not a matter of balancing the well-being of the greatest number against that of the least number. Thus, if there is ever a choice between the rights of the innocent and the requirements of utility, the former should be given priority.

So understood, the moral appeal of social defense over deterrence resides in its stress on the rights of the innocent, a feature that precludes actions that would harm some innocent individuals to benefit others. That is, on my reading of the theory of social defense, the principle of utility is always constrained by a deontological principle that rules out the abuses to which a purely utilitarian theory might be open.

For some a moral deficiency of this theory—in its pure form—is that it does not require punishment of the guilty: it is a nonpunitive theory that provides no notion of what offenders deserve. Incapacitation, not punishment, is the objective. If this is a flaw, we will have to see to what extent it is carried over in the application of the theory to defense policy.

Retribution

Retribution is a theory whose central concern is giving criminals what they deserve. The primary aim of retribution is, in a word, justice. To achieve this aim offenders must be made to suffer a punishment that is proportional to the seriousness of their crimes and their degree of culpability. From the retributive standpoint, justice is not served if offenders who are mentally competent and in control of their actions are not punished at all, or if they are punished too leniently or too severely. The two crucial principles that a correction system must focus on, therefore, are culpability and proportionality.

The function of a correction system, from a retributivist perspective, is to apply punishment appropriately—that is, in a fair and equitable way. Whether punishment deters crime or reforms offenders is secondary to its just application. Although the theory asserts that punishment should fit the crime, it does not require that the penalty match the crime in some literal way—for example, a torture for a torture (which, in fact, would violate justice by reducing the state to the moral level of the torturer)—but only that the penalty be determined by the seriousness of the crime. On this view, justice must not be compromised in the name of deterrence or social protection.

Classically, retribution has been grounded in deontological ethics, and especially a Kantian viewpoint. What is morally central is respect for persons. As we saw in Chapter Two, this view holds that offenders should be punished in proportion to their degree of responsibility for their crimes. The moral justification of punishment is always to be found in the fact that offenders, in so far as they are not insane or coerced, but free and responsible individuals (i.e., persons), deserve punishment. Offenders ought to suffer because they are culpable for their crimes. Punishment is never to be justified in terms of its consequences—for example, its benefits to society—but only in terms of its conformity to the requirements of justice, understood according to the principle of respect for persons.

Under no circumstances can punishment of the innocent be justified. Before punishment can be morally applied, guilt must be established, the gravity of the offense determined, and the degree of voluntariness of the offense established. If there are mitigating circumstances or if the degree of intent is minimal, the punishment must be reduced accordingly.

To what extent can this retributive model be duplicated in defense policy? Is it really possible in war to avoid punishing the innocent? On what grounds do we label someone guilty during a war? Assuming that we can decide who deserves retaliatory punishment in time of war, can the criterion of proportionality be satisfied by modern weapons? These are questions we will investigate in an attempt to determine to what degree retributive theory can be applied to the military domain.

Rehabilitation

The assumption behind rehabilitation theory is that crime is a product of alterable conditions. This assumption calls for a two-pronged strategy in response to criminal threats: (1) preventive measures designed to change the social conditions that generate or motivate criminal behavior (e.g., lack of education, poverty, unemployment, child abuse), and (2) corrective measures designed to reshape the offenders' psyches or behavior patterns so that they will be able to fit back into law-abiding society (ideally, a reformed and more humane society). In its humanitarian form, rehabilitation is opposed to the use of all punitive correction measures. The behavior and the minds of offenders are to be changed through humane, therapeutic, and nonviolent techniques. The objective is to help the offender overcome criminal tendencies and to return to society as a productive, law-abiding citizen.

Although rehabilitation is often associated with utilitarianism, it can also be viewed as rooted in a principle of respect for persons. The utilitarian justification turns on the view that society will benefit if the conditions conducive to crime are eliminated and if effective correction techniques are developed for reforming offenders. Moreover, to the extent that utilitarianism seeks to minimize suffering in all individuals, including offenders, the theory of rehabilitation is appealing because it promises to decrease criminal behavior in society without resort to the infliction of suffering on offenders (punishment).

The principle of respect for persons comes into play in rehabilitation's concern for the offender as an individual. In one of its variants, rehabilitation aims at the moral transformation of criminals: offenders are to be treated as moral agents capable of recognizing the wrongness of their actions and correcting their behavior. In contrast to deterrence, social defense and retribution, the approach of rehabilitation is sympathetic to the offender. Certain external conditions are viewed as contributing to the negative behavior of offenders, as distorting their thinking and relations with others; the point is to change these conditions and the psychological distortions that they have created.

What would it mean to apply the theory of rehabilitation to the domain of defense policy? What preventive actions can be taken to avert the international crime of nuclear aggression? Who is to be rehabilitated and how? These questions will be pursued in a chapter devoted to the exploration of a nonviolent security strategy, which is designed to translate rehabilitation into a policy of national defense.

Application of Correction Theories to Nuclear Policy

I suggest that, taking a lead from criminal correction theory, we have at least four ready-made, clear, and distinct candidates for policy alternatives. Specifically, when translated into nuclear policy options, the correction doctrines give us the four following strategies:

1. Deterrence: the inhibition of nuclear aggression through a nuclear counterthreat. This strategy requires us to convince the Soviet

Union that a nuclear attack would result in unacceptable losses for the USSR. This assumes the essential rationality of the adversary and holds that any risks generated by the strategy are outweighed by benefits.

2. *Social Defense:* the protection of society from nuclear attack through active and passive defense. This strategy requires an ability both to incapacitate Soviet weapons in flight (i.e., active defense) and to shelter the population from the effects of any nuclear forces that penetrate the defensive shield (i.e., passive defense). A concern with protecting the innocent and minimizing suffering requires a strategy designed to limit damage to the homeland while avoiding retaliation against population centers.

3. *Retribution:* the defense of the nation against nuclear attack through preparation for nonnuclear retaliation against the agents of nuclear aggression. This strategy demands that we have forces discriminating enough to inflict proportional punishment on those involved in nuclear aggression while avoiding attacks on noncombatants. The underlying principle is that the guilty and only the guilty should suffer retaliation.

4. *Rehabilitation:* the prevention of nuclear attack through nonmilitary preventive and corrective measures. This strategy requires that we seek to remove the conditions conducive to armed conflict in general and nuclear war in particular while training the population in the tactics of nonviolent resistance. The assumption is that without resort to force, we can prevent an aggressor from achieving military victory.

Each of these strategies constitutes an answer to the question of what the United States and its allies should do in response to the Soviet nuclear threat. In exploring these competing strategies I also sketch force systems appropriate to each.

My exposition of the first option will be a summary of competing approaches to nuclear deterrence. This option really breaks down into several suboptions or nuclear strategies. Deterrence, as I pointed out above, remains the dominant nuclear weapons policy option. The current debate within the defense establishment is about which form of nuclear deterrence is most credible.

The second correction framework, social defense, is developed in its most radical form—as a proposal for population defense against nuclear attack. This is strategic defense conceived as an astrodome: a protective shield over society. A more modest version of strategic defense, seeking to defend retaliatory nuclear forces rather than people, is designed to create uncertainty in the minds of potential aggressors, making them doubt the possibility of a successful attack. (I will consider this under the heading of hybrids in Chapter Eight: it is really an attempt to enhance rather than transcend nuclear deterrence.) I focus on the astrodome concept—Reagan's original ambitious proposal to make nuclear weapons impotent and obsolete—because it represents a significant break with "established" strategy: indeed, it calls into question the whole notion of security based on nuclear threats. Moreover, it is the version of strategic defense that logically follows from a social defense premise.

In developing the first two nuclear policy proposals, I do not break any new ground, but only place well-known policy alternatives within conceptual frameworks borrowed from criminal correction theory. I think it is interesting to see to what degree nuclear deterrence and strategic defense are logical—or analogical—extensions of the criminal correction models of deterrence and social defense. I explore the limits of the domestic analogy, indicating how it breaks down at certain points.

My exposition of policies based upon retribution and rehabilitation introduces relatively neglected options. The idea of applying the concepts of retribution and the just war to nuclear weapons policy has not been sufficiently explored: it provides us with a third path to nuclear security. Recently, there has been increased discussion of denuclearization and improvements in conventional weapons. These advances in nonnuclear weapons, we will see, offer the possibility of achieving the discrimination required by a policy of retribution. At least some prominent defense analysts have seriously considered the promise of the new conventional technology in relation to the attempt to restrict retaliation to military targets.

Finally, my application of the concept of rehabilitation to nuclear policy yields a strategy that—although dismissed by the defense establishment—deserves serious consideration if only because it demands that we think in new ways and question unchallenged assumptions about the requirements of national security. For example, it questions the assumption that security depends on military force. Rehabilitation, applied to nuclear defense policy, calls for the pursuit of security through a nonviolent transformation of the conditions that breed and sustain aggression.

I devote a chapter to each of the four policy options. Each option is analyzed in its pure form for the sake of simplicity and clarity, and my expositions are sympathetic: that is, as I develop each proposal I take the role of apologist for it, anticipating and answering objections.

Some mixture of options, however, may seem unavoidable. For example, it may appear that the aim of deterrence runs through all the other options. Wouldn't an advocate of any one of the other three policies welcome the potential for deterrence that the policy contains? Of course. But proponents of social defense, retribution, and rehabilitation will assert that deterrence is not the end-all but must be subordinated to another objective. From the perspective of retribution, for example, even if certain threats would be effective in deterring nuclear war, such threats will not be allowed if they violate the requirements of justice. Thus, holding the enemy's cities hostage to nuclear destruction might prove to be an efficacious deterrent, but it is unacceptable to retributivists because it calls for threats to punish the innocent.

A reader who is not satisfied with any of the pure types may find some mixture of strategies more appealing. As I indicated above, I also sketch some hybrids: policy proposals that combine different strategies. The only *logical* requirement is that the hybrid be a coherent synthesis. In Chapter Eight I describe a number of logically consistent combinations. First, however, I will consider nuclear deterrence in isolation from the other options.

CHAPTER FOUR

Deterrence Policy:
Security Through
Mutual Nuclear Threats

Initially, before Soviet acquisition of nuclear weapons, the United States used nuclear weapons to deter Soviet conventional aggression. The United States held out the threat of massive retaliation with nuclear weapons if the Soviets launched conventional aggression anywhere in the world.

Current U.S. nuclear policy has to address itself to a Soviet Union as well armed with nuclear weapons as the United States. Nuclear deterrence is now based upon two premises: (1) that the Soviet Union constitutes a threat to our security, and (2) that the best way to deal with this is through a nuclear counterthreat. Despite the so-called new Soviet thinking on defense, as long as the Soviet Union has thousands of nuclear weapons aimed at the United States, it can be plausibly argued that U.S. security requires some form of nuclear deterrence. We must, according to advocates of nuclear deterrence, retain our nuclear arsenal and keep it aimed at the Soviet Union.

A policy of deterrence is morally justified by its good consequences. Specifically, it can be argued that a strategy of deterrence has the effect of preserving free institutions, preventing Soviet nuclear blackmail, and keeping the peace between the superpowers. It allows individuals in the West to pursue their own happiness in their own way. It makes war between the superpowers too costly to be worth fighting. On this view, if we did not threaten the Soviets with nuclear retaliation, then our freedom would be less secure and war would be more likely. The gains of a strategy of deterrence are said to outweigh the small risk of its failure. The moral justification of deterrence is thus essentially utilitarian: this strategy is efficacious, working to keep the peace and to preserve liberty.

The Requirements of Deterrence

Deterrence involves the use of threats for the purpose of discouraging conduct that the deterrer condemns or prohibits. It is supposed to operate on the psyche of the potential offender: the assumption is that a subject can be dissuaded from engaging in proscribed behavior if its goal is made to appear unattainable, excessively costly, or both. On the standard view, in order for deterrence threats to work, they must be: (1) clearly communicated, (2) credible, and (3) directed at subjects who are rational calculators.[1]

Communication. The threatener must make clear to potential offenders both the action or actions that are prohibited and the penalty for engaging in the proscribed behavior. That is, potential offenders must be informed about what constitutes an offense and what price they will pay for committing one. If there is a failure to communicate either of these two things, a potential offender may inadvertently become an actual offender.

Credibility. Credibility turns on what the potential offender thinks about the deterrer's power and will. *Power* refers to the capacity to inflict excessive costs (in relation to possible gains) on offenders and/or to deny offenders their objectives. Power is something that can in principle be empirically confirmed: the deterrer can show the offender that it has the physical ability to inflict unacceptable losses by, for example, displaying its weapons. *Will* means the resolve to use one's power. This is a psychological disposition that cannot be empirically demonstrated—at least not until it is tested by an act of aggression.

Credibility is a concept that is very hard to nail down. Claims about what is required for credibility are claims about what potential violators need to think in order to be deterred, not about whether *in fact* the deterrer has the power and the resolve to punish offenders. Thoughts are as good as reality in the realm of credibility. The question is, what thoughts must we put into the minds of potential offenders to inhibit proscribed actions? In the case of nuclear deterrence, there is profound disagreement concerning what a potential nuclear offender must believe in order to be deterred. At least four views are logically distinguishable.

1. An extreme view is that a potential offender will not be deterred unless it is certain that the deterrer has both the power and the will to inflict unacceptable losses. On this view, in order for deterrence to work, the potential offender must be absolutely convinced that the

deterrer has the capacity and resolve to inflict on the attacker excessive losses or to deny the attacker its objectives. Serious doubts about the deterrer's power or will to retaliate may tempt the potential offender to engage in prohibited actions.

2. A weaker requirement is that although a potential offender must feel certain that the deterrer has the *power*, it need not feel certain that the deterrer has the *will*. In other words, uncertainty about will, if coupled with certainty about power, is sufficient to deter. On this view, a potential offender—provided it is convinced that the deterrer has the power to inflict unacceptable punishment or to deny the potential offender its objectives—will be deterred simply because it is uncertain about the threatener's will to use this feared power. For all the potential attacker knows, the deterrer *may* use its retaliatory power: the mere possibility of retaliation brings with it the unacceptable risk of massive destruction.

3. A third view is the reverse of (2): it asserts that to be deterred, the potential offender only needs to feel certain that the deterrer has the *will* to retaliate; this is sufficient, provided that the potential violator cannot rule out the possibility that the deterrer—if it has so claimed—has the power to inflict unacceptable losses. If the penalty for an attack is heavy enough, certainty about resolve combined with uncertainty about capacity may be enough to dissuade the potential offender. If it is convinced of the deterrer's resolve, the potential offender will err on the side of safety, assuming, for the sake of its own security, that the deterrer has retaliatory forces sufficient to inflict excessive costs or to deny the potential attacker its objectives.

4. The weakest requirement is that it is enough for the potential offender to believe that the deterrer *might* have the power and the will to retaliate. On this view, if the prospective losses are high enough, uncertainty in the mind of a potential aggressor about will and power will be sufficient to deter an attack.

Proponents of competing nuclear deterrent strategies disagree about which of the above views is correct. We cannot in fact know which of the above, if any, is the correct interpretation of the credibility requirement. Since the credibility requirement involves perception—a subjective factor—the question demands that the deterrer try to get inside the head of the potential attacker, a difficult, if not impossible, task. The deterrer will have to judge whether the potential aggressor, in order to be deterred, needs to feel certain (or merely uncertain) about the deterrer's retaliatory power, will, or both. The only noncontroversial thing that can be said about the credibility requirement is negative: the potential attacker will not be deterred if it feels certain that the threatener lacks the power or the will to carry out the threat.

Rationality. Finally, in order for deterrence to work, the potential offender must be a rational agent. The assumption of the rationality of the adversary is a fundamental element in nuclear deterrence strategy. There has also been a long and complex debate about the meaning of rationality. All that is meant here is that a potential attacker can be deterred only if (1) it is capable of weighing the consequences of alternative actions, and (2) it will not engage in actions that (a) have little chance of achieving its objectives or (b) will, even if successful in achieving its objectives, result in excessive costs. If the potential aggressor is disposed to act rashly, or if it deliberately disregards all the probable negative (counterproductive) consequences of contemplated actions, then all threats will prove impotent. An agent who is heedless of the consequences of its actions, or who knows but does not care that its actions are likely to result in failure or in costs that exceed benefits, is not a rational calculator.

This does not mean that all rational agents will be deterred by the same kinds of threats. Indeed, an empirically minded deterrer will construct a system of threats that takes into consideration the peculiar psychology of the individual or group that is to be deterred. To be rational in the required sense, a potential violator does not need to share the values and fears of the deterrer: that is, the concept of rationality used here is open enough to apply to agents who, from the point of view of the deterrer, hold an irrational worldview. The kind of rationality required for effective deterrence does not even presuppose that those to be deterred are sane. This is because even an incorrigibly insane individual can be manipulated and controlled by threats, provided that the deterrer can discover this individual's peculiar objectives and deepest fears. All that is required for an efficacious deterrent is to make it undesirable *from the potential offender's perspective* to engage in actions prohibited by the threatener. To achieve this, the deterrer needs to know what potential offenders highly value, what losses they are unprepared to accept, and what they most fear. It will be seen that those who disagree about nuclear deterrent strategies disagree in part because they have conflicting views of what the Soviets most value and most fear.

Differences Between Domestic and Nuclear Deterrence

Although deterrence in the criminal justice context and deterrence in the nuclear context share a common structure—namely, the attempt to inhibit proscribed behavior through the use of threats—a radical difference appears when we consider the *utility* of punishment.

Although we can meaningfully talk about the utility of punishment in the domestic sphere, utility in the strategic domain seems to apply only to the instruments of punishment, not to punishment itself.

For example, let us assume that law enforcement officials seek to deter the crime of murder by threatening to electrocute murderers. Also let us assume that these officials believe in the deterrence efficacy of capital punishment in general and electrocution in particular. Granted this, it could be argued that the death penalty exists, for these officials, in order to be applied—that capital punishment has utility. After all, electric chairs are constructed for the purpose of being used.

By contrast, under nuclear strategy (even the war-fighting variety), nuclear weapons are constructed and deployed so that (ideally) they will *never* be used. If we reverse the analogy and transfer the logic of nuclear deterrence to the domestic sphere, this would be like training executioners and constructing the machinery of execution on the assumption that their existence will prevent their use. That is, the success of the system would require that executioners never have to do what they were trained to do and that electric chairs remain forever unoccupied.

In a criminal justice system, however, the use of the death penalty is not in fact considered a failure in the same sense as the use of nuclear weapons would be under a system of nuclear deterrence. The practice of execution can be *accepted* in a way that the practice of nuclear retaliation cannot. Anyone who argues, "If we ever have to execute a criminal (i.e., carry out the threat), then deterrence has failed us," has not understood the nature of criminal deterrence.

Deterrence in criminal correction theory is concerned with *discouraging* or *minimizing* prohibited behavior: it does not promise to eliminate or prevent criminal behavior altogether. Domestic deterrence theorists are not utopians who expect that simply by threatening to inflict punishment, a criminal justice system can produce perfect conformity to criminal law. The fact that, despite the threatened punishment, crimes still occur does not invalidate deterrent threats, unless, of course, crime becomes epidemic.

Indeed—here the analogy clearly breaks down—it can be plausibly argued that domestic deterrence *requires* some intermittent failures in order to satisfy the requirement of credibility and show new generations of potential offenders what will happen if they break the law. Fresh examples are periodically needed in order to demonstrate that crime does not pay. This is the paradox of domestic deterrence: to prevent crimes, some crimes are needed. The paradox is that the deterrer values the (occasional) occurrence of the prohibited behavior. If the general population is not periodically reminded of the negative consequences of criminal behavior, punishment will become an abstraction, and willingness to break the law will eventually increase. Threats lose their meaning unless they are sometimes cashed in reality. For educational purposes, the authorities need some criminals (incorrigible and irrational offenders will do): the punishment of these individuals will serve as examples—for the general (deterrable) population—of what happens to those who break the law. If there were no crimes for a long period (and thus no examples of the costs of crime for a new generation), those charged with deterring crime might feel tempted to invent some during the drought.

Under nuclear strategy, by contrast, a single failure of deterrence would be disastrous, not educative: it would be the ultimate disaster. Nuclear deterrence requires us to rely on an impressive *display* of threatening hardware instead of on the *periodic use* of these punitive instruments. Nuclear deterrence is based upon a threat whose utility collapses as soon as it has to be carried out. The point is that once nuclear weapons are used in an act of retaliation, their utility for preventing war has obviously been reduced to zero. Unlike domestic deterrence, once nuclear retaliation occurs, deterrence of the prohibited criminal act (in this case a Soviet first strike or act of aggression) is no longer possible: "If these buttons are ever pushed, they have completely failed in their purpose. The equipment is useful only if not used."[2]

Although in theory the utility of nuclear weapons lies in their nonuse in a military sense (that is, in an act of retaliation), in fact, if they are to achieve deterrence, their use cannot be ruled out by either the potential aggressor or the threatener. The Soviets must, in order to be deterred, believe that we will (or might) use our nuclear weapons, and—unless we are bluffing—we must be ready to use them. These conflicting intentions—to use and not to use them—are somehow immanent in these weapons. The fact that we build weapons that embody contradictory intentions is the paradox of nuclear deterrence.

To ensure its continued success, advocates of nuclear deterrence have to face the question of whether they can find an adequate substitute for the feature that domestic deterrence finds necessary for continued success—namely intermittent, fear-inducing illustrations that remind new generations of the consequences of "crime." Otherwise, won't there be a serious credibility problem? It would appear that all illustrations of the negative consequences of nuclear aggression must be purely imaginary.

It is, of course, instructive to have Hiroshima and Nagasaki as antique examples because they enable the nuclear deterrer to point to the past and say to the potential nuclear aggressor: if you attack us, we will inflict upon you a hundred thousand Hiroshimas. Moreover, these "illustrations" of nuclear punishment give the United States a deterrence edge: the Soviet Union has to recognize that the United States is the only nation that has actually used nuclear weapons. Although forty-five years after Hiroshima the meaning of the nuclear threat is vague, it is horribly and frighteningly vague, as the image of hell's fiery punishment must be to a fundamentalist.

Undeniably there remains a significant disanalogy between domestic and nuclear deterrence: namely, the essential utility of the act of punishment for the former and its unquestionable disutility for the latter. The threat can be made credible only indirectly, in nonnuclear contexts—by, for example, engaging in conventional retaliation against nations or groups who attack U.S. interests, such as the U.S. air attack on Libya as reprisal for its alleged involvement in a terrorist act. Perhaps such limited conventional military reprisals, which do not involve the danger of global confrontation, can help show the United States' resolve to make offenders pay.

The problem, of course, is that deterrence, as applied to nuclear policy, is a two-way street. This is another important disanalogy between nuclear and domestic deterrence: the aim of nuclear deterrence is to create a situation of *mutual* deterrence. In domestic deterrence, social peace is not typically maintained by a stand-off between criminals and authorities: in fact, the efficacy of domestic deterrence depends on the capacity of the state to intimidate the criminal more effectively than the criminal can intimidate the state; the state must possess a capability to inflict punishment that the offender lacks.

By contrast, nuclear deterrence (in most of its varieties) requires, in order to preserve a stable international peace and prevent nuclear aggression, that each side be able to inflict unacceptable punishment on the other side. This is a requirement of nuclear crisis stability: that neither side should be vulnerable to one-sided punishment, or to defeat, by the other side. *Crisis stability* refers to "a situation in which, in times of crisis or high tension, no country would see the advantages of attacking first with nuclear weapons as outweighing the disadvantages."[3] The lower the degree of crisis stability, the greater the probability that one side will launch a preemptive nuclear attack in a period of high tension. (This remains a requirement unless one assumes the essential goodness or nonaggressiveness of one side—as do the advocates of U.S. nuclear superiority.)

For there to be mutual deterrence, (1) each side must communicate to the other side that it has (or may have) the nuclear means, if attacked, to deny the attacker its objectives and/or to inflict losses in excess of any gains; although it may not be necessary that each side be *certain* that the other side will retaliate, (2) neither side must be able to rule out that the other side might retaliate, if attacked;[4] and (3) each side, before considering a nuclear attack, must be disposed to weigh carefully the threat of nuclear retaliation, while also being disposed against engaging in highly risky—possibly suicidal—actions.

Types of Nuclear Deterrence

The specific nature of the required retaliatory forces and the appropriate targets of retaliation are, as we will see, matters of heated debate among proponents of nuclear deterrence. Competing nuclear deterrence options are typically classified under one of two headings: deterrence-only or deterrence-plus.

Before explaining these two types, it should be noted that the concept of extended deterrence applies to both types in so far as we are dealing with current U.S. commitments, especially its membership in NATO. *Extended deterrence* refers to the role U.S. nuclear forces play in deterring attacks other than those on the U.S. homeland, such as attacks on U.S. forces overseas or aggression against allied nations (e.g., Western Europe). Under extended deterrence the Soviet Union cannot attack an ally of the United States without risking nuclear retaliation by the United States. In addition, extended deterrence covers such vital interests as the protection of the flow of oil from the Persian Gulf to the United States and its allies. Sometimes it is hinted that even aggression against another communist power might elicit nuclear retaliation—for example, an attack against China. Does U.S. deterrence really extend to China? Should it? Whatever the status of these murky cases, there are enough clear cases of extended deterrence—specifically, the official U.S. commitment to defend Western Europe and Japan with nuclear weapons, even at the risk that the conflict will escalate to a Soviet nuclear attack on the U.S. homeland. Extended deterrence requires the coupling of the security of the United States and its allies in such a way that the USSR clearly understands that aggression against a U.S. ally or an area of vital U.S. interest involves the risk of U.S. nuclear retaliation against Soviet assets.

Pure Deterrence Strategies

The objective of *deterrence-only* (also called *pure deterrence*) strategy vis-à-vis the Soviet Union is the prevention of threats to U.S. security. It makes no provision for failure: the whole point is to make the consequences of aggression so costly that nuclear war becomes unthinkable for either side. Pure deterrence holds that the utility of nuclear weapons lies exclusively in their deterrence value. The function of U.S. nuclear weapons is to prevent a nuclear attack, nuclear blackmail, or conventional aggression. On this view, nuclear forces have no military function in any standard sense: that is, they have no value as weapons that could be rationally used to achieve victory in an armed conflict. Robert McNamara represents this perspective when he states that "nuclear weapons serve no military purpose whatsoever."[5] There are at least two species of deterrence-only strategy: mutual assured destruction and existential deterrence.

Mutual Assured Destruction

Mutual assured destruction (MAD) is a well-known example of pure deterrence. MAD was, for a time, official policy (under McNamara, during the Kennedy administration); it is no longer official U.S. policy. The basic assumption of MAD is that neither side will start a nuclear war if each side can arrange things so that nuclear aggression means national suicide. This is what Jonathan Schell has in mind when he states that "the central proposition of the deterrence doctrine is that a nuclear holocaust can best be prevented if each nuclear power holds in readiness a nuclear force with which it 'credibly' threatens to destroy the entire society of the attacker, even after suffering the worst possible 'first strike' that the attacker can launch."[6] More formally, the strategy, conceived as a means to realize the objective of deterrence, requires the following.

1. Each side must perceive the other side as having the capacity—even after suffering an all-out surprise nuclear attack—to destroy it as a functioning society. That is, each side must believe (or, on a more modest view, must be unable to rule out) that the other side has retaliatory nuclear forces capable of inflicting unacceptable damage on its society.

2. Each side must believe that the other side will (or might) use its retaliatory capacity if attacked. Given the enormous losses that a nuclear aggressor would suffer, unless one side can be certain that the other is bluffing in its threat to retaliate, neither side will be reckless enough to attack the other.

3. Neither side must perceive the other side as doing anything to protect or save its population from nuclear attack: each must be seen as leaving its people hostage to the nuclear forces of the other side. This is the meaning of *mutual assured destruction:* each side must somehow assure the other that its population is vulnerable to devastating nuclear retaliation.

4. Neither side must perceive the other side as doing anything to threaten its retaliatory forces. The only acceptable target is the other side's civilian assets, including the population and the industry of the attacker—this is called *countervalue* targeting. This means two things: (a) neither side must perceive the other as targeting its retaliatory forces, and (b) neither side must be perceived as having the capability of destroying the retaliatory forces of the other side. (MAD therefore excludes *counterforce* targeting and *counterforce* weapons—accurate nuclear weapons designed and deployed to destroy the retaliatory nuclear forces of the other side.) In sum, MAD requires that each side convince the other that it possesses only inaccurate *retaliatory* weapons.

Although MAD is, in my special sense, a nuclear defense strategy, technically speaking it is incompatible with the traditional concept of national defense. Defense of one's population against nuclear attack— whether by a program of civil defense, air defense, or a missile defense system—is in fact inconsistent with deterrence conceived as mutual assured destruction. As indicated in the third requirement above, MAD is a policy of mutual homeland vulnerability. Schell, again identifying nuclear deterrence with MAD, puts it this way:

> The adoption of the aim of preventing rather than winning war requires the adoption of other policies that fly in the face of military tradition. One is the abandonment of the military defense of one's nation—of what used to be the center of all military planning and was the most hallowed justification of the military calling. The policy of deterrence does not contemplate doing anything in defense of the homeland; it only promises that if the homeland is annihilated the aggressor's homeland will be annihilated. . . . It positively requires that each side leave its population open to attack, and make no serious effort to protect it.[7]

Force Requirements

Assured destruction capability has been quantified in terms of the minimum number of deliverable *retaliatory* warheads necessary to destroy a specified percentage of the Soviet Union's population and industrial capacity. For example, Pentagon staff during McNamara's tenure as secretary of defense estimated that we must ensure the invulnerability of the equivalent of 400 one-megaton warheads in order to destroy one-quarter to one-third of the Soviet Union's population and two-thirds of its industry.[8] These percentages were taken to constitute the quantitative meaning of the term *unacceptable damage*.

Distribution Requirements

To ensure sufficient retaliatory forces, numbers alone are not sufficient: the deployment strategy is also crucial. One way the survivability of nuclear weapons has been enhanced is through a triadic method of distribution: on land in silos, in the sea on submarines, and in the air on bombers. The point is to have enough warheads so distributed that the ability to inflict unacceptable damage is assured—even after absorbing the worst possible first strike. If, for example, it was decided that only 400 warheads were needed to inflict the desired levels of destruction, then the United States would obviously need—for an assured destruction capacity—more than 400 weapons in its arsenal, to allow for failure in launches, weapons going off course, and the destruction of U.S. retaliatory weapons by a Soviet first strike. Some advocates of MAD have recommended, as insurance, that *each leg* of the U.S. nuclear triad possess the capability of delivering 400 one-megaton warheads.[9]

From the standpoint of pure deterrence, however, the number of warheads can and should be kept limited because (1) the production of warheads beyond the number capable of inflicting unacceptable damage would not be cost-effective, and (2) an excess of weapons erodes rather than ensures security by suggesting to the Soviet Union that we are interested in something more than simply deterring war—perhaps in building toward a disarming first strike. Thus, MAD is also sometimes described as a doctrine of *finite deterrence*.

The Credibility Problem

It is usually pointed out by critics of MAD that it lacks credibility—that the Soviets will not believe that, once deterrence has failed, we will carry out the threat of all-out retaliation. If our only available choices were massive retaliation or surrender, the Soviets might find it tempting to contemplate a limited first strike against the United States, on the assumption that it would be irrational for the United States to respond to limited nuclear strikes with an all-out nuclear attack against the USSR. Faced with MAD, the Soviets might, in a crisis,* find the following strategy attractive: (1) launch a limited first strike against military targets (including nuclear forces) in the United States, and then (2) threaten to launch a devastating second strike against our cities if the United States refused to capitulate.

Soviet leaders could very logically ask themselves what meaning-

---

*It is, for example, conceivable that a new hard-line leadership in the Soviet Union might decide to retake parts of Eastern Europe. They would know that this is likely to provoke a U.S. reprisal.

ful objective the United States could achieve by retaliating. The Soviets might reason that the United States would see that MAD retaliation would simply be the mindless slaughter of Soviet civilians, which would trigger a massive Soviet attack against American civilians. In sum, critics of MAD claim that the Soviet Union might conclude that the United States would have nothing to gain and everything to lose if it responded to a limited Soviet counterforce attack by a mass countervalue attack on Soviet urban and industrial centers.

Which would the Soviet Union perceive as the more reasonable response to a limited first strike against the United States: an agreement to surrender that would save millions of American lives (and civilization) or pointless (i.e., merely vengeful) retaliation that would mean the total destruction of U.S. society? The credibility objection is simply this: under MAD, capitulation after a limited nuclear attack looks like the more rational option. MAD therefore creates a condition of crisis instability by making it rational to strike first and irrational to retaliate.

The Meaning of MAD Rationality

In response to the credibility objection, an advocate of MAD can point out that rational political leaders who are contemplating launching a nuclear attack must weigh possible gains against the possible losses. The potential attacker must ask, *what if* the victim of nuclear aggression were, against reason, to retaliate? Granting the irrationality of retaliation, it does not follow that a potential aggressor can rest assured that retaliation will not occur. Schell observes:

> The irrationality of the threat to commit suicide probably doesn't do a great deal to reduce effectiveness. There has been enough insanity in history to lend credibility to even the maddest threats, and for governments to threaten to do something irrational is quite enough to get everybody to believe they will do it.[10]

Governments and leaders are, Patrick Morgan reminds us in *Deterrence: A Conceptual Analysis,* quite capable of nonrational behavior, and "in the nuclear age this is what makes a threat to retaliate plausible."[11] The only sensible course of action for a nation that confronts a nuclear adversary is to avoid unnecessary provocation—that is, to try to minimize risk and to be, above all, prudent and cautious.

Although it may be *theoretically* true, according to an ideal model of rationality projected onto a victim of nuclear aggression, that it would be irrational for the victim to retaliate, thus making it *theoretically* rational for one side to attack first, in the real world of multiplying uncertainties and irrationalities, prudence recommends against such aggression.[12] Even if the probability of retaliation were small, the risks are so enormous that betting on the perfect rationality of the victim of nuclear aggression is not itself a rational wager. On this view, uncertainty about response is enough to deter a rational nation from attacking a nuclear power. Therefore, the requirement of rationality applies not to the nation attacked but to the nation contemplating a nuclear attack: if the latter is sensible, it will not risk everything on the chance that the other side will see the pointlessness of retaliation. If there is even a possibility that the other side might act on its threat to retaliate, that is enough to deter a sensible nation from aggression. It is the potential attacker's uncertainty about the potential victim's response, combined with the severity of the losses, that deters an attack.

According to the logic of MAD, therefore, a nuclear attack can be deterred if the potential aggressor runs the risk of incurring losses greater than any possible gains. What are the possible losses, and do Soviet leaders really value what we threaten to destroy under this policy? MAD obviously depends upon a crucial assumption concerning what each side values, and thus it turns on a concept of what each side most fears losing. MAD's countervalue targeting plan assumes that both sides ultimately value civilian assets and thus will avoid actions that risk significant civilian losses.

The assumption underlying MAD is that Soviet leaders would never risk the assured destruction of a significant percentage of their population and industry. In this sense, the Soviet leaders must be seen as sharing the values of U.S. leaders. The conviction that the mass destruction of civilian assets constitutes unacceptable damage makes sense only if we assume that those in power in the Soviet Union, as well as in the United States, care about their people. Furthermore, we must assume that Soviet leaders, despite their admission of the failures of centralized socialism, take pride in what the Communist Party has achieved industrially and socially since 1917, and that they wish to build on these accomplishments. It is reasonable, on these assumptions, to conclude that the threat to destroy the Soviet Union as a functioning society will be enough to dissuade the Soviets from launching an attack on the United States or any of the nations we have pledged to defend.

The Case for MAD

The case for MAD can be summarized as follows.

1. The threat of mutual annihilation has worked for decades: that is, the existence of mutual nuclear threats has prevented war between the United States and the Soviet Union. It is reasonable to hold that the

mutual capacity for annihilation has contributed significantly to the prevention of world war by making both superpowers extremely anxious to avoid any armed conflict that might lead to a nuclear war.

2. There is every reason to believe that MAD will continue to work indefinitely into the future. As long as each society can hold the other's population hostage to the threat of annihilation, conventional and nuclear war between the superpowers will remain irrational. So long as each side continues to have nothing to gain and everything to lose by going to war, neither side will launch an attack against the other.

3. Acceptance of points 1 and 2 leads us to the conclusion that if the United States and the USSR did not have retaliatory nuclear forces, conventional war would become more likely. In the absence of mutual fear of annihilation, war might again become thinkable and worth the risk.

4. The threat of assured destruction prevents Soviet blackmail and defends Western democracy. If the Soviet Union had nuclear weapons and the West did not, the Soviet government might in the future, under more aggressive leadership, use their conventional forces for expansionist purposes, keeping the United States from intervening by threatening nuclear strikes against the American homeland. The preservation of democracy in the West is worth the small risk of a nuclear war.

5. There is no reasonable alternative to MAD. Any deterrence strategy that stops short of the threat of mutual annihilation will increase the probability of war: any decrease in the horror of nuclear war increases its likelihood. Any move toward unilateral disarmament will invite a renewal of Soviet aggression and expansion: for all we know, the Soviets are still committed to the goal of world domination and will exploit any new opportunity to achieve this objective. Any attempt to protect the homeland from nuclear attack (such as anti-missile defenses) will lead to massive countermeasures, including the multiplication of nuclear weapons and thus an endless arms race.

6. MAD is consistent with a radical nuclear arms reduction. Embracing a regime of finite deterrence, MAD allows for substantial cuts in current arsenals: the United States and the Soviet Union would only need a small percentage of the thousands of warheads each presently possesses. Rejecting the indefinite proliferation of nuclear weapons, advocates of MAD recognize a point of diminishing returns—in terms of security as well as expenditures—in nuclear arms production. MAD allows us to test the Soviet Union's sincerity about working toward a goal of minimal deterrence.

7. In providing extended deterrence through relatively inexpensive nuclear forces and in not requiring expensive modernization (e.g., improvements in accuracy) of retaliatory nuclear forces, MAD is a cost-

efficient means of achieving security. It costs far less to deter potential Soviet aggression against Europe, the Middle East, or Japan through finite retaliatory nuclear forces (the U.S. nuclear umbrella) than it would to establish conventional armies capable of matching those of the Soviet Union. Furthermore, it costs less to maintain countervalue retaliatory forces than to create a counterforce arsenal.

8. MAD is a cooperative strategy: it requires cooperation between the Soviet Union and the United States in arms control. In order for MAD to work, both sides must agree (formally or informally) that they will not construct weapons in a quantity or of a quality that could be used to threaten the nuclear forces of the other side. The ABM Treaty of 1972, which prohibits territorial defenses, is an example of a document that embodies cooperation in promoting the objective of mutual vulnerability. MAD is compatible with a policy of testing bold new Soviet proposals in nuclear arms reduction.

Existential Deterrence

Existential deterrence (EXDET for short) is a second example of a deterrence-only policy. It exploits the deterrence value implicit in the mere possession of nuclear weapons. EXDET differs from MAD in its silence concerning employment policy: it makes no declarations about how or whether the nuclear forces will be used. This form of pure deterrence rests, in the words of former National Security Advisor McGeorge Bundy, on "the uncertainty about what could happen, not in what has been asserted."[13] The assumption of EXDET is that mere possession prevents use.

On this view, it is the uncertainty of a nuclear nation's response to a nuclear attack that deters. Neither the promise of restraint (e.g., a policy of no first use) nor threats of proportional punishment (e.g., a policy of limited nuclear reprisal) can be confidently relied on: knowledge of the devastating power of the weapons is sufficient to prevent nuclear aggression. Given the enormous destructive power of nuclear weapons, declarations of intentions are seen as unnecessary. Indeed, threatening the other side with annihilation can be viewed as provocative, as creating a destabilizing insecurity in the nation threatened. Under certain conditions—for example, a crisis in which nerves are frayed and the fear of an attack is high—a threatening posture may provoke the action it seeks to prevent.

Given an enemy who is averse to great risk, nuclear deterrence, according to EXDET, is easy: to deter a risk-averse enemy, what matters is the adversary's perception of our military *capacity*, not our public statements about how we will use this capacity. In sum, the enemy will be deterred by its awareness of the *existence* of weapons capable of inflicting great destruction. So long as both sides appear to have nuclear weapons designed to be used after an attack, there should be mutual deterrence and therefore crisis stability.

Force Requirements

EXDET is similar to MAD in so far as it requires only a finite deterrent—a limited nuclear retaliatory force. This might be achieved through the triadic arrangement described above; or, if it was possible to guarantee an invulnerable retaliatory force with only one kind of delivery vehicle (such as a submarine force or mobile land-based missiles), the other legs of the triad could be dismantled. Since existential deterrence makes no declaratory threats about, for example, what percentage of Soviet industry or population would be destroyed in a retaliatory strike, it would appear to require fewer warheads than MAD. McGeorge Bundy has stated: "One bomb on a city would be a catastrophe without precedent."[14] Although we can be sure that more than one warhead would be required in order to have a credible deterrent, at least for some proponents of existential deterrence the number might be considerably less than 400 invulnerable one-megaton warheads, even allowing for failed launches, weapons going off course, and Soviet damage to U.S. weapons.

The point is that there is no need to try to match the adversary in numbers and kinds of weapons. Strategic superiority does not have much meaning in a world of nuclear weapons. If the United States retained only a small number of survivable nuclear forces, the fear of the destruction they could wreak on Soviet society would be enough to deter a Soviet nuclear attack. If that were not the case, the Soviet Union would long ago have taken care of Communist China. Only if the adversary appears capable of making a dramatic breakthrough that would threaten our retaliatory force would a change in the force structure be necessary. We must, of course, do what is necessary to offset any technological threat to the survivability of our nuclear arsenal, but no more than is necessary. If it is considered important to cultivate ambiguity in terms of targeting plans, then it might be prudent to modernize our nuclear arsenal enough to create a mix of countervalue and counterforce weapons—but not so many of the latter as to threaten the Soviet Union's retaliatory forces.

The Case for EXDET

The case for existential deterrence can be summed up as follows.
1. EXDET follows MAD in asserting that (a) nuclear weapons have prevented a Soviet–American war; (b) if neither side possessed nuclear

forces, conventional war would be more likely to occur; and (c) if the Soviet Union alone possessed nuclear weapons, a more aggressive Soviet leadership might, in the future, be tempted to use its substantial conventional forces to threaten free institutions while exploiting a nuclear monopoly to prevent the United States from countering this threat.

2. EXDET, unlike MAD, does not require threatening the other side. The language of threats is provocative and intensifies the tensions between the superpowers without adding anything to mutual security. Moreover, there is really no need to increase hostility by making threats of annihilation: the weapons speak for themselves. It is wise to leave their use ambiguous: speak softly and carry a nuclear stick.

3. This strategy, unlike MAD, does not require the United States to endorse population targeting and proclaim that our policy is to kill millions of Soviet citizens. Thus, it avoids making immoral threats and, indeed, *all* statements about how or whether the United States intends to use its nuclear arsenal.

4. If this policy does not endorse counterpopulation targeting, neither does it call for counterforce targeting. Although it does not rule out the possession of some modernized, accurate nuclear forces, it does not require the mass production of a destabilizing (potentially first-strike) counterforce arsenal designed for a first strike or protracted war-fighting. It requires neither a significant number of nuclear weapons nor their endless modernization—only the existence of a finite and survivable deterrent force. It thus cannot be misinterpreted as a war-winning posture.

5. EXDET recognizes the cautious and conservative nature of Soviet thinking. Given their uncertainty about the West's response to a Soviet attack, Soviet leaders will not wager on gaining Western territory if that means taking even a small risk of suffering nuclear retaliation. No matter how one views new Soviet thinking, EXDET makes a Soviet nuclear attack unthinkable.

6. The strategy is realistic: it accepts the fact that we must live with nuclear weapons. The knowledge of how to construct nuclear warheads makes their abolition improbable. No matter how many promises the Soviets make about eliminating nuclear weapons, real security will depend on the retention by the United States of at least some invulnerable nuclear forces as a guarantee against cheating. Indeed, mutual security may be enhanced if both sides, while making significant progress in arms control, agree to keep a minimal nuclear deterrent. Given this, existential deterrence simply exploits the deterrent value inherent in their possession.

7. Existential deterrence is conducive to improved relations with the Soviet Union: it fits in with a policy of reasonable accommodation

and detente. This nonprovocative form of deterrence is consistent with an easing of Soviet–American tensions. Under this strategy, the psychology of threats can be replaced by a psychology of cooperation (placed, of course, within the context of our unspoken capacity for retaliation). EXDET fits in well with a willingness to take seriously new Soviet declarations on nuclear strategy, and specifically the declared Soviet policy of reasonable sufficiency.

8. This strategy allows for significant arms reductions, bilateral or unilateral. Since strategic superiority has lost its meaning in the nuclear world, we can reduce our forces without threatening our security. We should, of course, invite the Soviets to follow suit and attempt to achieve reductions based on verifiable, negotiated agreements.

9. The adoption of EXDET would be comparable to MAD in cost-efficiency. It would allow us to retain nuclear forces for extended deterrence, making it unnecessary to engage in an expensive arms race with the Soviet Union if, in violation of their proclamations, they keep building nuclear weapons. Unlike MAD, EXDET might involve the development of some counterforce weapons, requiring somewhat more investment than MAD in nuclear weapon design. (This might, of course, be offset by the need for fewer weapons.) Any modernization program under existential deterrence would be prudent and modest, calling for only those improvements necessary to give the United States a limited counterforce capability while avoiding the expensive and destabilizing improvements needed for nuclear war–fighting.

Deterrence-Plus

Critique of Pure Deterrence

Deterrence-plus (or enhanced deterrence), which is current U.S. policy, is designed to correct what its proponents perceive to be two fundamental weaknesses of deterrence-only. The first basic weakness of pure deterrence is its lack of a rational plan in case nuclear deterrence fails. It is, according to advocates of deterrence-plus, morally, strategically, and intellectually irresponsible not to anticipate the failure of deterrence and to plan for it. Pure deterrence theorists dogmatically assume that nuclear weapons lack military utility and that neither we nor the Soviets will ever use nuclear forces. But, as Leon Wieseltier asks: "What if the Russians, however, use them? Of what use will the truth about the military inutility of nuclear weapons be to the President who will be faced with the responsibility of nuclear retaliation?"[15]

Wieseltier points out that the view that nuclear weapons must never be used leaves us at a loss about what to do once they have been used by the other side.[16] The important point is this: a policy of pure deterrence provides the president with no guidance about the courses of action that he should follow in case nuclear weapons fail to deter a Soviet nuclear attack. What if there is a limited Soviet nuclear attack? Is the president to launch all U.S. nuclear weapons and bring about a holocaust? Or should the commander-in-chief have more flexible options that allow at least the possibility of keeping the war limited? If the president is forced to choose between all-out retaliation and doing nothing, then— given the suicidal consequences of an unlimited response—capitulation might be the most rational choice.

Thus, technically speaking, pure deterrence is not a strategy. To have a strategy is to have a plan for the purposeful application of military force to achieve political ends, such as restoring a meaningful peace, terminating the war on terms not unfavorable to the United States, or even victory over the aggressor. MAD, for example, is the negation of strategy because it denies that nuclear weapons can have a purposeful application to any political ends.[17] The impression left is that once deterrence of a nuclear attack has failed, nothing of political value can be attained by using nuclear weapons. This is a strategic black hole out of which there is no escape.

The second fundamental weakness of pure deterrence, from the perspective of advocates of enhanced deterrence, is that it is destabilizing in so far as its failure to provide a nuclear war–fighting strategy erodes the credibility of U.S. nuclear use. If the Soviets do not believe that we have any rational *plan* for the use of our nuclear weapons in the event of a limited nuclear attack on the United States, then they may conclude that it would be improbable that we would really use these weapons that we have declared to lack all military utility. Even if, as defenders of MAD argue, the Soviets are too sensible to attack us out of the blue, the Soviets might reason very differently in a crisis in which nuclear war appeared imminent. If in a crisis they believed (mistakenly) that war was likely, it might seem rational, from the Soviet point of view, to launch a damage-limiting attack against our nuclear forces. That is, if (under new hard-line Soviet leaders) tensions were building toward war, the Soviets might be tempted to launch a first strike against our nuclear forces for self-protection, to reduce the damage we could inflict upon them, rationally wagering that since we have no war-fighting plan, we will probably not use our nuclear forces in pointless retaliation. Thus, the lack of an announced plan for fighting a nuclear war may make a nuclear attack more probable.

Aims and Requirements of Deterrence-Plus

The primary aim of deterrence-plus is, its advocates insist, to make deterrence more credible by creating a believable war-waging strategy, including a plan—in case deterrence fails—for war termination short of an all-out exchange. Supporters of deterrence-plus deny the assumption that once *any* nuclear weapons are used, *all* nuclear weapons will be used. Pure deterrence takes an apocalyptic approach to nuclear weapons by dismissing as delusive all possibilities of forestalling or moderating nuclear war before it reaches an all-out exchange. Advocates of enhanced deterrence, by contrast, entertain instead the possibility that in a nuclear conflict the arsenals may not have to be emptied, so that a nuclear exchange might involve a small number of weapons. The point is that there are more catastrophic and less catastrophic things that can be done with nuclear weapons.

Enhanced deterrence moves radically beyond the purity of nuclear threats toward the complexity of plans for fighting a protracted nuclear war. While pure deterrence theories concentrate exclusively on the prevention of an all-out nuclear attack through the (explicit or implicit) threat of unacceptable damage (deterrence by punishment), theories of enhanced deterrence, while retaining the option of massive retaliation, add a capacity to respond with less than all-out nuclear attacks. The idea is to develop the nuclear flexibility to deny the Soviets military and political gains they might hope to achieve at any level of nuclear aggression (deterrence by denial). That is, the enhanced deterrence strategy is designed to convince the Soviets that we have the capability to prevent them from attaining their objectives at any level of nuclear conflict.

So long as our only option in the face of any Soviet attack, no matter how limited, is a massive response with all our surviving weapons, we forgo the possibility of preventing mutual annihilation. Defenders of a nuclear war–fighting capability argue that we must not lose any chance to keep a nuclear war limited and avoid the destruction of both societies. Enhanced deterrence strategists seek to provide opportunities for limiting destruction and achieving de-escalation.

The primary objective of nuclear policy, defenders of enhanced deterrence wish to emphasize, remains deterrence. Advocates of the development of a nuclear war–fighting strategy believe that the best way to prevent a nuclear war is to convince the Soviet Union (no matter who is in charge) that we are able to fight such a war. The assumption is that the most likely crisis scenario is a limited nuclear attack on Western nuclear forces. To achieve the objective of deterrence, it is argued, the

United States needs, in addition to an assured destruction capacity, the ability to respond to selective attacks on Western military targets (e.g., U.S. ICBMs) by retaliating in kind, with limited nuclear reprisals against Soviet military assets. This means that we need a capacity for flexible nuclear responses—for example, the ability to target transportation routes of advancing Soviet forces and military installations within the Soviet Union.

The point is that deterrence can be enhanced if we can develop a strategy suitable not only for *prewar* deterrence, but also for *intrawar* deterrence—that is, a strategy not only suitable for deterring a first strike, but capable of deterring further attacks in case the enemy initiates a nuclear war. From the perspective of deterrence-plus, an adequate deterrence doctrine must be both designed to dissuade the enemy from initiating nuclear war and capable of terminating the nuclear aggression of a nation that, for whatever reason, has miscalculated what it can gain from such aggression. Our strategic capability must be such as to convince the nuclear adversary that the attack was a miscalculation.

In other words, the idea of deterrence is to be extended to the sphere of nuclear war–fighting with the aim, in the event of the failure of deterrence, of preventing greater violence against the United States or its allies by threatening the Soviet Union with denial of its nuclear war objectives, or—if that does not stop the Soviets—graduated nuclear punishment (short of annihilation). James Schlesinger as secretary of defense officially affirmed this concept of deterrence: "What we need is a series of measured responses to aggression which bear some relation to the provocation, have prospects of terminating hostilities before general nuclear war breaks out, and leave some possibility of restoring deterrence."[18] The point is to convince the Soviets that should they initiate a nuclear war, the continuation of nuclear attacks will not enable them to achieve their war aims and, if they persist, will cost them more than they can gain—in sum, that further aggression is not worth the progressively higher price they will have to pay.

Force Requirements

A credible war-fighting strategy requires a large force system containing a variety of weapons. Given the wide range of options needed to carry out this strategy, an arsenal of ten thousand strategic warheads can no longer be described as overkill, because weapons are needed not only to obliterate cities, but to destroy the enemy's forces and war-support systems.

The number of weapons called for will be large because (1) in some cases at least two weapons will be needed to ensure the destruction of a single target (e.g., a missile in its silo); (2) some weapons will malfunction and become inoperable; and (3) some weapons will be destroyed by the enemy either in a preemptive attack or by defensive interception. In the face of the possible targets, defenders of a nuclear war–fighting capability argue, the problem is not one of overkill but of a scarcity of nuclear forces.[19]

Command, Control, Communications, and Intelligence

In addition to a large number and variety of nuclear forces, enhanced deterrence—unlike pure deterrence—requires an elaborate system for monitoring and managing the course of a nuclear exchange. To be able to fight a prolonged nuclear war and to ensure intrawar deterrence—the capacity for controlled nuclear reprisals, with pauses for the purpose of negotiation—a survivable and enduring C^3I is essential. C^3I is the nervous system of the nuclear war–fighting structure: it consists of warning sensors, command posts, and communication systems. Pronounced "C-cubed-I," the term stands for the Pentagon's capacity for *command* and *control* of, and *communication* with, its nuclear forces, and to the collection of military *intelligence* relevant to targeting and fighting a nuclear war. Such a system must survive a nuclear attack and endure in the midst of a nuclear exchange. Some would say that under a nuclear strategy of deterrence-plus, endurance (of forces and C^3I) replaces an assured destruction capability as an essential requirement of U.S. strategic forces.[20] Under enhanced deterrence American forces must be able to fight a prolonged nuclear war, one that could last for months.

In summary, a believable enhanced deterrence strategy requires a variety of survivable nuclear forces and an enduring C^3I. Deterrence is weakened to the extent that forces are vulnerable and C^3I is subject to being knocked out by a first strike. Indeed, if the enemy can immediately paralyze command, control, and communications systems, there will be no need to destroy our nuclear arsenal, because the forces, minus the brain and eyes, will be useless.

Countervailing Strategy

Deterrence-plus includes at least two options: countervailing and prevailing strategies. Countervailing strategy (cvL) was initially formulated under the Carter administration. One of its advocates, Walter Slocombe, explains its basic aim:

> Its fundamental feature is the proposition that deterrence over the full range of contingencies of concern requires in an age of strategic parity that the United States have forces, and plans for their use, such that the Soviet Union, applying its own standards and models, would recognize that no plausible outcome of aggression would represent victory on any plausible definition of victory. In short, the policy dictated that the United States must have *countervailing* strategic options such that at a variety of levels of exchange, aggression would either be defeated or would result in unacceptable costs that exceed gains. [21]

This strategy is premised upon an interpretation of Soviet military doctrine that differs substantially from the interpretation that is the premise of pure deterrence. Specifically, CVL is based upon the following understanding of Soviet thinking:

- The Soviets do not accept the doctrine of mutual assured destruction. Protection of the homeland is central to their policy, which means that they are serious about civil and strategic defense. [22]
- Soviet military doctrine contemplates and prepares for the possibility of a relatively prolonged nuclear exchange. [23]
- The Soviets emphasize the initial targeting of military forces rather than economic installations or urban centers. [24]
- Soviet leaders highly value the preservation of the Soviet state and its coercive machinery—at least as much as they value the general population. [25]
- The Soviet military takes seriously the possibility of a Soviet victory in nuclear war. Although there is no evidence that they are interested in starting a nuclear war, if one should become imminent, their military doctrine suggests that the best way to limit damage to the homeland is the preemptive destruction of the enemy's nuclear forces—and ultimately the military defeat of the United States. [26]

Defenders of CVL remain skeptical of proclaimed changes in Soviet military doctrine. In light of what they claim is actual Soviet strategy as reflected in the Soviet force structure and Soviet military writings, countervailing theorists argue that we must convince Soviet leaders that no nuclear attack, on any scale, at any stage of conflict, could lead to victory. To deter Soviet aggression means sending the message that the United States is capable not only of annihilating Soviet society, but also, short of that, of destroying—or at least seriously undermining—other assets that the Soviet leadership values: its means of political control; Soviet conventional and nuclear forces; the economic capacity to sustain military operations; and the industrial potential to recover from a nuclear war. According to Slocombe, deterrence will be enhanced to the degree that the USSR recognizes that aggression entails not only the risk of unlimited retaliation against the whole Soviet target system, but also the choice of a more selective and measured response that would deny the Soviets any advantage from having initiated the conflict.[27] Thus, CVL is a flexible strategy encompassing a variety of force and target options. Two major principles guide it: deterrence and insurance.

Deterrence. Countervailing strategists see no contradiction between the development of a war-fighting capability and deterrence. Nuclear forces are to be designed primarily for the purpose of convincing the Soviet Union that the costs of nuclear aggression, at any level, would be too high to justify a nuclear attack, and that nuclear aggression will never be successful, no matter how the Soviets define success. A capacity to inflict costs in excess of gains and to deny the Soviets their objectives will make a Soviet nuclear attack extremely improbable.

Insurance. Despite the asserted credibility of CVL, its supporters recognize that no system of deterrence can dismiss the possibility of failure. Unlike pure deterrence, a countervailing strategy contains a plan for restoring deterrence in the midst of a nuclear war, so that even if the strategy fails to deter a nuclear attack, Soviet leaders can still be dissuaded in the course of the conflict—by U.S. threats of limited but costly nuclear counterattacks—from escalating their nuclear attacks to a higher level. Should prewar deterrence fail, the aim of the strategy is (1) to limit the scope and duration of the conflict and the damage, and (2) to restore peace on terms acceptable, or at least not unfavorable, to the United States. In other words, the United States will be able to defeat any attack while limiting—to the extent possible—the level of violence.[28] In sum, the war-fighting objective of CVL is to deny the Soviets their political and military goals and to counterattack with sufficient force to terminate hostilities at the lowest possible level of damage to the United States and its allies.

Force Requirements

In order to realize these principles, three requirements are placed on nuclear forces.

Force Variability. There must be a continuum of forces, ranging from low-yield, highly accurate theater and strategic nuclear weapons to intercontinental nuclear forces capable of massive area destruction. Thus, counterforce as well as countervalue nuclear weapons will be required. CVL does not call for superior military forces, or even for a force structure that mirrors that of the Soviets, provided that the overall military capability of the United States is not allowed to become inferior to that of the Soviets in reality or appearance. The Soviets must believe that we have sufficient forces so organized that Soviet aggression—at any level—would either be defeated or would result in costs that exceed gains.

Escalation Control. The United States must be able to monitor the level of the enemy's attack and fine-tune our response. This requires survivable intelligence-gathering technologies as well as blast-resistant facilities for communication with and command over nuclear forces. In addition, U.S. leaders must be able to communicate with Soviet leaders, who in turn must have a capacity to monitor the level of our attack and to control the response of their nuclear forces. Restoring a durable peace may require an agreement between leaders of both countries: thus, some provision must be made for peace negotiations during a nuclear conflict. This may require pauses for the purpose of assessing the response of the other side, after which we can either escalate to a higher level of destruction or de-escalate. Whether or not such escalation control will in fact be possible in a nuclear war, we must—for the sake of deterrence—try to convince the Soviet Union that we can adjust our response to the level of their attack, denying them victory at any level of escalation.[29]

Flexible Targeting. We must design a targeting policy that threatens to destroy what the Soviet leaders value: themselves, their military forces and their support facilities, the means of domestic control, and their capacity for economic recovery from a nuclear war. Two targets deserve special discussion: cities and the Soviet leadership.

The CVL targeting plan does not call for substituting combatant for noncombatant targets, nor does it rule out massive retaliation against Soviet cities, population, and industry. Indeed, to deter attacks on our population, a general urban targeting option must be retained. That is, Soviet cities will be retained as hostages to be threatened with destruction in order to prevent attacks on U.S. cities. If the Soviets should nonetheless attack American cities, then we could respond accordingly.

There is disagreement among countervailing strategists about the advisability of destroying the leadership. If the aim is to reach a negotiated settlement—not to achieve victory over the Soviet state—it would appear that we need to spare the leadership in order to have agents with the authority to limit the nuclear attacks (to sustain escalation control) and ultimately to terminate the war. In Presidential Directive 59, formulated as the targeting plan for countervailing strategy under the Carter administration, the president was apparently given the flexibility to kill, in the initial phase of the fighting, second-echelon military and political leaders, thereby seriously impairing the command/communication systems needed to conduct detailed combat operations, while sparing the top Soviet leaders who started and could stop the war.[30] The president could then threaten to destroy the top Soviet leaders in their bunkers unless they terminated all attacks. The point would be to leave the top leadership on the target list—communicating this for the purpose of intrawar deterrence—while delaying their destruction until it was apparent that nothing could be gained (e.g., limitation of violence or de-escalation of hostilities) by merely threatening to destroy them, at which point they could be attacked.

The Case for CVL

The following points can be made in favor of countervailing strategy.

1. It provides a plausible answer to the question, what happens if (prewar) deterrence fails? CVL does not leave us with the dilemma of pure deterrence: suicide or surrender. It provides a way of terminating the conflict short of all-out war.

2. By providing a broad range of options—from limited reprisals to mass retaliation—and by promising to defeat Soviet aggression at all levels, CVL makes U.S. nuclear counterthreats more credible. The Soviets will be hesitant to attack us if they know that we can match them at every level of nuclear war–fighting.

3. This doctrine takes into account actual Soviet strategy: it recognizes that the Soviets refuse to play by the rules that two must obey if MAD is to work; the rule of not protecting one's population and the rule of not trying to win a nuclear war.

4. The strategy is not a destabilizing and provocative one. Its aim is not superiority or victory, but rather the countervailing aim of denying victory.

5. Although it allows for the failure of prewar deterrence, it does not give up the objective of deterrence. In the event of nuclear attack, it will enable us to restore deterrence by using flexible forces and flexible targeting strategy to dissuade the Soviets from further aggression.

Prevailing Strategy

Prevailing strategy (PVL) has many of the same features as countervailing strategy. It shares CVL's view of Soviet thinking, especially the perception of the Soviets as committed to victory in nuclear war. In addition to the three nuclear force requirements affirmed by CVL—force variability, escalation control, and flexible targeting—prevailing theorists call for strategic superiority. A condition of parity or essential equivalence would not permit the realization of the overriding wartime objective that should emerge, according to prevailing strategists, in case (prewar) nuclear deterrence fails—namely, termination of the war on conditions favorable to the United States and the forces of freedom.[31]

Advocates of this strategy would also argue that their primary objective is the same as that of MAD and CVL: to deter a Soviet nuclear attack. Deterrence is, according to these thinkers, best achieved by threatening not only to defeat Soviet *objectives*, but by threatening to defeat the Soviet *state*. On this view, we must not allow the Soviets to think that both sides would lose a nuclear war: advocates of PVL believe an effective deterrence strategy requires that we persuade Soviet leaders that our government and society will prevail in a nuclear war. The aim is to convince the Soviets that the United States is capable of fighting and defeating them under conditions that ensure that the United States and its allies will emerge with relative advantage.

For advocates of this strategy, the distinction between *prevailing* and *countervailing* in a nuclear war is not a trivial one. Unlike countervailing strategists, who seek to avoid the choice between surrender and suicide by striving to convince the Soviets that the United States can defeat their objectives at any level of nuclear conflict, proponents of prevailing strategy want something much more positive and decisive—a strategic edge over the Soviet Union.

Force Requirements

PVL has certain distinctive force requirements.

Escalation Dominance. To will the positive end is necessarily to will superior means. Among the necessary means is escalation dominance, the ability to dominate the conflict at all levels of violence in order to deter the Soviets from escalating to higher levels of destruction. In order to prevail in a nuclear war, the United States must have a qualitative advantage that will enable it to do much more than merely deny the Soviets their objectives. We must have the superior forces necessary not only to compel the Soviets to terminate their attacks but to terminate the hostilities on terms advantageous to the United States.[32]

If a nuclear war is to be worth fighting, we must have reason to believe that we can come out of the war in significantly better condition than the Soviet Union. The problem with CVL, from the perspective of proponents of PVL, is that—aside from the largely negative notion of denying victory to the enemy—CVL lacks a definition of success.[33] Its system of flexible options is not informed by any concept of how the application of a variety of nuclear forces and the utilization of a survivable C^3I would promote the attainment of a meaningful political goal for the United States. In other words, strategic flexibility, unless guided by a plausible theory of how to achieve a decisive and favorable conclusion of the hostilities, does not provide the United States with a credible war-fighting goal. Therefore, we are left with only the negative vision of not allowing the Soviet Union to win, without an affirmative concept of what the United States would gain in the process of victory denial.

It is sometimes said in jest that the superpower that has more survivors at the end of a nuclear war is the side that has prevailed. Colin Gray, a military doctrine analyst who supports a victory strategy, a strong version of PVL, has given this question of relative losses serious consideration. Although Gray does not argue that the side with the greatest number of survivors wins, he does appear to think that losses on each side have a bearing on who prevails. It is for him a necessary, although not a sufficient, condition of success in nuclear war that we convince the Soviets that we will not be self-deterred by fear of heavy casualties during the course of a war. In other words, U.S. resolve and capability must appear such that the Soviets can never reason that if they escalate U.S. losses to a certain predetermined level, we will capitulate.[34] If we give the impression in advance that, for example, the loss of a quarter of our population is unacceptable damage, and Soviet leaders are willing to go much higher in terms of both enduring and inflicting losses, then they will have an incentive to raise the ante—that is, to threaten to inflict a higher level of destruction. Even if we have the technical capability to dominate them at each level on the ladder of escalation, this strategic superiority will not allow us to prevail if the Soviet Union is able to tolerate more losses than we can.

Requirements of Intrawar Deterrence. There are two sides to intrawar deterrence—that is, two dimensions to any plan, in the course of a nuclear war, for deterring the other side from escalating attacks and for compelling them to terminate further attacks: (1) the enemy's understanding of the physical damage it can inflict on the things we highly value (e.g., population and industry), and (2) the damage to these valued assets the enemy believes that we can psychologically endure.

The extent of the destruction the enemy can inflict upon us depends, of course, on the extent to which we try to save population and industry through civil defense, strategic defense, and other damage-limitation measures. If, as under MAD, we leave our cities completely vulnerable while the Soviets strive for maximum self-protection, then they have an advantage in damage-infliction. The greater our efforts to protect what we highly value, the less confidence the Soviets will have in their ability to threaten our assets.

The other dimension of intrawar deterrence is the Soviet perception of our tolerance for losses. If they perceive that we cannot tolerate
the loss of more than a particular percentage of population and industry,
then—as pointed out above—they will try to inflict a level of destruction that exceeds this percentage. In other words, during a nuclear
exchange, the Soviets will have an incentive to press past the point of
(what they perceive to be) our tolerance for destruction in order to
induce surrender. Beyond this destruction threshold, they will expect
us to be self-deterred—that is, discouraged from escalating attacks
(despite our physical capacity to do so) by our inability to endure greater
destruction. If, however, we can convince them that we have a capacity
to endure destruction to a point equivalent to their maximum destructive potential and that we have a plausible recovery plan, then they will
have very little incentive to press on.[35]

Of course, the more we strengthen the first side of intrawar deterrence—the protection of the American homeland—the less we will
have to worry about any Soviet testing of our tolerance for destruction.
The more uncertain the Soviets are of the damage they can inflict, the
weaker their threats of nuclear escalation become. U.S. damage limitation, to be successful, must involve both counterforce targeting (i.e.,
the destruction of as many Soviet "sitting" nuclear forces as possible)
and active and passive defense (i.e., ballistic missile defense, air defense, and civil defense). U.S. strategic forces, the American population, and U.S. industry must be protected as far as possible.[36] On the
other hand, if we could convince Soviet leaders that no amount of destruction would induce us to surrender, then we would not have to worry
about credible damage-limitation measures. The Soviets might, however, find it difficult to believe that we could reasonably consider the destruction of more than half the U.S. population as acceptable damage.

The capacity to withstand Soviet attacks—considered in terms of
tolerance for punishment or protective measures—is only one necessary
condition of a strategy of successful nuclear war–fighting. Such a strategy requires, in addition, a concrete vision of the *advantageous* termination of a nuclear war. This concept of successful war termination contains two dimensions: a concept of Soviet defeat and a concept of
postwar U.S. recovery.

Targeting the Soviet State. The first dimension of success is the
counterpart of our capacity for punishment: it is a concept of the degree
and kind of losses that would be intolerable for the Soviet Union and
inconsistent with *its* theory of victory. MAD assumes that the assured
destruction of a certain percentage of the population and industry of the
Soviet Union would constitute unacceptable punishment. Advocates of
PVL believe that population targeting by itself lacks deterrent value

because Soviet leaders may be willing to absorb enormous human losses to achieve their goals. According to Gray, for example, what is most valuable from the standpoint of the leadership is the political system and the means of political control. Therefore, proponents of PVL stress the deterrence value of a declaratory strategy that calls for making the state apparatus the primary target, allowing for targeting of the Soviet economy only to the extent that its disintegration would play a role in the defeat of the Soviet state. Gray sums up this thinking as follows:

> The Soviet Union, like Czarist Russia, knows that it can absorb an enormous amount of punishment (loss of life, industry, productive agricultural land, and even territory), recover, and endure until final victory—provided the *essential assets of the state* remain intact. The principal assets are the political control structure of the highly centralized CPSU and the governmental bureaucracy; the transmission belts of communication from the center to the regions; the instruments of central official coercion (the KGB and the armed forces); and the reputation of the Soviet state in the eyes of its citizens. Counter-economic targeting should have a place in intelligent war planning, but only to the extent to which such targeting would impair the functioning of the Soviet state.[37]

Thus, a clear and meaningful war aim would be the dissolution of the Soviet political system. With the destruction of the Soviet state as the maximum objective of nuclear war–fighting, other objectives, subordinate to this goal, can be identified. For example, attacks that weakened the coercive instruments of the Soviet state, or that weakened the control of the state over disaffected masses in the USSR, might provide conditions for the erosion of Soviet power or for successful revolts of constituent republics in the Soviet Union.[38] Despite *glasnost* and more democratic elections, there are republics in the Soviet Union that perceive Moscow as a repressive center, denying them opportunity for self-determination, freedom, and independence—conditions they would establish if Moscow lost its ability to control them.

Even if there is no certainty that the United States could destroy the political control structure of the Soviet Union, Soviet leaders cannot be sure that they would prevail. The awareness by Soviet leaders that the political control structure is a primary target, along with their uncertainty about the survivability of this structure, could serve as a powerful deterrent. If the leadership of the USSR sees its control apparatus as being at serious risk, it will not find the possible gains of starting a nuclear war (or nuclear retaliation in a war in which the United States resorted to first-use or launched a first-strike) worth the possible costs.

Indeed, this threat alone may be sufficient to prevent Soviet leaders from launching a first strike.

What about targeting the leadership? The same dilemma faces PVL and CVL: the deterrence value of threatening to kill the leadership versus the need to preserve the leadership for war termination. Does the wartime objective of defeating the Soviet state require as an option a decapitation strike: an attack against the leadership that would paralyze the Soviets' war-fighting capacity? Or does a rational PVL require us to leave the Soviet leadership in a "withhold" category so that we have someone with whom to negotiate war termination on favorable terms?

The decapitation dilemma may, however, be a false one in so far as it is assumed that to sever the head of the Soviet C^{3}I is the same as killing the political leadership. That is, the political leadership needs to be distinguished from the military command and control apparatus. It might be possible to decapitate the military leadership needed to conduct the war while at the same time preserving the political leadership needed to negotiate a surrender.[39]

Success as Postwar Recovery. Assuming we can destroy the Soviet state—or weaken it to the point of virtually finishing it as a coercive apparatus—what more is required of a theory of success? As Gray points out, the destruction of the Soviet state is not the same as victory for the United States.[40] It will, after all, be a Pyrrhic victory if the Soviets can do the same to us. In summarizing his vision of both aspects of successful nuclear–war fighting—defeat of the Soviet state and victory for the United States—Gray sketches a concept of meaningful victory:

> For the United States to win a central war, the Soviet Union would have to surrender—or be in such poor political-military condition that the issue of an instrumental surrender would be an irrelevance—and the United States would have to be intact as a political entity, able to recover on fairly short order from the damage suffered (courtesy of voluntary, and some no-doubt coerced, assistance from undamaged economies abroad), able to continue or resume military operations, and generally be in a position to organize, and enforce, the terms of the new post-war international order.[41]

Thus, in addition to a capacity to threaten the survival of the Soviet state, we must have a credible plan to preserve the U.S. governing apparatus, along with the means for economic recovery (provided from abroad, if necessary), with military forces capable of establishing a new international order compatible with U.S. interests and values. Along these lines, Paul Nitze argued many years ago that in a successful campaign, the victor will be in a position to issue orders to the loser and the loser will have to obey them or face complete chaos or extinction. The victor will then go on to organize what remains of the world as best he can. Certainly he will try to see to it that there is never again a possibility that the loser possesses nuclear weapons.[42]

This is clearly a vision of a world in which the possibility of Soviet domination and expansion no longer exists and in which freedom and human rights in general will no longer be threatened by the goal of world communism. But, as Nitze points out, the closer we can get to the attainment of the capability necessary to achieve victory, the less likely it is that nuclear war will ever occur.[43] A prevailing strategy remains (even in its extreme form as a victory doctrine) in the end primarily a deterrent doctrine.

The Case for PVL

The case for a prevailing strategy can be summed up as follows:

1. The strategy will strengthen deterrence by threatening what the Soviets highly value—the Soviet state and its instruments of control.

2. In case deterrence fails, this doctrine provides a meaningful objective for nuclear war fighting: a concept of success in which the Soviet threat to freedom is ultimately removed and there is a world order consistent with U.S. interests and values.

3. The doctrine not only takes into account Soviet strategy but provides a way of militarily dominating the Soviets. It thus provides a credible strategy of intrawar deterrence: the Soviets, if ever involved in war with the United States, will have no incentive to continue hostilities. They will have nothing to gain and everything to lose in continuing a nuclear exchange.

4. PVL returns nuclear deterrence to the standards of traditional military strategy, providing nuclear weapons with real strategic utility. Thus, these weapons will be constructed for meaningful strategic use, which will add to their ultimate deterrent value.

5. Ultimately, the doctrine offers the best chance for deterring a Soviet nuclear attack. By placing nuclear weapons and nuclear strategy within the realm of credible war fighting—a strategy in which the U.S. possesses military superiority and the capacity to dominate the Soviet Union at all levels—we make Soviet nuclear aggression against the United States or its allies irrational.

6. PVL is based upon a healthy skepticism about Soviet pronouncements. We must take a long historical view of Soviet strategy. In the past the Soviets have announced conciliatory changes that ultimately gave

way to aggressive actions. Those who declare that the Cold War is over fail to consider that Soviet military and foreign policy declarations may represent only tactical shifts conceived to encourage Western disarmament rather than an actual transformation of Soviet strategy or objectives.

Guarding Against the Failure of Deterrence

Even if tensions between the Soviet Union and the United States are reduced substantially, as long as each side has thousands of weapons aimed at the other, flaws in the C^3I systems on either side could lead to inadvertent warfare. Each side relies on elaborate detection and tracking systems that are fallible and capable of giving misinformation that could lead to accidental nuclear war. Moreover, each side must balance procedures that prevent the unauthorized use of nuclear weapons with procedures that guarantee that nuclear weapons will be used once the correct command is given. A breakdown in this balance, too, could lead to inadvertent nuclear war.

Supporters of all the deterrence strategies described above are concerned with guarding against the failure of nuclear deterrence. After all, a major objection to all forms of nuclear deterrence is that misinterpreted incidents, accidents, unauthorized use of nuclear weapons, and crisis situations could ignite a nuclear war that might, despite every effort to terminate it, result in an all-out exchange of nuclear weapons. Such a failure of nuclear deterrence would mean—even in the case of limited nuclear exchanges—catastrophe.

Accidents include computer malfunctions and false alarms that result in an erroneous warning of an enemy attack.[44] *Unauthorized use* refers to the initiation of nuclear war by individuals at lower levels who exceed their authority by firing the nuclear weapons in their charge without orders to do so. During a *crisis* or a period of high tension, with each nation's forces on alert, neither nation might want to go to war, but, sensing that war was imminent, each might feel driven to hit first rather than second. That is, during a crisis, if a nation saw the decision not as one of war versus peace, but as one of striking first versus striking second, then, to minimize damage to its society and its forces, a preemptive strike might appear to be the only rational course.

Measures taken to prevent inadvertent nuclear war as a result of accidents, unauthorized use, and crises include the development of accident-prevention and crisis-control procedures and improved weapon security. Since nuclear deterrence is current U.S. policy and will be with us—in some form—for the foreseeable future, the general case for nuclear deterrence is not complete without some mention of these preventive efforts.

The Prevention of Unauthorized Use

One public worry involves the unauthorized launching of nuclear weapons. Arrangements have been made to minimize the danger of such a launch in the strategic triad (bombers, ICBMs, and submarines) and in theater forces. Each system has its control provisions.

Could a single individual at a lower level start a nuclear war? Defenders of nuclear deterrence will answer no for at least two reasons. First, there is the "two-person rule," which states that launching a nuclear weapon of any kind, anywhere—on a submarine or bomber or in an ICBM launch control center—requires at least two people. "This means that, at all stages of arming and firing nuclear weapons, the control mechanisms are such that it is physically impossible for one person to perform the task."[45]

Second, military personnel whose jobs involve handling nuclear weapons or nuclear materials must be periodically evaluated under the Personnel Reliability Program (PRP) of the Army, Navy, Air Force, and Marines. The objective of the PRP is to ensure that only individuals who meet the highest suitability and reliability standards are assigned to nuclear duty positions. Personnel are neither trained for nuclear weapon duties nor assigned to them until they have been properly screened. Deviations from exacting standards of reliability, or aberrant personal behavior, will result in immediate scrutiny, and probably removal from nuclear weapons duties. Thousands of people have been decertified and removed from "nuclear" jobs after failing reliability tests.[46]

Permissive Action Links (PALs). It is important to remember that the thousands of young soldiers, sailors, and airmen with their fingers on the button "only perform the final act in the nuclear weapons chain."[47] The U.S. military has developed elaborate mechanical safety catches to prevent unauthorized use of nuclear forces. Numerous pre-launch codes and procedures must be performed before a weapon can be armed and the firing keys will work.[48]

The United States has developed an electro-mechanical lock for many of its missiles. Only an insertion of the correct code can unlock the PALs and arm the nuclear warheads. There are over 16 million possible PAL codes for ICBMs, and insertion of the incorrect code sets off a warning light at higher headquarters. Many nuclear warheads now contain "command disable" devices that, if activated by insertion of the incorrect code, will render the warhead useless. That is, repeated insertion of the incorrect code would lock the weapon and make certain key components unusable: to be again functional, the warhead would have to be taken to the factory for repair. Beyond this, several other devices have been incorporated into certain nuclear weapons to prevent unauthorized or inadvertent detonation. For instance, many newer nuclear warheads contain what are called "insensitive high explosives," which prevent them from being detonated by fires, gun shots, aircraft crashes, or inadvertent release.[49]

Bombers. At bomber bases throughout the United States, the crews, living in partially underground rooms at the end of the runways near their bombers, spend seven days of each month on alert duty. The fact that bombers are easy to recall gives the Strategic Air Command (SAC) commander, a four-star general, great control over them. The general can send his bombers to a holding position after receiving an alert from the North American Aerospace Defense Command (NORAD), before any orders come down from the National Command Authority (NCA). From the holding positions, the bombers can be recalled or they can be given their go codes to turn north and fly over the North Pole to their Soviet targets. With a flying time to the Soviet Union of anywhere between six and nine hours, they are obviously the most controllable of all nuclear weapons delivery vehicles. In each bomber cockpit there is a red box with validation codes for authentication of the missile control order and two keys for missile bomb release. The nuclear weapons carried by U.S. strategic bombers have PALs that must be unlocked before they can be armed. Paul Bracken in *The Command and Control of Nuclear Forces* asserts that caution has been carried so far here that the bomber force might be wiped out in an actual Soviet attack.[50]

ICBMs. Intercontinental ballistic missiles are controlled by SAC. All ICBMs are equipped with PALs that prevent unauthorized arming and firing: to arm and fire them, a prescribed code (frequently changed) must be inserted. Launch control officers cannot fire the missiles without receiving the PAL codes: they do not have copies of the PAL codes in their possession. Two launch control officers sit in each launch control center near the ICBMs that are in their charge. Each center is sealed off from the outside by four-ton blast doors. In the case of Minuteman forces, ICBMs are organized into squadrons, each squadron consisting of five separate launch control centers from which two launch control officers oversee ten ICBMs.

Set (by regulation) twelve feet apart, the two launch control officers in each center face identical computer consoles that monitor the status of the missiles. A red metal box, secured with two combination locks, sits perched on a shelf between the two officers. If there is an attack, an alarm bell inside the capsule will ring in response to the initial alert from the SAC controller at Offutt Air Force Base in Nebraska. (It is at this base that the Joint Strategic Planning Staff develops the plans for fighting a nuclear war and coordinates the nuclear forces to strike targets under preplanned "options" available to the NCA.) When the red phone rings, the senior crew member picks it up and may be told by the Strategic Missile Wing Command Post that an Emergency Action Message—an authorized launch instruction from the NCA—has been received and will be conveyed over the SAC automated command and control system to the center. An "enabling" or PAL code—an oral code consisting of twelve numbers and letters—is immediately given over the red phone, and the crew commander copies it down on a piece of white paper. Over a teletype machine, a "hard copy" of the code simultaneously confirms the oral message. After this, each crew member opens one of the two combination locks on the red metal box, and each removes his copy of the code book, which contains the sealed emergency war order: special instructions for firing the missiles. They also take out their silver firing keys.

After the Emergency Action Message sent over the red telephone has been jointly validated by the launch officers, the next step is to wait for the "Nuclear Control Order"—the release message. This message may instruct the officers to launch all their missiles, to launch some of them, or simply to prepare them for launching. The message may even require the missile crew to change the targets of their missiles by dialing a new set of numbers into the missiles' memory. The crew does not, however, know what the changes mean in terms of the location of specific targets in the Soviet Union.[51]

Peter Pringle and William Arkin—specialists on nuclear operations—describe the next stage:

> Before the crews are able to turn their keys to launch their missiles there are two more checks. A second crew, in one of the other four launch control centers attached to their "squadron," must go through the same operations, "voting" positively that the launch command is valid. Also, any one of the crews in the other capsules can delay, and ultimately prevent, a launch if they believe it is being made as a result of an invalid order. The delay lasts for a few minutes only, after which it is automatically cancelled. But the delay mechanism can be introduced any number of times, thus ensuring that any crew can be permanently prevented from launching its missiles.[52]

If all the above procedures have been followed and the crews all vote to launch, the final step requires the two crew members to turn their keys *simultaneously* and hold them in position for at least five seconds.[53] (The twelve-foot space between the key "ignitions" ensures that one person could not turn both keys.) During this whole procedure the lit panels on the crewmen's consoles have passed through the following progressive launch sequences: "strategic alert," "warhead armed," "launch in progress," and (finally) "missiles away." Once a missile is fired, of course, there is no recall.

SLBMs. Submarine-launched ballistic missiles constitute the third leg of the nuclear triad. Submarines, although the least vulnerable of strategic nuclear vehicles, are the most difficult to maintain communication with; indeed, some forms of communication can make a submarine vulnerable to detection. To avoid detection, the submarines are never required to report to base while they are on patrol. Consequently, the commander is given a unique degree of autonomy.[54] In fact, submarine commanders are permitted to give the order to fire their weapons if communications with land-, sea-, or air-based command posts are cut. The fact that the missiles can be physically armed and fired without the external enabling codes qualitatively distinguishes submarine-based nuclear forces from the other two legs of the strategic triad. That is, there are no external controls such as PALs to prevent unauthorized launch of any of the SLBM's. According to the Navy, the absence of PALs is due to fear of losing contact with submarines during a war: if communications were cut, then PALs would prevent the submarines from launching a retaliatory strike. Moreover, it is argued, since the threat of capture or seizure of nuclear weapons on submarines is minimal, there is not the same need for PALs on submarine-based nuclear missiles as there is on the more vulnerable land-based systems.[55]

The autonomy of the sea-based leg of the strategic triad has been exaggerated by those who speculate that a mad submarine commander could start a nuclear war. In fact, the command authority of a commander on a submarine is not unchecked or absolute. Although SLBM's lack the physical locks that protect other nuclear weapons, they cannot be fired by the commander without cooperation from members of the crew. Richard Ned Lebow, professor of government and director of the Peace Studies Program at Cornell University, summarizes what is known about the procedure:

> To prevent unauthorized launch, the navy relies . . . on institutional safeguards. The launching of a missile requires the concerted action of four officers and eleven seamen at various stations of the boat. All four officers must throw switches or turn keys within moments of one another; the missile cannot be fired if any one of them fails or refuses to participate.[56]

NATO *Nuclear Forces.* Most, if not all, U.S. nuclear weapons based in Europe contain PAL locks with codes held solely by the NCA. (However, in the initial stage of a crisis, it is believed that the president would turn over the codes to the commander-in-chief of U.S. forces in Europe and his deputy to permit fairly quick release of nuclear weapons.) For many U.S. nuclear forces deployed in Europe, there is a "dual-key" arrangement (in fact, no physical keys are involved): the U.S. controls the nuclear warhead, and the NATO host country controls the delivery vehicle.[57] (Britain and France, of course, maintain independent nuclear arsenals over which the United States has no control.)

In summary, there are elaborate procedures to prevent any single individual—among the thousands with their fingers on the nuclear trigger—from launching a nuclear weapon without authorization. Moreover, the weapons themselves are usually equipped with electronic safeguards that make it impossible to fire them without proper authority—that is, there are safeguards that render the weapon inoperable if tampered with.[58]

Soviet Nuclear Forces. Given the Soviet Union's highly centralized command hierarchy, it appears probable that responsibility for ordering the use of nuclear forces rests in the hands of a very small number of individuals within the Politburo, and is perhaps limited to the general secretary of the Communist Party, although it must be assumed that, as in the case of the United States, arrangements exist for the delegation of launch authority in the event that the Soviet leadership is killed. We can also assume that mechanical safeguards protect against unauthorized use of nuclear forces. It is believed that Soviet launch control centers for the ICBMs contain four individuals: two KGB officers who would arm the missiles' nuclear warheads and two regular officers who would launch the missiles; it is also assumed that all four officers would have to vote to launch in order for a missile to be fired. As for theater nuclear forces, it has been reported that nuclear stockpiles are controlled by special forces of the KGB rather than regular military officers.[59]

The Authorization Dilemma

U.S. nuclear weapons are subject to two kinds of control: negative and positive. *Negative control* consists of efforts to prevent unauthorized use of nuclear weapons through concentration of control in the hands of the president or his designated successor, the two-person rule, and PALS. *Positive control* consists of efforts, in a crisis, to ensure the capacity to retaliate through the dissemination of go codes and launch authority— that is, the delegation of nuclear release authority to subordinate commanders.

Deterrence theorists face a difficult choice in their effort to achieve two goals: the prevention of unauthorized use of nuclear weapons and the avoidance of command paralysis. Absolute protection against unauthorized use of nuclear forces would require direct presidential approval, but such centralization of command invites a decapitating strike. If command and control of nuclear forces were in fact concentrated in the hands of the president, then it would be possible for the Soviets to disarm us without destroying our nuclear forces: they need only destroy the president and his designated successor. On the other hand, a decentralized arrangement that gave people in the "field" immediate launch authority would eliminate the risk of decapitation while increasing the risk of unauthorized use. If, in a crisis, control over nuclear weapons devolves on hundreds or thousands of individuals, the chances of inadvertent nuclear war increase substantially.

Thus, there is an inherent tension between negative and positive control. While negative control must operate in peacetime, in wartime positive control must be given precedence. The problem—faced by the Soviets as well—is the orderly transition from one form of control to the other.[60]

Accident and Crisis Control Measures

One way around the negative–positive control dilemma is to avoid situations that allow us to move too hastily from negative to positive control or, conversely, situations in which we fail to move quickly enough from negative to positive control. In addition to procedural checks and mechanical devices for preventing the unauthorized use of nuclear weapons, there are numerous accident-prevention and crisis control measures to avert nuclear war. If we can avoid, or at least manage, crises with the Soviet Union, we can avoid facing the nuclear control dilemma.

The Hotline. One of the earliest crisis control measures—which followed upon the slow, indirect, and clumsy communications between John Kennedy and Nikita Khrushchev during the Cuban missile crisis of 1962—was the Washington–Moscow Hotline, a teletype located in the Pentagon with an extension to the White House. (Notice that the Hotline is not a red telephone: it was feared that voice communication would create too great a risk of misunderstanding through immediate translation and hasty response.) The Hotline was instituted in 1963 to reduce the likelihood of provocative behavior, improve crisis communication, and prevent crises in the first place.[61]

Other Agreements. In addition to the 1963 Hotline agreement, the following Soviet–American accords have already been established in the area of crisis control:

1. The Accidents Agreement (1971) commits each side to inform the other at once in the event of an accidental unauthorized event that could lead to a threatening detonation of nuclear warheads. It requires that each side give the other warning of any missile test firings in the direction of the other's homeland. Each side is "to act in such a way as to reduce the possibility of actions being misinterpreted should a nuclear incident occur, and to maintain and improve internal arrangements intended to prevent unauthorized or accidental nuclear war."

2. The Incidents at Sea Agreement (1972) establishes navigation rules for naval vessels and procedures for dealing with accidental collisions and near-misses.

3. The Prevention of Nuclear War Agreement (1973) requires consultation between Washington and Moscow in any situation involving a greater-than-normal risk of nuclear war.

4. The Hotline was improved (1984) and given the capability to transmit whole pages of text, photographs, and graphics.

5. The Stockholm Confidence- and Security-Building Accord (1986), signed by NATO and Warsaw Pact countries, requires that the signatories give forty-two days' advance notice of military maneuvers involving 13,000 soldiers or more, or 300 tanks or more. If the maneuvers involve 17,000 soldiers or more, two observers must be invited from other participants in the Stockholm Conference. These provisions reduce the risk of war breaking out behind the cover of maneuvers. If one country suspects another of cheating, it can demand on-site inspection in airplanes or land vehicles.

6. The Agreement on Nuclear-Risk Reduction Centers (1987) calls for centers designed to reduce the risk of conflict between the United States and the Soviet Union, particularly nuclear conflict that might result from accident, misinterpretation, or miscalculation. The centers would be used to trade information on such things as nuclear or missile tests.[62]

7. The Accidental War Prevention Agreement (1989) is designed to prevent or contain accidental military encounters before they escalate into critical confrontations. The agreement covers four main areas: (1) the crossing of national boundaries by military aircraft or troops because of accident or emergency; (2) the hazardous use of range-finding laser beams (which can blind humans) during military tests and maneuvers; (3) interference with the two sides' command and control networks of communications during peaceful operations; and (4) possible creation of "special caution areas" in tense areas like the Persian Gulf, where military maneuvers have been known to exacerbate political problems. The agreement calls for designation of special radio frequencies to allow direct communications between the two nations' military units in the

field to prevent misunderstandings. It will also seek to develop mutual cooperation in the wording of training manuals to reduce the risks of accidental encounters.[63]

Proposal for a Crisis Control Center. Another proposal goes beyond the Hotline, which, although extremely important, has significant limitations in cases that require face to face conversations or working-level discussions. It also goes beyond the risk reduction centers. Military and diplomatic officers from the United States and the Soviet Union would jointly staff this center around the clock. At the beginning it might have twin locations—in Washington and Moscow—electronically linked by telephone, computer, facsimile transmission, and teleconferencing. In Washington there could be eight Americans and four Soviets; in Moscow the numbers would be reversed. Staff would rotate between the two sites.

The center and its staff in Moscow and Washington could perform five tasks in a crisis. The following description of these tasks comes from William Ury's *Beyond the Hotline:*

> Exchanging, clarifying, authenticating complex information. Back and forth communication to eliminate dangerous misunderstandings is the essence of what the center would do. . . . The opportunity to question and challenge the authenticity of the other side's information and interpretation is crucial.
>
> Carrying out emergency safety procedures. . . . Consider, for instance, what might have happened if the center had existed in September 1983, when the Korean Air Lines flight 007 strayed into Soviet airspace. The Soviet air defense command might have immediately queried the American experts at the Moscow crisis control center about the nature and mission of the Korean airliner as it intruded. . . . The American experts could have worked together with their Soviet counterparts to make radio contact with the plane in order to direct it immediately out of Soviet territory or to a safe landing spot for Soviet inspection.
>
> Technical problem solving. Perhaps the most dangerous crises are those least expected. When every minute may count, a trained binational staff used to working with each other and ready on an instant's notice to engage in intensive ad hoc problem solving could make a critical difference. The staff could not make political decisions, but once the leaders decided, they could work out the technical details of implementation. In certain cases, they might even be called upon to explore creative options, especially if it was understood from the start that they did not have the authority to negotiate for their governments.

Experts on call. In focusing on what role the institution could play, it is vital not to overlook the individuals involved, for they might prove to be the chief resource in a crisis. From studying past crises and current leadership styles, they would be uniquely knowledgeable. . . . They would serve as a human repository of the accumulated wisdom from past crises and of expertise for handling future ones.

Building public confidence. The center would be more visible than the Hotline has become. The public knowledge that Americans and Soviets were working intensively side by side at the center to avoid war might allay anxiety and give the leaders of the United States and the USSR some time and room to communicate and deliberate.[64]

In normal times the center's staff would work hard to prevent crises from occurring. It could perform the following five functions during calm periods:

Developing technical procedures. How can one side prove to the other that a launch was really an accident or was unauthorized? . . . Center staff could engage in simulations to develop these procedures and to test them before using them in a crisis. . . .

Identifying new dangers. Discussing past unintended incidents and analyzing hypothetical ones could reveal risks of runaway escalation that the two sides had not talked about together, nor perhaps even fully appreciated themselves. . . .

Exchanging information about global nuclear dangers. Building on their tradition of cooperation in trying to control nuclear proliferation, the United States and the Soviet Union could exchange information about potential sources of nuclear terrorism, and perhaps information about emerging risks of nuclear war in the Third World. . . .

Questioning military movements and other threatening actions. The center could be as effective in normal times as during crises, clarifying the meaning of suspicious events (e.g., the unusual movements of naval vessels or troops).

Staffing cabinet-level talks on crisis control. The center would be able to provide staff support, briefings, and a logical site for meetings on crisis control between cabinet-level officers from each side. Such close work during normal times would make it more likely that high-level decision makers would avail themselves of the center's expertise should a crisis erupt.[65]

Awareness of the catastrophic consequences of the failure of nuclear deterrence has led deterrence strategists to search for supplements to deterrence, such as the crisis control centers and the other measures discussed here. Critics of nuclear deterrence do not, however, think that the answer lies in supplements but only in the development of an alternative to nuclear deterrence. One of the most ambitious alternatives is the proposal to construct a defensive system to protect American society from nuclear attack. In the next chapter, I explore this option.

CHAPTER FIVE

Social Defense:
Security Through Protection of
the Homeland

For decades nuclear deterrence was never seriously questioned—
at least in public—by those in power. The only real questions for the
makers of nuclear policy were what kind of nuclear weapons do we
need, and how many, to deter a Soviet first strike. Even when the
United States briefly flirted with an anti-ballistic missile system during
the late 1960s and early 1970s, it was for the purpose of enhancing
nuclear deterrence.[1] And, as we have seen, the various nuclear war–
fighting doctrines are really only different attempts to improve nuclear
deterrence—that is, to make U.S. nuclear threats more credible. In
general, defense theorists in search of security in the face of the Soviet
nuclear threat have treated the United States nuclear arsenal as a given.

With President Ronald Reagan's proposal for research on a comprehensive missile defense system (the strategic defense initiative, or
sDI), deterrence based on nuclear threats was officially called into question. In March 1983 Reagan presented a vision of a world in which the
security of the United States would no longer rely on the threat of
nuclear retaliation:

> Wouldn't it be better to save lives than to avenge them? Are we
> capable of demonstrating our peaceful intentions by applying our
> abilities and our ingenuity to achieving a truly lasting stability? I
> think we are. Indeed, we must. . . . After careful consultation
> with my advisers, including the Joint Chiefs of Staff, I believe
> there is a way. Let me share with you a vision that offers hope. It is
> that we embark on a program to counter the awesome Soviet

109

missile threat with measures that are defensive. . . . What if a free people could live in the secure knowledge that their security did not rest upon the threat of instant U.S. retaliation to deter a Soviet attack, that we could intercept and destroy strategic ballistic missiles before they reached our own soil or that of our allies. . . . ? I call upon the scientific community in our country, those who gave us nuclear weapons, to turn their great talents now to the cause of mankind and world peace, to give us the means of rendering these weapons impotent and obsolete. . . . We seek neither military superiority nor political advantage. Our only purpose—one all people share—is to search for ways to reduce the danger of nuclear war.[2]

This strategic policy would deal with the Soviet nuclear threat in a manner completely different from the psychology of counterthreat that characterizes all nuclear deterrence policies. Some members of the Reagan administration subsequently revised the mission of strategic defense, placing it within the framework of nuclear deterrence, reassuring a skeptical strategic community that its purpose was really to enhance deterrence by creating uncertainty in the minds of Soviet military planners. In place of Reagan's sweeping nonnuclear, purely defensive strategy, a more modest mission was assigned to SDI: the protection of our nuclear retaliatory forces.[3] Robert McNamara has called this revised version of SDI "Star Wars II," in contrast to Reagan's original vision, which McNamara labeled "Star Wars I."[4]

Since my objective is to explore qualitatively different strategic options, I will focus exclusively on the more ambitious version of SDI, Star Wars I, found in Reagan's 1983 speech. Star Wars I represents a break with the tradition of nuclear deterrence—of security through the threat of nuclear retaliation. Strategic defense, in its comprehensive form, embraces the same nonpunitive objective that characterizes the domestic theory of social defense: the protection of society.

Application of Social Defense to Nuclear Policy

As a proposal for dealing with the domestic threat of violent crime—internal aggression against the social order—social defense theory asserts that protection of the population should be the goal of correction policy and incapacitation of dangerous agents the means. In a correction system based on social defense, incapacitation measures, whether imprisonment, exile, or even execution, are not imposed as penalties. The violent offender who is securely incarcerated is thereby prevented from harming the public; the murderer who is given the death penalty is permanently incapacitated.

To distinguish the social defense perspective from punitive perspectives such as deterrence and retribution, this approach must be understood as growing out of a skepticism concerning the value of punishment. Its supporters have no confidence in punitive measures, whether for deterrence or retributive purposes. They are skeptical of deterrence doctrine in so far as it assumes the essential rationality of potential offenders—assumes, that is, that individuals can be expected to weigh consequences and do the sensible thing. They are also suspicious of the retributive attempt to match penalties to crimes: they call into question the assumption that we can discover a formula for truly just punishment. In place of a punitive objective, the primary aim of domestic social defense is to *shield* law-abiding citizens from violent attacks on their persons and property. The point is to find ways to make the agents of violence incapable of injury—to render dangerous individuals harmless.

Applied to nuclear policy, social defense would call for the development of means to shield citizens from nuclear attack. In other words, its project would coincide with that of Star Wars I. In line with its domestic counterpart, the moral foundation of national social defense is both teleological and deontological. Its teleological aim is to minimize the terrible suffering of nuclear war by minimizing casualties on both sides. Its underlying deontological principle is that government has an obligation to protect its citizens from harm and to avoid harming innocent individuals in other nations. No matter how beneficial the policy of nuclear deterrence has been, it is morally objectionable because it maintains peace by threatening to incinerate millions of innocent people. The utility of a policy, on this view, must not conflict with the government's moral obligation to protect its own citizens and to avoid attacking civilians in an adversary's society. Citizens have a fundamental right to security against attack, and noncombatants have a fundamental right not to be treated as hostages or targeted in time of war. As a nuclear weapons policy, social defense promises to satisfy the principle of utility while also fulfilling the principle of respect for the innocent.

From the perspective of social defense, a government that intentionally leaves its population exposed to nuclear attack (in the manner of MAD) is as immoral as a government that deliberately leaves its citizens exposed to dangerous criminals. Advocates of strategic defense believe that a strategy must be found that achieves the opposite of mutual assured destruction: this means that military forces must be designed for the purpose of making the homeland as invulnerable as possible.[5] Since the assured survival of population is a fundamental objective of strategic defense, many of SDI's advocates welcome the adoption of this defensive strategy by the Soviet Union. Indeed, some proponents have even called for sharing our achievements in defensive technology with the Soviets.[6] The point of mutual assured security is to create a world in which nuclear weapons can no longer be used to murder millions of innocent individuals and to inflict unimaginable suffering on survivors. On this view, the immoral strategy of MAD must be replaced by the moral strategy of MAS.

Of course, defenders of nuclear deterrence maintain that their policy also protects society from nuclear attack by making nuclear aggression so costly for the Soviet Union that it cannot rationally choose to use its nuclear arsenal against the United States. From the perspective of social defense, however, the problem with the claim that nuclear deterrence provides protection for the population is that advocates of nuclear deterrence can provide no satisfactory moral explanation of what will happen if their strategy fails. The argument that nuclear deterrence protects the population is circular: deterrence protects society as long as deterrence works. But, as critics frequently point out, time and fallibility are not on the side of nuclear deterrence. No matter how intimidating the nuclear threat, the strategy of deterrence is unlikely to work forever, and the consequences of its failure would be catastrophic for civilization. Colin Gray recognizes the difficulty:

> The problem, indeed the enduring problem, is that the future rests upon a nuclear deterrence system concerning which even a single serious malfunction cannot be tolerated. So 40 years into the nuclear age it is uncertain whether the absence of bilateral nuclear war should be attributed more to luck than to sound policy. The question is, for how long should this system of reciprocated retaliatory threats be expected to work satisfactorily? One may be confident that stability reigns today, but how confident can one be for the next 50 or 100 years?[7]

There are thus two problems with claims about the efficacy of nuclear deterrence. First, one cannot convincingly demonstrate that nuclear threats alone have prevented Soviet nuclear (or conventional) attacks against the United States or Western Europe: other factors and conditions may have significantly contributed to the maintenance of peace. Perhaps the Soviet Union has never really had aggressive intentions toward Western Europe or the United States. Or perhaps the Soviet Union would not have thought the costs of even a conventional war worth any possible gains. Second, even if one could somehow establish that nuclear threats have kept the peace for decades, it does not follow that this arrangement will continue to work indefinitely.

When it comes to the question of what the United States should do in the event of a nuclear attack, no version of nuclear deterrence seems plausible. Mutual assured destruction tells us that if there is a Soviet nuclear attack, we must be ready to incinerate millions of innocent Soviet citizens and accept in return an even more devastating second attack on our citizens. Countervailing and prevailing strategies require us to believe something implausible: that we can fight a limited nuclear war and keep it from escalating into an all-out exchange. Even if we could control the level of violence—which is unlikely, because nuclear explosions will probably nullify all means of communication and control—the devastation produced by even a "small" nuclear war will cause massive destruction to human life and the global environment.

In the end, all forms of nuclear deterrence, including the detailed limited war options of some nuclear strategies, involve a desperate bet against failure, a wager largely based on belief in the rationality of the adversary and in the infallibility of mechanical systems. Unlike nuclear strategists, advocates of social defense do not want Western security to rest upon dubious assumptions about Soviet rationality, faith in the reliability of warning systems, and disregard for the possibility of an accidental launch.

The widespread disagreement among nuclear strategists about what sorts of threatened losses would effectively deter Soviet aggression reflects great uncertainty about the nature of Soviet reasoning. From the perspective of social defense, our survival should not depend on faith in Soviet rationality or automated systems, but on our capacity to protect society against an irrational Soviet attack or mechanical breakdown.[8]

A comprehensive defensive system that could incapacitate the Soviet arsenal would, of course, simultaneously operate as an indirect deterrent by rendering Soviet nuclear weapons impotent. That is, deterrence would be a bonus of an essentially defensive policy. If the policy of social defense brings deterrence with it, however, it is deterrence by denial of objectives rather than deterrence by threat of punishment. The aim of a purely defensive strategy is not to inflict damage or pain on the aggressor's society or even its military personnel: the aim is instead to neutralize the instruments of aggression.

Avoiding Destabilizing Ambiguity

If, on the way to a purely defensive strategy, the United States is not to send a threatening, and therefore destabilizing, message to the Soviet Union, it is important that while the nation builds up its defenses it simultaneously reduces its offensive forces. There is an ambiguity in the concept of social defense that must not be retained in its translation into a national security doctrine. President Reagan acknowledged this problem in his March 1983 announcement of SDI: "I clearly recognize that defensive systems have limitations and raise certain problems and ambiguities. If paired with offensive systems, they can be viewed as fostering an aggressive policy, and no one wants that."[9]

That is, if the United States continues to build counterforce offensive weapons as it is constructing a defensive system, the Soviet Union might conclude that America is developing a first-strike strategy, a conviction that might motivate the Soviets to launch a preventive attack before the defensive system is completed. This is precisely what many critics of strategic defense charge—that far from being a purely defensive system, SDI is really a component of an offensive war–winning policy. This charge will appear to have credibility if the United States does not decrease its arsenal of accurate counterforce nuclear weapons as it constructs a system of defenses. The involvement of nuclear victory strategists such as Colin Gray in the SDI movement makes Soviet suspicion that SDI advocates aim at a war-winning strategy *prima facie* plausible.

The destabilizing ambiguity that lies at the heart of the very concept of social defense is captured by the following question: in seeking to realize the objective of social defense, should it be our goal only to counter an act of aggression, or should we also be prepared to incapacitate an adversary whose forces merely threaten our security (i.e., to disarm a *potentially* dangerous power)? That is, does social defense justify incapacitation only after an act of aggression has been initiated? Or does it also justify preventive action? If the answer to the second half of that question is yes, then the theory appears to sanction attacks on the Soviet nuclear arsenal even in the absence of Soviet aggression—in other words, a first-strike strategy. Certainly nations have justified unprovoked attacks on adversaries in the name of defense. Consider, for example, the 1981 Israeli raid on an Iraqi nuclear reactor then under construction. Israel argued that the possession of nuclear weapons by the Iraqis would constitute a serious threat to the security of the state of Israel, thus justifying the attack as defensive.

The domestic version of social defense may appear to permit preventive incapacitation of individuals identified by the state as dangerous. If society's fundamental concern is protection of citizens from harmful individuals, and if we have reason to believe that certain individuals will one day soon commit acts of violence (crimes), then—it can be argued—we ought to incapacitate them in order to prevent their probable criminal behavior and thereby protect society. On this view, it does not appear that a social defense perspective requires an actual crime—as does, for example, a retributive perspective. In order to authorize an act of incapacitation, it requires only the probability of dangerousness. If priority is given to protecting citizens from harmful individuals (as opposed to protecting the rights of those who are categorized as dangerous), then, in the name of domestic social defense, we could justify the incarceration of probable, as well as actual, offenders.

That, at least, would be reasoning appropriate to a crudely utilitarian reading of social defense. It must, however, be balanced against the Kantian reading, which would require us to protect the innocent, including those who have not yet committed crimes, no matter how probable their future criminal behavior appears to be. Of course, in the case of American society, the constitutional guarantee of due process would lead us to condemn acts of preventive incapacitation.

Analogically extending the concept of preventive incapacitation to the nuclear context would mean justifying a policy of preventive war and, with it, the requisite counterforce first-strike capability. Although we could work out a consequentialist interpretation of national social defense that parallels the domestic idea of preventive incapacitation, there are overriding prudential and deontological reasons not to do so.

First, a strategy authorizing preventive defense will require a destabilizing arsenal of superaccurate, offensive, first-strike weapons. It would be a crisis-destabilizing strategy likely to encourage a Soviet preventive attack on the "defensive" system before it was completed— or to encourage the Soviets to adopt a finger-on-the-trigger launch-on-warning posture. Crisis stability depends on the force structures and doctrines of both sides and on each side's perception of the other. As we have seen, crisis instability is synonymous with any situation in which one side has an incentive to initiate hostilities. If the Soviet Union believed that unless it used its forces first, it would lose them, then it would clearly have an incentive for a first strike.

Second, if a *purely defensive* system designed only to neutralize weapons in flight is feasible, there is no reason to supplement it with an offensive system capable of destroying stationary weapons. Given an effective defensive system, it would be redundant and provocative to add a comprehensive preventive-strike arsenal. Moreover, if our policy is truly defensive, then we should not use our weapons until the other side launches an attack. This means that we should construct defensive systems that by their very nature can go into action only when the missiles or aircraft of the aggressor take to their flight paths—that is, only when the act of aggression has been initiated.[10] The system should be such that it will not work unless an aggressor's weapons are confirmed as in flight.

Third, it should be recalled that a moral concern to protect the innocent—in the Soviet Union as well as the United States—was part of the motivation behind the original SDI proposal. This precludes a first strike on Soviet nuclear forces because (1) the Soviet military, given this scenario, would not be guilty of aggression (thus, an attack on them would be an attack on innocents), and (2) any attack on Soviet nuclear silos, given their proximity to population centers in the USSR, would cause significant civilian casualties.

The most fragile and potentially destabilizing period will be the transitional one between the offense-dominated present and the defense-dominated future. If the United States relies on nuclear deterrence while it is building an adequate defensive system, care must be taken in mixing nuclear forces with an improving defensive capability. To avoid sending the wrong strategic message to the Soviet Union—namely, an offensive one—and thus violating the requirement of crisis stability, the United States needs an interim strategy and force system that will provide security for the nation without creating insecurity for the other side. Several possibilities need to be explored.

For example, during the transitional period, we might dismantle our multiwarhead missiles and build a minimal deterrence force based on mobile Midgetman missiles. We could adopt a minimal deterrence posture and reduce our arsenal to 500 retaliatory Midgetman missiles, thereby giving ourselves a relatively modest, more survivable, and less threatening nuclear deterrent.[11] The Midgetman missile's small size—37,000 pounds, compared with the huge MX missile (190,000 pounds)—allows it to be deployed and moved about on trucks. It is less threatening to the Soviets because it carries only one warhead (compared with ten for the MX) and, unless built in large numbers, poses no threat of a first strike. Moreover, having one warhead makes it a less attractive target for a Soviet first strike—assuming they could locate it—than a multiple-warhead missile.[12] In sum, a mobile and small Midgetman arsenal would promote crisis stability by being difficult to hit (making it survivable) and by being incapable of a disarming first strike (making it nonthreatening). Thus, as an interim nuclear deterrence force—one designed to ensure a stable transition to a purely defensive strategy—Midgetman missiles may be appropriate weapons.

Another possibility for a stabilizing transitional posture is the elimination of all nuclear weapons except those of the air-breathing variety: bombers and long-range cruise missiles. The speed of ballistic missiles may count against them as interim weapons; fast-flying ballistic missiles, which can reach their targets in twenty to thirty minutes, put pressure on decision-makers to respond quickly to a *possible* attack. For this reason, some defense analysts think ICBMs invite a preemptive strike or are likely to cause an accidental war. Bombers and long-range cruise missiles, on the other hand, may promote crisis stability because of their slower speeds. According to Bruce G. Blair, an expert on command and control systems, reliance on bombers and long-range cruise missiles would allow decision-makers to "conduct a cooler, more reasonable and reasoned decision process."[13] In the event of a Soviet–American agreement to eliminate ballistic missiles, these weapons might guard against the risk of cheating while providing a way to defend the United States and Western Europe.[14]

A third suggestion for an interim strategy is the early deployment of a primitive terminal defensive system—the first (and easiest to construct) component in a layered defense—to protect command and control facilities and a relatively small (and therefore nonthreatening) but sufficient retaliatory nuclear force, perhaps 50 percent or less of our current ICBM force.[15] Not having to adopt a use-them-or-lose-them strategy, we would have time to assess attack warnings and to make a rational decision about the need for a retaliatory strike.

A fourth possibility is to retain only a submarine force because it is the least vulnerable leg of our nuclear triad. This would require improving communications with this force, so that it would not have to be autonomous and would not be endangered by having to come close to the surface for messages.[16] In addition, to discourage the Soviets from adopting a launch-on-warning strategy, U.S. submarines should not be positioned close to the Soviet homeland.

In summary, a movement toward defense ought to be accompanied by a nuclear build-down and the retention of interim offensive forces that could not be construed as part of a war-winning strategy. In eliminating weapon systems we must not, of course, so reduce our offensive forces as to invite Soviet adventurism and aggression: that would be equally destabilizing. Two things invite an attack: the appearance of first-strike preparation and the appearance of weakness. Both must be avoided if the transitional period is to be a stable one.

None of the above suggestions for a transitional strategy may prove adequate. That is a technical problem for professional strategists: they must work on several options that satisfy the requirement of crisis stability and present them to elected officials (the president and the Congress) for debate. The main point is that a transitional strategy—one on the way to comprehensive national social defense—should be unambiguous and should in no way threaten Soviet security while providing real security for the United States and its allies. The initial stages of a defensive system could enhance nuclear deterrence as we build toward a purely defensive system—a system that will further our security and that of our allies without threatening to destroy millions of people.

It is, of course, important to convince the Soviets that a transition to defense is in their best interests. In fact, strategic defense is a policy that fits in well with Soviet military doctrine. The objective of defending the homeland is central to Soviet strategic thinking. The Soviets appear prepared—if war seems imminent—to use their counterforce weapons to destroy U.S. nuclear forces in order to limit damage to Soviet forces and Soviet society. It is their concern with damage limitation that led the Soviets to adopt the dangerous doctrine of preemption: in a crisis where nuclear war seems unavoidable, Soviet strategy appears to call for striking first. It is reasonable to assume that Soviet strategy, despite disclaimers, still calls for a preemptive nuclear attack on U.S. nuclear forces as a way of minimizing Soviet losses. Of course, to the extent that this strategy is premised on the threat posed by U.S. counterforce (potentially first-strike) weapons, we should be able to remove the motivation for preemption by cutting the number of counterforce weapons as we build up our defenses.[17] In that case, the Soviet leaders will no longer have a basis for preemption or for a large counterforce arsenal. At this writing the Soviets seem ready to reduce their arsenal significantly and to move toward a purely defensive doctrine. The task is to convince them that strategic defense is the best way to achieve this.

We must persuade the Soviets that a shift from offensive nuclear forces to strategic defenses is a more direct way of realizing their central strategic objective. After all, they have been working for decades on their own strategic defense program. The transition to defense could provide the damage-limiting capability required by Soviet doctrine, with defensive forces replacing the Soviet offensive arsenal as the principal means for limiting damage.[18]

Many supporters of SDI have emphasized that the best transition from an offensive to a defensive strategy would be a cooperative endeavor with the Soviet Union in which arms control would play a critical role.[19] Arms control and defenses have a symbiotic relationship: significant mutual arms reductions make the work of defenses feasible and manageable, while mutual advances in defenses make significant force reductions thinkable and stable. Arms control is important in guaranteeing that the task of defenses will not be overwhelming. Facing ten thousand warheads is a dizzying prospect, but as mutual reductions move toward zero or even a few hundred weapons on both sides, an effective comprehensive defense becomes a real possibility.

The ideal of a truly leak-proof shield becomes realizable as the number of threatening weapons is reduced. Even if one side secretly retained some nuclear weapons, a comprehensive defensive system could confidently handle the accidental or intentional launching of these warheads. Moreover, as defenses improve, the problem of verification and the fear of cheating disappear as stumbling blocks to the mutual acceptance of very deep reductions and even complete nuclear disarmament.[20] Mutual strategic defense could provide both countries with an insurance policy against cheating. Trust would no longer be an essential requirement for an agreement on the elimination of nuclear weapons.

A Unilateral Initiative and the Problem of Countermeasures

If there is no such cooperation, then we can expect the Soviet Union to invest in offensive measures in order to defeat our defense. These are called *countermeasures*. For example, along with nuclear warheads the Soviets might pack their missiles with hundreds of decoys, chaff (metal strips), or other materials designed to confuse the defensive system. If the Soviets refuse to cooperate on arms control agreements that permit a stable transition to defense, the possibility of successful defense depends, according to some of its advocates, on the satisfaction of two criteria advanced by Paul Nitze: survivability and cost-effectiveness at the margin.[21]

Survivability. Survivability means survival of the defensive system in the face of Soviet attempts to destroy it. If the system is not survivable, the Soviet Union has an incentive in a crisis to strike first at vulnerable elements of the defense. Satisfaction of this criterion ensures that the Soviets will have no prospect of nullifying the defensive apparatus.

One proposal for ensuring survivability is to have lots of independent and separate systems—a decentralized arrangement instead of one large centralized system. Richard Lipton, professor of computer science at Princeton University, sums up the idea in this way:

> You might have dozens or even hundreds of separate pieces, each capable of tracking, each capable of targeting, each capable of shooting at and eventually destroying targets coming at the United States. Now, each of those systems would be possibly different kinds of systems with different kinds of weapons and different kinds of sensors. They might be built by different contractors, different vendors, perhaps at different times, using different technology. The Russians would be faced, or anyone attacking us would be faced, with something like a triad, but it would be a many-legged defensive system.[22]

In other words, this collection of nonnuclear defensive units would be analogous to our current offensive nuclear triad. Even if one system misfired or fired at decoys instead of warheads, the adversary would still have to worry about the other systems. With many legs of defense, the destruction of all the legs becomes too difficult to make a successful Soviet attack plausible. Whether or not such a decentralized, redundant system is feasible, it illustrates the kind of thinking that is necessary for the satisfaction of the criterion of survivability.

Cost-Effectiveness. The criterion of survivability cannot be completely separated from that of cost-effectiveness. Since nothing is absolutely survivable, the question that must be asked is what price the defense must force the Soviets to pay to negate a particular defensive asset. The cost-effectiveness criterion demands assurance that any deployed defensive system will create a powerful incentive not to respond with additional offensive measures, requiring, in effect, that countermeasures cost more than the additional defensive capability (counter-countermeasures) needed to defeat them. In other words, defenses should be deployed only if the cost of deploying them is less than the cost of offsetting them.

Consider, for example, a layer of a defensive system that has a 90 percent probability of destroying any warhead that comes its way. In other words, for each 100 interceptors launched, 90 warheads would be destroyed. The cost-effectiveness criterion requires us to ask whether, at the margin, 100 interceptors cost more or less than 90 additional warheads or whatever countermeasures might be employed. If the interceptors cost more than the aggressor's off-setting measures, then the system is not cost-effective; if the interceptors cost less, then the defense is cost-effective.[23]

This means that we should seek defensive options that provide clear disincentives to efforts to counter them with additional offensive weapons or countermeasures. Lt. Gen. James Abrahamson, former director of the Strategic Defense Initiative Organization, put it this way:

> We must ensure that the kind of defenses that we have chosen, and the systems that we have chosen to be part of the defenses, would be the kind that would discourage the Soviets from wanting to build more missiles or from undertaking a course that would force us into a very expensive reaction. It must be cost-imposing on the Soviets. We are . . . looking for the kinds of characteristics of our system that would be most expensive for them and most difficult for them to overcome, so that what we are really after is behavior modification. . . . The course of action that we want is for them to begin to recognize that their ballistic missiles do not have the same omnipotent military value that they had in the past, and therefore see that the proper and reasonable course is to shift

to their own defenses as opposed to continuing to try to build up offensive weapons.[24]

If it is cheap enough to add additional defensive capability, the Soviet Union will have no incentive to construct additional offensive weapons (or countermeasures) to overcome the deployed defenses: put positively, the Soviets will have an incentive to redirect their efforts from offense to defense. Again, this can be achieved only if we are able to impose a cost on the Soviets that is greater than the cost we are incurring in developing the system.

This means that we must develop devices that are not easily countermeasured by the Soviets. The ultimate aim, of course, would be to get the Soviets to the bargaining table for the purpose of mutual reduction of nuclear arms and a cooperative transition to strategic defense, because even if we could establish a cost-effective survivable system, its technical effectiveness would be stretched to the limits by a multiplication of Soviet offensive weapons or other countermeasures. On the other hand, as noted above, the ambitious goal of providing the population with comprehensive protection becomes more feasible as the number of threatening weapons is reduced.

Not all supporters of a policy of social defense agree that the proposal should stand or fall on whether it satisfies the criterion of cost-effectiveness at the margin. For instance, Michael Altfeld, strategic policy analyst at the U.S. Army War College, points out that some people may, at the margin, value a highly effective defensive system more than they value the other things that might be purchased with the funds required for such a system. That is, if one sees innocent human life as an ultimate value and one is convinced of the effectiveness of the defenses, it is one's obligation to support the development of a defensive system, despite any unfavorable cost-exchange ratio.[25]

If we consider the question within the domestic context, the issue becomes clearer. What if, at the margin, the incapacitation of dangerous criminals failed the cost-effectiveness test? What if, after a certain point, the building of additional maximum-security prison units to house violent, dangerous offenders cost society enormous sums, so that the additional expenditures, even though they did protect additional people from murder, robbery, assault, and rape, were not really cost-effective. Would we then settle for these additional but avoidable human losses in order to satisfy the criterion of cost-effectiveness at the margin? Social defense theorists could persuasively argue that cost-efficiency should not take priority over the government's obligation to protect the lives and bodily security of its citizens.

Likewise, in the domain of national security, the protection of citizens can be considered a government obligation so important that it should be implemented, even if very costly in economic terms. On this view, one simply cannot and should not weigh human lives against economic gains and losses. As one early proponent of strategic defense put it:

> Some persons reason thus: Which is cheaper, to have offensive weapons that can destroy cities and entire states or to have defensive weapons that can prevent this destruction? At present the theory is current in some places that one should develop whichever system is cheaper. Such "theoreticians" argue also about how much it costs to kill a person, $500,000 or $100,000. An anti-missile system may cost more than an offensive one, but it is intended not for killing people but for saving lives.[26]

The source is Alexei N. Kosygin, who was chairman of the USSR Council of Ministers from 1964 to 1980. In the mid-sixties Kosygin and other Soviet officials were openly supportive of strategic defense. As SDI supporters remind us, the Soviets during this period made a powerful moral case for defenses—one that should not be forgotten as we listen to the Soviets' less credible case against SDI.

Implementation of Social Defense

The idea behind national social defense is the same as that underlying domestic social defense: the protection of society through the incapacitation of threatening agents. The aim of national social defense is to disarm and render harmless acts of nuclear aggression. A comprehensive defensive system designed to satisfy this objective is called an *astrodome* or a *peace shield*. This total protective umbrella would include both active and passive components. Active defense seeks to neutralize or destroy the attacking weapons before they hit. Passive defense attempts to save the population from weapons that penetrate the active defense.

Active Defense: Strategic Defense

A fully comprehensive active defense must intercept intercontinental ballistic missiles, bombers, cruise missiles, submarine-launched missiles, and all other methods of delivering nuclear warheads. Most of the research has focused on the interception of ICBMs—the mode of delivery that constitutes about 70 percent of Soviet nuclear forces. The proposal most frequently discussed is for a layered defense that would attempt to destroy the ICBM in one or all of its four phases of flight. Destruction in earlier stages of missile flight would reduce the number of warheads that later defensive layers would have to attack; later layers would supposedly mop up the weapons that got through earlier ones. To convey a better idea of what such a system would have to achieve, it will be helpful to sketch the phases of ICBM flight.[27]

1. Boost Phase. The first period covers the time from launch to burnout of the booster rockets. The phase lasts as long as there are booster rockets attached to the warhead bus, the carrier of reentry vehicles with warheads. During this phase the hot gases from the initial booster rocket exhaust produce a large, easily detected infrared signal or signature, especially as the rocket rises above the clouds and the dense layers of the atmosphere. For current missiles, it lasts from three to five minutes. Of course, not all of this short period is available for attack. The defensive system must first detect the missile launchings, target the missiles, and then order a kill. The advantage of a kill at this stage is that the destruction of the target results in the elimination of all its warheads and decoys. In the case of a single Soviet SS-18, that means the destruction of as many as ten 600-kiloton independently targeted nuclear warheads, along with perhaps hundreds of decoys. This means, on the other hand, that each missile that survives the boost phase may produce hundreds of objects that must be individually tracked, discriminated, and destroyed in a later defensive layer.[28]

2. Postboost Phase. After the booster rockets have dropped away, a postboost vehicle (PBV, or bus) continues toward the target. This stage starts after the last booster stage has finished firing and covers the time during which the remaining reentry vehicles (RVs)—separate, heat-shield-protected vehicles, each containing a warhead—are dispersed by the PBV and placed on independent ballistic trajectories toward their targets. Decoys and other defense-penetration aids can also be dispersed during this phase. This period may last as long as six minutes, but it could be much shorter. As this phase progresses, the PBV dispenses all its RVs and decoys and consequently depreciates in value as a target. Hence, the destruction of the PBV at the beginning of this stage is most important.[29]

3. Midcourse Phase. In the next period, lasting about twenty minutes, the warheads coast toward their targets. Most of the warheads' flight time is spent in midcourse—the period between release from the bus and reentry into the earth's atmosphere. Although there is much more time to destroy the targets, there are many more targets to destroy than in the earlier phases. Before a warhead can be destroyed, it must be discriminated from the decoys and debris. Whereas in the boost phase the defense needs to locate and destroy only one object to kill the ten warheads on an SS-18, in the midcourse phase the destruction of the same ten warheads requires sorting through hundreds of objects within a period of twenty minutes. In a massive launch of missiles, this would mean sorting through thousands of objects.[30]

4. Terminal Phase. This reentry phase, which starts when the warheads reenter the earth's atmosphere and the lighter decoys burn up, lasts a minute or less. To protect the population in this phase, interception must take place at the highest possible altitude. A few tens of seconds would be available for this task as atmospheric effects begin to sort out decoys from warheads. The terminal defense would, of course, have almost thirty minutes to get ready to destroy these warheads— assuming that information about the location of the surviving warheads could be communicated to the terminal interceptors.[31]

While the exact shape of a comprehensive defensive system is not yet clear, it should be evident from what was said above that the system will have to perform the following tasks:

- Surveillance and acquisition: missile launchings must be detected and all threatening weapons must be identified.
- Discrimination: missile buses and warheads must be distinguished from nonthreatening decoys and other debris.
- Pointing and tracking: the target must be tracked and that information communicated to the defensive weapon.
- Target destruction: a defensive weapon must deliver sufficient energy or appropriate force to the target rapidly enough to destroy it.
- Kill assessment: targets destroyed must be identified and distinguished from survivors. This information must be passed on to subsequent layers.

In sum, the system that is ultimately chosen must be able, in the face of all Soviet countermeasures, to detect and disable the attacking weapons in seconds as well as rapidly communicate to later layers information about surviving warheads. Such a system must include sensors to perform the tasks of tracking, discriminating, and pointing; computers to calculate flight trajectories, order attacks, assess the success of an attack on a target, and perform many other tasks; communication links to ensure that each part of the system knows what the other parts are doing; and weapons with which to kill the attacking warheads or delivery vehicles.[32] The weapons requirements of a ballistic missile defense system have led to talk of *directed energy interceptors*—laser,

particle beam, and microwave weapons that kill through heat or pulse—
because the speed of destruction would be near the speed of light,
arriving at the target in less than a tenth of a second. There has also been
discussion of the use of kinetic-energy weapons (so-called smart rocks)
that destroy their targets through direct collision at very high velocity.[33]

Another plan is that of "brilliant pebbles"—several thousand
space-based rockets designed to intercept ballistic missiles in the first
minutes of flight, before the release of their multiple warheads and decoys. In place of battle stations, each interceptor would orbit individually, and each would include a rocket capable of boosting the interceptor
to near-ICBM velocities. The "pebbles" would be put on war alert when
ground controllers sent them a special encrypted signal. To achieve its
purpose each pebble would have, according to Lt. Gen. Abrahamson,
"sophisticated sensors to independently detect and track Soviet missiles; a high-speed computer capable of identifying Soviet missiles by
type, judging which missile to shoot at, predicting its trajectory, and
plotting a flight path for interception."[34] The idea is to place in orbit
between ten thousand and a hundred thousand small weapons that
would home in on enemy missiles and destroy them by force of impact.
These interceptors would be hardened against nuclear and laser attack.
In theory these devices would not require much in the way of outside
guidance from sensor satellites and ground stations. This relative autonomy, as well as the sheer number of pebbles, would make the system
much harder to attack effectively and less vulnerable to disruption.

Whatever weapons are eventually chosen must, of course, be
adequate to the task of destroying "attacking" Soviet nuclear forces and
not be subject to a destabilizing ambiguity of the kind discussed above.
That is to say, since the Soviets infer U.S. "action" policy from our
weapons capability—and not from our "declaratory" doctrine—the
weapons we choose for strategic defense should not be such that the
Soviets could interpret them as part of an offensive war–winning strategy. The appeal of directed-energy weapons is, according to SDI advocates, that they are not subject to misinterpretation. Defending research
on these weapons, Lt. Gen. Abrahamson made this point in testimony
before the Senate:

> We are really looking for weapons concepts that will be ideal for
> the specific tasks that were outlined, and that is to destroy a
> ballistic missile. Contrary to all of the marvelous cartoons, a laser
> does not put a great deal of energy at its point of impact. It is like
> perhaps several hand grenades or a stick of TNT or something of
> that kind, quite adequate under certain conditions to destroy a
> booster, but certainly it is not a weapon of mass destruction. A

neutral particle beam, which is another idea that we are research-
ing very carefully—and by the way, the Soviets are doing exactly
the same thing in that area—while it could be a very capable
weapon in space against electronic systems and perhaps even
against warheads themselves, cannot even penetrate the atmosphere. That does not mean that some energy of some of these
kinds of systems might not be able to leak down to the ground.
Yes, that is possible, but it would not be of the character or the
kind that it would make an ideal weapon of mass destruction to be
used against populations in the same way that a ballistic missile
would.[35]

The same could be said of the brilliant pebbles concept: since
they would be designed to destroy missiles in flight by force of impact,
they would not be suitable either for the destruction of missiles in silos
or for mass destruction.

The objective guiding weapons design should be the destruction
of attacking weapons or weapons in flight—with no potential for killing
"stationary" weapons or for destroying large area targets. That is, such
weapons should not be capable of a disarming first strike or the destruction of industrial–urban centers.

If we add to the challenge of ballistic missile defense that of
defense against low-flying cruise missiles and submarine-launched missiles (whose flight time off the coast of the United States is only a few
minutes), the defensive project may seem overwhelming, indeed impossible. Advocates are well aware of the difficulties and often remind
critics of the enormous challenge posed by the Manhattan Project, the
plan to build an atomic bomb. They ask citizens to be skeptical of
experts who deny the possibility of strategic defense. They point out
that in 1932 Einstein stated: "There is not the slightest indication that
nuclear energy will ever be obtainable,"[36] and that Admiral Leahy said
as late as 1945: "The atomic bomb will not go off and I speak as an
expert on explosives."[37] Breakthroughs have repeatedly achieved what
was previously thought to be impossible. As Lt. Gen. Abrahamson
stated: "Our history shows that when we decide that something is truly
worthwhile and we maintain the rational will to proceed, technical
solutions can be found."[38]

Passive Defense: Civil Defense

The problem with any system of active defense is leakage. We
cannot expect the defensive astrodome to be completely impenetrable.
Thus, there is a need for passive forms of defense to compensate for

such penetration. Passive defense attempts to limit the damage resulting from the aggressor's penetration of the active defense system—that is, it is designed to minimize the destructive effects of nuclear weapons that cannot be intercepted. Passive efforts fall under the heading of civil defense.

Civil defense is the nonmilitary protection of a society's nonmilitary assets, including civilians, government operations, vital records, and economic infrastructure. It may involve various contingency plans for a nation's political and economic recovery after an attack. Some studies have suggested that U.S. casualties could be reduced from 48 to 75 percent of the population without civil defense to 10 to 26 percent of the population with such measures.[39] Plans to move the population from target areas to safer regions, construction of blast and fallout shelters, the stockpiling of critical supplies such as food and medicine, and the training of the population in preparation for a nuclear attack are concrete passive defense measures. Comprehensive civil defense plans will prepare the nation for a surprise attack as well as for an attack after days of rising tension.

Evacuation procedures are, of course, relevant only to the second attack scenario, in which Soviet–American tensions build over days or weeks. With sufficient planning and periodic practice, the evacuation of target areas (e.g., communities near nuclear missile sites) could take place within twenty-four hours. The idea is to evacuate citizens from high-risk areas (probable targets) to host communities at low risk of direct attack. Provision would have to be made to relocate the evacuees to host homes, churches, or schools. Destination plans and host city arrangements would have to exist and be made known to everyone in advance. There are precedents for this: mass civilian evacuations prior to natural disasters such as hurricanes have proceeded without panic.[40]

In the event of surprise attack by ICBMs, there could be as little as twenty minutes' warning, since it takes ballistic missiles from the Soviet Union approximately thirty minutes to reach the U.S. mainland. People would have to be able to get to nearby bomb shelters. Only if shelters were available close to home and places of work and play—and only if warnings were given quickly—could civil defense work in the face of a sudden attack. These shelters must contain food, medical supplies, communications equipment, and radiation detectors.

Shelters are of two kinds: blast and fallout. Blast shelters are designed to afford protection against the extreme overpressure of nuclear attacks: against blast, area fires, and prompt gamma radiation. An adequate urban shelter might need both its own oxygen supply and a cooling system. A shelter can be hardened to withstand 50 to 100 pounds per square inch (psi) without great difficulty. (Some advocates of civil defense assert that less than 0.05 percent of the area of the United

States would be exposed to an overpressure of 50 psi or more.)[41] Such shelters would be crucial to places designated as target areas.

A Soviet counterforce attack against U.S. military installations would endanger civilians primarily through fallout effects. Fallout shelters are designed for long-term occupancy in order to provide protection from radioactive fallout. Radioactive fallout tends to decay rapidly: two days after an attack it is reduced to about one percent of its original level, and after two weeks to a tenth of one percent.[42] Citizens could safely emerge after several weeks underground. Prolonging the stay in a fallout shelter beyond a couple of weeks—unless it is extended for months—will probably not significantly reduce the total fallout dosage received.[43]

A social defense policy would appear to require a comprehensive federal shelter program, something comparable to the Swiss plan. In Switzerland it is required by law that every new house or public building have a blast and fallout shelter. Within a few decades every Swiss citizen will have this kind of passive protection.[44]

If protection from the threat of nuclear attack is considered as much a right as protection from criminal violence, then shelter protection must not be the privilege of the wealthy few who can afford fallout shelters. It must be—as Freeman Dyson argues—public and universal, equally available to all citizens.[45] If criminal justice authorities incapacitated only the criminals who threatened the wealthy sections of society while ignoring criminal threats to poorer sections, this would violate the requirement of equal protection. If shelter protection were a contingent matter of affordability, it would take on a class character that would violate the same fundamental principle.

The Problem of Fallibility

The combination of layered interception and passive defense should significantly minimize population vulnerability to a nuclear attack. Proponents of strategic defense believe that the use of active and passive defense could reduce the civilian casualties from an all-out Soviet attack from as many as 100 million members of an unprotected population to a small percentage.

Critics of Star Wars I who are advocates of nuclear deterrence seem to find it morally reprehensible that supporters of population defense are willing to spend billions of dollars on a system that will not be a perfect shield against Soviet missiles. Advocates of population defense must, of course, grant that the task of protecting society from nuclear attack is enormous. To justify their proposal, they need not, however, claim that a perfect shield or impenetrable system of defenses can be built: they need only make the case that casualties can be significantly reduced and civilian assets substantially protected by a comprehensive program of active and passive defenses. Proponents of a defensive strategy can even grant—without making their position inferior to that of nuclear deterrence—that there is no way to test the technological components of a defensive system to determine how they will perform under realistic battle conditions, or to know in advance all the counter-measures that the system will have to handle.

Once put in place, a defensive system may not operate perfectly. There are two ways in which the system might fail: it could be triggered mistakenly, responding as if a Soviet attack had occurred when in fact there was no such attack, or it might fail to achieve its mission and allow a devastating number of weapons to penetrate. The system can really be tested only during an actual attack, which is, of course, too late to find out if it works. Despite these admissions, a social defense advocate might respond to the fallibility objection as follows.

First, to be fair, nuclear deterrence advocates must acknowledge that a deterrence system can also be mistakenly triggered. One must then ask oneself which is worse—an erroneous nuclear reprisal against the other side or an erroneous nonnuclear defensive reaction directed against targets that have not materialized (i.e., nuclear weapons in flight)? It is the difference between weapons that will mistakenly kill thousands or millions of human beings and interceptors that, being incapable of mass destruction, will find no real weapons to attack. The scale of disaster in the case of accidental nuclear retaliation would be qualitatively different from that of accidental anti–nuclear weapons retaliation. Under nuclear deterrence, our only response to an indication that we are under nuclear attack is nuclear retaliation, which may lead to a holocaust, whereas mistakes in the same situation with a defensive system are less irreversible and less costly.[46]

What about the failure of the system to achieve its mission? If the Soviets came up with just one special trick to spoof the defensive system and we did not design the system to cope with it, then it will be a Maginot Line in space.[47] But, again, a defensive system is not really unique in this regard, because the existing nuclear triad has never been put to a real test. Indeed, no ICBM has been fired in the north–south route it will have to take in an actual war, and no one has launched thousands of ICBMs at once—yet advocates of nuclear retaliation are willing to believe the system will work.[48] Missiles may fail to fire, fall back to earth, or miss their targets. Thus, failure can be expected in retaliatory as well as defensive systems. The fact that the effectiveness of a defensive system is ultimately uncertain and that it can only be tested in wartime does not distinguish it from the present deterrence system, which is also full of uncertainties.

In summary, both deterrence and defensive systems can be accidentally triggered, and neither can be fully tested. Both are fallible. The important difference, according to SDI advocates, lies in the scale of disaster that would accompany the failure of each system. Defensive systems, it is argued, have a significant advantage over offensive systems in terms of the types of catastrophes that can occur.[49] From the perspective of social defense, there is something morally strange about the deterrence advocate's unwillingness to settle for a defensive strategy because it can protect only a percentage, and not all, of the U.S. population, while embracing a retaliatory strategy that could result in the mass destruction not only of Soviet and U.S. populations, but perhaps of life on the planet.

The ABM Treaty

In addition to economic, technical, and moral objections to strategic defense, there is a legal objection. Many critics assert that it violates one of the most important Soviet–American arms control agreements ever signed—the 1972 Anti-Ballistic Missile Treaty. The treaty is considered by many to be the foundation of arms control. James Rubin, speaking as assistant director for research at the Arms Control Association in Washington, sums up this view: "Because the treaty prohibits either side from developing and deploying a nationwide defense, or a base for such a defense, both sides can retain confidence in the effectiveness of their deterrent forces even at reduced levels."[50] This agreement in effect prohibits the construction of a comprehensive system of ballistic missile defense. Article I states: "Each Party undertakes not to deploy ABM systems for a defense of the territory of its country and not to provide a base for such a defense, and not to deploy ABM systems for defense of an individual region except as provided for in Article III."[51] Article III allows for the defense of two sites (amended to one in a 1974 protocol) with a limit of 100 interceptors and 100 launchers. The treaty defines an ABM system as "a system to counter strategic ballistic missiles or their elements in flight trajectory"—including interceptor missiles, ABM launchers, and ABM radars.[52] The treaty was intended to be of unlimited duration, although it was to be reviewed for possible amendment every five years.[53]

In addition to limiting the kind and number of fixed land-based ABM systems, the treaty forbids either side to develop, test, or deploy mobile ABM systems or components that are based on land, sea, in the air, and in space.[54] On the traditional or restrictive interpretation, the agreement also prohibits the testing and development of exotic ABM systems, such as the particle beam and laser weapons, that are based on physical principles other than those on which interceptor missiles are based.[55] There has been disagreement about the portion of the treaty that deals with the testing and development of exotic systems, and a new broad interpretation asserts that the agreement allows extensive tests of such defensive systems. On this broad reading, testing and development of systems based on new physical principles are not prohibited.[56]

Whatever the correct interpretation concerning testing, it is clear that the treaty prohibits deployment of territorial ballistic missile defenses. The important point, according to SDI advocates, is that the ABM agreement is premised upon MAD: each side's population is to be kept defenseless against enemy missiles. The effect of the treaty is to leave essentially unimpaired the penetration capacity of either side's ballistic missile force. That is, the treaty is designed to keep both societies vulnerable to attack.

Of course, the original idea was that neither side would feel compelled to build more weapons as long as the other side was kept vulnerable to attack. Strategic defenses were to be constrained so that even a small number of retaliatory missiles surviving an attack could be certain of penetrating the attacker's territory and inflicting massive damage.[57] Moreover, the accompanying Strategic Arms Limitation Agreements (SALT I and II) were designed to limit the number of offensive weapons so that there would be too few to destroy military targets (in a first strike) but more than enough to wipe out most of the opponent's cities (in an act of retaliation).[58]

According to SDI proponents, the problem with the SALT and ABM treaties is that the Soviets never accepted MAD: rather, they used these agreements to gain a strategic edge. The Soviets supposedly believed that the treaties would retard U.S. ABM progress while allowing them to catch up in the race for defenses; is also allowed them to enhance their offensive arsenals through the exploitation of loopholes in the SALT agreement (e.g., they called a *second* new Soviet ICBM—prohibited by the treaty—a mere modification of an existing one).[59] Even within the ABM Treaty's restraints, the Soviets knew they could continue to deploy and improve their ABM system around Moscow, to build air defenses (not covered by the treaty), and to pursue passive defense by improving civil defense and hardening command bunkers and missile silos—actions that violate the requirements of MAD.

Until recently, the Soviets were less coy about their work on defensive strategy; at the time of the signing of the ABM Treaty, the minister of defense, Marshall Andrei Grechko, stated that the agreement "imposes no limitation on the performance of research and experimental work aimed at resolving the problem of defending the country against missile attack."[60] In 1976 Marshall G. V. Zimin, chief of PVO Strany (a separate military service involved in strategic defense), asserted:

> Now victory or defeat in war has become dependent on how much the state is in a position to reliably defend the important objects on its territory from the destruction of strikes from air or space.
>
> The enormous destructive power of nuclear warheads raises the necessity of destroying all targets without exception, which accomplish a breakthrough into the interior of the country from air or space.
>
> All of these conditions put before the air defense complex and responsible tasks, the resolution of which will be determined by the ability to repulse strikes not only of aerodynamic but also of ballistic means of attack.[61]

Since, according to advocates of SDI, it is clear that the Soviets reject MAD, new arms control agreements can no longer be premised on mutual vulnerability. New treaties must combine meaningful offensive arms reduction with a mutual transition to comprehensive strategic defense. The point is that a bilateral agreement to adopt strategic defense would only formalize the de facto policy of the Soviet Union. That is, arms control, if it is to be faithful to actuality and morality, must take a new direction.

From the fact that strategic defense is inconsistent with the requirements of the ABM Treaty, it does not follow that SDI is inconsistent with arms control. It depends on what one means by arms control. John Bosma, editor of *Military Space* and *SDI Monitor*, asserts that to understand how SDI fits in with meaningful arms control requires foundational thinking about what arms control is supposed to do. The technological advances that make strategic defense a real possibility also make possible, according to Bosma, a recovery of the original meaning of arms control:

> The German death camps of World War II shocked the Allies into codifying the immunity of noncombatants in the 1949 Geneva Conventions. In the same way, an SDI-abetted resurgence of "classical" arms control analysis may permit an equally historic repudiation of the underlying logic of the ABM Treaty—the hostaging of entire noncombatant populations on a scale far greater than the Nazis sought in World War II.[62]

The United States is a signatory to the 1977 Protocols that amended the 1949 Geneva Conventions. Bosma maintains that the Protocols legally require signatories to protect their own populations in wartime, perhaps the first codification of such a requirement.[63] He further asserts that the 1977 Protocols would unhesitatingly classify the MAD logic underlying the 1972 ABM Treaty—"the mutual hostaging of noncombatant populations and the intentionality suggested by the treaty's rigid constraints on defenses for protecting people and cities"—as a "war crimes" strategy.[64]

For Bosma, the ABM Treaty represents a barbarization of a once "ethically resonant" arms control tradition.[65] The ABM Treaty, according to Bosma, sanctions the terroristic strategy of population bombing; it violates the "classical" arms control tradition the just war tradition that seeks to place humane limits on the use of arms.[66] On this view, the mainstream arms control community has deviated so radically from the classical tradition that it has become ideologically hardened to population bombing and dismissive of any ideas about defense. Mainstream arms controllers adhere to MAD, Bosma insists, because they believe it is the only appropriate way to conceptualize the weapons that they regard as uniquely exempted from "traditional" views of the just use of force.[67]

Assuming that we face a conflict between two international obligations—one to the ABM Treaty and the other to the Geneva Conventions—we must decide which is to be given moral priority. How do we decide which obligation is overriding? Bosma suggests that the answer is clear: our commitment to respect the laws of war is historically prior to, and morally more compelling than, our commitment to adhere to a treaty signed in 1972. He wonders, however, whether these alternatives are genuine, given the conditional nature of the ABM agreement and the unconditional nature of the morality underlying the laws of war.

He points out that Gerald Smith, chief of the U.S. delegation, asserted during the ABM talks that the United States would withdraw from the treaty if the Soviets continued arms-racing; Smith's interpretation, according to Bosma, became the Senate's official understanding of the treaty.[68]

In fact, Bosma argues, the Soviets have proceeded apace with the construction of counterforce missiles like the SS-9, as well as surprise missiles like the SS-17 and SS-19, all of which the U.S. delegation thought it had outlawed.[69] Moreover, the Soviet construction in the interior USSR (Krasnoyarsk) of a large phased array radar suitable for tracking hundreds of separate ballistic missiles is now acknowledged by the Soviets to be a violation of the treaty.[70] Thus, on this view, Soviet violations of the agreement throw doubt on our obligation to adhere to it.

In sum, America's obligation to live up to the terms of the ABM Treaty is conditional in two senses. First, it is contingent upon Soviet compliance, which is questionable. Second, it is conditional in the sense that it can be overridden by a more substantive obligation: even if the Soviets were faithful to the ABM Treaty, the United States' legal and moral commitment to the laws of warfare and the obligation of the U.S. government to protect its population would constitute sufficient justification for repudiation of the treaty. The United States, on Bosma's view, has been adhering to "an arms control regime premised on the commission of war crimes—specifically, the deliberate slaughter of noncombatant hostages."[71] A territorial astrodome, on the other hand, brings with it the possibility of a nonretaliatory defense, which moves us away from the immoral policy of population hostaging and toward a moral policy of population protection.

John Coffey, staff assistant in the Office of Negotiations Policy in the Department of Defense, also supports the view that SDI is a response to the requirements of just war principles. Specifically, he believes the concept of strategic defense conforms to the principles of proportionality and discrimination.[72] The principle of proportionality, when applied to the decision to resort to war, requires that the harm a nation contemplates inflicting and suffering in war should not be disproportionate to the good it expects to achieve by resort to force. Assuming that a nation decides that a war is worth the costs in human suffering, the principle of discrimination requires that noncombatant life not be directly or intentionally attacked and that every effort be made, in attacks on combatants, to limit collateral damage to noncombatants.

Coffey points out that for the just war philosopher, the probability of success is a corollary of proportionality: the principle would rule out, for example, utterly futile, reckless resistance to aggression.[73] The principle of discrimination rules out direct attacks on population. It can be argued that the MAD doctrine embodied in the ABM Treaty violates both proportionality and discrimination: it sanctions a disproportionate response that has no hope of success, and it involves the deliberate (indiscriminate) destruction of noncombatants. (It should be pointed out that many advocates of SDI do not think that nuclear war–fighting doctrines are any better than MAD: such strategies can only *pretend* to respect the two just war principles.)

By contrast, a social defense strategy would conform to the principle of discrimination by targeting only enemy nuclear weapons, thereby imposing no harm on innocent noncombatants. This defense strategy, according to Coffey, also "respects proportionality, since it inflicts damage only on enemy military forces and necessarily lessens the suffering incurred by the victim of aggression."[74] Moreover, a defensive response is by definition proportional in another sense: it does not exceed the level of the aggression because the level of response precisely matches the level of the attack.

Strategic Defense and NATO

Some Europeans have objected to SDI on the grounds that it strengthens American tendencies toward unilateralism and isolationism—it will protect the United States while leaving Europe safe for conventional or nuclear war and vulnerable to a Soviet tactical or theater attack.[75] That is, strategic defense has been accused of undercutting extended deterrence and decoupling American and Western European security.

In response, advocates of a comprehensive defensive system argue that far from undercutting the United States' ability to protect Europe, a system effective in protecting the United States from a Soviet strategic attack would increase U.S. readiness to retaliate (with conventional forces) against the Soviet Union. The U.S. decision to come to the aid of Western Europe would not be inhibited by the fear of Soviet strategic retaliation against the American homeland.

Nuclear deterrence strains credibility as a strategy of extended deterrence because it calls for the president to risk—and perhaps commit—national suicide in defense of NATO allies. By contrast, a comprehensive system for the protection of U.S. territory would make the willingness of the United States to fulfill its alliance obligations more, not less, believable.[76]

There is, however, another objection to a defensive system from the perspective of European security: if the Soviet Union develops effective defenses in response to U.S. efforts, then NATO will no longer be able to use the nuclear card to counter the Soviet Union's conventional forces. A Soviet ballistic missile defense system would seriously undercut threats by European countries to escalate from conventional to nuclear war in the event that a Soviet conventional attack overruns NATO conventional armed forces. The possession by Moscow of territorial defenses could lead Soviet military planners to calculate that they can launch a successful conventional attack against Europe because NATO's nuclear weapons would be neutralized. Valued Soviet assets—targets such as military forces, command posts, and the leadership—would be less vulnerable to attack from Europe or the United States. A NATO objection to a social defense strategy, therefore, is that Western European security requires the preservation of nuclear deterrence and a capacity for effective escalation from conventional to nuclear retaliation. The ABM Treaty, it will be argued, must be preserved and every effort made to prevent the deployment of strategic defenses on both sides.

In response to this claim, supporters of a defensive strategy can point out that, as mentioned above, Moscow is already working on a system of missile defenses that the ABM agreement has not stopped and will not stop; in addition, the United States can share its defensive technology with Europeans and invite allies to contribute to research on a defensive technology that can be used to counter tactical and intermediate as well as strategic nuclear weapons. Moreover, it appears that Soviet nuclear parity in theater and battlefield nuclear weapons has nullified NATO's threat to escalate to a nuclear level: that is, the Soviet Union's capacity to match NATO at every level of escalation renders the threat of nuclear retaliation empty. Finally, in a battle with Soviet forces crossing into Western Europe, escalation to the nuclear level would mean the destruction of the territory being defended.

NATO needs a capability that will allow Europeans (those in the East as well as the West) to achieve security without reliance on the first use—or even the second use—of nuclear weapons. Even if one doubts the capacity of a missile defense system to protect European populations completely, its ability to protect military point targets—conventional forces, command centers, and radars—will introduce sufficient uncertainty into Soviet calculations regarding the likely success of their offensive operations to deter an attack.

Some of the technology used in constructing defenses against nuclear weapons can be used in improving the technology of conventional defense, allowing improvements against, for example, tanks and conventionally armed aircraft. Indeed, the greatest threat against NATO forces may be a preemptive missile strike by the Soviet Union using nuclear or even nonnuclear missile forces against NATO's airfields, special weapons storage sites, command centers, and air defense systems, as well as ports and other infrastructures for NATO reinforcements. Manfred Wörner, writing as minister of defense of the Federal Republic of Germany, concludes that the only politically and strategically acceptable alternative for NATO is a direct defense against Soviet missiles:

> A defense against attacking missiles is consistent with—indeed, reinforcing of—the defensive cast of the NATO Alliance. Such a defense could only contribute to the stability of the military relationship between opposing blocs in Europe.
>
> Acquisition of such a defense capability has to be a common alliance initiative. It should be seen in the context of a strengthening of NATO's conventional defenses; thus it represents a special challenge to the European members of the Alliance. Yet it cannot be a purely European decision or project. The United States must be involved: not only does it bear a substantial share of the integrated defenses of Western Europe, but the large U.S. force presence on the continent also yields a direct interest in safeguarding those forces from the enhanced conventional threat generated by Soviet conventional missile capabilities.[77]

Wörner asserts that the necessary technologies for upgrading existing air defenses and defense capabilities against cruise missiles, including aircraft-delivered stand-off weapons, as well as medium-range and short-range ballistic missiles, "are either available or within reach."[78] Several examples point the way. The United States is developing for the Patriot air defense system a limited self-defense capability against tactical ballistic missiles. The arming of available and planned airborne platforms with anti-tactical missiles (ATM)—or even anti-tactical ballistic missiles (ATBM)—could, according to Wörner, come onto the technological agenda as well.[79]

A social defense policy would fit in well with a NATO strategy that is evolving away from deterrence based on a threat of nuclear retaliation to a concept of nonoffensive defense and deterrence by denial. It also fits in well with the declared Soviet strategy of defensive defense.

The United States could continue to symbolize its commitment to Europe through the presence of several thousand U.S. troops. In sum, a defensive strategy is consistent with the coupling of U.S. and European security—with extended deterrence—so long as the technology is shared with European NATO members and the U.S. maintains a force presence in Europe.

The Case for a Social Defense Policy

The points in favor of adopting a policy of national social defense can be summarized as follows.

1. This policy would provide real national defense. That is, it reinstates the traditional military principle that arms are for the purpose of protecting the homeland: that defense means the security of persons and property from harm.

2. Social defense offers a rational response to the question of what we should do if nuclear weapons are launched against us. Unlike MAD and nuclear war–fighting doctrines, it does not require either a suicidal response or an unwinnable nuclear exchange. Its answer is a response that reduces rather than increases nuclear destruction.

3. It is a nonprovocative strategy. In its purely defensive form, the strategy in no way threatens Soviet security, and hence is not destabilizing. It is not aggressive or provocative, but strictly reactive and protective.

4. This strategy satisfies the moral objective of *democratic* social defense: equal protection of all citizens' lives and property. In this sense, it is in the tradition of policies that guard equal rights. If the government has an obligation to protect its citizens from danger, whether it

comes from within or from outside the society, then it must be able to incapacitate both internal and external agents of harm.

5. It is a humane policy in its exclusive focus on the destruction of weapons instead of persons. It does not require the mass killing of noncombatants, or, for that matter, even combatants. It protects human lives, Soviet as well as American. It fits in well with the Geneva Conventions that forbid attacks on civilians and require nations to protect their populations.

6. In neutralizing the Soviet Union's offensive nuclear weapons, strategic defense will function as a deterrent. The Soviets will not launch an attack if they believe it cannot achieve their objectives. The defensive apparatus will create sufficient uncertainty in the minds of Soviet military planners about the prospects for achieving their objectives to deter a Soviet nuclear attack. Deterrence by denial would replace deterrence by threat. (All forms of nuclear deterrence, no matter what their proponents assert, involve deterrence by threat.)

7. The new policy would promote a defensive arms race. SDI could be the beginning of a new kind of competition—one oriented toward the protection of one's society rather than the destruction of the other's society. This would be a less dangerous kind of arms race.

8. Active defense enables a nation to counter an accidental or third-party launching of nuclear weapons. It could easily handle a few weapons launched by mistake (by the USSR or another nuclear power), thus preventing an accidental war.

9. A defensive strategy fits in best with operational Soviet doctrine. Defense of the homeland has always been central to Soviet military strategy. The Soviet Union now describes its policy as defensive defense. A joint move toward social defense policy offers a way to realize this objective without risking the destruction of either society. The objective of social defense fits Soviet national self-interest as well as it fits ours. Moreover, it is a fact that the Soviet Union has been working on strategic defense for a long time.

10. The construction of comprehensive defensive systems by the Soviet Union and the United States would make significant arms reduction, and even nuclear disarmament, a real possibility. To the extent that defenses can reduce the effectiveness and thus the value of ballistic missiles, they can also increase the incentive for negotiated reductions. Moreover, neither side would have to worry about the other cheating or about elaborate systems of verification because the launching of any hidden weapons could be neutralized by the active defenses. The United States could accept the Soviet Union's call for the abolition of nuclear weapons by the year 2000. Active defense would constitute our insurance policy.

11. The new policy does not make Western security depend on the rationality of the Soviet leaders; rather, our security would be based on the inability of the Soviet Union to inflict mortal damage on us.

12. This strategy does not require us to make immoral threats of mass retaliation or indiscriminate attacks—or, for that matter, to make any threats at all. Social defense abandons security through intimidation altogether.

13. If the Soviet Union should try to counter our defensive measures with offensive ones—instead of joining in the defense race—the United States would bankrupt their system because our economy is capable of outspending theirs. Indeed, such an economic contest would seriously injure the Soviet system, perhaps doing it irreparable harm.

14. To reject the promise of SDI is to accept an endless offensive arms race, the consequence of which will probably be the most devastating war the world has ever experienced. Without a plan for strategic defense, it is likely that arms control will fail because of lack of trust between the superpowers and the lack of acceptable methods of verification.

15. Strategic defense is the only way to prevent the climatic catastrophe that would result from even a small nuclear exchange (500 to 2,000 detonations). Whether or not one accepts the nuclear winter hypothesis, it is agreed that the detonation of even a small percentage of the 50,000-plus nuclear warheads in the world would cause serious damage to all forms of life affected by these weapons. Active defenses could disable many of these weapons before they detonate.

The exotic, expensive, and futuristic nature of strategic defense may lead policymakers to seek a more immediate and conventional solution to U.S. defense needs. That is precisely what supporters of a policy of retribution could claim for their proposal, which I will examine in the next chapter.

CHAPTER SIX

Retribution Policy:
Security Through
Measured Retaliation

Strategic defense is only an idea: it is no more than a research program that may or may not prove feasible. Its opponents view it as a dangerous and costly illusion. Some critics of strategic defense may, however, agree with its initial premise: namely, that if one is not satisfied with a doctrine whose failure means global disaster, then some workable alternative to nuclear deterrence is needed. No matter what form it takes, nuclear deterrence, it can be argued, is a policy that does not allow for failure. The previous success of the policy—the fact that nuclear threats in various forms have worked for decades—can be rendered meaningless by a single event: the triggering of a nuclear exchange, whether by deliberate decision or mechanical failure. With weapons on both sides ready to be launched at a moment's notice, the end of the world is not far to seek. Belief in nuclear deterrence appears to require a wager on eternal success—on the infallibility of this system for the indefinite future. This would seem to be an irrational bet, given the fallibility of human beings and warning systems.

Supporters of deterrence-plus, of course, hold out the possibility of keeping the violence contained. But a limited nuclear war, even if possible, would still be a disaster beyond imagination. In fact, it might be difficult to distinguish, in terms of consequences, from an all-out nuclear exchange. If both sides fire nuclear weapons at each other, then—regardless of declaratory policy—mutual assured destruction is the probable consequence.

No matter how significantly Soviet–American relations improve, so long as each nation has thousands of nuclear weapons aimed at the other, there is no foolproof way to prevent inadvertent nuclear war and the indiscriminate death it would bring. Reliance on a strategy of nuclear deterrence involves, even in an era of good relations, the ever-present possibility of global catastrophe.

There is a third policy option—one standing between the present reality of mutual assured destruction and the futuristic vision of mutual assured survival. It is a strategy that could further the objectives of both deterrence and defense while achieving a moral end that neither *nuclear* deterrence nor *strategic* defense can provide—to wit, justice. In response to a Soviet nuclear attack, nuclear deterrence, in its preoccupation with terroristic intimidation, authorizes (de facto, if not officially) indiscriminate punishment of Soviet society, while strategic defense, in concentrating on the destruction of attacking weapons, provides no idea of how, if at all, the aggressor will be punished.

Although (as we saw in Chapter Six) defenders of the peace shield concept argue that a social defense strategy would restore just war principles, in fact such a strategy lacks a crucial just war element: it provides no concept of just retaliation. In itself social defense is a policy of security through population protection that makes no provision for punishment of a nuclear aggressor.

What is missing in a purely defensive strategy is a concept of punishment. What is not practically possible in any nuclear deterrence strategy is proportional punishment. These deficiencies can be remedied by a strategy of retribution. The concept of retribution, at least as I will develop it, has nothing to do with revenge: rather, it is a sophisticated moral notion that fits in well with the just war tradition.

The Just War Tradition

If one takes seriously the just war tradition, neither nuclear deterrence nor strategic defense appears satisfactory. This tradition involves two components: the concept of *jus ad bellum* (justice of war), and the concept of *jus in bello* (justice in war).

Jus ad bellum refers to the idea that a nation or subnational group must have a morally defensible reason—or just cause—for using military force against another nation or subnational group. If the cause is not just, then the use of violence is not morally defensible. For example, using force for the purpose of appropriating the resources of another sovereign state is a violation of the justice of war requirement. On the other hand, using armed force to repel aggression constitutes a just use of violence.

When translated into international law, *jus ad bellum* takes the form of a prohibition against aggression. For instance, the International Tribunal at Nuremberg formulated a category of war crime it called "crimes against peace," by which it meant planning, initiating, and/or waging a war of aggression or a war in violation of international treaties, or conspiring to do so.[1] The Charter of the United Nations enjoins all nations to "refrain in their international relations from the threat or use of force against the territorial integrity or political independence of any state."[2] The Charter allows for the legitimate use of force in self-defense if an armed attack occurs.[3]

The second component of just war theory, *jus in bello*, affirms the notion of moral limits within war. According to this concept, certain forms of violence are not permissible even in the course of waging a legitimate war, such as deliberately targeting civilians or killing prisoners of war. *Jus in bello* has to do with the way the war is fought: it provides criteria for assessing methods of fighting and targets to be destroyed. In terms of international law, the *jus in bello* requirement is reflected in the so-called laws of war, which constitute an attempt to codify rules of humane warfare.

Numerous international conferences have established the conventions of war. The Declaration of St. Petersburg in 1868 was the product of one of the first such conferences: the signatories agreed that "the right to adopt means of injuring the enemy is not unlimited" and that "the only legitimate object which states should endeavor to accomplish during war is to weaken the military forces of the enemy."[4] Thus, it was agreed that weapons that cause unnecessary suffering should be prohibited. Other international conferences took place in the Hague and Geneva. At the 1907 Hague Convention the participants agreed to prohibit "the attack or bombardment, by whatever means, of towns, villages (and even individual) dwellings or buildings which are undefended."[5] This conference also formulated the Mertens clause, which held that the rules of "humane warfare" would apply to other technology not then developed.[6] Various additions or protocols have been added to war conventions to update them. For example, the United States ratified the 1977 Protocols to the 1949 Geneva Conventions, Article 85 of which states:

> The following shall be regarded as grave breaches of this Protocol: (a) making the civilian population or individual civilians the object of an attack; (b) launching an indiscriminate attack affecting the civilian population or civilian objects in the knowledge that such an attack will cause excessive loss of life, injury, or damage to civilian objects.[7]

In addition, as pointed out in Chapter Two, the U.S. Department of Defense Instruction 5500.15, dated 16 October 1974,[8] requires that all Defense Department actions concerning acquisition and procurement of weapons and their planned use be consistent with all U.S. international obligations, including obedience to the laws of war.

It should be emphasized that the two components of just war theory—justice of war and justice in war—are logically independent. That is, it is logically possible for a war fought for an unjust or illegal cause to be fought justly and according to the laws of war, and for a war fought for a just or legal cause to be fought unjustly and in violation of the laws of war. For example, although the fight against Nazism was obviously a cause that satisfied the requirement of *jus ad bellum,* the allies' indiscriminate fire-bombing of Dresden, which resulted in the death of over a hundred thousand civilians, was a violation of *jus in bello* conventions prohibiting direct attacks on civilians. On the other hand, the Nazi general Erwin Rommel, while fighting for an unjust cause in violation of *jus ad bellum,* nonetheless, in refusing to obey Hitler's orders commanding him to kill prisoners of war, conformed to *jus in bello:* it could be said that he fought justly for an unjust cause.

But can the concept of justice be meaningfully applied either to war's ends or its means? Both pacifists and realists answer no. Although they have fundamentally different starting points—with the realists staking their ground on national interest and the pacifists on moral principle—they are unified in their rejection of the just war doctrine. For neither school of thought does it make sense to apply morality either to the causes for which wars are fought or to the ways in which combat is conducted.

The realists argue that nations do not go to war to achieve just objectives but to further or protect national self-interest. For the pacifists, no cause can morally justify using violence against another society. Both realists and pacifists deny that human beings will respect rules of humane warfare during an armed conflict. Both see war as inherently unlimited. Once a war begins, they will ask rhetorically, isn't the overriding aim to win, with everything being considered (by the participants) fair in the pursuit of that end? Is not war by definition *hell*—a domain of excess within which the law (whether moral or juridical) is silent and impotent? Is it not a contradiction in terms to talk about "humane warfare" or "killing according to the rules"? On the realist/pacifist view, war is a realm of necessity and duress in which moral responsibility and legal limits can play no meaningful role.

Since a retributive policy asserts the possibility of achieving justice within war, it is necessary at the outset, in order to construct a reasonable case for retributivism, to make the concept of limits plausible. Despite its *prima facie* absurdity, a persuasive case can be made for applying the concept of justice to war. In the arguments presented below, there will be a number of references to "ordinary soldiers." It may appear that these traditional combatants of conventional war have no relevance to nuclear policy—that is, to any meaningful response to the Soviet nuclear threat. It will, however, become clear in the course of this chapter that a retributive response to the Soviet Union requires, among other things, that NATO replace its current policy of nuclear first use with a nonnuclear policy that gives ordinary soldiers a greater role in the preservation of the security of Western Europe. Indeed, it can be argued here (as it was in the chapter on social defense) that a move toward the denuclearization of NATO forces fits in well with current Soviet thinking about defense. As will be seen, the point is that fidelity to the laws of war requires the replacement of nuclear forces with more discriminating nonnuclear weapons.

The Rationale of Laws of War

The following reasons can be given in defense of applying a concept of limits, or rules, to war.

1. Laws of war constitute a moral statement. The first reason is a moral one: members of the military who participate in war do not by that fact cease to be moral beings. War conventions assert that despite their status as "combatants," soldiers retain specific rights and have definite responsibilities. For example, there is no justification for inflicting excess suffering on combatants (by, for instance, using weapons that cause prolonged agony). And soldiers who have surrendered and put down their weapons are no longer legitimate targets: they have a right to proper respect and care. On the other hand, soldiers have responsibilities as well as rights, not only to respect the rights of enemy soldiers, but also to avoid deliberately killing noncombatants. In sum, war conventions serve the function of making a moral statement that educates national leaders, military commanders, and ordinary soldiers about the rights and obligations of combatants.

2. Formal laws legitimate punishment. The international condemnation of aggression (as a crime against peace that violates *jus ad bellum*) and the international codification of rules of war (the specification of what is to count as *jus ad bellum* and *jus in bello* war crimes) legitimates, under a kind of global social contract, two acts: resort to armed force to repel and punish an aggressor during the course of a war

and, at the end of a war, the process of trying and sentencing those guilty of atrocities.

It is fair to punish individuals *only* if they have engaged in explicitly prohibited actions. *Nullum crimin sine lege, nulla poena sine lege* is a fundamental principle of just punishment: "no crime without a law, no punishment without a law." Under the principle of legality, as it is called, it is the establishment of agreed-upon war conventions that enables the international community to distinguish legitimate from illegitimate uses of armed force, and that justifies, after a war, the prosecution of leaders and combatants for crimes against peace or for war crimes committed during a conflict. If there were no agreed-upon international laws of war, or specification of what constitutes a war crime, then there could be no legitimate prosecution of individuals who plan, or who engage in, excesses.

3. Laws of war may have deterrence value. If combatants know that certain actions are officially prohibited and that they *may* be punished (whether by the enemy, a third party, or their own nation) for engaging in the prohibited behavior, they may be less likely to commit atrocities. If the existence of such laws of war and fear of their enforcement have even a minimal humanizing effect on the way commanders and ordinary soldiers treat enemy combatants and civilians, then there will be fewer atrocities than would otherwise occur. If proclaimed rules of humane warfare have even minimal deterrent value, the result will be less suffering and less death in time of war. Respect for human life and a concern to minimize the agony of war obligate us to do whatever we can to discourage excessive violence within war. This is why some limits are better than no limits.

The very existence of internationally agreed-upon conventions places a burden on each nation to explain apparent excesses, to defend itself against charges of criminal behavior when there is evidence it is violating the laws of armed conflict. Although some nations may openly defy the conventions (as Iraq did in its use of chemical weapons during the war with Iran), other nations will be inhibited by the conventions and by concern about world opinion. For example, although the Soviet Union apparently violated war conventions in Afghanistan (by, for instance, rigging toys to explosives and thus maiming and killing children as a way of destroying enemy morale), Soviet leaders felt compelled to deny this and perhaps subsequently to moderate the use of such methods. The pressure on belligerents to deny or cover up their crimes may create restraints on the employment of inhumane practices—restraints that would not exist if such behavior were not morally condemned and proscribed by international law.

4. The absence of agreed-upon limits may encourage excesses. Failure to codify just war principles could actually provide an incentive to combatants to commit unjust acts. That is, the absence of war conventions may encourage excesses in war. If the international community were to concede the pessimistic thesis of pacifists and realists—that limits are not possible—and make no attempt to impose restraints on wartime violence, then the implicit message to national leaders, commanders, and ordinary combatants might be this: in time of war everything is permissible; no attempt will be made to punish you, no matter what you do. Moral and legal silence, the absence of any asserted limits or laws of war, might, in effect, increase violence by giving combatants a free hand. If national leaders and combatants operate in a world in which nothing is officially prohibited and in which there is no possibility of punishment for their acts against the enemy population, then they may feel *encouraged* to indulge in violent excesses.

5. Excessive violence is a sign of undisciplined soldiers. Soldiers who commit excesses are—in a technical sense—poor soldiers. To commit excesses in time of war is to exhibit a lack of military discipline. As Michael Walzer states: "It is almost certainly true that [soldiers] fight best when they are in most control of themselves and committed to the restraints of their trade. Extra killing is less a sign of toughness than hysteria."[9] To allow soldiers to indulge in atrocities is to permit a corrosive disorder to slip into their behavior, which, even in strictly military terms, may be counterproductive to the ethos of efficient fighting. By sanctioning uncontrolled behavior, a nation may ultimately weaken the self-mastery essential to the "good soldier." Thus, it is in the interest of the military in all societies to acknowledge—and condition their soldiers to obey—laws of war.

6. Wanton violence is inefficient. Destruction of nonmilitary targets is wasteful. If the central aim of war is to defeat the agents of aggression as quickly and as effectively as possible, then we should aim exclusively at military targets. In the name of economy of forces, we should not spend time and resources destroying civilian objects when the same resources could be used more efficiently in purely counterforce attacks.[10]

7. The state needs to avoid alienating potential friends and allies. Excessive destruction—especially of civilians and civilian property—may alienate people who might otherwise be friendly to our side. If, for example, dissident minorities within the enemy territory, or even a majority of the enemy population, support our efforts to win the war, then engaging in indiscriminate destruction may in fact cause these potential allies to turn against us and begin to support those in power whom they once opposed. In addition, indiscriminate attacks may cause

third parties, such as neutral nations, to condemn us and ally themselves with our enemy.

8. Observance of the laws of war may be reciprocated. Our conformity to limits such as avoidance of attacks on the enemy's population centers may lead to reciprocal action. It may be in the self-interest of all belligerents to obey laws of war in order to limit the damage to their societies and therefore recover more quickly after the war. The general avoidance of the use of poison gas in World War II can be seen as an example of reciprocal adherence to a prohibition.

In retrospect, all nations that engaged in strategic bombing during World War II might admit—if completely honest—that these terroristic attacks on population centers were often pointless and inconclusive.

9. The possibility of shortening the war and promoting the requirements of an enduring peace is the final consideration. It is wise to use only force sufficient to defeat and punish the military forces of the other side. A nation should not commit acts that will so outrage enemy combatants and the adversary's civilian population as to motivate them to fight to the last breath. Moreover, if the peace to come is to be a lasting one, a nation should, for prudential reasons, avoid crimes of war because they might create such bitterness that the enemy, even if defeated for the time being, may seek to rebuild its forces with the aim of eventually attacking and punishing the victor. In sum, excessive violence may create a powerful desire for revenge and make an enduring peace less likely. To do anything and everything to win, even if it leads to success, may ultimately be short-sighted and counterproductive.

Retribution as a Just War Objective

Defenders of the concept of just war can argue that what is missing in the policies of both nuclear deterrence and strategic defense is a notion of retribution, a concept that fits in well with *jus ad bellum* and the international laws prohibiting aggression, while also fitting in well with the kind of measured retaliation called for by *jus in bello* and the laws of war. A commitment to retribution would require the subordination of deterrence and defense to the requirements of justice. Retribution, if applied in its most sophisticated form to nuclear defense policy, would be continuous with the just war tradition.

In what follows I will (1) explain the constitutive principles of retribution; (2) translate these constitutive principles into military principles; (3) explain the implications of retribution for weapons development; and (4) anticipate and answer some major objections to a retributive strategy.

In order to apply the retributivist model to defense policy, it is first necessary to make explicit the constitutive or fundamental principles underlying the doctrine of *legal* (or domestic) retributivism. A criminal justice system that has retribution as its primary objective will require a system of punishment to satisfy two principles: culpability and proportionality.[11]

The principle of culpability holds that we ought to punish those who are guilty of criminal acts. The legally guilty are individuals who have voluntarily engaged in criminal acts (*actus reus*) with criminal intent, criminal negligence, or criminal recklessness (*mens rea*). This principle asserts two things. First, in opposition to any exculpatory correction doctrine, such as rehabilitation, that seeks to replace penalties with compassion, the principle of culpability holds that *criminals ought to be punished:* justice, according to retributivism, requires that offenders be made to suffer for their crimes. Second, against any correction doctrine, such as utilitarian deterrence, that could, in principle, authorize punishment of the innocent, if that was likely to produce more good than evil, retributivism asserts that only those who are guilty of a crime should be punished.

The principle of proportionality requires that punishment of offenders be meted out according to the gravity of the offense and the level of responsibility. According to retributivism, two elements should determine the kind and degree of punishment: the kind of crime and the degree of liability. The more serious the nature of the crime, the more severe should be the form of punishment. This rules out the infliction of penalties that are, in relation to the offense, either too lenient or too harsh. After deciding the appropriate type of punishment (e.g., imprisonment) for a particular crime (e.g., armed robbery), we must determine the degree of punishment (i.e., how many years). To decide the degree of punishment, we must weight such factors as the offender's original mental state and the degree of voluntariness of the offender's behavior at the time of the crime. The greater the reflectiveness preceding the crime and the greater the freedom of action, the closer the punishment should approach the maximum allowed for the particular crime. As criminal intent and the ability to conform conduct to the law diminish, so should punishment.

Culpability and Military Policy

The use of military violence against aggressors is the international equivalent of domestic punishment. Translated into military terms, the principle of culpability requires that armed force be used only to punish aggression and that, so far as possible, retaliation be limited to combatants. The principle of culpability, while requiring retaliation against the aggressing nation, forbids intentional, direct attacks on the innocent, and its demands that, in attacking the guilty, every effort be made to limit collateral harm to the innocent. In other words, while demanding that the guilty nation be punished, retributivists would also seek to minimize the chances that the innocent will be harmed in the process. This means that, ideally, in carrying out acts of retaliation, the targets chosen and the weapons used should enable us to punish the guilty without harming the innocent.

But who are the guilty and the innocent in a nation guilty of aggression? The standard answer is that the guilty are combatants and the innocent are noncombatants. The translation of the (legal) guilt/innocence distinction into the combatant/noncombatant distinction may, however, be problematic. George Mavrodes has argued that the guilty are as likely to be noncombatants (e.g., civilian supporters of a war of aggression), and the innocent are as likely to be soldiers (e.g., immature draftees coerced into fighting).[12] This raises doubts about the justice of making combatants targets of punitive retaliation. One can reasonably question whether combatants satisfy the requirements of legal culpability—specifically, the capacity for voluntary criminal behavior (*actus reus*) and criminal intent (*mens rea*). The fundamental question is, can it meaningfully be said about combatants that they have, with a guilty mind, voluntarily committed criminal acts?

Any defense of the claim that combatants are culpable individuals who may be justly targeted for punitive retaliation will have to make use of a revised concept of criminal liability. Criminal intent and voluntariness will have to be automatically ascribed to certain forms of military behavior. Participation in this prohibited behavior will have to be construed as decisive evidence of criminality. More specifically, the participation of soldiers in internationally proscribed forms of behavior must by itself constitute a justification for inflicting punishment (i.e., retaliatory military force) on them.

The standard legal concept of criminal culpability requires, of course, the establishment of *mens rea* and *actus reus* prior to punishment. According to the revised concept of culpability that would have to operate under conditions of war, a prohibited *act* by itself must be taken as presumptive evidence of culpability. The weakened notion of culpability introduced here circumvents the requirement that punishment follow the establishment of guilty mind and voluntary behavior: instead, it imputes *mens rea* and voluntariness to, and authorizes punitive action against, persons engaged in internationally proscribed actions.

In a sense, this revised concept of culpability is similar to the notion of strict liability, which makes proof of criminal *conduct* a sufficient basis for punishment. The revised concept substantially differs from strict liability, however, in that, unlike the latter, it is concerned to retain the notions of *mens rea* and voluntariness. This is because retributive justice requires that punishment be applied only to those who voluntarily, and with criminal intent, engage in criminal behavior.

In fine, the idea is to construe participation in a certain type of action as sufficient to "convict" individuals of criminality, even in cases where there is evidence of duress—for example, where soldiers are conscripted and acting under orders. Retributivists need not view conscription or acting under orders as exculpatory conditions in the sense of altogether removing liability and invalidating punitive retaliation. At best, such conditions *mitigate* culpability and justify a reduction in the severity of punishment.

The Nature of Combatant Culpability

But what behavior, in time of war, would distinguish the culpable from the innocent? That is, what behavior can be legitimately punished by retaliatory actions? One answer is this: culpable behavior in time of war is to be understood in terms of a negation of the original meaning of innocent—that is, the guilty are the *nocent* (harmful). Whether individuals in the enemy nation deserve to be attacked would depend on, in Paul Ramsey's words, their degree of "actual participation in hostile force."[13] The culpable in war, therefore, are individuals engaged in unprovoked, harmful activities against another nation. More specifically, the culpable are combatants engaged in aggression against a sovereign state. David Fisher, of the British Ministry of Defense, justifies the use of retaliatory armed force in precisely these terms:

> If—as just war theory claims—war can be justified to stop harm being done . . . then the use of proportionate force against those doing the harm must also be conceded: for how else can the harm be stopped? Those engaged in doing or threatening the harm will, of course, usually be the combatants and those not so engaged, the non-combatants. . . . The moral distinction between non-combatants and combatants rests simply on the question of who is doing *nocent*—regardless of their personal moral guilt or innocence.[14]

From a retributivist perspective, however, Fisher's assertion that force is justified if it serves the purpose of stopping harm—regardless of the guilt or innocence of the harmers—violates the principle of culpability. To repeat: the use of force in war is the international equivalent of domestic punishment. From a retributivist perspective, the individuals we retaliate against should be subject to attack not simply because they threaten us with immediate harm, but because they are participants in a crime—specifically, the international crime of aggression. In retaliating against agents of aggression, we are not only stopping their harmful activity: in addition, we are punishing the harmers. Thus, the retributive justification for using force against combatants must fit within a legal framework that condemns aggression as a crime against peace and calls for punishment of the aggressors.

Obviously, in the heat of war, there is no time to establish an international tribunal to determine which members of the aggressing society may be legitimately attacked. This is where the analogy with domestic retribution breaks down and why direct participation in the prohibited behavior itself (i.e., aggression) must be taken as evidence of criminality. The nation that is a victim of aggression does not have the luxury of waiting—in this supreme emergency—for a global authority to establish guilt, contain the aggression, and swiftly punish the aggressors.

Despite the anarchic nature of relations among nations, retributivism still requires that a nation that uses force against another nation be able to point to the culpability not only of the nation it attacks, but also of the specific groups it targets within that nation. In the absence of world government, the nation that acts to "correct" aggression must perform the tasks of jury and judge, deciding who in the enemy nation is culpable and determining the appropriate punishment. This places an enormous burden on the nation that retaliates: it must use enough force to stop aggression while at the same time restricting its punitive reprisals to the culpable.

It might seem that this demand for evidence of culpability needlessly complicates things. After all, it may appear that all we need to say to justify retaliation against an aggressor is that it is an act of national self-defense designed to terminate harmful action. Given their commitment to the principle of culpability, however, retributivists cannot limit retaliatory action to the objective of stopping harmful attacks.

There are several reasons why—from the retributivist point of view—a purely defensive justification of retaliation is inadequate. First, it is not enough to *repel* aggression: to satisfy the requirements of retributive justice, aggression must also be *punished*. That is, retributive justice requires that the guilty suffer a penalty: the culpability principle demands that offenders be made to pay for their crimes.

Second, the principle of national self-defense, by itself, does not rule out the targeting of civilians, and it has in practice often justified indiscriminate attacks: noncombatants in the enemy nation have been—in the name of national defense—viewed as fair game for retaliation. In fact, it has been argued that to defend the nation and to stop aggression we need to attack enemy population centers and destroy the morale of the people, so that they will put pressure on their government to terminate the aggression.[15] Therefore, if our only concern is national self-defense, and we believe that a "hostage" strategy will effectively and quickly terminate aggression against our country, it is possible to make a case for the terror bombing of enemy cities. Contemporary U.S. nuclear war–fighting plans call for holding back on attacks of Soviet cities for this very reason—namely, to use them as hostage targets for the purpose of coercing the Soviets into terminating their nuclear attacks against the United States or its allies.[16]

In order to rule out attacks on civilians, it is necessary to explain why, regardless of the efficacy of such attacks for self-defense, certain groups are not legitimate targets. We need, therefore, a deontological principle that transcends national self-defense—a rule of discriminate retaliation. More precisely, we need a principle that asserts that only those directly involved in illegal harmful action against the United States or its allies can justly be attacked, a principle that asserts that we should target for punitive retaliation only those who are directly participating in the international crime of aggression. That is exactly what the military version of the principle of culpability asserts.

On this view, participation in aggression must, of course, be considered sufficiently intentional and voluntary to deserve punishment. Retributivists who call for punitive retaliation against enemy combatants must hold, therefore, that even if acting under duress, enemy combatants, in general, are not absolutely compelled to participate in the crime of aggression. It must be assumed that these combatants have, in a significant sense, consented to participation in the aggression that they carry out. Conscription and obedience to orders do not exonerate the agents of aggression, because—in the face of commands to engage in harmful actions against the innocent—they remain free human beings with a *capacity* to desert, to feign illness, or to refuse to obey orders. Elaine Scarry in *The Body in Pain* describes the role of consent in the behavior of the conscript soldier:

> He chooses to go, rather than be jailed or go into hiding. Though a constrained act, some level of consent has occurred. He now goes to his job to announce his future departure, gets his papers in order, says goodbye to his friends. . . . With each of these small acts, his level of consent and participation is growing. He walks to

the ship, he picks up his gun, he puts on his uniform, not once, but each morning, day after day, he reputs it on, renewing each time his act of consent. He could have, on the first day, refused to go; or he could now on the three hundredth day, feign injury or appendicitis and so, for a time, exempt himself from further combat; he may stay on the front and fire at the enemy, or stay on the front and fire straight up into the air. . . . Government leaders, military commanders, and comrades will work to sustain his "consent." . . . The war cannot be executed without his consent.[17]

In addition, retributivists can argue that the obligation to respect international law overrides the national duty to obey commands or to continue serving in a conscript army. Fear of demotion, reprimand, or imprisonment is no excuse for the willingness to participate in violating the rights of the innocent (in the victim nation), which aggression necessarily involves. Some retributivists, finding support in the Anglo-American legal tradition (Blackstone), might refuse to recognize *any* compulsion, even the threat of death (e.g., the threat of execution by a superior officer), as sufficient to excuse attacks on innocent and unoffending persons.

Consider, for example, what may now appear to be a remote possibility (but which remains the *raison d'être* for NATO): a Soviet-directed invasion of Western Europe. As far as ordinary Soviet soldiers are concerned, a retributivist could assert this: since obedience to orders is no excuse for participation in aggression (for reasons given above), the use of punitive violence against these agents of a crime against peace is justified. Acting under orders cannot justify their criminal attack on the innocent: all victims of aggression within Western Europe (including members of the armed forces) must be considered innocent from the standpoint of international law. Participation of Soviet soldiers in aggression against Western Europe would therefore constitute their punishable offense. In the course of an invasion of Western Europe, we can reasonably presume, Soviet combatants would know that they were crossing international borders and entering Western territory in violation of international law. That they have been told they are participating in the liberation of the West cannot exonerate them from the charge that they possess the intent to participate in a crime against peace.

Of course, there is a possibility that those we retaliate against were deceived by their government into believing that they were responding to *our* aggression, in which case our presumption of their intent to violate international law would be mistaken. Just as a jury can erroneously bring in a verdict of guilty, so a nation responding to aggression can mistakenly impute guilt to the innocent. If this should be discovered later, retributivists can always fall back on the more modest justification of self-defense. Having retribution as a primary objective does not rule out also retaining the objective of self-defense and invoking it to justify the use of force.

Ideally, for retributivism, retaliatory military force should fulfill the principle of culpability, but in cases where the presumption of culpability proves unfounded, the use of force can still be justified as an act of national self-defense as long as it was directed against agents of aggression. The point is that from a retributivist perspective, we must try, whenever possible, to go beyond the limited objective of self-defense, just as we must try to transcend the limited objective of deterrence.

The Nature of Noncombatant Innocence

One might question the assumption—so far undefended—that persons in the enemy nation who are not directly involved in aggression should be classified as noncombatants and should not be made deliberate targets. The fundamental justification for excluding civilians from acts of punitive retaliation is that they are not directly involved in harmful actions. Making civilian status an exculpatory condition might be criticized on the grounds that in a modern war almost every member of society is involved, in some fashion, in contributing to the war. Therefore, it could be argued, even civilians should be treated as contributing to harm.

Such logic ignores the substantial differences between the actions of those participating directly in aggression and those who are not. Clearly, no one could reasonably consider as combatants entire classes of individuals such as—to quote the U.S. Catholic bishops—"school children, hospital patients, the elderly, the ill, the average industrial worker producing goods not directly related to military purposes, farmers and many others."[18]

Moreover, in focusing on the Soviet threat, we are dealing with a society in which, despite some incipient democratization under *glasnost*, there is not yet popular control over defense policy. Therefore, in the event of a Soviet attack, Soviet citizens who are engaged in ordinary (non-military-related) tasks should neither be considered direct participants in an act of Soviet aggression nor viewed as having played a direct or indirect role in deciding on such aggression. Since in an act of aggression Soviet civilians will not be directly involved in harmful actions against us—not be directly involved in the international crime of aggression—they ought not to be subjected to punitive retaliation.

A Paradox of Retributive Targeting

It might appear that in the event of aggression, the least controversial and most appropriate targets, from a retributive perspective, would be the political leadership—the individuals who make the decision to attack. The next most logical targets would seem to be those in military command who orchestrate the attack. Given the principle of culpability, it is only logical that those most responsible for aggression should be made to pay. That is, just retaliation, from a retributive perspective, would seem to imply an endorsement of what is called *decapitation* targeting: attacks on the political leadership and those in military command positions. In his important book *Can Modern War Be Just?* James Turner Johnson sums up this reasoning:

> In essence, decapitation strategy in contemporary form is a prolongation of the realization that without leadership a military force is powerless, and without a particular political leadership in some instances the war would not be waged at all. Such strategy dictates that officers are to be preferred as targets over enlisted men on the battlefields, sergeants preferred targets over privates. It implies putting command posts and headquarters out of action and, frequently in past wars, capturing the capital city of an enemy nation and with it as much of the government machinery as possible. The principle involved is the same one established classically in international law that makes rulers liable for wars waged at their behest.[19]

If we could effectively prevent an attack from escalating by killing the Soviet leadership (which, in the case of aggression, is the unambiguously culpable group), this would satisfy the objective of retribution with moral economy. There are, however, serious objections to decapitation targeting, some of which we have already examined in a previous chapter. First, arrangements might be such that, in the event of decapitation, military personnel who lose communication with their superiors have standing orders to execute an all-out attack. Second, in the case of limited nuclear strikes against the West, we may need to preserve the Soviet leadership in order to preserve officials with the power to prevent escalation to an all-out attack and with the authority to negotiate a termination of the war.

Without Soviet leaders and the military commanders under them who direct the attacks, there might be no chance of limiting the violence that the USSR could inflict on us. *Escalation control* is so important from the retributivist standpoint that it may, paradoxically, require a prohibition on targeting those most responsible for criminal aggression—certainly in the initial phases of the war and perhaps during the course of the entire conflict.

Even if all efforts to dissuade the Soviet leaders from further attacks failed, so that nothing more could be gained through negotiations with them—any plan to destroy this most culpable group would, of course, require that every effort be made to minimize civilian casualties. A strict adherence by the West to the principle of discrimination would no doubt be welcomed by Soviet leaders as they situated themselves in such a fashion as to make Soviet civilians their protective shields.

Even though threatening to kill the Soviet leadership might have great deterrent value, retributivists would have to forgo this ploy if it became clear that this threat could not be carried out without risking massive civilian casualties. If retaliation against the leadership will bring with it significant collateral damage to civilians, such an attack will never be appropriate—even if that means that those most responsible for the aggression must be indefinitely spared. This is the paradox of retribution when it is applied to military strategy: the most culpable individuals in the enemy nation may have to be given immunity.

In sum, although retributivists might be willing, if armistice negotiations proved impossible, to attack the Soviet leadership, provided that this involved a risk of only limited civilian casualties, they could not justify risking massive noncombatant fatalities as "side effects" of an attempt to destroy well-hidden Soviet leaders. Practically minded retributivists realize that any attempt to administer just punishment may from time to time result in the deaths of innocent individuals—for example, on the domestic level, the wrongful imprisonment or execution of the innocent may occur. The point, however, is to construct a system so that wrongful punishment is kept to a minimum. In the case of military reprisals, this means attending to the rights of civilians to the point of avoiding any military actions that involve the foreseen, even if unintended, killing of large numbers of noncombatants, no matter how well the proportions work out on the macro-war level in terms of total lives saved versus those lost.

If, for example, there was evidence that a war with the Soviet Union could be terminated by the annihilation of Moscow, then, in terms of saving lives, it might appear that such an act would be justified. If the only way to ensure the destruction of the leadership and save millions of lives in the Soviet Union and the United States was the destruction of Moscow, why not do so?

If our intention is to destroy the leadership and the only way to destroy the leadership is to destroy Moscow, would the classical *principle of double effect* allow us to do this? First developed by Catholic moralists in the Middle Ages, this principle tells us under what conditions it is permissible to carry out acts that have both good and bad consequences. This principle tells us that it is permissible to commit an act that has evil consequences so long as (1) our intention is to bring about a good effect (to end the war in this case); (2) the bad effect is merely foreseen and not intended (i.e., we do not intend the bad effect either as a means to the good effect or as an end itself); and (3) the bad effect is not disproportionate to the good aimed at (i.e., the good effect is sufficiently good to compensate for allowing the evil effect). Note that the notion of proportionality invoked here is not the same as the one embodied in the retributive principle.

It appears that a decision to destroy Moscow could be made to satisfy the principle of double effect so long as the following conditions obtain: the intended target is the culpable leadership, the objective is to bring the war to an end, and the number of lives saved far outweighs those lost. The deaths of hundreds of thousands that would occur as a result of an attempt to kill Soviet leaders could be looked upon as collateral damage.

The retributive response to such reasoning would be this: we cannot justify the killing of hundreds of thousands to save millions, even if the intended target is a culpable leadership. (It should be noted that retributivism will not allow even the *threat* to do this for the purpose of deterrence.) Retributivism can no more accept this double-effect reasoning than it could accept—on the domestic level—a plan by the police to destroy a small town and all its inhabitants in order to kill a gang of dangerous murderers who, if allowed to escape, would probably kill enough people to populate several towns the same size. Assuming for the sake of the analogy that there is no other way to stop these murderers, the police would still not be, from a retributivist standpoint, justified in doing this—or threatening to do this, even if there was a high probability that they would not have to act on the threat. From a retributivist point of view, it is better to suffer evil than to commit evil or even threaten it. This is one of the few features retributivism has in common with pacifism. The Kantian imperative that prohibits us from treating *some* persons as mere means, even if doing so is likely to benefit many other persons, operates to rule out the Moscow-annihilation option.

Appropriate Nonleadership Targets

Since Soviet leaders would be (under the conditions specified above) at best a late target in any retaliation plan, the problem, then, is to find other targets that would satisfy the principle of culpability while fulfilling the pragmatic need for a threat that has substantial deterrent value.

Countersilo Targeting. The question of the appropriate targets—which targets, short of the leadership, would fulfill the requirement of culpability while providing deterrence—has been answered in various ways. One targeting strategy is countersilo or counter-ICBM targeting. This would involve, in the event of a Soviet attack, the destruction of ICBMs in their silos (or, if detectable, on mobile platforms) and/or the killing of the missile command officers in charge of these weapons of mass destruction. The objective would be to destroy the launch control facilities and the officers who fire the missiles.

If, however, we are retaliating against a massive first strike, we may end up destroying empty silos or platforms. Of course, from a retributive point of view, it would still make sense to "execute" missile officers who had participated in the "war crime" of obeying orders to fire these immoral weapons. (Even if these officers were deceived into thinking they were responding to a U.S. attack, they would still be guilty from the retributivist perspective because they would have consented to the use of unjust weapons.) To deterrence theorists, by contrast, it will seem pointless to kill missile officers who control empty silos—unless the public declaration that we plan to do so could be judged as having deterrence value: that is, unless such a declaration could credibly deter Soviet officers in charge of firing missiles from doing so.

There is, however, another practical reason for "executing" at least some missile control officers after they have launched a salvo of ICBMs. It is known that the Soviets have—or, at least, are working on—a capacity to quickly reload a number of their silos or launchers after firing. Given the possibility of reload rounds, the capability to destroy missile launchers and launch control officers could serve the end of damage limitation while satisfying the culpability requirement of retribution. That is, in retaliating against those directly involved in a nuclear attack on the United States, we may at the same time be eliminating facilities capable of inflicting additional destruction on our society.

On the other hand if—in a crisis—the Soviet Union believes that we have a capacity to destroy Soviet ICBMs before they can be used, that would provide them with an incentive to use them before they lose them. A preemptive strike by the United States would, of course, violate the principle of culpability, which asserts that force should be used only in response to aggression. Since, however, a *declaration* that we will not use our weapons unless we are attacked would not be convincing to the Soviets if they believed that we had the *capacity* to destroy Soviet ICBMs, a comprehensive counter-ICBM targeting strategy could be destabilizing. In other words, despite a U.S. declaratory policy of retaliation-only, the Soviets might reasonably infer, if the United States had a massive counterforce capability, that we had a first-strike action policy: they could, despite declarations to the contrary, plausibly interpret our forces as signaling a U.S. first-strike plan. In that case, in a crisis they might be tempted into a preemptive attack on our strategic weapons.

A compromise position is to develop only a limited countersilo (or counterlauncher) capacity—in other words, a finite counterforce targeting strategy. The aim would be to have a modest counterforce capacity: enough weapons to survive a first strike and be able to destroy enough launchers (or missile launch centers) to reduce damage to our society, but not enough forces to give us a disarming first-strike capacity. That is, we would strive for a limited second-strike counterforce capability—a capacity to put together an effective attack out of what remains of our partly destroyed forces, against what remains of the enemy's partly expended forces. This, of course, would require survivable command, control, and intelligence facilities that would be capable of (1) discovering what the enemy had left after an attack and (2) destroying these remaining forces. Thus, the ability to protect C^3I facilities is crucial to this retaliatory strategy.

Countercombatant Targeting. A third alternative, put forward by Bruce Russett, is a silo-avoiding countercombatant strategy:

> A strategy of countercombatant targeting must preserve the confidence of Soviet leaders that they have an invulnerable second-strike force capable of surviving any American first strike. But it could be consistent with strategic stability if it depended for its effectiveness primarily not on a threat to enemy nuclear retaliatory capabilities but to the enemy's ability to maintain internal security and to control its borders and neighbors by tactical means. Thus, special targets would be arms factories and concentration of troops and materials for tactical military forces (headquarters, supply centers, marshalling yards and repair facilities, transportation centers, pipelines and fuel-distribution centers, and power plants), particularly those isolated enough to be destroyed with minimum residual damage to the civilian population. Particular attention would be given to Soviet divisions in Eastern Europe and along the Chinese border and to KGB (Soviet internal police) units, often of substantial size, intended for deployment against Soviet unrest.[20]

Russett's conviction is that, next to itself, the Soviet leadership most values its ability to control Soviet society and guard Soviet borders. (If *glasnost* expands, the means of control may become less valuable targets; for the foreseeable future, however, Soviet society will remain highly controlled.) Soviet leaders realize that Soviet government would cease to function if its internal and external security agencies—its internal police and its armies—were crippled. According to Russett, by declaring that in the event of a Soviet nuclear attack, we will launch a countercombatant strategic attack, we could effectively threaten to impair the Soviet Union's power to resist a conventional invasion and to maintain domestic order.

The appeal of this strategy is threefold: its deterrence value, moral defensibility, and credibility. First, such a strategy would exploit a longstanding Soviet fear, based on historical experience: vulnerability to foreign invasion. Second, from a retributive standpoint, it is appealing because it restricts targets to combatant forces. Finally, it would be a more credible policy than a threat to destroy Soviet population centers after a limited attack on the United States—the kind of U.S. response that would bring massive retaliation against the U.S. population.[21]

An objection to Russett's countercombatant targeting strategy is that under certain attack scenarios, it does not fit the concept of culpability sketched above. For example, in a Soviet first strike against the mainland of the United States, the KGB and the Red Army would not be the agents involved in the attack and thus would not satisfy the principle that retaliation should be limited to *harmers*.

This objection can be answered. Although in such a strategic attack Soviet ground forces and the KGB (except for those involved in launching nuclear weapons) would not be the immediate harmers of U.S. citizens, they could be retained as *justifiable* targets for two reasons. First, NATO member nations in Western Europe are pledged to view an armed attack against any member as an attack against all members—one that must be met by action, including the use of armed force. Thus, our NATO allies are pledged to target Soviet forces and can expect the Soviet armed forces to mobilize for war against Western Europe in advance of an attack on U.S. territory. Second, the United States may legitimately target Soviet regular army and KGB forces because both are likely to be the instruments used in a Soviet plan to make Western Europe a recovery base after a devastating strategic war with the United States. Thus, to create a deterrent threat consistent with retribution, we can justly declare that the Soviet army and the KGB are on our target list.

Summary

Whatever targeting strategy is ultimately chosen, it must satisfy the principle of culpability, which requires (1) that we target only combatant forces (agents and instruments of harm) and (2) that in targeting combatant forces we make every effort to minimize collateral civilian casualties. A retributivist who is a realist will, of course, acknowledge that in war it is impossible to avoid actions that result in the unintended killing of noncombatants or even innocent combatants (ones lacking criminal intent or freedom of action). The objective is to develop a military strategy and a system of forces that will permit a practical application of this principle and a minimum number of foreseen but unintended noncombatant casualties.

Proportionality and Military Policy

Applied to military policy, retributive proportionality requires that the retaliatory acts directed at the "harmers" be proportional to the aggression suffered. This is not the same as the standard just war notion of proportionality, which requires that the evil done be balanced by the good achieved. *Proportionality* here refers to the need to inflict on the guilty a just measure of punishment. According to retributivism, retaliation against the harmers is not to be viewed as a necessary evil: it is not an evil at all, but a requirement of justice. To the degree possible, retaliation must be in proportion to the nature of the attack and the degree of culpability of the attackers.

Retaliation against Soviet harmers should be proportional to the level of harm they inflict. Consider again the possibility of aggression against Western Europe. (No matter how unlikely such aggression may appear during a period of good relations, Western security requires preparation for this contingency.) During the early stages of such an attack, retaliation could be limited to attacks on advancing Soviet forces as well as the bridges, railheads, and various points through which they must pass. No more force should be used than is necessary to stop the advance. If the aggression continued after this limited and proportionate response to the initial phase of invasive action, retaliation could then be escalated to include back-up Soviet forces and facilities within the Soviet Union for supporting the invasion. The retaliation would proceed in this graduated and measured fashion. Soviet leaders would be warned that if all these measured responses failed to stop the attack, then the headquarters of the internal police and other instruments of Soviet political control would be attacked—and ultimately the leadership itself.

If, on the other hand, a Soviet nuclear attack is restricted to the United States—a first strike—then the strategic response must be proportionate to the damage inflicted on U.S. assets. If we were to adopt a limited counterforce strategy, our declared initial targets of retaliation in the event of a Soviet strategic attack would include Soviet strategic and support facilities such as silos (if we can achieve this without causing crisis instability), air fields, and submarine ports. Attacks against these assets could escalate in a manner that matched the level of Soviet attacks.

Every effort would be made to keep lines of communication open so that we could make clear the intention to keep our retaliation limited and proportional, while also making it clear that we plan to match the Soviets at every level of aggression. The aim would be—in addition to administering proportionate punishment—to deter further attacks and to terminate hostilities with the least possible destruction to civilians on both sides.

From the standpoint of retributivism, a proportionate response obviously does not mean matching the Soviets in terms of equivalent target destruction—that is, responding in kind. Although we can hope that our avoidance of retaliation against Soviet cities will bring reciprocation, we cannot rule out the possibility that the Soviets might, in the course of strategic war, intentionally destroy American cities. Even if they deliberately attacked our cities, we would—if we adopted a retributivist policy—refuse to retaliate in kind. It should be clear by now that retribution, contrary to popular belief, rules out such a tit-for-tat strategy. Being willing to retaliate against *x* number of Soviet cities if *x* number of American cities are attacked is a violation of retributive justice, comparable to murdering the family of a criminal who murdered members of one's own family.

The point is that a proportionate response under retribution must always be governed by the principle of culpability: we should respond in a manner proportional to the attack while at the same time limiting our retaliation to the agents and instruments of aggression. No rule tells us the kinds of counterforce attacks that would constitute sufficient and proportionate punishment for the deliberate destruction of our cities (assuming, of course, that intelligence was capable of distinguishing intentional from accidental attacks). Yet the difficulty of proportioning the punishment to the crime is not peculiar to the military domain. On the domestic level, it is just as difficult to determine what penalty is appropriate for a particular crime—for example, rape. Justice does not require a city for a city any more than it requires a rape for a rape. Again, retributivism is not concerned with finding an exact equivalent but with proportioning punishment to offense in a fair and reasonable manner.

The difficulty of arriving at a defensible punishment—one that is reasonably commensurate with the crime—does not invalidate retributivism, but it does make the application of the principle of proportionality somewhat arbitrary. There is no mechanical formula for proportionate response in the area of military justice, any more than there is such a formula in the area of domestic criminal justice. Those committed to retribution can only try to establish penalties roughly proportional to the seriousness of the offenses to which they are applied. The point is to recognize differences in the nature of transgressions and to try to respond in a way that reasonably takes those differences into consideration.

Implications for Force Development

What forces are required in order to satisfy the requirements of a retributive defense policy—a policy that seeks to address the Soviet nuclear threat in a manner consistent with the principles of culpability and proportionality? Some have mistakenly viewed the strategy of assured destruction as a retributive doctrine. Given the above account of retributive principles, it should by now be obvious that any attempt to construe MAD as a retributive policy reflects a crude and incorrect understanding of retribution.

The use of inaccurate city-busting nuclear weapons has the look of revenge, not retribution. Where retributivism requires a proportionate and discriminating response, the logic of MAD retaliation seems to be this: because those in power in the aggressing nation have ordered a nuclear attack against us, we are going to punish all of the citizens in the enemy society. Despite popular prejudice, revenge and retribution are not the same. An act of revenge may be indiscriminate in terms of its victims; for example, it may involve the punishment of the innocent in exchange for attacks on the innocent, as MAD does. The crucial difference resides in the principles of culpability and proportionality, which retribution requires and MAD violates.

The adoption of a limited war–fighting strategy, which makes use of highly accurate low-yield nuclear weapons, may appear to satisfy the requirements of retribution. Certainly, the strategies of limited nuclear options (LNO) and flexible response (FR) are *prima facie* suited to meeting culpability and proportionality criteria. Historically, however, counterforce nuclear weapons were not developed to satisfy just war doctrine but to provide the West with nuclear options beyond massive retaliation and thus improve its bargaining position. Cities were not morally prohibited targets but rather "withholds" within a strategy designed to give the West—in James Schlesinger's view—the ability to withhold population destruction for an extended period of time.[22] The point was to provide the West with the capacity for graduated response or escalation control, holding out as a final threat a massive attack on Soviet cities.

The idea behind limited nuclear options was not the achievement of justice: it was the ability to engage in terroristic bargaining, with civilians held back as the final chips. As Bernard Brodie put it many years ago, cities would be "targets to be hit or threatened because they are the ultimate tokens in whatever armistice negotiations may develop."[23] Therefore, the moral objective of avoiding attacks on noncombatants was never a central concern of the various U.S. limited nuclear war–fighting strategies.

Retributivists would, of course, reject the idea of using graduated nuclear retaliation for bargaining purposes—for a strategy in which populations are retained as possible targets in order to achieve escalation control. The important question for retributivists is whether nuclear weapons, even if absolutely restricted to military targets, can be used in such a way as to satisfy the principles of culpability and proportionality: punishment being limited to harmers, and harmers being given a just measure of punishment.

Of course, not all advocates of flexible nuclear forces seek more variegated and accurate nuclear weapons for purely strategic purposes— that is, simply to make deterrence more credible and, in case deterrence fails, to have a strong (coercive) intrawar bargaining position through a capacity for controlled nuclear destruction. On the contrary, some proponents of a limited nuclear war–fighting doctrine seek to create a morally defensible force system. Beyond the goal of escalation control, these advocates of a graduated response are also concerned to have—in case deterrence fails—a *just* form of retaliation. That is, they do not want the failure of deterrence to require immoral attacks on the Soviet people. Their language fits in with a retributive theory of punishment.

For example, former U.S. Secretary of Defense Caspar Weinberger, an advocate of a limited nuclear war–fighting capability, has condemned as immoral any retaliation against the Soviet people for "an attack launched by the Soviet leadership—a leadership for which the Soviet people are not responsible and cannot control."[24] The implication is that nuclear retaliation should target the "guilty," not the "innocent." There is, however, good reason to doubt that the goal of just retaliation can be realized by a system of nuclear retaliatory forces, no matter how accurate.

Improvements in the accuracy of delivery vehicles do, of course, allow us to reduce the destructive power of nuclear warheads and to engage in more precise counterforce nuclear retaliation. The problem is that the present generation of nuclear weapons, no matter how accurately they are delivered to military targets, will have grossly indiscriminate effects. The collateral damage to civilians from even limited counterforce attacks may be so great as to make them indistinguishable from counterpopulation attacks, especially when one considers the combined effects of nuclear blast, heat, and radiation.

Within the realm of "new" nuclear weapons (modified fusion bombs), the neutron bomb, an enhanced radiation weapon, might be thought the appropriate retributive weapon. If we are required to choose from the nuclear arsenal, then, according to James Turner Johnson, this fusion device is the morally superior weapon:

> That property is left undamaged, whether by blast or lingering radiation, is significant for protecting the rights of noncombatants, who must have buildings in which to live, work, and shop, means of transportation, land to farm, and so on. The neutron warhead is definitely superior morally to tactical fission warheads in these terms; it is both more inherently discriminate and more proportionate.[25]

The reason for its alleged superiority is that neutron radiation, while deadly for those in the affected region, is not long-lasting, so that the lingering effect of radioactive contamination is significantly reduced, compared, at least, with the effects of other nuclear warheads of similar yield.[26] Moreover, compared with other nuclear weapons, the neutron warhead produces less blast and thus less destruction to the surrounding environment. Johnson asserts that a weapon's long-term harm to property and to the environment on which people depend for the conditions of normal living is morally significant because

> the amount and types of such effects help to determine whether the intention was in fact to disregard the rights of noncombatants, either immediately or through the lasting impact of the weapon on their lives, or whether the damage caused to noncombatants was, by the moral rule of double effect, a secondary effect, a secondary and indirect result of a permitted action against combatants.[27]

Strategies designed to prevent Soviet economic recovery by making the target areas, whether the countryside or cities, uninhabitable after the war would violate Johnson's enlarged temporal notion of noncombatant immunity. The deliberate nuclear attack on an urban or agricultural area—even territory not inhabited at the time of the attack (as a result, for example, of evacuation)—in order to cause long-term contamination and make it unlivable after the war is as much a violation of the rights of noncombatants as a direct attack upon civilians. It may destroy their means of survival (farmland) or livelihood (factories in a contaminated city). For this reason, the short-term radioactivity produced by neutron weapons makes them less objectionable than standard nuclear weapons.

In terms of immediate effects, too, neutron attacks, because of their limited blast and heat, can be restricted to a prescribed area—a zone of combat. The neutron warhead's enhanced short-lived, restricted radiation would thus (allegedly) be morally superior to the more indiscriminate blast-enhancing nuclear weapons in NATO's arsenal. Its heat and blast effects would be less severe than those of NATO's current nuclear weapons designed for battlefield use: the neutron warhead could be used against tank and troop concentrations with less destruction of built-up surroundings.[28]

Although he believes neutron weapons would be preferable to less discriminating kinds of nuclear forces, Johnson admits that even these are too grossly destructive to be employed with restraint in nearly any conceivable military situation because their use even against a legitimate (that is, combatant) target would entail such foreseeable collateral harm to noncombatants as to cast grave doubt on the morality of such use.[29] For example, given the density of population in Western Europe, the use of the neutron bomb by NATO against advancing Soviet forces would result in indiscriminate destruction. Even the smallest nuclear warheads (including tactical neutron weapons) are, Johnson concedes, "too large for proportionate use except against fairly large targets."[30]

Even if the effects of neutron weapons could be limited to combatants, it is not clear that the moral requirements of retribution would be satisfied. The retributive viewpoint requires a measured response in two senses: (1) it should be limited (at least in terms of its intended target) to offenders; and (2) it ought to be proportional to the offense and to the offender's level of culpability. The second requirement can be interpreted as implying that it is impermissible to inflict wanton suffering on combatant forces. The retributive perspective would endorse the principle expressed in the 1907 Hague Convention: "The rights of belligerents to adopt means of injuring the enemy are not unlimited."[31] This law can be interpreted as prohibiting weapons that cause unnecessary suffering to combatants.

The neutron bomb kills people by a slow lingering death from radiation sickness: a very large proportion of its victims would take from a few days to a month to die. Thus, combatants who did not die immediately would face a relatively slow, agonizing death. Within a few hours of the blast, severe shock sets in, accompanied by vomiting and diarrhea. Because of massive internal injury, the victims start passing blood. Fever then sets in, making the victims feel weak and ill. Hair falls out, and ulcers cover the throat and intestines. Bone marrow rots in the living body, and individuals become unable to resist even the mildest infection.[32] This appears to be cruel and unusual punishment for anyone. From a retributivist viewpoint, a nation that uses such weapons reduces itself to a criminal level. It must be emphasized again that retribution aims at justice—not cruel vengeance.

We must keep in mind that although ordinary soldiers are (as argued above) consenting participants who are not absolutely compelled to behave as ordered, they have little responsibility for the inception of the war or influence over its continuation. If ordinary combatants are not as fully culpable as political leaders, this should in fact mitigate their punishment. (Indeed, the use of neutron weapons even against the leadership would be excessive.) No more force should be used than is necessary to repel and punish the agents of aggression.

In contrast to the area of domestic criminal justice, where punishment can be reduced (e.g., by lessening the period of imprisonment) to reflect mitigating factors, the domain of military retaliation does not allow for finely tuned punishment. Punitive military retaliation either kills, wounds, or terrifies the agents of aggression. To reflect the low degree of culpability of ordinary soldiers, the least that can be done is to prohibit weapons that cause unnecessary or prolonged suffering. The act of imposing on soldiers the constant threat of injury and death is perhaps punishment enough for their participation in aggression.

In addition, there is a tactical reason for rejecting neutron weapons. Because the neutron warhead kills its victims slowly while sparing the instruments of war—such as tanks—"terminally ill" Soviet tank forces could (theoretically) continue to fight in kamikaze fashion. Therefore, not only is using neutron weapons against advancing tank crews a violation of proportionality, but it also appears unsatisfactory in military terms. Thus, from the standpoints of both retributivism, which requires that we inflict the least force necessary to punish ordinary combatants, and military efficacy, which requires that we prevent enemy soldiers from accomplishing their goals, it appears inadvisable to use neutron weapons.[33]

In sum, whether we are concerned with the capacity for discrimination, escalation control, or the suffering of combatants, it is doubtful that the current generation of nuclear weapons—strategic, intermediate, or tactical—can satisfy the requirements of justice. To repeat what was stated above: the consequences of a limited strategic nuclear war may not differ substantially from unlimited nuclear exchanges. The authors of one study dealing with the effects of a limited nuclear conflict conclude: "Either superpower contemplating such an attack should be well aware that nuclear attacks—even limited to military targets— could cause casualties that approach those from all-out attacks."[34]

Furthermore, even if one doubts that a limited (strategic) nuclear war will produce the catastrophe of nuclear winter, the long-range cumulative effects on the environments of neutrals as well as belligerents make it a threat to "noncombatants" throughout the world for the indefinite future. It would be a global Chernobyl. Desmond Ball warns:

The gross uncertainties that surround any significant use of nuclear weapons make them inherently ill-suited to policies requiring precision and discrimination. . . . In the end, a better understanding of force employment policy might lead to the realization that the limited nuclear war–fighting option is a chimera, and that policies which depend upon the ability to maintain escalation control of a nuclear exchange are ultimately incredible.[35]

The Search for Precision Retaliatory Forces

For retributivists it is a moral imperative to seek an alternative to reliance on current nuclear weapons, even the most accurate types. Two new weapons concepts offer promise in the search for accurate, discriminating forces: third-generation nuclear weapons and the possibility of replacing all nuclear warheads with precision-guided nonnuclear ones. After a brief discussion of the new direction in nuclear weaponry, I will devote substantially more space to new nonnuclear options because (1) these weapons allow us to avoid the ambiguity the new nuclear weapons would create, and (2) the military applications of the new nonnuclear weapons have been more thoroughly explored.

Third-Generation Nuclear Weapons

The first generation of nuclear weapons comprised the fission bombs of the 1940s and the early 1950s. To satisfy the quest for even more powerful weapons, the superexplosives were developed—the fusion (hydrogen) bombs. The possibility of a third generation of nuclear weapons is now being explored with a stress on pinpoint targeting. For example, research is being conducted to create a weapon that could concentrate the force of its nuclear blast on a small target, such as the Kremlin, while leaving the rest of Moscow intact. The result of this research will be, according to the physicist Theodore Taylor, a weapon as different from current nuclear weapons as a rifle is from gunpowder. Taylor, a nuclear weapons designer at Los Alamos from 1949 to 1956 who later worked for General Dynamics' atomic division and served as deputy director of what is now the Defense Nuclear Agency, contends that third-generation work constitutes "a qualitative new phase of nuclear weapons development."[36] Weapon designers can now enhance or suppress any of a bomb's destructive effects, including shock waves, heat, and various types of electromagnetic radiation.

The important point, from a retributive standpoint, is that the destructive energy of the third-generation nuclear weapons, instead of being radiated uniformly and indiscriminately outward, as occurs with current nuclear warheads, can be concentrated in a certain direction; for example, a significant fraction of the explosive energy could be transformed into microwaves that are concentrated in a precise way on targets. The effects of a nuclear explosion could also be made directional in the same way high-explosive devices such as conventional shaped charges can produce armor-penetrating jets of molten metal or directional shrapnel. Furthermore, the new weapons could be so constructed that the quantities of radioactive fission products (the main component of fallout among the weapon debris) could be controlled over very wide ranges.

Furthermore, microwaves generated by third-generation nuclear weapons could be useful in retaliation designed to incapacitate enemy forces in a countermissile attack, especially if the remaining weapons were on mobile launchers. Should the Soviet Union increase its mobile-based weapons to try to achieve invulnerable second-strike ICBM forces as a follow-on to a first-strike strategy, we need some way to take out these remaining weapons. John Pike, a weapons expert with the Federation of American Scientists, points out that "a single third-generation nuke could blanket a wide area with microwaves, which would short-circuit the electronic mechanisms, disabling the missiles."[37]

Is it desirable to move in this direction rather than making a complete break with nuclear weaponry? During a transitional period from nuclear forces of mass destruction to weapons of great accuracy, could it be dangerous to have third-generation weapons mixed with an arsenal of indiscriminate nuclear weapons? Given the fact that the new nuclear weapons will be less destructive and more discriminating, isn't it likely that they will blur the line between nonnuclear and nuclear weapons, thus making it more probable that a conventional conflict would escalate into an all-out nuclear war involving the most destructive weapons? That is, it would be tempting to introduce these accurate nuclear forces into a conventional war, thus crossing the firebreak more quickly than might be done with more destructive nuclear forces; once this step is taken, there may be no way of halting nuclear escalation. This is a serious problem for retributivists who are attracted by the third-generation work yet concerned to make a stable transition to more discriminating weapons.

The Substitution of Nonnuclear for Nuclear Weapons

In order to avoid blurring the line between conventional and nuclear weapons, it might be prudential to search for a nonnuclear alternative. Some defense specialists believe that current technological progress has made it possible to substitute nonnuclear for nuclear forces at the tactical, intermediate, and strategic levels. Albert Wohlstetter, a respected professional strategist, supports the development of these conventional warheads: "My own research and that of others has for many years pointed to the need for a much higher priority on improving our ability to hit what we aim at. That would mean, in particular, that effective conventional weapons could drastically reduce the West's reliance on nuclear weapons."[38] In discussing the substitution of nonnuclear for nuclear forces, I will consider what this change would mean on the tactical, intermediate, and intercontinental levels.

NATO's reliance on the threat of first use of nuclear weapons has been based mainly on the assumption of NATO inferiority to Soviet-led Warsaw Pact forces. The assumption of inferiority is now undercut by two facts: (1) the weakening (and perhaps de facto dissolution) of the Warsaw Pact as a result of upheavals in Eastern Europe; and (2) the reduction and pullback of Soviet troops from Eastern Europe. These facts alone undermine the case for first use and even the need for nuclear forces.

The only conceivable Soviet threat to Western Europe is the possibility that, in the event of the failure of *perestroika*, hard-liners bent on expansion (perhaps to gain valuable economic resources to relieve Soviet scarcity) will come to power in the Soviet Union. In that case the new leadership would have to reconstitute Soviet forces so that they could achieve aggressive objectives without assistance from East European "allies." Even if retributivists grant this worst-case possibility, they can still argue that nonnuclear forces are sufficient on all levels: tactical, intermediate, and strategic. In the following sections, I elaborate on this.

Tactical Level

The tactical level is the level of battlefield combat within a range of 310 miles. This level is crucial because alleged NATO conventional inferiority here has been used to justify not only the possession of nuclear weapons but an announced NATO readiness to use them first.

The substitution by NATO of nonnuclear for nuclear forces could involve three separate yet closely interwoven elements: improvement of armed forces, emerging technologies (ET), and improved tactical schemes.[39] The objective would be to correct the imbalance that justifies the current NATO strategy of flexible response, which calls for the first use of tactical nuclear weapons to stop Soviet forces in the event that they overrun NATO's conventional defenses. A greater range of conventional flexibility is needed within the strategy of flexible response. It is the impoverished nature of NATO nonnuclear options that makes the Alliance dependent not only upon nuclear weapons but, what is more frightening, upon their early use. As it now stands, according to some estimates, the Supreme Allied Commander of Europe (SACEUR) has the means to provide a conventional defense only for two weeks (and probably less) before it would be necessary to resort to nuclear forces.[40]

There is, of course, nothing novel in the suggestion that NATO should aim at improvements in its conventional forces on the Central Front, making the changes necessary to overcome its numerical inferiority. First-use policy has been justified by claims that the Warsaw Pact has overwhelming superiority—close to two-to-one (or higher) in the categories of tanks, men, artillery, and tactical aircraft.[41] The attempt to counter Soviet conventional forces with nonnuclear forces would not necessarily require matching the enemy tank for tank, plane for plane, soldier for soldier, and so on. Rather, NATO could organize a variety of effective nonnuclear retaliatory forces—technological and human—capable of stopping a Soviet invasion.

What if the Soviets somehow—through stealth or a change in strategy—retain or reestablish superiority in numbers? Let us consider a worst-case possibility in which Soviet cheating allows them to maintain forces much larger than those of NATO. Critics of denuclearization will argue that to guard against such a contingency, the West should retain some nuclear weapons for insurance.

Even without nuclear weapons, and even granting Soviet numerical superiority, however, NATO could still defend the West. Two reasons can be given for not having to match Soviet forces item for item: namely, the strategic advantage of defense and new emerging technologies (ET). First, it can be argued, the Soviet Union's wartime military task, offense, is inherently more difficult than NATO's, defense. Success is not just a function of overwhelming numbers: it also turns on the respective tasks of the belligerents. The Soviet general staff knows what the great Prussian theorist von Clausewitz stated—that "the defensive form of warfare is intrinsically stronger than the offensive."[42] This means that the defender normally needs fewer forces than the attacker. In the prenuclear age, the rule of thumb was that a three-to-one advantage was required to ensure victory for the attacker. Military specialist A. A. Sidorenko states that the lessons of World War II still apply in showing the "decisive superiority" needed for an offense to be "3 to 5 times for infantry, 6 to 8 times for artillery, 3 to 4 times for tanks and self-propelled artillery, and 5 to 10 times for aircraft."[43]

The fact that NATO's task is defensive gives it three advantages:
1. The ability to fight from prepared, even fortified, positions. The attacking forces, by contrast, must, in order to advance, come into the open, exposing themselves to fire.[44]

2. Familiar terrain. This advantage can be exploited by forcing Soviet armor into poor tank country, especially if the terrain is prepared with field fortifications.[45] John Mearsheimer, a NATO specialist, asserts that the terrain works to NATO's advantage: the area that encompasses the Central Front is riddled with obstacles that make it very difficult to move large armored formations.[46]

3. Motivation. NATO forces will be fighting to save their free institutions; by contrast, Soviet forces (especially soldiers from a re-Stalinized Soviet Union) may develop a morale problem and become unreliable when asked to carry out the dubious mission of imposing upon the West the same bleak Communist system from which many of them would like to be liberated. Is a Russian soldier likely to support, and give his blood for, the extension of a hated system into Western Europe?[47] Is it conceivable that troops from Eastern Europe will join in a Soviet invasion? Is it likely, for example, that Polish soldiers would be willing and enthusiastic participants in an invasion of the West? The likelihood of a successful invasion is, of course, greatly reduced if there is no significant support from European countries such as Poland or Czechoslovakia.[48] Soviet troops may, in fact, meet as much resistance in the East as in the West. There is a psychological advantage to defense when the defenders believe in what they are defending, while the agents of aggression are subject to serious doubts about the justice of their mission.

In addition to the advantages of defense, NATO forces need not match Soviet forces quantitatively, item for item, at the tactical level because of the qualitatively superior technological potential of the West. The side with the greatest number of guns and soldiers cannot be presumed to have superiority at the tactical level. There is emerging the possibility of more discriminating conventional tactical weapons that will make it possible to destroy by nonnuclear means targets that previously required nuclear warheads. New propulsion fuels and guidance systems will make missiles more accurate. It is becoming easier to detect and identify targets as a result of the new high-resolution radar. More sophisticated satellite surveillance allows for more detailed monitoring of enemy positions. Moreover, new computer technology makes it possible to carry out the complex tasks of "target acquisition" (relaying the information from the satellites or radar system back to a central point for assessment) and "battle management" (coordinating a series of precision strikes against a huge number of small targets).[49] Here is how Richard D. DeLauer, former undersecretary of defense for research and engineering, describes the new or emerging technologies and their relevance for NATO:

They are hardware and software that can accomplish a rapid assimilation of intelligence and operational data from many independent sources and sensors. They can quickly—essentially at the speed of light—analyze these data, select the necessary battle management option and present it to the field commanders in a form that will permit the most effective decision for retaliation. The weapons will be carried on low-observable platforms, which are not detectable by radar, and will attack the enemy with munitions that are highly effective against his mobile forces and accurate within a few meters. Such a response will result in high attrition of the attacker's forces and high survivability for the defender.[50]

Moreover, what is important from the retributivist standpoint is that these munitions would have few, if any, of the collateral effects of nuclear weapons, such as blast, heat, fallout, or neutron flux. In addition, the new conventional forces need not be subject to the formal release procedures (negative control) required for the use of tactical nuclear weapons and thus, unlike the latter, would be employable from the outset of any hostilities.[51] In sum, ET involves three major developments: advanced sensors to locate enemy units precisely, precision-guided munitions to strike them, and an elaborate command system to coordinate the entire battle.

What makes the emerging technologies devastating to the invasion forces is the possibility that the defense can score a hit every time a weapon is fired. "That's been the Holy Grail of tactical warfare," says Robert Cooper, former head of the Defense Advanced Research Projects Agency (DARPA).[52] A new generation of "smart" weapons—which, once fired, can search out and strike targets on their own with devastating accuracy—are starting to emerge from the laboratories and into America's Army, Navy, and Air Force arsenals. What distinguishes the smart weapons from previous conventional ones is that they can detect specific types and levels of heat and sound, as well as electronic signals from radar, and analyze them with their own tiny computers to recognize and select a target from the infinite variety of "signatures" around it.[53] The aim is to develop a new generation of "fire and forget" smart weapons that will, after launching, find targets on their own, with no human intercession.

Consider, for example, the Soviet challenge: thousands of tanks advancing through a probably resistant Eastern Europe toward unified Germany. One ET method of countering any Soviet advantage in tanks might be the Army's Sense and Destroy Armor (SADARM) smart weapon system, which uses advanced radar, heat sensors, and a miniature onboard computer to provide precision aiming. Fired by soldiers out of sight of the target, it would, from above a targeted tank, aim for the center (where the armor is thin) and fire an explosively formed slug of metal, killing the crew and disabling the tank. Also, smart SADARM mines can be shot into place immediately in front of advancing tanks: once the target is in range, the mine kicks up a SADARM-like weapon, much like a skeet launcher tossing up a clay pigeon, which precisely locates the target and fires, propelling itself to the target to destroy it.[54] The memoirs of former Soviet leader Nikita S. Khrushchev appear to foretell the "death" of offensive tank strategy; after observing war-game maneuvers of Soviet army units, he wrote: "When I arrived at the exercise area and saw how the tanks were attacked and were put out of action in no time by anti-tank missiles, I felt sick. After all, we are spending a lot of money to build tanks, but if . . . a war breaks out, these tanks will get burnt out before they have reached the line to which the high command ordered them."[55]

In addition, NATO stealth fighter-bombers could make use of "autonomous guided bombs" from safe distances to destroy bridges or rail yards that advancing reinforcements must pass through. Launched by a stealthy (i.e., invisible to radar) aircraft at a very low level, this bomb flies a planned route and uses an on-board television camera and computer to search for the target that matches a programed description, ultimately attacking the object that matches its computer picture.[56]

This brings us to the third component of a denuclearized NATO strategy. The aim of such smart weapons is to hit the Soviets where they are vulnerable. Soviet doctrine, according to Maj. Gen. Wilson Shoffner (U.S. Army), calls for a continuous forward flow of forces—that is, it is central to Soviet doctrine that fresh formations are continuously fed in to sustain the momentum of the offensive in the hope of cracking the defense apart.[57] To do this the Soviet commander knows that he must continue to have overwhelming numbers at the point of decision—the front. Each Soviet unit is on a strict timetable, with little room for individual initiative. On the other hand, a successful Soviet blitzkrieg depends on split-second timing, since opportunity on the battlefield is so fleeting: it demands a flexible command structure peopled from top to bottom with soldiers capable of exercising initiative in combat.[58] According to Stephen J. Cimbala, a specialist in strategic studies, the success of the blitzkrieg approach depends upon

> the willingness of lower-level commanders to take risks and to understand orders in other than literal terms. The combat effectiveness of fighting battalions and the regiments under such conditions depends as much on qualitative factors as it does on quantitative variables: the qualities include small-group cohesion, morale, leadership, and willingness to improvise.[59]

These are, Cimbala points out, the very qualities that appear to be lacking in modern Soviet ground forces.[60] When Soviet plans are disrupted, Soviet soldiers appear not to improvise very well. Soviet military tradition requires rigid central command and discourages low-level initiative. As James Dunnigan puts it: "In the Russian Army no one does anything without detailed instructions from the central command."[61] It is well known that junior officers lack independent leadership capabilities. John Mearsheimer believes that there is substantial evidence that Soviet officers and NCOs are deficient in individual initiative.[62] A survey of Soviet Army veterans by Richard A. Gabriel revealed that about two-thirds felt that their officers and NCOs did not have the kind of judgment they would trust in combat.[63] Soviet commanders write frequently in their journals about the inability of their troops to take the initiative.[64] Cimbala points out that the conditions under which Soviet conscripts are trained do not encourage initiative, small-group cohesion, or respect for officers.[65] Mearsheimer asserts that Soviet awareness of this problem and attempts to correct it are thwarted by historical and political forces:

> The Soviets are well aware of the need for initiative and flexibility, and they go to great lengths to stress the importance of these qualities in their military journals. They are not, however, attributes which can be willed into existence. Their absence is largely a result of powerful historical forces. Fundamental structural change in Soviet society and the Soviet military would be necessary before there would be any significant increase in flexibility and initiative.[66]

Andreas von Bulow, head of the Commission on Security Policy of Germany's Social Democratic Party, makes a similar point: "A society that promotes private initiative so little and stakes nearly everything on centralized planning cannot realize the opposite ideal in the military sphere. All our intelligence and observations confirm this."[67] Although the Gorbachev-initiated restructuring of Soviet society may eventually reduce its heavy centralism, it may be a long time before any significant societal change filters down to the military.

Anything that interrupts or impairs the Soviets' ponderous, massive, planned advance, the echelon attack, will significantly weaken the chances for a successful Soviet blitzkrieg. If one takes Murphy's Law seriously, we can expect rigid Soviet plans to go awry, with the West as the beneficiary of Soviet inflexibility and lack of initiative. *Soviet Army Operations*—a handbook prepared by the U.S. Army Intelligence and Threats Analysis Center (hardly an institution given to underestimating the Soviet Army)—discusses the Soviet addiction to set formulas:

Primarily, there is no provision for the unexpected. When initiative is seen in terms of finding a correct solution with normative patterns, a sudden lack of norms may place a commander, at whatever level, in an unexpected and perilous situation. The Soviet leader who can assess his situation and select the "proper" tactical guidelines based on appropriate norms is lauded. However, despite all the exhortations for a commander's use of initiative, he will be condemned if his initiative fails and he has not followed prescribed norms.[68]

Reports on the Red Army's performance in Afghanistan have provided no indication that Soviet soldiers were any different from the ones described in *Soviet Army Operations*. Even struggling against a technologically backward and ill-equipped guerrilla force, they did not show sufficient tactical flexibility to gain any significant hope of victory.

The Soviet Army is composed largely of conscripts who serve only two years. Since new conscripts are trained in actual combat units, at any one time significant numbers of soldiers are either untrained or only partially trained. (This, of course, will change if the Soviets institute an all-volunteer professional force.) By contrast, Western troops are provided with substantial training.[69] Also, reports indicate that Soviet soldiers, unlike Western ones, are deficient in map reading, a skill that is crucial for an army attempting to launch a blitzkrieg.[70]

As Mearsheimer envisions it, the Soviets plan to establish a breakthrough battle operation by concentrating their armored forces at one or two points along the Western front, hoping to achieve an overwhelming force advantage that will allow them to pierce NATO's forward line.[71] Once this breakthrough is achieved, the tactic is to avoid further contact with NATO's main body of forces, concentrating instead on driving as rapidly as possible into the defender's rear, in a deep strategic penetration, to sever lines of communication and destroy key points in the defender's command and control network. They plan thereby to disrupt NATO's ability to make decisions and control its forces.[72] If deep penetration is achieved, the Soviets can maneuver to encircle the various bypassed NATO forces, who will be cut off from each other and from their command posts.

The Soviet attack would (theoretically) unfold in waves, or echelons. After the first echelon broke through NATO's front line, a second wave would move up from deeper within Eastern Europe within forty-eight hours. A third echelon from the western USSR itself would finish the job, like a bloody battering ram thrust into the NATO front. According to an earlier version of the Soviet plan for overrunning Europe, the armies in East Germany would constitute the first wave, taking West

Germany to the Rhine; the armies of Poland and the Slovak part of Czechoslovakia would constitute the second echelon, advancing to take the Low Countries; and the armies of the western Soviet Union would constitute the third echelon, completing the conquest.[73] Given the changes in Eastern Europe, this plan of attack now appears to be part of the history of Soviet military doctrine.

Could even a huge Soviet army go it alone and succeed? An important prerequisite of a successful solo Soviet invasion, surprise, is unlikely to be achieved, because the USSR could not initiate an attack without bringing its forces to a war footing, preparations for which would be highly visible to the West. As Cimbala puts it: "Strategic warning would come in the form of the accumulation of indicators regarded by NATO as suggestive of a buildup beyond normal exercises or troop rotations."[74] The time required for the Soviets to complete their massive preparations for a blitzkrieg attack would be sufficient for the West to mobilize its superior technological resources. An invasion out of the blue would simply not allow the Soviets to throw a sufficient portion of their conventional forces at the allies.[75]

The only way they could surprise the West would be through a large-scale tactical nuclear strike. Wouldn't a Soviet monopoly of battlefield nuclear weapons allow them quickly to defeat a denuclearized Western Europe? If they no longer had to fear nuclear retaliation, they could strike quickly, with devastating effect. A tactical-nuclear surprise attack would, however, be counterproductive: any "victory" over Western Europe so achieved would be at the cost of resources they wanted to "win." As Eugene V. Rostow has observed: "After all, the Soviet leadership does not want to inherit the great Western centers of economic power as smoking ruins, contaminated by radiation and poison gases."[76] Moreover, after Chernobyl, the risk of nuclear fallout should deter the Soviet Union from a tactical nuclear attack on territory so close to western Russia.[77]

Thus, a Soviet attack, if it occurs at all, is likely to be a conventional one. Since Soviet doctrine calls for the rapid reinforcement of the forward line of troops (FLOT) by second and follow-on echelons deployed to the rear, it is wholly logical for NATO to develop a strategy for an attack on, and disruption/delay of, reinforcing formations (and the ever-lengthening lines of supply) before they can reach the battlefield. This is precisely the aim of a Follow-on-Forces Attack (FOFA) strategy, formally endorsed by the NATO Defense Planning Committee on 9 November 1984.[78] "A few high-precision hits on railroad bridges and switching areas, etc., using conventional smart weapons could," according to von Bulow, "sever the lifelines of the Soviets' first ring in Eastern Europe."[79] Specifically, such precision strikes could leave the Soviet divisions in East Germany without reinforcements and supplies by keeping the materiel in depots in the rear from coming through.[80] This NATO strategy involves purely conventional strikes on rear echelons of Soviet forces up to 250 miles behind the battle front.[81]

Of course, the interdiction of the enemy's rear area by way of attacks on bridges, railways, and reinforcing formations has been for many decades part of military plans and doctrine. In the past the means of attack have been manned aircraft, which, given modern radars and missiles, would today probably experience a high loss rate. In the near future these attacks could be undertaken by nonnuclear precision guided munitions (PGM). Emerging technological advances mean that the warheads could be conventional and the delivery means unmanned. Thus, fewer soldiers would be able to do more jobs with less loss of life in the process of defending against attacks.

Indeed, there is the prospect of more and more missions being done by smart machines. DARPA, the Pentagon's advanced weapons center, is working on a number of projects that would enable automated devices to perform dangerous combat missions that previously required human agents.[82] The picture of more automated battle agents begins to emerge. In short, the *quality* of Western defense—based on its strength in the area of high technology—could offset any quantitative Soviet superiority.

If a Soviet blitzkrieg is prevented from quickly breaking through the Western front, the war will then probably take the form of a traditional war of attrition, with the new technologies inflicting a heavy toll on front-line and follow-on forces. Whether the Soviet Union can mobilize sufficient manpower and reliable equipment to logistically sustain a protracted conflict in Europe is probably something about which the Soviets have their own significant doubts. We know that their efforts to mobilize reserves during three major operations (Czechoslovakia, Afghanistan, and Poland) were plagued with problems of command incompetence and/or troop noncompliance, including desertion.[83]

Such operations put far less stress on Soviet capabilities than a war with NATO. In a protracted conventional conflict, argues von Bulow, the overwhelming population superiority of the Alliance over Soviet and any supportive East European nations "would come to bear not only on the number of soldiers but on the industrial reserve capacity."[84] Given the economic superiority of the NATO states to the Warsaw Pact nations, would the Soviet Union really dare to wage war against them?[85]

Thus, in contemplating an invasion of Western Europe, the Soviets face a serious dilemma. To avoid the strain of a protracted war, they need to exploit the advantage of surprise, but to avoid telegraphing their plans, they must launch a war with as little mobilization as possible.

This means that their forces will be thin compared with what they could be with full mobilization—perhaps too thin to break through the front. On the other hand, if they take the time for mobilization to full strength, they lose the element of surprise, which might mean having to fight the kind of protracted war that their resources would not permit them to sustain—at least not as well as the West with its greater productivity can.[86]

In sum, even granting Soviet superiority in troops, guns, and armored vehicles, the West (with probable help from a number of East European governments) can still effectively counter this quantitatively superior offensive force by (1) exploiting defensive advantages, (2) making use of emerging technologies that allow precision retaliation against the agents of aggression, (3) exercising a military flexibility and initiative that the Soviets lack, and (4) making the most of the superior training and the greater reliability of its soldiers.

The above represents a tactical plan that would be consistent with retributivism. It may turn out that there are alternative tactics better suited to a retributive policy. The point was to give an idea of what a retributive tactical plan would look like. From a retributivist viewpoint, whatever ultimate tactical arrangement is developed, it should have the capability of avoiding the kind of indiscriminate destruction that tactical nuclear forces now threaten to inflict on both the enemy and the inhabitants of the territory to be defended. A tactical system should be capable of inflicting sufficient punishment on advancing troops to stop their forward movement and defeat their tactical objectives, but it should not be capable of causing prolonged and unnecessary suffering to the combatants who are targeted.

If the Soviets really implement a defensive strategy that would make it physically difficult for them to invade Western Europe, that would be a mirror image of what is being proposed here in the spirit of a retributive policy. There would thus be an isomorphism between NATO and Soviet doctrines. Until the evidence is palpable, we cannot take the Soviets at their word. What Soviet political leaders assert may have little to do with what the military is in fact doing. The proposal here does not, however, depend on trusting Soviet claims about the adoption of a purely defensive posture.

Intermediate Level

Forces at the intermediate level (including land-based missiles and aircraft) are less than intercontinental in range yet capable of reaching significantly beyond the battlefield. The Intermediate Nuclear Forces Treaty called for the elimination of all American and Soviet land-based intermediate nuclear forces, and it is doubtful whether replacing nuclear with conventional warheads is permissible under the treaty. Thus, what is proposed here would probably require either an abrogation or a renegotiation of the treaty. I am simply exploring the concept of conventionally armed intermediate delivery systems in order to show what is possible.

These systems, which include long-range and short-range intermediate forces, can reach targets within a range of 310 to 3,500 miles. Thus, when situated in certain NATO countries, long-range intermediate weapons can reach major targets in the Soviet homeland, including Moscow. Cruise missiles, for example, belong to the class of long-range intermediate nuclear weapons, being capable of reaching targets at a distance of up to 1,550 miles. With advances in accuracy, land-based intermediate delivery systems for nuclear weapons (now prohibited), such as the low-altitude radar-evasive cruise missiles, could be used for conventional warheads, according to James Turner Johnson:

> The capability of contemporary cruise missiles to discriminate among targets at long range appears to open up the possibility of replacing nuclear warheads with conventional high explosives for some tactical and even some strategic use. . . . Generally speaking, the moral advantage lies with highly controllable weapons of limited destructiveness and little redundancy of destructive power. The cruise missile armed with an appropriate conventional warhead appears to approach this moral goal quite closely in terms of technical characteristics; what remains necessary is the intention, expressed in tactical and strategic plans and decisions during battle, to serve this same goal.[87]

If improved tactical forces did not stop advancing Soviet troops, then it might be necessary to escalate to the intermediate level. Having a conventional capability at the intermediate level would make a nuclear capability unnecessary. If it becomes desirable to strike deeper into enemy territory than tactical weapons permit, then delivery systems hitherto designed for the delivery of nuclear warheads beyond the battlefield can carry conventional warheads to the appropriate targets. In addition to cruise missiles, Pershing II missiles (also now outlawed)—highly accurate ballistic missiles with a range of 1,100 miles—could be used to deliver conventional munitions for deep-strike targeting.

The point would be to destroy or impair the movement of succeeding waves of Soviet troops, tanks, and so on while they are still in East European territory, perhaps hundreds of miles into the interior, or while they are on their way from the western Soviet Union to Poland. In addition, intermediate conventional warheads could be used to destroy airfields, air-defense sites, command centers for waging war, communications facilities, railway lines (specifically the power stations that feed them and the rail yards where troops brought from the Soviet Union would disembark), and logistical supplies deeper in Eastern Europe and the western USSR.

The success of a Soviet offensive depends on the successful combination of air and ground attacks. We have already seen the kinds of attacks and weapons that could disrupt ground forces. The disruption of coordinated air attacks could be achieved by destroying runways, preventing Soviet aircraft from getting airborne. Nonnuclear munitions specifically designed for runway destruction could be used to cause an upheaval of the runway surface, closing all airfields within minutes and making the damage time consuming and difficult to repair.

Just as high-quality conventional anti-tank weapons could substitute for tactical nuclear weapons, so a conventional-for-nuclear substitution might be feasible for various kinds of longer-range counterforce strikes at Soviet military targets. As Soviet reinforcements moved forward from the USSR and crossed East European territory on the way to the West, an array of cruise missiles could be used to destroy significant portions of the railways and highway bridges on which the Soviet advance depended. George Quester, an authority on military strategy, states:

> Bridges are not so easily rebuilt once they have been destroyed, nor are tunnels. The gauge-change points between the Soviet and East European railways have always looked like inviting targets, and they might indeed be vulnerable to conventional attack as well, if the CEP [circular error probable] is brought down enough.[88]

If, in addition to the prospect, at the tactical level, of having thousands of their advancing tanks destroyed by anti-tank guided missiles (ATGM), the Soviets must also confront, at the intermediate level, the prospect that their reinforcements will have difficulty getting through because too many bridges have been destroyed by accurate nonnuclear missiles, all this may be sufficient to deter the Soviet leaders from launching an invasion into Western Europe in the first place.[89]

For a successful invasion the Soviets require that reserves be available to sustain and exploit the momentum of the initial attack. Interdiction of the second echelon and other reserves, together with denial of logistical support, could deny the Soviets their objectives. What is significant, from a retributive perspective, is that well-placed warheads could disrupt operations without destroying follow-on forces. It may be possible to avoid the mass destruction of follow-on troops (which would not be possible if nuclear weapons were used) if we can instead use precision-guided nonnuclear munitions to destroy bridges, other key travel points, and logistical support vehicles.

In short, intermediate nonnuclear strikes against rear-echelon targets would be designed not to destroy mass numbers of soldiers, but to destroy the tempo of the invasion. If a successful Soviet invasion depends on both mass and timing, the denial of victory can be achieved as well by temporary delay and disruption (by throwing off the tempo of the combined operations) as by attrition (the destruction of combatants). The West can cause an attack to come unhinged by putting obstacles in the way of reinforcements, resupply, and synchronized combined arms co-ordination.[90]

Ultimately, if these countercombatant shorter-range intermediate-level attacks fail to halt Soviet advances, longer-range attacks could be used to weaken the Soviet means of political control and coerce Soviet leaders into terminating aggression by inflicting heavy losses on the KGB border police, the MVD (internal security) forces, and the forces that guard the border with China. Since Pershing II missiles, if properly located, can be six to ten minutes away from significant military and political targets in the Western USSR (including Moscow), they may quickly provide the next step on the escalatory ladder if the Soviets should be successful in breaking through the front battle lines. If in the midst of impairment of Soviet means of political control, there emerge popular uprisings of disaffected groups in greater Russia, significant numbers of Soviet forces will be tied down in internal struggles— perhaps the gravest danger of all in the eyes of Soviet leaders.[91]

If all proportionate retaliatory responses fail to stop Soviet aggression, retributive policy would of course seek, in the name of justice, to destroy the most culpable group, the leadership. Ideally, they would be "executed" by strikes on their bunkers with powerful shaped conventional charges capable of digging into hardened sites. I say *ideally* because the permissibility of an attack on the leadership depends, as I pointed out above, on the expected collateral damage to civilian populations.

The well-known Soviet civil defense and evacuation plans might in fact work in favor of forms of attack directed at destroying, or at least impairing, the Soviet state: Soviet plans for passive defense—assuming they separate the population from the leadership in such a way as to allow for discriminatory attacks—might enable the West to hold down Soviet civilian casualties as it attacked underground bunkers believed to house government officials and security forces.[92]

In addition to attacking sites believed to be occupied by the leadership and its instruments of political control, strikes could be directed against transmission belts of communication from the center to the regions, so that even if the leadership survived the attack, they would emerge from their shelters to confront a capital cut off from the rest of the country—a situation in which their means of control would be significantly degraded; if communication links were severed with the rest of the country, they might face a de facto decentralized society.[93]

The declared Western objective would be to use precision-guided conventional weapons to destroy the Soviet leadership, or at least isolate it from the great non-Russian "minority" peoples who have been traditionally discouraged from seeking independence and who have no great love for the Soviet leadership.[94] The Soviet leaders would have to ask themselves whether they were willing to risk retaliation that *might* create a postwar world in which, even if most high Soviet officials survived attacks on their bunkers, the central government was unable to restore the Soviet empire.

Thus, on the intermediate level, a retributive strategy would involve the development of a capacity for measured retaliation and a targeting plan capable of deterring or halting Soviet aggression. The knowledge that the West, even though denuclearized, had a conventional military technology capable of threatening its most valued assets—the means of political control and ultimately the Soviet leadership itself—might be sufficient to discourage the Soviets (no matter how aggressive the leadership) from undertaking an invasion of Western Europe.

Strategic Level

Technically speaking, strategic forces are those with a range of 3,500 miles or more—that is, forces capable of being delivered from the territory of the United States to targets within the Soviet Union. A nonnuclear intercontinental strategy would rest on a trend that "suggests that fundamental strategic objectives could be pursued with nonnuclear strikes against strategic targets, using technical means that, while not yet assembled, have already been revealed in their components."[95] That is, precision-guided conventional munitions can be carried to the other side of the globe by long-range delivery vehicles. With substantial improvements in the accuracy of delivery systems, such as the MX missile, and the capacity of shaped nonnuclear charges to dig deep within hardened sites, conventional warheads might usefully substitute for nuclear warheads on intercontinental ballistic missiles. If the Soviet Union decided to launch a nuclear attack on the United States, powerful conventional warheads could be delivered by precision-guided vehicles to valued military and political assets in the Soviet homeland—again with the leadership targeted in case all attempts at negotiated settlement fail. (To repeat: the leaders would be attacked only if all calls for negotiated settlement failed and if surgical attacks on them were possible.) The important point is that even without nuclear weapons, the United States could threaten highly valued noncivilian assets in the Soviet Union.

Summary

The general aim of a retributive policy would be to achieve the fundamental objective of nuclear defense policy—the protection of free institutions—by developing a countercombatant strategy that exploits advances in nonnuclear tactical, intermediate, and strategic weapons. Those committed to retributive principles would demand research that could determine the feasibility of making a transition to nonnuclear weapons. Over a decade ago Fred Ikle called for the exploration of nonnuclear weapons as a way to avoid countervalue (i.e., population) targeting without giving up deterrence:

> By taking advantage of modern technology, we should be able to escape the evil dilemma that the strategic forces on both sides must either be designed to kill people or else jeopardize the opponent's confidence in his deterrent. The potential accuracy of "smart" bombs and missiles and current choices in weapon effects could enable both sides to avoid the killing of vast millions and yet inflict assured destruction on military, industrial, and transportation assets—the sinews and muscles of the regime initiating war.[96]

The emerging new weapons have been described by some analysts as signaling a revolution in military technology:

> The political taboo against the use of nuclear weapons is very real, and exists for convincing reasons. Therefore the ability to destroy vital target systems efficiently and cheaply and with a modest force, without much by-product damage, and without nuclear weapons, is a capability of potentially revolutionary importance: probably the most important development since the A-bomb.[97]

Objections to a Retribution Policy

In addition to doubts about its technical feasibility, there are several other objections to the above proposal. A deontological moral point of view has been emphasized in this exposition of retributive policy, especially the just war concept as interpreted in retributivist terms. The moral appeal of such a policy—even if it proves technically feasible—will not be sufficient to convince the public and policymakers if other problems are not addressed, such as (1) a Soviet refusal to give up nuclear weapons, (2) crisis stability, and (3) affordability. Taking the point of view of an advocate of a retributive policy, I will briefly address the difficulties in each area.

Soviet Policy

There is evidence that the Soviets are receptive to a policy of increasing, if not complete, denuclearization. In terms of policy intentions, it can be argued that a retributive doctrine fits in well with current Soviet declaratory policy. A retributive policy does not call for large offensive forces capable of threatening Soviet territory: rather, it calls for the capability to punish aggression proportionally. The new Soviet emphasis on defensive defense is in keeping with the spirit of a retributive policy.

Although a retributivist might hope that U.S. denuclearization would lead to Soviet reciprocation—on the strategic as well as the theater level—a Soviet refusal to structure their forces to conform to retributive principles would not be taken as an indictment of retributive policy. The principles of culpability and proportionality are nonnegotiable: they are not conventions the adherence to which is contingent upon what the other side does.

Still, every effort could be made to encourage reciprocity by publicly declaring (1) our plan to use force only in response to Soviet aggression, and (2) our intention to respect the principles of culpability and proportionality in so far as possible by using, in the event of war, accurate nonnuclear counterforce weapons against Soviet military forces and support facilities, with the Soviet leadership held as a final target in case all attempts at a negotiated settlement of hostilities fail.

Again, even if the Soviet Union refused to renounce weapons of mass destruction and the targeting of urban–industrial centers, retributivists would not for that reason abandon their principles of restraint. As Bruce Russett states: "We ought to care about what happens to Soviet civilians even if the Soviet Union does not care what happens to ours."[98] Russett believes, however, that there is good reason to think that the Soviet government might reciprocate and seek to limit American and European civilian casualties. He points out that they have repeatedly declared that they are in a struggle with the capitalist governments, not the peoples of capitalist societies.[99] According to new Soviet thinking, this struggle is giving way to cooperation. In addition, as pointed out above, a nuclear attack on Western Europe or the United States would be counterproductive, not only because of the collateral damage (from fallout) to the Soviet Union and Eastern Europe, but because it would destroy much of the valuable natural resources and productive forces of these societies—something valued by any Marxist society, especially one as economically troubled as the USSR.

Stability

The transition to the new strategy—whether unilateral or bilateral—could be profoundly destabilizing. If the West were to move unilaterally toward a retributive strategy while the Soviet Union retained its arsenal of thermonuclear weapons, this might encourage a renewal of Soviet adventurism throughout the world, especially against Western Europe. The standard objection to unilateral *nuclear* disarmament (understood as the elimination of weapons of mass destruction) is that the Soviet Union would be able to blackmail the United States, threatening to destroy selected North American cities should the United States attempt conventional intervention to save NATO countries. On this view, the Soviet Union might gamble that it could take Western Europe without actually having to use any nuclear weapons against either Western Europe or United States, simply by threatening to do to the West what the West could no longer do to the Soviet Union: namely, inflict assured destruction. That is, it could be argued that the force imbalance would make Soviet aggression more probable.

Obviously, the West—without an arsenal of nuclear weapons—could not match a nuclear-armed Soviet Union in the capacity for mass destruction. Stability and the mutual capacity for mass destruction are not, however, necessarily equivalent. To repeat a point made above: the assumption behind a retributive strategy is that a credible threat to the Soviet leadership's military forces or its means of political domination is as good as any kind of nuclear threat.

Of course, even if the Soviet Union reciprocated and adopted a nonnuclear strategy, it is not clear that the problem of stability would be solved. Again, stability should not be equated with equivalence of forces. Successful efforts to reduce the horror of Soviet–American war might be profoundly destabilizing if they made armed conflict more tolerable, thus reducing the inhibitions against starting a war. If the balance of nuclear terror has kept the peace between the superpowers for over forty years, isn't the "humanization" of war likely to degrade this terrifying but stable order? Would it not be better to live with the small risk of nuclear war and its indiscriminate slaughter than to live without the fear of nuclear holocaust but with a substantially greater danger of world war? This is no doubt a powerful argument for both sides' retaining world-threatening forces: namely, that war between nations with weapons of mass destruction promises horrors that make a Soviet–American armed conflict irrational and therefore unlikely.

The defender of a retributive strategy could respond that the enormous casualties of a conventional conflict between the United States and the Soviet Union—even if limited to combatants—would be of significant deterrent value by themselves. Both sides realize the enormous power of modern conventional weapons: they would not easily risk the destruction that such weapons could inflict on their respective assets.

Moreover, as we have observed, if Soviet leaders and their means of domination are both targets of a countercombatant strategy, they will have a great incentive not to attack Western Europe or the United States. Although it would be impossible to completely destroy the Red Army and the internal police in retaliation for an attack on the U.S. homeland, it might be possible to threaten these valued assets enough to create doubt in the minds of the Soviet leadership that their remaining forces would be sufficient to repress internal resistance, to control dissident Soviet republics, or to appropriate Western Europe as a recovery base.

In addition, the possession of an effective counterforce (battlefield and intermediate) deterrent by NATO could strengthen rather than weaken the credibility of the Alliance's retaliatory threats. For example, by modernizing its conventional forces, including its ground armies, NATO could abandon the dangerous nuclear first-use option, a threat that if acted upon, would surely bring about devastating nuclear retaliation.

The retributivist is concerned to achieve a stable deterrent based on counterforce arsenals so constructed that they fit in with the principles of culpability and proportionality. But the retributivist qua retributivist will refuse to subordinate the requirements of justice to those of deterrence efficacy—even if refusing to do so slightly increases the chances of war. The retributivist will not trade justice for efficacious deterrence purchased through immoral nuclear threats. The fact is that deterrence—whether nuclear or nonnuclear—may fail. The question is, what *action* policy best fits the requirements of justice?

It should be remembered that in choosing a strategic policy, it may be necessary to decide which is more important: deterrence or damage-limitation. Retributivists give priority to the latter because they believe it is crucial to have a morally defensible answer to the question of what we are to do if deterrence fails. If the proposed policy was officially accepted and deterrence failed, the result is likely to be (given the limited nature of the weapons themselves) *less* indiscriminate slaughter and *less* harm to noncombatants in neutral as well as belligerent nations.

Cost

Lying behind NATO's doctrine of first use and the proliferation of nuclear weapons in the West is, of course, the fact that compared with (human and mechanical) conventional forces, "traditional" nuclear weapons are a relatively inexpensive path to military security. If it requires expensive conventional (or a costly new generation of nuclear) weapons and a significant increase in troop strength to achieve the objectives of a retributive strategy, this policy proposal might appear prohibitively expensive. No matter how morally desirable, a policy that threatens to bankrupt the West will be rejected.

If the new forces required were, for example, a hundred times more expensive than current nuclear forces, the retributive option would appear impractical, even if technically feasible. All that can be said in advance is this: we should face the alternatives squarely. Should we be willing to spend substantially more to get out from under a strategy of (in effect if not in intention) indiscriminate slaughter, which threatens the planet in ways we never want to discover? Carl Builder, in referring to the first- and second-generation nuclear forces, puts it this way:

> Nuclear weapons have always been recognized as the cheap way to military power, but the cost is now being reckoned in survival of societies, not just in money spent on arms. Achieving a specific military objective at say five times the cost, but without having to resort to nuclear weapons, is almost certain to be a welcome bargain to most political leaders at the brink of nuclear war.[100]

The Case for a Retribution Policy

A counterforce strategy based on the concept of retribution, while retaining the aim of deterrence, affirms as more fundamental an objective that, retributivists believe, eludes contemporary nuclear deterrence doctrines: justice. In the event that deterrence fails, a retributive policy calls for a strategy and system of forces capable of inflicting proportionate punishment on the agents of aggression. Although supporters of a retributive policy will have to acknowledge that this policy involves significant risks, they can point out that the same is true of nuclear deterrence.

The arguments for a retributive policy can be summarized as follows.

1. The policy objective—retribution—is morally superior to pure deterrence and pure defense in its concern to achieve a just response, demanding that retaliation satisfy the requirements of culpability and proportionality. It is the only military option that is continuous with the just war tradition.

2. A counterforce strategy based on a concept of retribution is more credible as a war-fighting strategy than either a countervailing or a prevailing (nuclear) strategy. It offers the possibility of meaningful discrimination and less destruction. Even if we grant that a nuclear war can be kept limited and terminated within a short period, the consequences of current nuclear weapons—including blast, heat, and fallout—will be devastating to civilians in all societies attacked, and even to neutral nations affected by radioactive fallout. It must be remembered that countervailing and prevailing strategies call for the retention of nuclear weapons capable of destroying cities in order to coerce termination of war. To the extent that war is fought with nonnuclear weapons with accurate and limited destructive force, it will be possible to conduct the conflict along traditional military lines. With advances in precision targeting, and with low-yield weapons, it will be possible to minimize collateral damage to civilians.

3. It offers a meaningful alternative to MAD. No matter how hard nuclear deterrence strategies—strategies based on threats—try on paper to avoid the massive response of MAD, they will ultimately, as a result of escalation, be indistinguishable from a strategy of assured destruction. The very idea of an escalation ladder, which requires a capacity to move from tactical to city-busting nuclear retaliation, opens the door to an uncontrolled ("spasm") nuclear war.

4. A retributive policy implemented by the use of precision weapons is a more realistic path to protection of civilians than the enormously expensive and morally dubious strategic defense initiative. The technologies it requires are not as demanding or as exotic as those of SDI. They amount to a further refinement of existing war-fighting technologies. Instead of pursuing the illusion of comprehensive population defense, it pursues the real possibility of population avoidance in targeting and weapons development.

5. In threatening assets highly valued by Soviet leaders—their means of coercion and themselves—while providing weapons that can discriminate in a far more precise way than the most accurate nuclear forces, retributive policy provides a form of deterrence consistent with justice: it gives us a doctrine of just deterrence. The only permissible threats under retribution are ones directed at the agents of harm and those who are culpable. To achieve deterrence, retributive policy re-

fuses to threaten mass murder. The point is that immoral nuclear threats are not necessary in order to satisfy the requirements of deterrence.

6. Recognizing the fallibility of its deterrent component, a retributive strategy provides a rational and ethically acceptable answer to the question of what the West should do if deterrence fails. Indeed, the point of retributive policy is to have a morally defensible retaliation plan in the event that deterrence fails.

7. The adoption of this strategy, even unilaterally, provides a way of avoiding the environmental and climatic catastrophe that would result from even a limited exchange with existing nuclear arsenals. Given Soviet awareness of the counterproductive nature of a nuclear war fought with weapons of mass destruction—the boomerang effect— the Soviet leaders have a great incentive not to attack us with weapons that would not only poison the environment they breathe, but destroy valuable resources they need.

8. The adoption by the United States and NATO of a countercombatant strategy would provide a powerful incentive for Soviet moves in the same direction. With the elimination of weapons of mass destruction from the U.S. arsenal, the Soviets also have a good reason to reduce radically, if not eliminate, their indiscriminate nuclear forces. Moreover, if they were convinced that conventional forces could provide them with sufficient security—and a U.S. transition to such a system would be a compelling example—they might eventually dismantle their arsenal of weapons of mass destruction. In fact, there is evidence that the Soviets are moving away from the nuclear option toward more reliance on conventional weapons.[101]

The idea of denuclearizing U.S. military forces may seem like a radical proposal. There are, however, those who do not think that it is radical enough and who call for a complete demilitarization of U.S. defense policy. I examine this nonmilitary option in the next chapter.

CHAPTER SEVEN

Rehabilitation Policy:
Security Through Nonviolent Prevention and Correction

In formulating nuclear weapons policy options, I have made use of concepts borrowed from domestic correction theory—deterrence, social defense, and retribution—as if I were developing in each case, by way of extended analogy, an international version of the domestic theory. A theory of criminal correction that may not seem to lend itself to such analogical extension is rehabilitation. *Prima facie* it is not clear how this concept can be applied to nuclear weapons policy. After all, what would it mean to rehabilitate a nuclear-armed adversary?

To get an idea of how we might transfer the concept of rehabilitation from the domestic to the international level, we must first review what the domestic theory of rehabilitation asserts. It should be recalled that it is concerned with both prevention and correction. The *preventive* aim of rehabilitation is to remove the circumstances that generate criminal intentions and criminal behavior. In case prevention fails, the *corrective* goal is to use humane (nonviolent) methods to help offenders fit back into law-abiding society. The assumption underlying the theory of rehabilitation is that criminal behavior is a consequence of particular, alterable conditions. In sum, the doctrine holds that criminal behavior can be extinguished through two kinds of reforms: (1) measures that eliminate the external conditions that provoke or reward crime, and (2) measures that remold or re-form offenders so that they change their behavior and, if possible, their thinking. The preventive side cannot be neglected, because corrective efforts are doomed to failure if the environmental factors that provoke and reinforce criminal behavior remain unchanged. If, for example, an impoverished and unemployed high school drop-out who committed a robbery to feed his family is sent through a rehabilitation program, only to be returned to a jobless, impoverished environment, then—even if his thinking and behavior are temporarily reshaped within the correctional institution—the unchanged circumstances of poverty and unemployment may again induce him to commit new criminal acts.

Globalizing the Concept of Rehabilitation

A defense strategy based upon rehabilitation would involve a combination of preventive and corrective measures designed to extinguish the sources of armed aggression and to reinforce lawful national behavior. More specifically, applied to nuclear weapons policy, the concept of rehabilitation would translate into a program of international economic reconstruction, creative diplomacy, military disarmament, Soviet–American cooperation, pursuit of various methods for nonviolent conflict resolution, and adoption of a strategy of civilian-based defense. The objectives of a policy of rehabilitation would be (1) to eliminate the circumstances conducive to aggression and war, and (2)—in case these preventive measures fail—to find nonmilitary methods of correction that will persuade or nonviolently coerce a "criminal" nation (i.e., aggressor) to fit back into a civilized international community.

The ethical foundation of this policy is both utilitarian and Kantian. The utilitarian claim is that a nonviolent defense strategy is likely to produce fewer casualties and less suffering, as well as less destruction to valued nonhuman resources (animal and plant life, productive farmland, factories, and the environment in general) than a military strategy. The Kantian dimension of this policy is manifest in the corrective phase, in which enemy soldiers are, in so far as possible, to be treated as autonomous moral agents (i.e., persons in Kant's sense).

Preventive Measures

The program of prevention would involve doing all that is possible—through nonviolent measures—to eliminate the conditions that could lead to a Soviet–American conflict. The term *prevention*, as it is used here, is closer to its use in a therapeutic context (the prevention of disease through appropriate measures) than to its use in a deterrence context (e.g., the prevention of crime through punitive threats). On this view, since nuclear weapons are symptomatic of a disorder, their abolition will not by itself cure the pathological condition that gives rise to them.[1] Nuclear weapons might be interpreted as the prime symptom of the war-disease, whose prevention lies in the elimination of war-generating circumstances. Although there may be no permanent cure for the disease, it may be possible to perform "surgery" that will, at the least, limit its spread.[2]

Conditions that breed revolution are one possible cause of nuclear conflict. By drawing the superpowers into a possible face-to-face confrontation, revolutions (for instance, in Central America) could escalate into nuclear conflicts. It is therefore crucial to prevent, so far as possible, such armed struggles in all regions at all levels of violence. We might begin by excising elements that contribute to violent conflict, by, for example, attacking poverty through material aid to societies whose economic conditions serve as breeding grounds for civil war and revolution. Assistance with economic development might help contain and reduce violent conflict in the third world.[3]

Not only poverty and hunger but also gross political injustice—the powerlessness of people in undeveloped societies or in subnational groups such as the Palestinians—contribute to revolutionary violence and terrorism. So long as governments imprison dissenters, deny their citizens basic freedoms, and torture opponents of the regime, there will be a motivation for armed insurrection. Thus, efforts must also be made to eliminate the political causes of violent conflict.

In sum, a policy of rehabilitation would require that we go to the root of conflict by eliminating all the conditions that stimulate violence and war. The policy would begin with the recognition that many armed conflicts, especially civil wars, are the product of economic and political powerlessness. Liberation movements would receive nonmilitary support from the United States, including training in techniques of non-violent resistance. This country could also, by putting diplomatic and economic pressure on oppressive regimes to make economic and political changes, use its influence and resources to empower oppressed classes.[4] Such actions might reverse the perception of the United States as an imperialistic and extractive power—that is, as a nation that exploits undeveloped countries without regard to the economic or political well-being of their populations. It would also correct the impression that the United States is always willing to aid in the repression of underclasses as long as the regime is right-wing and anti-communist (e.g., Marcos in the Philippines, the Somozas in Nicaragua), which has contributed to the tendency of insurrectionary movements to turn to the Soviet Union for military aid in order to offset U.S. support for a reactionary dictatorship.

This approach will be enhanced, of course, if the Soviet Union keeps its promise not to provide military aid to third-world insurrectionary movements. The cause of peace will be further enhanced if both nations avoid military intervention (direct or indirect, through surrogates) in the affairs of other nations—if both stop providing weapons and military support to every movement that is sympathetic to its ideology. The Soviet Union's current commitment to avoid providing military aid to third-world revolutionary movements could be strengthened if we show the same kind of commitment.

The relevance of such changes in foreign policy to nuclear defense policy is this: one way to avert nuclear war is for the United States and the Soviet Union to refuse to provide military support for a proxy that faces a proxy of the other (e.g., South Vietnam against North Vietnam), because such wars may tempt one side to introduce nuclear weapons as a way of quickly defeating the other side (an option considered by the United States in both the Korean and the Vietnam wars).[5]

Of course, the danger of a Soviet–American war cannot be prevented simply by avoiding military entanglements in the third world—that is, by staying out of conflicts that might lead to a nuclear confrontation with the Soviet Union. The temptation to use nuclear weapons may also occur in a direct conventional confrontation between the superpowers (e.g., a war between NATO and the Soviet forces) if, in the course of the conflict, either power sees that it cannot win at the conventional level.

Or, in an international crisis, if Soviet leaders believe that nuclear war is imminent, they may conclude that victory depends upon a preemptive nuclear attack. The point, which bears repeating, is this: so long as each side has nuclear weapons aimed at the other, any sudden increase in tensions—any unexpected international incident—could put each nation on nuclear alert status, perhaps to the point of a changeover from negative to positive control of nuclear forces, in which case the danger of inadvertent nuclear war will increase.

One obvious way to eliminate any Soviet motivation to deliver a preemptive nuclear strike is to remove the military forces that the Soviets perceive as threatening to their security. The fact that the United States has accurate nuclear forces that, in a crisis, might be used to destroy Soviet nuclear forces may tempt the Soviet Union, in a crisis, to launch a preemptive attack. No such temptation would exist if we removed the stimulus. Unilateral nuclear disarmament by the United States and NATO powers would be a radical preventive measure that would void any Soviet rationale for using nuclear weapons against the United States or its allies. This unilateral act of prevention—admittedly a kind of radical self-surgery—would remove a major source of Soviet insecurity.

The removal of Western nuclear weapons would also eliminate the danger of accidental nuclear war, in so far as fear of a first strike disposes both sides to place their forces on a hair trigger and creates a situation that could all too easily push one side toward an act of "retaliation" in response to a false warning of a nuclear attack. That is, possession of nuclear weapons appears to make a nuclear attack (whether deliberate or accidental) more, rather than less, likely. In effect, unilateral nuclear disarmament (and the elimination of all strategic delivery systems) would remove the threat of accidental nuclear warfare. If only one side was to eliminate its potential for a first strike by eliminating its nuclear forces and all strategic delivery vehicles (ICBMs, submarines, bombers), the world would be rid of the possibility of an American–Soviet *exchange* of thousands of nuclear warheads.

Is it unlikely that the Soviet Union would use nuclear weapons against a disarmed West? The Soviets would realize that such a nuclear attack on an unarmed nation would generate international condemnation, carrying with it the likelihood of diplomatic and economic sanctions throughout the world.[6] The international costs would be very high. Whether new Soviet thinking is for real or not, the Soviet Union would have nothing to gain from an unprovoked use of nuclear weapons.

Even if new hard-line Soviet leaders were indifferent to world opinion and global sanctions, it would—to repeat a point made in Chapter Six—be counterproductive for the Soviets to reduce the economic riches of the United States and/or Western Europe to irradiated ruins. Marxist theory calls for the preservation of all productive forces and natural resources; Soviet pragmatism calls for the exploitation of the achievements of Western industrial and technological progress.

Moreover, since the winds usually move from west to east, fallout from a nuclear attack on Western Europe would probably adversely affect the Soviet Union.[7] This means that even the unilateral use of nuclear weapons could have a significant destructive impact on the environment of the Soviet Union. Thus, Soviet leaders would have to deal not only with the loss of the Western economic productive forces and resources, but most probably with the contamination of their own people, water supply, farm land, and food. The effect would be like a giant western Chernobyl.

If, despite all this, the Soviet Union decided to engage in a limited attack on the United States or its allies—selective strikes for the purpose of intimidation and coercion (in the event that nuclear threats alone did not achieve its purposes)—civil defense planning in the West might provide significant protection and save thousands of lives. Civil defense measures are likely to be effective in the case of limited nuclear strikes.[8]

Soviet self-interest in keeping nuclear attacks small (in order to preserve valuable resources and minimize worldwide fallout) would also contribute to the protective value of a civil defense program in a society without nuclear arms. It really would be possible for a denuclearized nation—provided it had an adequate civil defense program and economic recovery plans—to rehabilitate itself after a limited nuclear attack.

The utility of civil defense in a nonnuclear United States should be contrasted with the relative fruitlessness of civil defense preparations in a U.S. society whose policy calls for the readiness to engage in a nuclear exchange. The latter may have to deal with the incredible devastation and fallout caused by thousands of warheads. Meaningful recovery would not be possible after such an attack. In addition, massive civil defense preparations by a United States with an enormous arsenal of counterforce weapons may look like part of a plan designed to limit damage to the U.S. homeland after a first strike on the USSR's nuclear forces. That is, from the perspective of Soviet leaders, such preparations appear aggressive, not defensive.[9]

Although under a rehabilitation policy the United States would not make its nuclear disarmament plans contingent upon Soviet reciprocation, the United States could encourage Soviet reciprocity by allowing on-site inspection, permitting the naturally suspicious Soviets to verify that nuclear disarmament was a reality. Since the Soviets have frequently asserted that they are prepared to get rid of all their nuclear weapons[10]—they are officially committed to nuclear disarmament—the dismantling of the U.S. nuclear arsenal would put enormous world pressure on them to keep their word. Therefore, an open and bold act of unilateral disarmament offers a real possibility of ending the nuclear arms race.

Moreover, if the two major nuclear powers set this example, the smaller nuclear powers—if convinced that their national security needs could still be met—might be influenced to imitate them. The United States and the Soviet Union could exert moral and economic pressure on the remaining nuclear powers to abolish these weapons. Clearly, if the superpowers led the move toward denuclearization, their condemnation of nuclear proliferation would gain moral force.

As pointed out above, the elimination of nuclear weapons by both sides will not, by itself, remove all tension between the Soviet Union and the United States. It has been said that nations do not distrust each other because they are armed: rather, they are armed because they distrust each other.[11] In the case of nuclear weapons, this may not be entirely true. Although nuclear weapons have not been the cause of Soviet–American tensions, it is reasonable to conclude that the mutual possession of weapons of mass destruction aggravates existing tensions and significantly contributes to Soviet–American mistrust and paranoia (e.g., the fear of a first strike).

With the elimination of these weapons (if only by the West), assuming we also pursue conciliatory measures, there is no reason why Soviet–American tensions cannot be significantly reduced, if not eliminated. We are just discovering that we are not eternally bound to be enemies. During World War II, any suggestion that the hatred between the United States and Japan would shortly after the war give way to friendly relations would have been dismissed as preposterous. Recent changes in the Soviet Union bode well for a new, friendly relationship. As long, however, as one side has nuclear weapons aimed at the other, the relationship will always be somewhat strained.

We should begin by giving the Soviets the benefit of the doubt and taking seriously their proposals for disarmament and cooperation. We should initiate projects that will make friendly relations more rewarding than hostile ones. Indeed, the Soviet Union may no longer need to be persuaded that keeping the peace is better for its interests than resorting to aggression. A rehabilitation policy would emphasize the importance of providing greatly expanded positive peaceful incentives, rather than relying largely on negative military incentives (that is, threats) to convince the Soviets that the tangible benefits of peace outweigh any anticipated benefits of aggression.[12] We should encourage and reward their announced repudiation of violence as an instrument of national policy and their proclaimed intention to develop a strategy of defensive defense, perhaps by helping them, in any way we can, to make a successful transition to a productive economy in which their military plays a diminishing role.

Some have argued that the Soviets will never give up their nuclear arsenal because, given their third-world economy, such weaponry is the only thing that makes them a superpower. If so, we need to help them to become a second- if not a first-world economy. We need to convince them, if they need convincing, that they can significantly improve their economy only if they radically reduce their investment in the military sector. If the Western military threat to their security is removed, we will provide Soviet political leaders with the incentive they need for such a transformation. Japan, of course, provides a powerful example of what can be achieved when a nation's economy is not drained by an arms race.

We can, in addition, begin to multiply the number of Soviet–American cooperative projects in science, the arts, medicine, and the exploration of space. Cultural, scientific, and educational exchanges— as well as increased trade—could be increased to further improve Soviet–American relations. In addition, both societies have a common interest in seeking ways of preserving the integrity of the biosphere and helping to solve the problem of world hunger.

Beyond these cooperative enterprises, a rehabilitation policy would place a new emphasis on the art of diplomacy. Negotiation theory could be given the detailed attention previously reserved for weapons development. Diplomats would be trained in techniques designed to resolve conflicts through creative bargaining—through sophisticated negotiation rather than through the threat and use of force. This would require that those who deal with Soviet representatives know the Russian language and understand the history, government, and cultures of the Soviet Union. To avoid misunderstandings they need to be masters of the nuances of Soviet thinking and speech, to comprehend what is peculiar about the Soviet psyche. Indeed, the attempt to understand the Soviets in their own terms, instead of judging them in terms of U.S. standards and values, might contribute substantially to the prevention of conflict.

Corrective Measures

Critics will respond that although unilateral nuclear disarmament and a new emphasis on cooperation might remove any Soviet motive for a nuclear attack on the United States, it will not provide the Soviets with a sufficient motive to eliminate their nuclear forces or to give up their plans for world domination. Some conservatives see Soviet plans for world domination as merely on hold.

Soviet self-interest (avoiding the loss of devastated territories and possible adverse effects on their own society, etc.) would, of course, be a good reason for their refraining from nuclear attacks on other societies. But their pledge about nuclear disarmament, conservatives will contend, the Soviet leaders will not take very seriously, especially if reneging on their promise to disarm allows them to achieve a unilateral advantage. The effect of unilateral disarmament, it can be argued, will be to rekindle—not extinguish—the Soviet will to dominate the world. The Soviets would be able to use their superior military forces for blackmail and limitless expansion.

In sum, skeptical conservatives will argue that improved diplomacy, cultural exchanges, and economic aid are not going to change the fact that the Soviets have a global design. If the United States allowed the Soviet Union to become—by our default—the most militarily powerful nation on the planet, the USSR would have for the first time since the 1917 Bolshevik Revolution a free hand in realizing the objective of world domination. Thus, avoidance of nuclear war will be attained at the expense of liberty and independence: in exchange for nuclear peace in our time, conservatives warn, we will give up the security of our free institutions that we have won by a strategy of peace through strength.

In addition to presupposing a dated Cold War–view of the Soviet Union, this criticism appears to assume that such preventive measures as improved diplomacy, economic aid, proposals for Soviet–American cooperative projects, and the unilateral elimination of nuclear weapons would be accompanied by the abandonment of the defense of the nation. If that were the case, the rehabilitation program would be incomplete, because the corrective component would be missing. The theory of rehabilitation is concerned not only with removing, so far as possible, the conditions that breed aggression: it is also concerned with correcting any aggression that the preventive measures fail to eliminate. Recognizing that no system of prevention is perfect, it also calls for nonviolent measures designed to reform or reeducate aggressors. This requires a strategy designed to alter (assuming it still exists) the aggressive mind-set—or at least the aggressive behavior—of the Soviet Union. Thus, a commitment to nonviolence does not imply passivity in the face of aggression: in conjunction with a long-term goal of complete (conventional and nuclear) disarmament, it requires a plan for nonviolently defeating aggression.

In other words, any dismantling of military forces must be part of a project of transarmament, understood as the transition from a military to a nonmilitary defense of free institutions. *Transarmament* means two things: (1) the gradual abolition of military forces, and (2) the emergence of a nonviolent strategy of national defense involving new forms of combat and struggle. The most systematically developed proposal for a nonmilitary strategy is called *civilian-based defense* (CBD): defense by civilians (as distinct from armed personnel) using civilian means of struggle (nonviolent forms of resistance).[13]

Far from being passive in the face of aggression, CBD calls for struggle against and victory over any invader. Indeed, one of the foremost proponents of this strategy, Gene Sharp, is uncompromising, even in the face of a threat of nuclear attack:

> A prudent nonviolent position in the face of such threats would be to refuse to bow even to nuclear blackmail. Submission to a particular threat would likely be the beginning of a series with escalating demands, with no end in sight.
>
> . . . In order to reduce or eliminate nuclear threats and attacks from hostile ruthless states, it is essential in civilian-based defense that potential attackers be made aware that even those threats will not achieve their objectives.[14]

Therefore, in proposing the abolition of military forces and the renunciation of the use of violence, a nonviolent policy does not call for appeasement, nor does it assume that the threat of aggression will be extinguished solely as a result of a new foreign policy and the unilateral elimination of provocative instruments of war. Neither does it presuppose the essential goodness of human nature or the eternal good will of Soviet leaders. Although a policy of rehabilitation holds that the elimination of offensive military forces will remove any Soviet motive for a preemptive nuclear strike, it does not conclude that unilateral military disarmament, even if combined with creative diplomacy and offers to cooperate with the USSR, will necessarily prevent all Soviet aggression.

Thus, in addition to preventive measures, the policy of rehabilitation—at least as conceived here—would strengthen security by introducing a new defense strategy. Specifically, a policy of rehabilitation would call for a plan of nonviolent resistance designed to send an assertive message: namely, that the nation is prepared to thwart the will of any aggressor, no matter how powerful its military forces happen to be. Moreover, it would back this warning with systematic and thorough training of its citizens in tactics designed to frustrate any nation that decides to invade and to occupy the society. Hence, a policy of rehabilitation can accommodate even the most cynical view of Soviet "new thinking" as a charade that buys time and conceals a Soviet plan to return later to aggressive expansion.

How can a nation committed to nonviolence effectively correct or reeducate a militarily powerful nation bent on occupying or coercing it? To answer this we must first understand that civilian-based defense calls into question two assumptions that have shaped our reliance on military power for national security: (1) that military power alone provides a nation with the power to defend itself against aggression, and (2) that military occupation necessarily gives the armed invader political control of the occupied country.[15]

Far from providing a real capacity to defend the homeland, Gene Sharp argues, military forces, especially nuclear weapons, threaten to bring about the annihilation of the society that possesses this destructive power: instead of guaranteeing national security, such forces create national insecurity.[16] And military occupation does not automatically provide political control because, according to Sharp, all political power is based on the cooperation and obedience of the subjects and the institutions of society.[17] This means that the exercise of power always depends on the consent of the ruled, who can, by withdrawing that consent, control and even extinguish the power of the ruler. (Recent events in Eastern Europe dramatically illustrate the power of mass nonviolent opposition.) This, on Sharp's view, is the revolutionary insight of civilian-based defense: that it is impossible to govern if cooperation and obedience are withdrawn.[18] The transformative insight is that power derives not, as so many people believe, from the barrel of a gun, but from the consent or acquiescence of the governed.[19] Sharp believes that this insight may have political consequences wider and deeper than the idea of releasing power from the atom.[20] Even the renowned professional nuclear strategist Thomas Schelling is sympathetic to the radical thesis that the potential of nonviolence "could be as important as that of nuclear fission."[21]

According to the theory of civilian-based resistance, it is possible for whole societies to apply this revolutionary insight for the purpose of nonviolently defeating a military invasion and occupation. Civilian-based defense shrewdly declines to meet the military aggressor on its own terms, where it is strongest, but shifts the ground of battle and the "weapons" themselves to a domain where the defender is strongest. By a disciplined refusal to acknowledge and accept alien authority, civilian-based defense makes use of what Sharp calls "political jiu-jitsu": the aggressor's "greater power is made ineffective and turned to its own disadvantage."[22] That is, nonviolent resistance uses the opponent's strength to upset its balance and contribute to its own defeat. The invading power is exposed to the world as a nation dependent upon and willing to use naked, brutal violence against nonviolent human beings—a perception that may increase the number of people inside and outside the invaded society who condemn and work to defeat the invader; in fact, it may eventually lead the occupying forces themselves to mutiny.

The purely defensive goal of civilian-based resistance is to deny the attacker its objectives, without resorting to any armed retaliation or physical intimidation. The objective is to spoil the spoils of war, depriving the aggressor of its anticipated fruits of victory.[23] Put more positively, CBD aims at protecting and preserving a country's independence and its people's lives, freedoms, and opportunities for future development.[24]

Nonviolent Strategies for Correcting Aggressors

The corrective instrument of civilian-based defense is nonviolent action: the use of nonviolent techniques to control, combat, and extinguish the opponent's sources of oppressive power. Civilian forms of struggle—social, economic, political, and psychological—are used to wage widespread noncooperation and to provide massive public defiance. In addition, every effort is made to subvert the loyalty of the aggressor's troops and functionaries and to encourage their unreliability in carrying out orders, even to the point of securing their conversion to the victim's viewpoint.[25]

This kind of resistance is based on advanced preparations, planning, and training. Since its agents are the whole civilian population, it requires, to some extent, the training of all citizens. In order for civilian-based defense to work, citizens *as a whole* must have both the training (i.e., the know-how) and the will (i.e., the resolve) to defend their society.[26] This strategy demands, therefore, much more of ordinary citizens than does nuclear deterrence, strategic defense, or nonnuclear retribution: it demands (of ordinary citizens) preparation, discipline, courage, and the capacity to endure suffering. In effect, the strategy transforms citizens into unarmed combatants. To have the motivation to endure in such a struggle, citizens must find the system they are defending preferable to any regime likely to be imposed by invaders or usurpers: they must perceive the invader as threatening to destroy things of ultimate value, such as individual freedom and collective self-determination. That is, the strategy presupposes that the society is in some meaningful sense a democracy worth defending.

Preparations for nonviolent resistance would be initiated when negotiated resolution of a conflict broke down. In the face of an impasse, CBD provides an alternative to imposing one's will on the enemy through violence or the threat of violence. In the face of an enemy's attempt to resolve the conflict by violently or coercively imposing its will, CBD provides an alternative to capitulation. Nonviolent national defense, it must be emphasized, is a strategy designed to halt aggression—not to appease the aggressor or give in to its demands. In the face of armed invasion and occupation, nonviolent resistance threatens an aggressor with (1) acts of omission (refusal to perform acts people are normally expected to perform by law or custom); (2) acts of commission (performance of acts people do not usually perform); and (3) a combination of the two.[27]

Sharp has identified 198 methods of nonviolent action, which he classifies under three headings.

1. Methods of nonviolent protest and persuasion. These are mainly symbolic acts designed to express dissent, to change opinions, or both: for example, parades, marches, teach-ins, personal conversations with occupying forces, vigils, pilgrimages, picketing, protest meetings, protest literature, renouncing honors.[28]

2. Methods of nonviolent noncooperation. These acts present the opponent with difficulties in maintaining the normal efficiency and operation of the occupied society. The nonviolent group withdraws or withholds social, economic, or political cooperation. This includes three subcategories: (a) social noncooperation (e.g., ostracism: treating occupying forces as if they did not exist by looking past them or refusing to speak to them); (b) economic noncooperation (e.g., economic boycotts, strikes by industrial workers); and (c) political noncooperation (e.g., strikes by government workers, giving speeches or distributing literature advocating resistance to an illegitimate government).[29]

3. *Methods of nonviolent intervention.* These methods involve nonviolent interference—positive or negative—with an imposed system. The means may be psychological, designed to win sympathy (e.g., hunger strikes in a city square); economic (e.g., stay-in strikes in which workers halt work but refuse to leave the workplace); or political (civil disobedience outside government offices, sit-ins in government offices, or the establishment of a parallel government).[30]

These latter actions, which involve physical confrontation with the opponent, are most effective when large masses of people engage in them over widely distributed areas of the country. Parallel government is said to exist when the resistance movement creates a new government and carries out programs of its own in defiance of the invader and in anticipation of the collapse of the occupation regime. Before the opposition can reach this stage, the invader will have to be significantly weakened. To work, the parallel government must have the support and the allegiance of the immense majority of the population.[31]

Civilian-based defense is similar to military defense in that it calls for strategic thinking and planning toward the objective of victory over the enemy or, short of that, the denial of the enemy's objectives. Specifically, it calls for two strategies—one for the initial period and one for the long run.

Initial Strategies

If, despite nonviolent preventive measures and a public declaration of intention to resist all attempts at occupation, an aggressor nevertheless decides to invade, the enemy forces will meet no armed resistance from a nation committed to civilian-based defense. From a traditional military perspective, such a "successful" invasion would be interpreted as a defeat for the nation so occupied. From the viewpoint of nonviolent national defense, however, the invasion is only the starting point of active resistance aimed at preserving the nation's social, cultural, and political institutions.[32] Defense is no longer conceived as the capacity to inflict military force but as the capacity to repel it.[33] Nonviolent national defense is defense without offense: it is a truly nonprovocative defense. In contrast to nuclear and conventional strategies, CBD offers a way to defend the homeland without destroying it or that of the aggressor. It has this much in common with strategic defense.

It differs from strategic defense in refusing to place its confidence in a technological solution to the problem of security. Advocates of CBD point out that with advances in military technology (such as air power and rocketry), even nations with heavily guarded borders can no longer prevent the penetration of their territory by aggressors.[34] There is no impenetrable Maginot Line that can guarantee the security of territorial borders. Long-range stealthy delivery systems enable one nation to penetrate another's borders, despite the best military defense of the latter. The question is no longer one of how to prevent the violation of one's borders but how to deal with an enemy who can penetrate one's territory.

An enemy that did not have to worry about retaliatory weapons would not need to precede an invasion with air or missile attacks designed to soften up the territory: it could simply send troops to the areas it intended to dominate or exploit. There would be no *physical* costs involved in invading and occupying the adversary's society. The invaders would, however, immediately begin to experience *psychological* costs.

In the beginning stages of an invasion, the aim of civilian-based resistance would be to shock the invaders into rethinking their actions and considering retreat. The plan behind nonviolent national defense is to arrange things so that invading enemy forces will in effect be walking into an ambush.[35] The initial strategies of civilian resistance policy might consist of communication and warning to the attacker, nonviolent blitzkrieg, and direct intervention and obstruction. These initial strategies are designed both to communicate to all concerned that the attack will be met by determined resistance and to accustom the home population from the start to active participation in the defense struggle.[36]

1. Communication and warning involve the use of words and actions to convey the message that a vigorous and powerful civilian struggle will be waged.[37] The tools include letters, leaflets, radio and television broadcasts, newspapers, posters, banners, and messages and slogans painted on walls.[38] The messages to be communicated (directed at occupying forces, the civilian population of the aggressor nation, and the world as well as the invasion forces and their leaders) include a statement of the issues at stake, the principles and practices of the attacked society, the unjust objectives of the aggressor, and the importance of the cessation of the attack.[39] It is also important to communicate to the invading army that the resisting population will try to defeat the aggression and defend their society without threatening the lives and the personal safety of the attacking forces.[40] Although this initial strategy appears mild, in reality, Sharp reminds us, it is mild only in the way that the cocking and aiming of a pistol are mild in relation to the subsequent firing.[41]

2. A bolder initial strategy would be direct intervention and ob-

struction. For example, citizens might use their bodies to block bridges, highways, streets, entrances to towns, and buildings. Or, to avoid risk to themselves, they could use thousands of abandoned vehicles to obstruct highways and airport runways.[42] Prior to the entry of attacking troops, citizens might demolish bridges or docks (depending on the model of invasion) and destroy or render useless anything that might be useful to the invading forces. For instance, parts could be removed from key machinery, and records and computer data that could be useful to the attacker might be destroyed.[43]

3. The most radical initial strategy would be the nonviolent blitz-krieg, involving a massive act of defiance and near total noncooperation in an effort to defeat the attack through a lightning quick response.[44] Its methods include the general strike, economic shut-down, emptying the streets, evacuating cities, refusing to leave homes, and paralyzing the commercial and political systems. Or a blitzkrieg might involve just the opposite: persistent and defiant operation of business as usual by gov-ernment and business employees. It could also involve filling the streets with demonstrators, massive attempts to subvert the attacker's troops or functionaries, or defiant publication of newspapers and radio broadcasts with news of the attack and resistance.[45] Whatever its form, this strat-egy is designed to induce immediate retreat on the part of the attackers. This massive defiance will warn of the population's resolve to defeat the attack. While conveying the nonviolent nature of the defense, it will also warn of future difficulties if the attackers do not withdraw. When nonviolent blitzkrieg is used, no sharp distinction can be drawn be-tween the initial stage of communication and warning and a substantive defense struggle.[46]

Powerful initial mass defiance by civilians in a society that has been invaded could, if used against enemy leaders capable of recogniz-ing error and reversing direction, make possible a quick end to the struggle and a swift victory for the defenders.[47] The leaders of the invasion have a variety of face-saving options: they could hold that the attack had been launched without authorization; they could say that the aims of the operations had been achieved; and so on.[48] Even if an initial blitzkrieg strategy is not successful, the resisters will have mobi-lized their forces, strengthened their sense of solidarity, communicated their intent to resist, and conveyed the special nature of their defense.[49]

Strategists will have to decide which of these options would be the most effective initial response. Whatever form it takes, this initial strategy is designed to convey to the attackers' leadership two things: (1) the aggressor is in for a struggle, perhaps a long one, in which citizens of the occupied country will do everything possible, within the limits of nonviolent methods, to deny the invader the fruits of victory; and (2) the struggle may have a fatal effect on the morale and loyalty of many of the attackers' troops and functionaries.[50]

The assumption behind these initial strategies is that an immediate show of nonviolent opposition—the demonstration of a resistance morale by the population—may shock the attacker into rethinking its plans. Since no deaths or injuries will be inflicted on invading personnel, the need to avenge losses will not motivate invading forces to continue the attack, as it would in the case of armed resistance or an armed ambush in which invading soldiers were killed or wounded.[51]

In stark contrast to the effects of military resistance, this immediate and sudden nonviolent ambush is meant to rattle invasion forces and convince the opponent that there will be an asymmetrical battle in which soldiers are denied an opportunity to display military virtues such as courage and heroism.[52] Indeed, because they have taken up arms against the unarmed, the leaders of the aggressing nation and their invasion forces will receive the contempt of the world—and perhaps will even experience self-contempt. The objective is to lower the morale of the occupation forces quickly and to place their political leaders on the political defensive. Every effort will be made to focus world opinion on the injustice of the invasion by communicating the situation (if possible, by graphic television reports showing the armed invaders occupying an unarmed, defiant people) to the world, by calling for a special United Nations session to require the aggressing nation to explain its actions, and by inviting neutral observers to see for themselves what is happening.[53]

Long-Term Strategies

If these initial strategies fail to induce a withdrawal of invasion forces, then it will be necessary to shift to more substantial long-term strategies. Civilian defenders can either mount a campaign of sustained total noncooperation and defiance (a kind of extended nonviolent blitzkrieg), or they can adopt forms of selective resistance.

Total Noncooperation. Since the strategy of massive, total defiance is difficult to sustain, the defenders must carefully choose the points in the struggle at which they believe total noncooperation may be effectively used. It could, for instance, be applied temporarily to achieve specific objectives, such as the termination of brutalities or conscript labor or restoration of food or medical supplies that have been cut off. More extended application of total noncooperation or defiance must be restricted to later periods, when the attackers' capacity to exercise control has been weakened, when troops appear ready to mutiny, or when some decisive condition exists.[54] In such cases the defenders must be able to sustain total noncooperation or mass defiance for an extended period, no matter how severe the repression. The strategy could be applied at a moment of enemy weakness or fatigue to secure final defeat, as a kind of knock-out blow.[55]

In February 1986 in the Philippines, for example, in an act of mass defiance, thousands of civilians confronted loyal military forces, including tanks and soldiers. Armed with nothing but flowers in their hands, they obstructed the loyalist soldiers' movement toward the rebel troops. Thousands of unarmed people filled the streets and turned back the tanks that had been ordered to attack the nonviolent rebel troops at Camp Crame.[56] This was the beginning of the end for the Marcos regime. Such an act of mass defiance might not have worked a few months earlier. By the time the people took to the streets, military morale was low and defections were high. It was a knock-out blow against a tired and weakened opponent—one ready to fall. Similar nonviolent actions in 1989 transformed the face of Eastern Europe.

Selective Resistance. A strategy of total noncooperation (for example, a complete economic shut-down) must be used cautiously and prudently because it imposes a heavy price on the defenders by shutting down necessary operations (e.g., economic production). It is difficult to sustain for long periods and requires a well-disciplined and well-prepared population.

For the duration of the struggle, therefore, the main strategy should be selective resistance. Selective resistance allows defenders to concentrate on specific points that are particularly important to the success of the resistance effort.[57] Selection of the forms of resistance that are least detrimental to the native population while still harmful to the opponent's plans and actions should be the general course of action.[58] Selective resistance does not diffuse attention and exhaust the defending population: it allows the burden of defense to be shifted from one section of the population to another as the point of attack and the issues change in the course of the struggle.[59] It allows nonviolent defenders to concentrate their energy on the vulnerable points in the attackers' forces and to disrupt plans, thus impairing the aggressor's ability to achieve its objectives. To decide on the points of selective resistance, one must understand the attacker's main objectives and concentrate on frustrating these.[60]

For example, let us imagine a future in which the West, including a unified Germany, has demilitarized and adopted a policy of civilian-based defense. Let us further imagine that a paranoid Soviet leadership invades and occupies the new Germany in order to make sure that it can never again militarily threaten Soviet security. In that case, German citizens could adopt a strategy designed to make Soviet control impossible. This should be achieved, of course, primarily by political non-cooperation: refusal to collaborate at all government levels, denial to invaders of control over various government departments (police, prison system, etc.), bureaucratic slow-downs, or even strikes by government workers. Energies would be focused on political resistance: economic strikes and boycotts on economic issues would unnecessarily diffuse human resources and should be avoided.[61] The objective of this political strategy would be close to that described by George Kennan in another context a quarter of a century ago:

> The purpose would be to place the country in a position where it could face the Kremlin and say to it: "Look here, you may be able to overrun us, if you are unwise enough to attempt it, but you will have a small profit from it; we are in a position to assure that not a single Communist or other person likely to perform your political business will be available to you for this purpose; you will find here no adequate nucleus of a puppet regime; on the contrary, you will be faced with the united and organized hostility of an entire nation; your stay among us will not be a happy one; we will make you pay bitterly for every day of it; and it will be without favorable long-term prospects."[62]

If, on the other hand, the invasion had been launched to gain economic objectives—for example, to extract certain products—then the whole arsenal of economic resistance would be brought into play: refusal of cooperation from workers, technicians, administrators, and scientists working in the targeted industries at all stages, such as processing of raw materials, research, planning, transportation, manufacture, and supply of energy.

The main point is that the choice of methods and specific strategy must always be determined by the attackers' objectives. The minimum aim of civilian-based defense is to deny the aggressors their primary objectives.[63] The maximum aim is to change the thinking of the aggressors so that they will see the injustice of their actions.

Three Levels of Rehabilitation

Does defeat of the enemy's objectives mean a victory for the victim of aggression? It depends, of course, on one's definition of *victory* or *success*. If by *success* one means an act of rehabilitation such that the aggressor's psyche is turned around, then we must conclude that an enemy may be denied its objectives while a victory for the civilian defenders remains out of sight. If, on the other hand, success is interpreted as meaning a change in the adversary's behavior such that its aggressive actions are terminated and the threat to the nation's independence and freedom is overcome, then victory *can* be identified with the defeat of the enemy's objectives, regardless of whether the adversary's mind has been changed.

Civilian-based defense may produce change in one of three ways, which Sharp calls "mechanisms of change": conversion, accommodation, and nonviolent coercion.[64] Although in practice these mechanisms may often be mixed, preference for one will strongly shape the grand strategy.[65] The preferred mechanism of change will reflect the defenders' concept of success or victory and the level of rehabilitation they strive to achieve.

Conversion

In *conversion* the attackers are brought to the realization that their objectives and their attacks are unjustified: that is, the aggressors are ultimately persuaded to accept the perspective of the defenders.[66] The adversary's attitudes and ideas are changed through rational, moral, and/or emotional means as a result of nonviolent action: in effect, the aggressor is converted to the victim's way of thinking.[67] This would be a maximal rehabilitation: a transformation of the adversary's psyche. For a strategist such as Gandhi, this was the definition of successful nonviolent action: "For my ambition is no less than to convert the British people through nonviolence, and thus make them see the wrong they have done to India."[68] The aim is not simply to liberate the oppressed group, but also to free the oppressor, who is believed to be imprisoned by his own policies and objectives.[69]

A strategy of conversion requires that invaders be treated as persons in two senses: (1) they are to be viewed as *autonomous beings* capable of free choice (including the choice to disobey orders), and (2) they are to be regarded as *moral beings* capable of understanding the injustice of their actions. The defender operates on the assumption that enemy soldiers and functionaries are self-determining human beings who can be induced, through reason or the example of suffering, to question the rightness of the invasion and, as a result of their moral conversion, to mutiny or desert.

For example, in conversations with occupation forces, defenders could repeatedly stress the immorality of the aggressing nation's practices and its continued military presence.[70] The aim would be to so affect the will of the invaders' troops and functionaries that they become inefficient and unreliable agents of occupation. At the same time, however, these agents of aggression would be made to understand that the native population does not attack them as individual persons, but as representatives of their government's policies and actions.[71]

Nonviolent conversion tactics are designed to loosen the psychological and moral ties that bind the invaders to their government and to the orders of their leaders, rendering the invaders hesitant and insecure. When the invader begins to consider the possibility that the demands of the nonviolent resisters are justified, he is on the way to conversion.

Let us consider the application of conversion strategy to Soviet troops. According to the advocates of NATO's doctrine of first use, if the West did not have nuclear weapons with which to threaten the Soviet Union, Soviet forces under the direction of aggressive leaders could not be effectively deterred from invading Western Europe. Given the inferiority of NATO conventional forces and the unlikelihood of NATO members' correcting this deficiency, the nuclear threat is said to be crucial to Western security. Thus, for the sake of deterrence, NATO's declared strategy calls for the Alliance to initiate the use of nuclear weapons if Soviet conventional forces appear to be overrunning Western Europe on the way to a victory.

Would the United States really come to the nuclear defense of Western Europe, at the risk of Soviet nuclear retaliation against the territory of the United States? And even if it did, what would be left of Western Europe or the United States after an all-out nuclear war? Would the concept of free institutions have any meaning after the territories of Western Europe and the United States were transformed into nuclear rubble?

Critics of a rehabilitation policy will probably predict that if Western Europe, along with the United States, unilaterally disarmed, any Soviet reluctance to invade Western territories would vanish—that, indeed, this would provide a substantial incentive for a Soviet invasion. New hard-line Soviet leaders would no longer have to fear retaliation against their territory. Given Soviet interest in the bountiful resources of Western Europe, this disarmed prize would be too tempting to pass up.

The answer to this prediction is as follows. Under a rehabilitation policy, a strategy of civilian-based defense would take the place of the current strategy of flexible response and extended deterrence, which makes much of Western Europe dependent on nuclear forces controlled by the United States—forces that, if used, would destroy the very countries they are supposed to defend. Civilian-based defense, by contrast, offers the option of self-reliance in national defense and the real possibility of preserving free institutions in the face of a Soviet threat.

The important point, from the perspective of civilian-based defense, is that in the unlikely event that leaders bent on restoring and expanding the Soviet empire come to power, a Soviet invasion and occupation of Eastern and Western Europe would not necessarily be the same as a Soviet political victory, especially if citizens habituated to democratic institutions and trained in the techniques of nonviolent resistance applied conversion tactics to Soviet forces.

Soviet soldiers might, of course, be told that their cause was just. But how long would Soviet soldiers continue to believe this lie in the face of mass noncooperation and mass defiance by Europeans? On the question of the stability of Soviet troops, there are historical precedents that make conversion tactics plausible, as Sharp points out:

> The impact on the morale of Soviet troops carrying out repression on nonviolent resisters in East Germany, Hungary, and Czechoslovakia was also considerable, leading at times to large-scale unreliability and troop replacement, and at other times to limited mutinies. . . . The Soviet morale and discipline problems in these several cases would be vastly aggravated by civilian-based defense, in which major preparations would have been made for deliberate subversion of occupation troops.[72]

In East Germany the largely nonviolent workers' uprising of 1953 so affected the morale of Soviet troops that seventeen Russian officers and soldiers refused to obey the orders of their superiors, knowing that this would result in their being court-martialed and executed. Given the likelihood that the Soviet occupation army called in to quell this nonviolent uprising was composed of the most trusted, disciplined, and thoroughly indoctrinated soldiers available, it is remarkable that there were men who were willing to pay with their lives rather than obey the orders of their superiors.[73]

The case of Czechoslovakia is more significant. In 1968 the Soviet invasion was designed to quickly replace the reform-minded Dubcek regime with a pro-Moscow conservative one. The Soviets assumed that the more than half a million Warsaw Pact troops could accomplish this task within days. Although the Czech army was easily defeated, nonviolent civilian resistance delayed the establishment of a collaborationist government for about eight months. Immediate nonviolent resistance came from the media, the uniformed public police, government ministers, and the National Assembly. According to some reports, the Soviet troops that initially invaded and occupied Czechoslovakia became so unreliable within a few days that they had to be sent back to the Soviet Union and replaced by non-Russian-speaking troops, with whom the Czechs and Slovaks could not easily communicate.[74]

The original troops, treated as oppressors instead of liberators, no doubt began to wonder why they had been sent to occupy Czechoslovakia in the first place. In fact, several hundred soldiers deserted across the frontier into Austria. One of the defectors, Viktor Suvorov, whose unit was one of those withdrawn in October 1968, recalls: "As they left Czechoslovakia, our divisions reminded one of the remnants of a defeated army, fleeing from the hot pursuit of a shattering defeat."[75] Sharp speculates that the lesson of 1968—that Soviet troops were highly vulnerable to a special kind of nonviolent resistance—was the reason Soviet troops were not used in the Polish uprisings of 1980 and 1981, where they would have faced a more sophisticated and more widespread nonviolent resistance movement in Solidarity.[76] The newly liberated Germans, Poles, and Czechs are likely to present a greater challenge to Soviet troops.

Western Europe would be equally difficult to subjugate. Would Soviet leaders want their troops to mix with the people and institutions of the West? Wouldn't the limited democracy and free enterprise of the Soviet Union pale in comparison with the greater liberties and economic abundance of occupied Western societies? Sharp points out that a large-scale Soviet invasion of Western Europe "would bring hundreds of thousands of ordinary soldiers, officers, and functionaries into direct contact with West European ways of life and with especially 'dangerous' populations."[77] These displaced Soviet soldiers, many of whom might already have doubts about the justification of their invasion, would face people who not only believed strongly in their own society and their right to control it, but were also "trained in how to subvert the loyalties of the invading personnel while resisting the occupation itself."[78] Training in the Russian language would be part of this education in subversive tactics.

Frequent rotation of Soviet troops would, of course, be one countermeasure, but it would bring a destabilizing possibility: Soviet personnel who had been converted would return to spread the truth about the democratic nature of European society. There is, of course, another solution: to have non-Russian-speaking troops occupy Europe. In fact, a sizable portion of the Soviet forces consists of non-Russian ethnic groups, many of whom speak little or no Russian.[79]

But is an invasion of Eastern and/or Western Europe to be led by Russian commanders giving orders to troops who barely understand the language? Such an invasion would be a dubious undertaking, involving serious difficulties in technical maneuvers and combat.[80] Even if these problems of communication and command could be solved, there is a question about the loyalty of non-Russian Soviet troops. For example, Central Asian conscripts were found to be politically unreliable in Afghanistan, passing ammunition to the locals, buying Korans in the bazaar, and possibly even handing over personal weapons; the Soviets, finally recognizing their error, sent these troops home.[81]

The Soviets could have similar problems with troops who might sympathize with people fighting to retain their liberties. If there was any potential for undercutting the loyalty of these troops to the Soviet regime, properly trained resisters could exploit it. No matter what their objectives (installation of a pro-Soviet government, economic appropriation, etc.), Soviet leaders would face great uncertainty in planning an invasion of an Eastern and/or Western Europe whose population was trained in conversion tactics. They would have to ask themselves if their troops could really defeat civilians who were prepared to apply a variety of tactics designed to undermine the morale of Soviet forces.

The conversion of invaders is, of course, the ideal—the maximum to be hoped for. The goal of conversion is nothing less than psychological rehabilitation: the extinction of aggressive behavior is to be a by-product of a transformation or re-formation of the aggressors' hearts and minds.

Conversion should not, however, according to Sharp, be the only criterion of success, because for a variety of reasons it may not be achievable. It may be impossible to change the hearts and minds of the aggressors because of the absence of shared beliefs and norms, a deep conflict of interests, the personality structure of members of the opponent group, training of the invasion forces that makes them immune to conversion tactics, and other factors.[82]

In that case, rehabilitationists must settle for partial rehabilitation—something less than psychological transformation. Just as there are hardened criminals whose minds can never be changed by any rehabilitation technique, so are there aggressors who will remain incorrigible in their intentions, feelings, and desires. The success of the rehabilitation project may, therefore, have to be measured in terms of altered behaviors rather than altered psyches, so that while the leaders of the aggressing nation would still like to impose their objectives, they will, despite their desire to subjugate a population, be influenced or compelled by the resisters either to compromise or to give up trying to achieve their objectives. This more modest notion of success might be called *behavioral rehabilitation*. It fits in with the other two mechanisms of change: accommodation and nonviolent coercion.

Accommodation

Accommodation may be the most that can be achieved in many cases. It is achieved when the opponent agrees to grant the demands of the nonviolent resisters without having changed its mind about the rightness of its action, or without having ceased wanting to realize its aggressive intention.[83] It occurs when an aggressor agrees to make concessions.

The leaders of the occupation may come to the realization that it is in their best interests to compromise in order to terminate problems caused by civilian resistance.[84] Some other factor or combination of factors—world opinion, economic losses, or opposition within the invader's own government, for example—may become more important than victory over the resisters: thus, accommodation means that the opponent is willing to yield rather than experience consequences that it considers worse than the frustration of its objectives.[85] This, then, is a situation in which the opponent *could* fight on but decides that the struggle is not worth the costs (moral, political, or economic).

In the U.S. colonial period, for instance, the British repeal of the Stamp Act was achieved in part because British merchants felt pressure as a result of the American colonists' cutting trade and refusing to pay commercial debts. As a Bristol merchant put it in 1765: "The Avenues of Trade are all shut up. . . . We are at our Witts End for Want of Money to fulfill our Engagement with our Tradesmen."[86] The merchants' pressure on the British government and their petitions for repeal of the relevant acts were a result of economic pressure—not a change in ideology or agreement with the justice of the colonists' complaints. The action of the British Parliament, in turn, was a response to protest from British commercial interests, not to the justice of the colonists' cause.

The nonviolent resistance of the Norwegian population during the Nazi occupation between 1940 and 1945 provides another example of accommodation. It is frequently asserted that nonviolent tactics will not work against a Nazi-type opponent. The Norwegian teachers who successfully resisted the Nazi effort to organize education along fascist lines constitute an impressive counterexample.

Although the Nazi-dominated government threatened the rebellious teachers with dismissal, closed all schools, and sent about a thousand uncooperative teachers to concentration camps (where they were reduced to starvation rations and tortured), the resistance of teachers and parents continued. The resolve of the incarcerated teachers strengthened the resistance on the homefront. Eight months after their arrest, the teachers were returned home, and Hitler ordered Vidkum Quisling, the minister of education, to abandon his educational plan.[87]

In the event of a Soviet invasion of Eastern and/or Western Europe, civilian resisters and a supportive world community (or, at the least, supportive allies) could make the invaders' costs so high that accommodation might become preferable to any gains the Soviets could achieve by continued occupation. Even if Soviet troops remained loyal, negative world opinion, economic boycotts, and the difficulty of ruling a recalcitrant population with no hope of a victory in the near future might be enough to persuade Soviet leaders, despite their strong desire and physical capacity to continue the occupation, to terminate it and withdraw.

Nonviolent Coercion

In nonviolent coercion, the opponent's behavior changes when it no longer has an effective choice between conceding or refusing to accept the resisters' demands. That is, the demands of the nonviolent group are achieved against the will and without the agreement of the opponent.[88] When nonviolent coercion is successful, the aggressor does not give in or compromise: it is simply incapable of governing the occupied population. Contrary to all its desires and plans, the aggressing nation is compelled to yield to the resisters.[89]

In nonviolent coercion the opponent's change of behavior is involuntary in the sense that the sources of its power have been so impaired by nonviolent means that it is no longer in control of things. Sources of power include respect for authority; general obedience and cooperation among those who sustain an oppressor's rule and keep the system operating; acceptance of the supporting ideology; and material factors such as control of the economy, transportation, means of communication, tax revenues, and raw materials. When the sources of power are withheld or withdrawn by nonviolent mass action, the opponent is deprived of the means of carrying out its objectives and *must* give in to the nonviolent demands.[90] When the sources of power are extinguished, the capacity to rule dissolves. Nonviolent coercion thus occurs when the leaders of the invasion/occupation are rendered impotent through acts of massive noncooperation by the occupied population and/or significant desertion in the ranks of the agents of occupation.[91]

Coercion does not require threats of physical violence. Crucial to coercion is the capacity to block the opponent's ability to implement its will. A will deprived of its sources of implementation is impotent. For example, the 1920 *Putsch* planned by Dr. Wolfgang Kapp against the new Weimar Republic was a successful *coup d'état* that was nevertheless defeated by coercion through noncooperation. Total economic and political resistance (in the form of a general strike and a shut-down of the bureaucracy) made it impossible for Kappists to rule.[92]

Nonviolent coercion may take place in one of three ways: (1) defiance may become so widespread and massive that it cannot be controlled through repression; (2) noncooperation and defiance may make it impossible for the social, economic, and political system to function unless defenders' demands are satisfied; and (3) the attackers' ability to apply repression may be internally undermined and may at times dissolve as a result of mutiny by the agents of repression.[93] Generally, nonviolent coercion is effective only where the number of nonviolent actionists is very large.[94]

Rehabilitation Failure Compared with Military Failure

Despite a careful choice of strategy, method, and mechanism of change, nonviolent defense could fail, and hundreds of unarmed defenders might be killed, wounded, and tortured in a vain effort to stop military aggression and occupation. Proponents of CBD do not guarantee that it will succeed (whether success is defined in terms of conversion, accommodation, or coercion), nor that, if it does succeed, it will do so without casualties. They admit that casualties and defeat are as possible with this policy as with other policies.

What the advocates of nonviolent national defense argue is that in thinking about the failure of this approach, two things should be recognized. First, to make a utilitarian point: the failure to stop or correct Soviet aggression through a policy of rehabilitation is preferable to any outcome of a nuclear war—or, for that matter, even a conventional war. Failure of CBD would mean at worst, in the case of a Soviet victory, a long, difficult, oppressive life under the domination of a tyrannical regime. Life would, however, go on, with the social infrastructure and the biosphere undamaged.

Second, to make a Kantian point, failure to achieve a total victory would not mean total defeat. Indeed, definitive defeat need never occur as long as the society survives, for the society always carries within it the possibility of eventual liberation and restoration of free institutions.[95] As long as the society remains intact, no matter how oppressive its structure, power still ultimately derives from the cooperation and the consent of the population, which means that with sufficient defiance and noncooperation, the sources of oppressive power may still one day be extinguished. Subjects in an oppressive society, so long as they respect and conceive of themselves as autonomous beings, can always collaborate in a collective refusal to obey those in power. On the other hand, when the infrastructure of a society has been torn apart by weapons of mass destruction and the physical landscape has been incinerated and irradiated, the ideas of democracy and freedom lose meaning; mere survival preoccupies and defines the daily existence of the remaining individuals.

Implementation of Rehabilitation Policy

It should now be clear that the proposal here is not a call for disarmament in the usual sense but for *transarmament*, the substitution of a civilian-based defensive strategy for military strategies. If we add to this nonviolent defensive strategy a strong emphasis on diplomacy, international cooperation, and the use of funds hitherto used for arms production to solve problems such as severe poverty and political injustice, then it becomes clear how a rehabilitation policy can significantly contribute to world peace.

If the West dismantled its weapons of mass destruction and military forces in adopting a policy of rehabilitation, it would greatly reduce Soviet insecurities. Moreover, far from appeasing (potential) Soviet aggressors, this policy calls for vigorous nonviolent resistance designed to correct (through psychological conversion or behavior modification) all aggressive actions.

The transition to a policy of rehabilitation would have to occur over an extended period, during which research on creative diplomacy, nonviolent conflict resolution, and CBD would be heavily funded. Pragmatic advocates of a policy of nonviolence realize that no society will abolish military defense until it has gained confidence in nonmilitary defense. A civilian-defense capacity could initially be introduced as a component of a total defense policy containing largely military forces, and then be gradually expanded. This means that, realistically, the new policy would have to be developed and practiced alongside military measures until it proved its efficacy in particular conflict situations.[96] This would then allow for a gradual phasing out of military forces— perhaps beginning with nuclear weapons and ending with a phasing out of conventional forces.

Evidence for the workability of the new system might have to be demonstrated initially by nonaligned countries such as Austria, Finland, and Switzerland.[97] If viewed as successful, it could later be adopted by NATO countries such as Germany and Denmark. Eventually, all European countries (including newly democratic Eastern governments) might adopt the new policy, making it unnecessary for them to rely on nuclear weapons—whether those of the United States or their own—to achieve national security. In a sense, most East European societies have already demonstrated the power of mass nonviolent protest.

This would not necessarily mean a complete decoupling of U.S. and Western European security; rather, it would mean that these nations would have the freedom to choose self-reliance in security matters and avoid the threat of nuclear destruction.[98] These societies would still be free to establish defense associations. In fact, NATO could be transformed into a civilian-based mutual-aid defense alliance.

If a majority of the citizens of the United States came to believe that the new defense strategy could provide better security for this country and its allies than military alternatives, then the strategy could be democratically adopted. It should be noted that to be successful, this policy must be developed openly and receive mass support. This distinguishes it from the other policy options, each of which could be imposed on a society or developed secretly.

Although a rehabilitation policy now seems alien to U.S. culture, given the national fascination with weapons and disposition to settle conflict through the use of armed force, success in other parts of the world might provide the compelling evidence required to persuade Americans of the value of nonmilitary defense. It is not likely that advocates of rehabilitation will succeed in persuading Americans to give up their weapons until a climate of security is created that renders arms obsolete.[99] Many Americans will not give civilian-based defense any credence unless and until they see it successfully used against armed aggression. The adoption and successful use of the policy by Western European NATO countries might provide the requisite evidence.

In any event, the introduction of a policy of rehabilitation might proceed along the following lines.

1. Education. A major educational program for the whole country on the nature and purpose of a policy of rehabilitation would be implemented. This would involve education concerning the role of constructive foreign aid (nutritional, medical, educational, etc.) in the prevention of destabilizing conflicts in the third world. The public would also have to be educated about the role of creative diplomacy in resolving conflicts with the USSR and the role of Soviet–American cooperation and exchanges in improving our relationship with the USSR. Furthermore, the public would also be informed about the largely neglected history of the successful use of nonviolent resistance—from the use of nonviolent techniques in the American revolt against the British to the successful use of nonviolent methods against the Nazis. Federal, state, and local government bodies, assisted by independent institutions such as schools, churches, trade unions, business groups, newspapers, television, and the like could undertake this educational program.[100] The task would be to inform citizens about the broad outlines of the new option, the ways it would operate, and the results expected.[101]

2. Research. Research would be conducted on how to improve nonviolent methods of preventing, deterring, defending against, and defeating aggression. In addition to Defense Department research, the government could fund and encourage private and university research in all aspects of rehabilitation policy. If even a small percentage of the funding and time that previously went into nuclear and conventional weapons research were put into nonviolent defense, there might be significant breakthroughs and discoveries that would, in their revolutionary significance, match the many variations introduced into nuclear weapons.

3. Diplomatic Training. State Department officials would receive thorough training in principles of nonviolent conflict resolution and negotiation. Since the first line of our response to a conflict or a threat would be diplomatic, all our ambassadors and diplomats would be required to master the art of negotiation and to have a substantial knowledge of the culture, language, political system, and history of any country to be served or bargained with. The Soviet Union would, of course, be given special attention.

4. Gradual Integration. During the process of transarmament, the new policy could be progressively integrated into an overall policy that still reserved a significant military component, perhaps as a last resort. For example, while conducting experiments in rehabilitation, the United States could maintain a minimum retaliatory nuclear force and adopt the doctrine of existential deterrence. A minimum deterrence force could serve as insurance as the policy of rehabilitation proved its utility in trial applications in various conflicts and crises. Nonintervention and a new emphasis on negotiation would be increasingly applied in foreign policy.

As for the U.S. application of CBD, it is unlikely that the United States will ever be invaded. Since Eastern and Western Europe are the more likely targets of any new Soviet expansionist ambitions, we could help these countries develop a nonviolent defensive strategy and pledge to offer them nonmilitary support in the event of an invasion. Although CBD allows for self-reliance in a way that the current NATO nuclear arrangement does not, this does not mean that outside help is excluded. As suggested above, the coupling of U.S. and Western European security that nuclear weapons now provide could be achieved by special mutual-aid treaty agreements.[102] Democratic countries committed to CBD could join together to make life unpleasant for the aggressor. For example, as mentioned above, they could economically boycott the Soviet Union, cutting off grain and other important goods.

Moreover, if non-NATO nations could be convinced of the injustice of an act of Soviet aggression, they might also apply pressure to the USSR. Other nations might reason that if this aggression is not defeated, they will find themselves the next victims of Soviet occupation. Widespread economic boycotts could imperil the Soviet Union's established trade relations throughout the world. No matter how large the Soviet armed forces, they are not large enough to invade and control all the nations that might choose to politically and economically punish the USSR for unprovoked aggression against an unarmed country. Before invading Europe or any other region, the Soviet Union would have to weigh all these negative consequences.

If Americans witnessed years of successful civilian-based defense in Europe—whether in the form of deterrence (the Soviet "failure" to invade unarmed allies) or in the form of a successful defeat of a Soviet attempt at occupation (the humiliating retreat of the Red Army in the face of massive nonviolent resistance), then they might become less skeptical of its application to the U.S. homeland, which is far less threatened by outside invasion. Not even the remote possibility of armed invasion from across the ocean by the Soviets or, for that matter, by Soviet-dominated Marxist nations south of the border—the new Nicaraguas so feared by the right wing—could be taken as an overwhelming threat to a nation thoroughly trained in strategies of nonviolent defense. We would, therefore, be no more defenseless than our European friends who had proved the efficacy of nonviolent techniques and tactics against the Soviets.

5. *Flexibility and Leadership.* Granting that not all conflicts can be resolved by negotiation and that an antagonist may elect to impose its will on us, the nation must know how, and be prepared, to apply a variety of strategies designed to achieve the nonviolent correction of such aggressive behavior. Workable strategies for dealing with aggression could be developed by an independent Department of Civilian-Based Defense and civilian defense counterparts of West Point for the education of civilian-based professionals who would operate local training centers throughout the country. The Department of Civilian-Based Defense could draw up and publish a resistance plan or a set of plans for different contingencies. [103]

To convince the general public of the value of nonviolent resistance and to give ordinary citizens sufficient training to make them unrulable by foreign powers, it will be necessary to have specialists or professionals who can serve as the leadership and vanguard for acts of mass resistance. The leadership—analogous to commanding officers in the military—would consist of those most knowledgeable in the theory of nonviolence and most experienced in its practical application. In the initial stages of an invasion these professionals would decide the initial strategies, based on their analysis of the enemy's objectives, and determine which sites were the most vital for the implementation of the strategies. [104]

It is, of course, important that CBD not become so centralized so that by killing or imprisoning the leadership the enemy could defeat the resistance movement. [105] That is, in addition to a professional leadership, it is desirable to have hundreds of thousands of citizens throughout the country, representing various occupational groups, who are trained resisters, specially educated in methods of nonviolent resistance.[106] This nonviolent civilian "army," consisting of the best organized and most disciplined force in the defense network, would be the backbone of the resistance movement.[107] These specially trained citizens would function in a manner similar to army reserves, training several weeks of every year in their communities or combining with groups from other communities for joint exercises. The general population would be expected to shelter and nonviolently protect those more actively involved in resistance. In addition, the general populace would receive sufficient training so that, when required, they could participate actively in resistance strategies that require greater numbers than could be supplied from the trained resistance group alone.[108]

6. Economic Conversion. Along with the gradual expansion of the nonviolent component of the defense establishment, there would be comprehensive plans for economic conversion from military to civilian production and service to avoid a sudden and traumatic displacement of workers in the (military) defense industry and military personnel in the armed services. Plans for such conversion could be worked out well in advance by joint conversion planning boards composed of both workers and management, with a gradual phasing out of weapons production along with retraining and relocation programs for members of the armed services and defense industry workers, engineers, and scientists.[109] The talent of these people could be creatively and constructively used in nonmilitary production and nonmilitary service—in the satisfaction of domestic needs that have been neglected. Those interested in defense strategy or in making a career in the defense of their country could, of course, find a place in the Department of Civilian-Based Defense; they could become members of a nonviolent army of disciplined and courageous professionals, including officers and regular "soldiers." These specially trained combatants would personify the national will to resist.[110]

7. Drills. Finally, with the completion of the transarmament program, it will be necessary to have regular drills, especially in the allied nations most threatened by invasion, to ensure the readiness of the defense professionals, the "reservists," and the general population. This might involve the periodic simulation of an attack and the playing of civilian defense war games. Once a year, in different sections of the country, the trained resisters could organize a simulated invasion so that problems of strategy and tactics could be posed and tested. In addition, material preparations will be necessary, including emergency fuel for transportation; equipment for underground communication (radio transmitters and the means to produce underground newspapers) so that defenders can communicate with each other and with the outside world; emergency medical supplies; emergency food supplies to counter starvation tactics by the aggressor; and independent sources of energy to operate underground equipment.

The Case of Rehabilitation

The elimination of spending on military forces—made possible by a complete transition to CBD—would allow us to satisfy domestic needs while providing constructive aid to other nations, which would in turn have the effect of increasing the number of allies and supporters who could impose sanctions and exert diplomatic pressure in case we were attacked. Aid to other countries does not necessarily have to take the form of handouts: it could include educational and technical assistance that would make them more self-reliant in terms of their economy and defense policies. If they adopted CBD, the currently poor nations could save the disproportionate funds they are now spending on armaments and purchase tools and commodities necessary to the fulfillment of their citizens' basic needs. Moreover, to the extent that political unrest and armed conflict result from economic deprivation, the number of revolutions and wars could be reduced.

To the extent that Soviet nuclear weapons and the readiness to use them result from the U.S. nuclear arsenal, the Soviet motivation to possess and use nuclear weapons should be reduced. With NATO's adoption of a rehabilitation policy—a policy that would not threaten Soviet security in the way present NATO policy does—there would be a real prospect of ending the nuclear arms race.

The main points in the case for a policy of rehabilitation can be summarized as follows.

1. Military strategies can no longer ensure national security. The very power of modern weapons is likely to result in the destruction of the society being defended. The Soviet Union obviously recognizes this.

2. Transarmament provides a way to end an otherwise endless nuclear arms race, which is likely—through accident or design—to result in a holocaust destroying much of civilization and life on the planet.

3. There are numerous past cases of successful nonviolent resistance, including its efficacious use against invasion and *coup d'état*. On the other hand, there are no historical illustrations of successful nuclear war–fighting strategies against a nuclear opponent.

4. The civilian resistance component provides a deterrent to armed attack by threatening to deny any aggressor its objectives and by threatening to make the costs exceed the gains. There is no good reason to assume that invaders can be deterred only by military means. That is, in abolishing weapons of war, we do not have to give up deterrence: indeed, rehabilitation policy establishes a form of deterrence that provides a credible nonmilitary way of warning an adversary against aggression. By communicating the likelihood of failure to establish political or economic control, as well as the unacceptable international costs in the form of world condemnation and economic boycotts by other nations, the strategy is likely to deter potential attackers. An important component of deterrence is the ability to make it clear to a potential aggressor, not simply that it cannot gain by aggression, but that it will positively lose.[111] A civilian-based defense strategy, in effect, tells a potential aggressor: if you attack us, you run the risk of losing control over your own troops and officials and of generating economically and diplomatically damaging adverse reaction from other countries.

5. In case deterrence fails, the policy offers a way to defend the homeland against aggression without destroying it. Unlike nuclear deterrence, it does not require carrying out a strategy that will do as much damage to native territory as to that of the adversary. It offers a way to successfully defend human lives and democratic institutions.

6. The defeat of nonviolent resisters—that is, the failure to defeat the aggressor—will be less disastrous than the failure of nuclear and conventional military strategies. Advocates of CBD do not deny that there will be fatalities and injuries. Despite the lack of armed resistance, the aggressor may deliberately kill unarmed defenders in order to coerce and intimidate the general population, who, as a result of such violence, may decide to surrender. What proponents of nonviolent national defense claim is that—compared with the alternatives—the application of this strategy will involve fewer casualties and less destruction of the social and biological environment. Its failure allows hope for eventual success in a way that the failure of the other policies does not. To repeat, the definitive defeat of CBD need never occur as long as the society survives.

7. This policy, given its requirement of mass support and mass participation, fits in with the values it is defending: democratic institutions and respect for human life, including the lives of invading enemy forces. *Civilian-based defense is a democratic defense of democracy.*[112] This nonviolent strategy involves a respect for enemy soldiers as persons: it treats them as autonomous, moral beings. No alternative fits in as well with democratic principles and a doctrine of human rights.

8. Rehabilitation policy repudiates *both* violence *and* appease-

ment. It provides a way of preventing *both* armed conflict *and* foreign domination. In stressing negotiation as the initial response to a crisis or conflict, the policy offers a means of peacefully resolving conflicts. In the event that negotiation fails and aggression occurs, it still gives us a way of nonviolently ending aggression. Thus, it repudiates violence while providing a way to "fight for" free institutions.

In summary, even granting the worst case scenario—a nuclear-armed and re-Stalinized Soviet Union committed to world domination—a policy of rehabilitation still provides a strategy that, according to its supporters, can ensure national security within a framework that is morally superior to the alternatives.

Those who are uneasy about this pacifistic proposal, and yet cannot unconditionally endorse any of the other three options, may want to consider a compromise—a combination of policy choices. The next chapter will explore a broad range of hybrids.

CHAPTER EIGHT

Hybrids

Borrowing from the domestic theories of deterrence, social defense, retribution, and rehabilitation, I have sketched several alternative nuclear weapons policy options. The major options can be graphed as shown in Figure 1. As I stated in the beginning, these alternatives are pure options. Additional, more complex options can be generated by marrying compatible aims, strategies, and forces. The only logical requirement is that the resulting mix be coherent. For example, we have seen that MAD deterrence and national social defense are incompatible, because MAD requires mutual population vulnerability, while national social defense requires mutual population invulnerability.

Hybrids, then, are policies that combine compatible features from two or more pure types to create a policy synthesis. A hybrid may involve marrying two strategies with the aim of using their complementary strengths to achieve a more efficacious nuclear weapons policy. Or a hybrid may retain the purity of a single strategy while borrowing from the force system of another option in order to enhance its own effectiveness. The following examples provide an idea of the way policy options can be multiplied by creating logically coherent hybrids.

National Social Defense plus Rehabilitation

National social defense and rehabilitation share a similar aim: to construct a defense that avoids the use of offensive military forces. The

Figure 1

POLICY	PRIMARY AIM	STRATEGY	FORCES
Pure deterrence (MAD version)	Prevention of nuclear war	Threat of assured destruction	Inaccurate nuclear forces
Enhanced deterrence (countervailing version)	Prevention of nuclear war + intrawar deterrence	Infliction of progressively greater damage + offering incentive for negotiations for war termination	Flexible nuclear forces: counterforce and countervalue
Social defense	Protection of society from nuclear attack	Active and passive defenses	Accurate forces capable of destroying attacking weapons
Retribution	Just punishment of the nuclear aggressor	Proportionate retaliation against combatants	Accurate forces capable of punishing military agents
Rehabilitation	Reform of the enemy	Nonviolent preventive and corrective measures	Civilian-based defense

strategies are compatible in the sense that both seek to avoid killing combatants and noncombatants while providing real security for free institutions. Both seek ways to minimize the destruction of the homeland. That is, social defense and rehabilitation complement each other: if combined, the resulting synthesis would provide a comprehensive program for national security that repudiates the current strategy of nuclear retaliation.

Proponents of CBD may find that—as insurance—investment in passive defense and in a purely defensive technology fits in well with their concerns. Gene Sharp states:

> In a civilian-based defense country, civil defense preparations become another part of a purely defensive posture. . . . Within the context of civilian-based defense efforts, attention should also

be given to the desirability and potential effectiveness of developing and deploying purely defensive technological measures against nuclear attacks (whether in the anti-ballistic missile form or some other). Work would be required on the likely effectiveness of such measures and their relative contribution to security, as compared with other means, alongside the civilian-based defense policy.[1]

Moreover, supporters of national social defense may want the kind of insurance that rehabilitation offers: removal of tension-producing conditions (through skillful negotiation and economic cooperation) and training of the population in nonviolent resistance. After all, the technical apparatus of strategic defense will not remove the still-opposed ideological interests of the USSR and the Western democracies. As long as the Soviet Union remains committed to a worldview at odds with that of the West, or as long as there remains the possibility of a reversion to its original vision of world domination, we cannot rule out the danger of conventional aggression. In the case of Western Europe, the Soviet Union, no longer having to fear nuclear retaliation, may be tempted to invade and occupy one or more NATO countries in order to expand its empire and extract the Western resources that its economy badly needs. In that event, assuming that all efforts at negotiation fail, it would be important for Europeans to be trained in the tactics of civilian-based defense.

This combination of elements from rehabilitation and social defense might yield as a bonus a new form of deterrence. The very knowledge that countries in Western Europe possessed defensive technologies and were trained in techniques of nonviolent resistance might be sufficient to deter such an invasion. The combination could create enough uncertainty in the minds of Soviet military planners to establish an effective strategy of deterrence by denial.

Existential Deterrence plus Unilateral Arms Reduction

Those who believe that we need only a small number of invulnerable nuclear weapons to achieve deterrence might favor a proposal put forward by Charles Osgood: GRIT (Graduated Reciprocation In Tension Reduction).[2] Given the surplus of nuclear warheads in the Western arsenal compared with the requirements of existential deterrence, there is room for radical, unilateral arms reduction. For example, compare Robert McNamara's requirement of 400 retaliatory warheads with our current arsenal of approximately 10,000 strategic weapons.

GRIT seeks an arms race in reverse: a graduated, unilaterally initiated tension-decreasing strategy would replace the tension-increasing arrangement that has resulted in an arms race. Osgood's plan assumes that nuclear deterrence will continue, but in a more modest form: he advocates that we retain only the minimum nuclear capacity required for deterrence. Arms-reduction plans would be announced publicly before their execution as part of a deliberate policy of improving Soviet–American relations. These plans would involve explicit invitations for Soviet reciprocation in some form. Unilateral arms-reduction moves would be continued for a period of time, regardless of whether reciprocation occurred. The goals of GRIT are the same as those of negotiated arms reduction: crisis stability, damage limitation, and reduction of expenditures on arms; these goals would simply be achieved by initial unilateral moves that hold out a promise of eventual bilateral agreements. An example of GRIT was President Kennedy's announced unilateral moratorium on atmospheric nuclear testing. The Soviets eventually followed the American example, and an agreement was negotiated.

GRIT moves fall short of the unilateral disarmament called for by rehabilitation policy, but they fit in with the latter's strategy of working to remove the sources of tension. Such unilateral moves allow for a radical reduction in nuclear weapons so long as the reduction is consistent with existential deterrence. While retaining the strategy of nuclear deterrence, GRIT takes risks for peace in the spirit of rehabilitation. For example, if, after a unilateral arms-reduction move (e.g., dismantling a particular weapons system such as MX land-based ICBMs), the Soviets did not reciprocate in some comparable fashion, we might still make further unilateral moves. If they reciprocated, we could then make another move and wait for reciprocation. The idea would be a build-down in which, ideally, the United States would sometimes lead and sometimes follow. (Lest it be thought that the USSR will never lead, consider the Soviet Union's own unilateral move of suspending underground nuclear tests for a year and a half.) As Osgood describes the process, it is more like courtship than marriage: "The players of GRIT move in complicated steps of their own, each keeping his eyes on the other, and leading or following, now one, now the other."[3]

The strategy would be to play GRIT until only very small retaliatory nuclear arsenals were left on both sides, the objective being to achieve a less destabilizing and less world-threatening level of mutual deterrence.

Countervailing Strategy plus Limited Strategic Defense

In exploring the policy of national social defense, I approached strategic defense as a revolutionary concept, using the comprehensive version introduced by President Reagan in his March 1983 speech. The original proposal called for substituting defensive for offensive forces—for creating a defense-dominated future in which the United States would be completely denuclearized.

A more modest form of strategic defense could be married to a countervailing nuclear deterrence strategy. Under this regime, the active defense system would not have as its goal the ambitious project of protecting the population but the more modest one of protecting retaliatory forces. Robert McNamara calls this "Star Wars II," Reagan's maximum vision being Star Wars I. Henry Kissinger has expressed support for this more modest version:

> Even granting—as I do—that a perfect defense of our population is almost certainly unattainable, the existence of some defense means that the attacker must plan on saturating it. This massively complicates the attacker's calculations. Anything that magnifies doubt inspires hesitation and adds to deterrence. The case grows stronger if one considers the case of Intercontinental Ballistic Missile launchers. . . . The incentive for a first strike would be sharply, and perhaps decisively, reduced if an aggressor knew that half his opponent's ICBM's would survive any foreseeable attack.[4]

This is, of course, an abandonment of the objective of national population defense. This hybrid strategy utilizes an element of strategic defense (point defenses) in order to enhance deterrence: it would achieve deterrence by denying the potential aggressor its objectives. Offensive and defensive weapons would be combined to meet the requirements of nuclear deterrence. The aim would be to create such uncertainty in the mind of the Soviet leaders about the prospects of a successful attack that they will see no advantage in attacking.

Existential Deterrence plus Nonoffensive Retribution

The premise of the hybrid strategy of nonprovocative defense is that preparations for offensive operations, on the nuclear or the conventional level, make war more likely. Such preparations give nations a general feeling of being under a threat. The solution is to shift to military doctrines and capabilities that make a nation incapable of conducting offensive military operations. The assumption is that a change on both the conventional and the nuclear levels is necessary to prevent nuclear war.

The Nuclear Level. Counterforce strategies are rejected in favor of a minimal deterrent. The nation should not have a capacity to disarm Soviet nuclear forces, whether by direct attacks on missiles or by attacks on C³I facilities. Arms control should work to reduce the number of weapons on both sides to a fraction of present arsenals, and to eliminate counterforce nuclear weapons. Even if the Soviet Union does not agree to reduce its arsenal, the United States should unilaterally begin changing the nature of its forces, thus providing the Soviets with an example.

A nonoffensive approach to nuclear forces must rely on weapons incapable of a first strike and on a principle of no first use. This should eventually render nuclear forces irrelevant to the point that most of them could be scrapped.[5] The only legitimate and credible role for nuclear weapons is, in the words of one defender of nonprovocative defense, "to deter nuclear attack and preclude nuclear blackmail."[6] The new strategy must reduce the role of nuclear weapons in the defense of Europe against a nonnuclear attack and renounce the first use of them. In order to reduce reliance on nuclear weapons, NATO must be satisfied that its conventional forces are sufficient to deter aggression.

The Conventional Level. Conventional forces should be small but credible enough to deter aggression. The point would be to rearrange conventional forces so that they can defend but not attack.[7] This strategy would be most relevant to the defense of Western Europe. It would make the NATO policy of nuclear first use unnecessary. Indeed, both NATO and the Soviet Union seem at this writing to be receptive to the implementation of this proposal. According to Stephen Flanagan, nonprovocative defense involves the following features:

- Territorial or area defense, in which defenders seek to exploit the natural terrain and, in some cases, urban sprawl to wear down an aggressor
- The assumption that defenders have a decisive advantage over aggressors
- The assumption that recent breakthroughs in military technology (new surveillance systems, precision-guided munitions, remotely piloted vehicles, and air defenses) will enhance the defender's natural advantage in future conflicts
- The assumption that crisis stability is furthered by providing few targets worth preempting before a war starts, something that could be achieved by deploying small, dispersed forces in less populated areas, forgoing military defense of urban centers, and limiting the role of the air forces (because they provide tempting targets)[8]

In sum, a nonprovocative conventional strategy is a form of deterrence by denial. If deterrence fails, the objective would be to "ensnare the aggressor in a web of small engagements, avoiding any decisive battle, thereby precluding a clear victory."[9]

A nonprovocative defense would reject the traditional notion of military balance based upon a "bean count" standard and concentrate instead on the ability to deny an aggressor victory without causing destruction to the civilian population. (There should be no deep-strike capability.) Preoccupation with balance in conventional forces has been for decades a justification for nuclear first use and pressure to increase conventional forces. There is no reason to believe that stability requires either a strategy of first use or conventional parity. In Anders Boserup's words:

> What matters is security, which depends on having forces sufficient to prevent or fend off an attack even in the least favorable circumstances. It does not depend on balance at all, but rather on an imbalance between defense and offense. . . . The only way military force can make a positive contribution to stability is through the preponderance of defense over offense. Bilateral stability depends on both sides having forces that are stronger in defense than those of the opponent when used in an attack.[10]

Defensive sufficiency for NATO can be achieved in two fundamentally different ways: (1) through bilateral action by both alliances in the form of a joint curtailment of offensive capabilities, or (2) through unilateral action that enables NATO to compensate for defensive deficiencies. The latter would be difficult, requiring NATO to increase its defense capability to match the offensive capability of the Soviet Union. The first alternative now seems a real possibility because the Soviet Union has announced a change in doctrine that amounts to an endorsement of nonprovocative defense.

According to Boserup, nonprovocative defense is more than a new military strategy:

> Nonoffensive defense is much more than a means to fend off an aggressor; it is also a political instrument specifically designed to undermine hostility, to facilitate disarmament, and to make itself superfluous. It is defensive only in the military sense. As an instrument of a broadly conceived security policy, nonoffensive defense is clearly an aggressive, "offensive" tool that each side can use to undermine militarism on the other side by denying it the benefit of a credible enemy.[11]

The Exclusion of World Government

Other policy options are, of course, possible. In this study I have tried to include the major options and their hybrids that are under discussion in the international security literature. Readers are encouraged to come up with their own syntheses.

Some will conclude that despite all the options I have explored, one of the most important has been neglected: international disarmament under the aegis of a world government. Indeed, it might be argued that this alone would give real meaning to the domestic analogy that I have used throughout this study.

The reason I have omitted a discussion of this path to the prevention of nuclear war is that I have been exclusively concerned with *national* defense policy options—proposals concerned with preserving the United States as a free, sovereign state. With this in mind, I have considered only proposals that promise to defuse the Soviet nuclear threat in a manner consistent with the continued existence of the United States as a nation–state.

It may turn out that the only adequate solution to the problem of nuclear security is a world government with the power to enforce world law and guarantee universal nuclear disarmament. In the absence of such a government, however, the more immediate practical problem is to find a way, in the midst of huge nuclear arsenals, to preserve free, sovereign nation–states without destroying the planet. That is the task of a nuclear weapons policy, the exclusive concern of this book. The problem is how to choose the most rational policy. I have tried to contribute to a solution to this problem by providing not only a broad spectrum of policy choices and the arguments in support of each, but criteria for evaluating them.

Conclusion

If any question deserves public consideration, it is this: in the face of new Soviet thinking, what nuclear weapons policy should the United States adopt? Robert Dahl has written: "No decision can be more fateful for Americans and for the world than the decision about nuclear weapons. Yet the decisions have largely escaped the control of the democratic process."[1] Dahl points out that for the better part of four decades questions about nuclear weapons policy were not subject to public debate, "much less to control by public opinion expressed through elections and congressional action."[2] Yet, as Walter Lipmann observed, public opinion can have little meaning unless the public understands the issues.[3]

This book was motivated by a desire to involve a wider public in the debate over nuclear weapons policy, to inform this public about alternative visions of nuclear security, and to provide a basis for the assessment of the competing visions. What this book will probably not do, despite its author's wishes, is generate greater interest in nuclear policy issues.

The lack of public involvement in issues connected with nuclear policy has been due in part to the secrecy that from the beginning surrounded this policy. The first nuclear devices were secretly built, and the decision to use them on Japan was made in secret. This initial secrecy can, of course, be justified in terms of national security: victory over Japan depended, it is argued, on surprise and on the concealment from Japan of the actual numbers of nuclear bombs. Moreover, after the crisis of war passed, we faced a new adversary, and those in charge of

233

national security advised against allowing the public to debate nuclear weapons policy on the grounds that such a debate could send to the Soviet Union a destabilizing message of a lack of resolve.

The general absence of public debate over nuclear weapons cannot, however, be blamed entirely on a government conspiracy of silence and secrecy. The fact is that the public has been willing to allow others to deliberate on nuclear policy and to make these fateful decisions. There have been, of course, brief periods of public interest in nuclear policy: during and shortly after the Cuban missile crisis, during the campaign against atmospheric testing of nuclear weapons, and during the freeze movement. Yet there has been no sustained effort by the public to involve itself in the formation of nuclear weapons policy. Indeed, the public seems largely ignorant of even fundamental features of nuclear policy that are officially a matter of "public" knowledge, such as the NATO strategy of first use—a strategy that allows the West to initiate a nuclear strike on Soviet forces even in the absence of a Soviet nuclear attack.[4] In fact, 81 percent of the American public believes that U.S. policy prohibits first use of nuclear weapons.[5] This is an example of what might be called a "public secret"—a fact that is publicly known but not known by the public.[6] The fact that 75 percent of the public opposes the use of nuclear weapons to repel a conventional attack is therefore irrelevant, because there has been no significant public debate in which its opinion might make a difference.[7]

Since public interest in nuclear weapons policy seems ascendant only during periods of high tension between the Soviet Union and the United States, it is likely that interest in nuclear policy questions will diminish as relations between the two superpowers improve. The problem is that improved Soviet–American relations do not mean that nuclear weapons no longer pose a threat. For all the public knows, both superpowers have thousands of nuclear warheads on a hair-trigger (i.e., a policy of launch on warning), ready to be launched in a "war" that will constitute a disaster beyond imagination. Even if START talks result in the elimination of close to half the weapons on both sides, the detonation of the remaining weapons would be no less a disaster. Is the public willing to live with nuclear deterrence and its risks indefinitely? Has it rationally chosen to do so? Is it aware of alternatives? There may be no rational alternative to the strategy of nuclear deterrence, but this needs to be demonstrated in a thorough national debate.

In addition to laying out the logic and ethics of nuclear deterrence (in its major variations), I have attempted to make the logic and ethics of other nuclear policy options transparent by placing them within the familiar framework of criminal correction theories. The domestic analogy has been a crucial feature of my exposition of competing nuclear policy proposals. It might be useful to end this study by weighing the strengths and weaknesses of this explanatory device—both in general and in its application to each option.

In general, the domestic analogy is fruitful because it allows us to see the policy decision we confront in the nuclear domain as analogous to the choice we face on the domestic level. Both defense policy and criminal correction theory are concerned with threats to the freedom, lives, and property of citizens. The one is responsive to external threats; the other, to internal threats. Moreover, it can be seen that similar ethical values operate in both domains. The values according to which we justify deterrence, social defense, retribution, and rehabilitation in the sphere of domestic crime are relevant to the justification of their respective counterparts in defense policy.

The question is, which correction model and set of values allows us to deal most effectively with the threat of nuclear aggression and nuclear blackmail? Critics may argue that this question is now dated and irrelevant because new Soviet thinking on security renders the domestic analogy invalid. Since the Soviet Union has announced a nonaggressive policy and is making moves to establish a force system that conforms to it, shouldn't we cease thinking of the Soviet Union as an international criminal and start thinking of this nation as a friend or partner?

In fact, the domestic analogy does not require us to impute criminality to the Soviet state. Rather, it requires us to develop a policy of correction that will enable us to deal with the threat that Soviet nuclear weapons still pose for U.S. security. If our relationship with the Soviet Union ever achieves the same degree of trust that we have with nuclear powers such as Britain and France, then the domestic analogy will no longer be appropriate. Obviously, we have not yet reached that point with the Soviet Union.

The fact is that the Soviet Union has a criminal record—a record of crimes against its own people and the world—which even it now acknowledges, at least in part. This record and Soviet political and economic instability provide grounds for caution in dealing with a nation that retains an enormous coercive and destructive capability. Recidivism cannot be ruled out. It must be kept in mind that, despite an improvement in relations, as long as Soviet nuclear forces remain aimed at the United States, U.S. security is endangered. Thus, the domestic analogy, which requires us to conceive of the Soviet Union as a *potential* international offender (a possible aggressor or coercer)–and protect U.S. institutions from the continuing Soviet nuclear threat—remains valid.

But, of course, the domestic analogy, like all analogies, breaks down at certain points. A general disanalogy already noted is that there is no central enforcing authority in the area of international law. Thus, an act of aggression—an international crime against peace—must be corrected by the victim and/or its allies. In terms of law enforcement, the injured nation is obviously not an impartial agent, yet it must serve as judge and jury in terms of deciding which individuals in the aggressor nation should be punished (or corrected) and the nature of the corrective response.

A second and related general disanalogy is that in time of war the enforcement authority (the victim of aggression and/or its allies) does not always have superior power. Indeed, in the case of some policy options (e.g., rehabilitation), the enforcer would be weaker than the offender. On the domestic level, in contrast, the criminal justice system typically has greater power than individual offenders: usually, the state can more effectively intimidate the criminal than the criminal can intimidate the state.

These disanalogies could be corrected if an international authority with powers of enforcement were established. But this solution to the disanalogy transcends defense policy and calls for a world in which national self-defense is superseded by something *sui generis*, and my aim, as stated above, is to explore what is possible within the limits of national self-defense. It may, of course, turn out that this is the only path to lasting security, the only way to solve the nuclear weapons problem. Einstein contended that there are only two alternatives for humankind: world government or nuclear holocaust.[8] Certainly, if one's goal is the denuclearization of the planet, this may be the only way to achieve it. The question is whether this solution would require the abandonment of something central to traditional security: the preservation of the nation–state.

The domestic analogy also appears to break down in specific ways with respect to each theory. For example, in the case of the theory of deterrence, the domestic doctrine does not call for threats to punish the innocent. No advocate of domestic deterrence would approve of having the police threaten to kill the family of potential murderers as a way of deterring murder—no matter how efficacious such a threat-strategy might be. The fact that deterrence advocates do not tolerate threats to innocents on the domestic level may tell us something about the inadequacy of deterrence efficacy as a criterion of policy, if separated from utilitarian moral concerns. That is, for domestic deterrence advocates, at a certain point respect for the well-being of innocents overrides deterrence value.

This, of course, raises a question of coherence for those who condemn threats to the innocent on the domestic level while approving such threats within the framework of defense policy. Those who condemn threats to innocents on one level and approve them on another need to explain the crucial difference. They might have to make the case that while threats to harm the innocent produce on balance negative utility at the domestic level, on the level of national defense such threats produce consequences that are overwhelmingly positive (i.e., substantial national security through the prevention of nuclear blackmail and the preservation of free institutions), compared with the slight "psychological" insecurity created in the small percentage of the population that worries about the failure of deterrence.

As we have seen, concern for the rights of the innocent is an unambiguous part of the rationale for social defense. The analogy between the domestic and the international versions of social defense does not appear to break down when it comes to the question of innocents: it is central to both levels. The disanalogy lies elsewhere. Specifically, the domestic version does not require for its success that the offender cooperate with criminal justice authorities. On the other hand, for the military version of social defense to be really effective, the adversary must be unwilling to try to overwhelm the defensive apparatus and ideally should agree to move toward a mutual strategy of defense dominance. Although there are advocates of strategic defense who believe we can build a successful defensive system even with Soviet noncooperation and Soviet multiplication of countermeasures, they are less than convincing. The disanalogy therefore seems real.

In the case of retribution there is also a significant disanalogy. The breakdown in the analogy lies in the attempt to conceive of military retaliation as a form of punishment. The fact that retaliatory "punishment" in war must be inflicted prior to the establishment of guilt raises questions about the meaningfulness of the application of the principle of culpability to war. The inability to fine-tune retaliation against the so-called culpable—many of whom may be conscript soldiers coerced or brain-washed into participating in aggression—raises questions about the meaningfulness of the application of the principle of proportionality to war. Punishment before proof of culpability and an inability to mitigate punishment strain the analogical move from the domestic to the international domain.

Finally, to what extent is it possible to base a national security policy on the concept of rehabilitation? To what extent does a single nation have the power to change the conditions conducive to armed aggression? On the domestic level, the government can initiate economic and social reforms that reshape the entire society. Is there anything comparable that a government can do, facing other sovereign states that exist, in spite of international law, in a virtual state of nature? And how can an aggressive nation's behavior be reshaped by another nation, especially if the latter is the victim of aggression, with no military power and no ability to project force on the aggressor? Under a policy of rehabilitation, the United States would in fact be a disarmed enforcer of international law. On the domestic level it is not the victim of crime who rehabilitates the offender, but rather a central authority with the power to reshape thinking and behavior. Rehabilitation, as a path to international security, seems to cry out for a world government to give it real meaning.

Despite these disanalogies the domestic analogy is, I believe, still fruitful. It gives us a sense of significant parallels on the domestic and international levels. Most important, each correction model becomes a vision, something to strive for. For example, although the retributive principles of culpability and proportionality can be only very roughly approximated in war, a nation that attempted to conform to them and a nation that was concerned only with winning would design their weapons and conceive their legitimate targets in significantly different ways. If nuclear deterrence differs from domestic deterrence in its willingness to "punish" the innocent, still the teleological concern to use threats in a beneficial manner ties them together in an important way. If social defense on the international level differs from its domestic counterpart in requiring that the potential "offender" cooperate, nonetheless the former's view that the government has an obligation to protect society (lives and property) through a strategy of incapacitation is very much in the spirit of its criminal correction counterpart. And although, within a chaotic world of sovereign nation–states, there are limits to how much a potential victim of aggression can reform the world to eliminate aggression, a policy that sought to achieve national security through a strategy of nonviolent prevention and correction would provide a defense alternative that significantly approximated rehabilitation.

Despite new thinking in the Soviet Union, each of these options (or some hybrid thereof) remains relevant. The relative negativity involved in applying a criminal correction model to our relationship with the Soviet Union cannot be avoided until relations qualitatively change. Certainly, we can look forward to the day when the domestic analogy will be inappropriate because the friendship between the two nations makes the notion of mutual threat meaningless. That day is not yet here.

APPENDIX

Criticisms of the Major Policy Options

I have provided an exposition of a variety of nuclear weapons policy proposals and criteria for evaluating them. Given my emphasis on autonomy—on allowing readers to make their own critical assessments and draw their own conclusions—it might appear that my task is completed. In order, however, to expedite critical assessment, I provide a summary of recurrent criticisms of four of the major policy proposals discussed above. The criticisms will illustrate how the seven criteria of policy assessment developed in Chapter Two can be applied. Specifically, I will provide a summary of objections to deterrence (in its MAD and countervailing forms), social defense, retribution, and rehabilitation. Some have already been touched on in previous chapters. Before embracing any policy, the reader should be aware of the major criticisms of it. If, in the face of substantive objections, a reader can still affirm a particular policy option, then the choice can be said to be based upon a critical analysis.

Critique of Deterrence Policies

Pure Deterrence: Critique of Mutual Assured Destruction

1. *MAD is an immoral strategy because it involves an immoral threat.* If it is immoral to threaten what it is immoral to do, then MAD is immoral.

MAD—as a declaratory policy—threatens to incinerate millions of innocent human beings in retaliation for an attack ordered by culpable leaders. The threat is, of course, supposed to prevent our actually having to murder innocent civilians: MAD advocates "wager" that the efficacy of the threat will prevent leaders from having to carry it out. It should be noted that terrorists, in the same way, often count on threats to achieve their objectives—threats that they may not really want to carry out, such as executing innocent hostages. MAD is de facto a form of state terrorism: it requires that we achieve our security objectives by holding an adversary's population hostage, threatening to murder innocent civilians if their leaders order an attack on our country. We cannot consistently condemn terrorism while approving a strategy of nuclear hostage taking.[1]

2. *In calling for an attack on civilians,* MAD *commits a nation to the violation of international law.* Unless this is a bluff strategy, we may one day have to carry it out. If we do, we will be guilty of war crimes. MAD—as an action policy—calls for the violation of laws of war that prohibit direct attacks on population centers and the use of weapons of indiscriminate destruction. The United States is a signatory to international agreements, such as the Geneva Conventions, that forbid what MAD requires.[2]

3. MAD *violates a fundamental obligation of government: to defend and protect society from harm.* It requires, on the contrary, that the population be exposed to attack—indeed, to annihilation. Security should mean protection from attacks by other nations. It is paradoxical, if not contradictory, to define security in terms of the guarantee that one's nation remain vulnerable to extermination by another nation. No citizen can feel secure in his person, property, or future well-being as long as there is the constant threat of nuclear annihilation. Thus, MAD does not satisfy the fundamental objective of nuclear policy: to defend society.

4. MAD *places the U.S. president in an unacceptable moral dilemma: suicide or surrender.* With its massive retaliation threat, MAD requires that once the United States is attacked, the president either bring down further ruin on the nation or capitulate to the other side in order to prevent further slaughter.

5. MAD *is not a military strategy, but the negation of all strategy.* Thus to call MAD a strategy is incoherent, a contradiction in terms. Strategy involves the use of a nation's forces for a political end: victory over an adversary, preservation of the nation's political institutions, terminating war on conditions favorable to the nation. MAD, if carried out, requires revenge serving no military or political purpose.

6. MAD *is not a credible policy.* Its threat of a suicidal response to even a limited nuclear attack is simply not believable. In failing to satisfy the

requirement of credibility, MAD is crisis-destabilizing. In a crisis, it provides an incentive for the Soviets to strike first. The Soviets would not believe that we would risk the destruction of American society to avenge a limited nuclear attack against our nuclear forces or those in NATO countries. Thus, MAD is likely to fail.

7. *MAD's claim to a long record of successful deterrence is dubious.* First, it is impossible to prove a negative: that war has not occurred as a result of the possession of nuclear weapons. War might have been avoided in the absence of such weapons; the fear of the destruction of conventional war might have been sufficient to deter war between the United States and the Soviet Union. Second, even if we grant that the threat of mutual annihilation has kept the peace for decades, it may fail to deter tomorrow or the next day. The point is that no deterrent can be expected to work indefinitely. The failure of MAD would be a disaster for civilization. In terms of magnitude of disaster, there can be no worse policy option.

8. MAD *requires an understanding with the Soviet Union that does not exist.* MAD is a game that two must play: we cannot play it alone. Specifically, MAD requires that the Soviets agree to leave their homeland vulnerable and renounce the idea of victory in nuclear war. The evidence is that the Soviets are preparing to defend their population through active and passive defenses and, if forced to fight a nuclear war, to win it. In other words, the Soviets reject the premises of MAD. MAD, therefore, is not an adequate policy vis-à-vis Soviet doctrine.

9. *Although advocates assert that* MAD *requires a minimal number of survivable retaliatory forces, in theory and practice it leads to an endless arms race.* Since the logic of MAD is that of the doomsday machine—a hypothetical device that blows up the world when one side launches an attack against the other—overkill enhances MAD deterrence. The more destruction we can inflict on each other and the planet, the closer we can get to world-annihilating retaliation, the madder war becomes. The logic of MAD is the logic of omnicide: a multiplication of nuclear weapons to the point of absurdity to ensure the irrationality of nuclear conflict.

Enhanced Deterrence: Critique of Countervailing Strategy

1. *In making nuclear retaliation more credible,* CVL *strategy makes nuclear war conceivable and therefore more likely.* As we decrease the horror associated with nuclear war by talking about limited nuclear war and damage limitation, we increase the probability that one nation or the other will find nuclear war more appealing. Thus, CVL makes nuclear disaster more, not less, likely.

2. CVL *erroneously assumes that each nation will limit its attacks—for*

example, to military targets—when it "sees" the other side doing so. There are two problems with this assumption. First, it presupposes that each superpower will be able to tell the difference between counterforce and countervalue strikes, an improbability given (1) the likelihood that some weapons will miss their military targets and hit civilian centers, and (2) the fact that the enormous destructive power of even the low-yield counterforce weapons will make it difficult to distinguish them from countervalue weapons. Second, it presupposes that we can force the Soviets to play by our limited nuclear war–fighting rules, when in fact their strategy calls for a maximum initial response to eliminate our forces and achieve victory as soon as possible. The policy is not realistic in its assumptions about superpower nuclear exchanges, and it is not responsive to actual Soviet doctrine.

3. *The likely destruction of command and control facilities by electromagnetic pulse (EMP) and other effects of nuclear detonations will nullify escalation control and communication between the two nations, leading to blind exchanges—a spasm war without limits.* The effects of nuclear explosions make any assumptions about each nation's capacity to control its nuclear forces dubious. The notion that each side will be able to monitor precisely the level of the other side's attacks (or even detect pauses in attacks) and respond in a manner that sends a clear message of controlled retaliation is unjustifiably optimistic. It is more likely that exploding nuclear weapons will blind all communications between the superpowers. In other words, CVL is not technically feasible.

4. *The Soviets do not believe in limited nuclear war.* They believe that once a nuclear war begins, it will go all the way—whether we or they like it or not. Unlike objection 2, this is a predictive claim, not a strategic principle. That is, the Soviets, over and above all strategic considerations, believe that nuclear war will become a spasm affair once it starts. This is a much more realistic view than that held by advocates of CVL.

5. *The Soviets will interpret our countervailing strategy as a disguised war-winning strategy.* To be able to destroy a wide array of targets, we must have thousands of counterforce—potentially first-strike—weapons. Such a strategy will be destabilizing because it will dispose the Soviets to strike first to prevent the United States from using its counterforce weapons to disarm them. The strategy is therefore destabilizing and inadequate vis-à-vis Soviet doctrine.

6. *Countervailing strategy is not morally superior to MAD.* CVL involves the willingness of the United States to kill millions of civilians indirectly as a result of collateral damage or directly as a result of "intimidation" attacks on population centers to coerce war termination. This is a terroristic strategy that calls for making the Soviet population a hostage.

Even with the best intentions to limit destruction, nuclear weapons do not allow for the kind of discriminate violence and fine-tuned war fighting that CVL requires. The important point is that this strategy does not rule out the intentional destruction of population centers: it only calls for delaying attacks on such targets for bargaining and coercive purposes. CVL violates, therefore, the ultimate values upon which democratic society is based.

7. *The maximum flexibility required by* CVL *calls for a full range of forces to cover all the plausible war-fighting scenarios, and hence an indefinite number of nuclear weapons.* This will be not only an expensive policy, demanding enough weapons to hit all major military targets and command and control centers as well as industrial targets and cities, but an arms race destabilizing policy that will force the Soviets to build a large array of weapons to match ours. If we are to have sufficient weapons for the full range of targets, and if we are not planning to strike first, then we must have enough weapons to hit all the required targets even after suffering the worst possible counterforce first strike. When we consider the worst-case losses in a first strike, along with the possibility of malfunctions in many weapons, it will require an enormous arsenal to satisfy the needs of a countervailing strategy. It will lead to a costly, endless arms race. CVL is an economically burdensome policy, requiring continual modernization of and increase in the number of nuclear weapons.

8. *The policy is incoherent in a number of ways.* First, it endorses parity of forces while at the same time implying the need for overall superiority. We cannot control escalation at all levels of nuclear conflict unless we have nuclear superiority so that no matter what the Soviets do, we can go them one better; we must be able to match their every move and raise the stakes by inflicting, or threatening to inflict, greater damage in response to their limited attacks. Second, it calls for targeting of C^3I facilities as a way of limiting damage to the United States and/or its allies, while at the same time requiring us to spare these facilities to limit the war and terminate it short of an all-out exchange. That is, it holds out the possibility that we can limit damage to our society by destroying centers of command, but it needs to preserve centers of command in order to provide the enemy with the means for controlling the level of violence and terminating hostilities. (Even if we do not target their command and control facilities, we cannot prevent them from targeting ours in their attempt to sever the head that commands attacks against them.)

9. *Countervailing strategy commits the fallacy of conventionalization.* It treats nuclear weapons as if they were conventional weapons, failing to recognize that these weapons are *sui generis*. In terms of magnitude of destruction and long-term consequences, these weapons cannot be

treated like conventional forces.[3] If cvl fails—which means not only that nuclear war occurs but that it defies limitation—then we will face a disaster of profound magnitude.

Critique of National Social Defense Policy

1. *The idea that we can provide significant protection for our population is an illusion.* If only a few nuclear weapons penetrate, the result will be the destruction of American society. For example, if we destroy 95 percent of 10,000 warheads launched, that leaves 500 warheads—close to the number that McNamara described as sufficient to achieve the assured destruction of a society. Even if we could achieve a 100 percent kill of attacking weapons (carried in missiles, aircraft, submarines), it would still be possible for the enemy to sneak nuclear weapons into the country and detonate them when they pleased.[4] Social defense is not feasible, because the Soviets will be able, by stealth, to get under or go around the system.

2. *Despite declarations to the contrary, the Soviet Union will interpret a plan for comprehensive national defense as an element of an offensive, war-winning strategy.* Knowing that such a system cannot be effective against a full-scale Soviet attack, they will infer that its utility lies in handling a ragged retaliation after most of the Soviet arsenal has been destroyed by a first strike. That is, the strategy produces a destabilizing ambiguity, making war more, not less, probable. The weapons we are contemplating in SDI research are not as intrinsically defensive as SDI advocates contend: they can be construed as offensive as well as defensive. Soviet strategists explain their suspicions:

> The dialectics of the development of weaponry testify that any division of weapons into offensive and defensive ones is arbitrary. . . . [The] EMP *weapon*, generalized as a microwave weapon, would be especially effective in first strikes for causing blackouts of command posts and communications of the other side. . . . The kill mechanism of the laser weapon . . . might be used more easily as offensive weapons than as planned in the SDI. . . . It becomes clear that the side that would create and deploy a space-based ballistic-missile defense system would, at the same time, be capable of effectively inflicting a preemptive strike with a view to black out simultaneously all the components of the command-and-control system of the other side. . . . Laser weapons . . . could be used to attack all sorts of civilian targets and components of the military infrastructure such as oil storages, refineries and depots.[5]

Thus, the strategy fails the instrumental coherence test in a way that makes it destabilizing.

3. *The Soviets will find countermeasures—such as additional warheads, chaff, decoys—to defeat the defenses.* Despite claims about economic limits, the Soviets will spend whatever is required to defeat the system. Indeed, the dependence of U.S. leaders on popular support for defense spending will put them at a disadvantage, because Soviet leaders can (even in the age of *perestroika*) disdain the needs of their citizenry and spend what they deem necessary for national security. The policy will accelerate the arms race, requiring us to spend enormous sums to counter Soviet countermeasures.

4. *This path to security places too much confidence in computer technology.* The computer requirements of a comprehensive defense may be beyond what can be technically achieved. It would require the largest computer programs ever conceived, containing millions of instructions.[6] Even if the enormous technical requirements were satisfied, the fact that automatic systems—not human beings—would be "deciding" to go to war makes the system highly questionable. In taking out the human factor, the automated defensive system removes the last element of representative government. A machine, not the president, will "declare" war. Computer scientists Greg Nelson and David Redell sum up the problems:

> The computer system required by the Strategic Defense Initiative is the most complicated integrated computer system ever proposed. . . . An attempt to build the system would not necessarily succeed, and if it did succeed, uncertainties would remain about its reliability. . . . Because of the time constraints for attacking boosters, the proposed system is required to activate itself within seconds of warning. This would require increasing the level of automation in threat assessment and weapons release. But automatic systems are unsuited for coping with the ambiguity, uncertainty, and unexpected events that are likely in a military crisis. Increasing the degree of automation in the handling of crises would increase the risk of nuclear war.[7]

That is, if the system is erroneously triggered and its weapons are fired at Soviet facilities, perhaps using up defensive firepower in the process, the Soviets will mistake this for U.S. aggression and order nuclear retaliation against us. Thus, an automated system, even if designed for pure defense, could bring about the very attack it was designed, in part at least, to prevent. In sum, the system is likely to produce a nuclear disaster.

5. *The cost of the system will put enormous strains on our economy.* It will

cost billions to develop and deploy the system. To pay for a comprehensive national defense, we will probably have to sacrifice other aspects of national security—including our conventional military forces—and neglect nonmilitary areas such as education and medicine. Given the enormous budget deficit we now face and the scarcity of resources, paying for this form of "security" could seriously weaken the American economy, creating, in the end, a less stable and less secure society.

6. *A purely defensive system designed to destroy nuclear weapons provides no answer to the problem of how to deal with the nuclear aggressor.* Even if the nuclear aggression is thwarted through the neutralization of the attacking weapons and the attack against the United States fails—that is, granting *per impossibile* that the system will work perfectly—how should we respond to the nuclear attacker? Will its leaders be punished for attempted mass murder? If so, how? By conventional forces? If we pay enormous sums for this defensive system, will we be able to afford conventional forces adequate to the task of making a failed nuclear aggressor pay? A successful shield against nuclear attacks does not end the possibility—perhaps even the moral necessity—of armed conflict with the Soviet Union. Perhaps a successful nuclear defense will only make the world safe for conventional war, where an edge in conventional forces will determine which society is ultimately more secure. In that event, we may be at a substantial disadvantage. Given their superior conventional forces, the Soviets will be able to impose their will on Western Europe and perhaps ultimately the rest of the world. In the end, even a workable defensive system may not achieve the fundamental objective of a defense policy: to preserve democracy against a renewed Soviet threat.

7. *This policy will in fact lead to a worsening of the Soviet nuclear threat.* To defeat the defensive system the Soviets will make two offensive countermoves that will lessen American security: (1) they will greatly increase the number of nuclear warheads that can be delivered to U.S. soil, and (2) they will aim many of these weapons at the targets that are the most difficult to protect: cities. In effect, the U.S. adoption of a policy of national social defense will redirect Soviet targeting from military forces to population centers, thereby increasing the threat to the very targets the policy was designed to protect. This is precisely the conclusion reached by the Union of Concerned Scientists: "The fewer warheads the Soviets can expect to arrive on U.S. territory, the more likely those warheads are to be assigned to the softest and most valuable targets—major urban areas. Warhead accuracy would become less important, and sheer destruction, with maximum collateral damage, more important, thus reversing the priorities associated with limited war strategies."[8] Thus, the strategy of SDI is ultimately inconsistent with protection of the population.

9. *It makes U.S. security contingent upon a system that can never be adequately tested.* There is no way to test a defensive system for reliability—except in a war. As Nelson and Redell put it: "It is impossible to test the system under operational conditions, yet component testing system simulations are totally inadequate substitutes. It would be folly to rely on such a system in the absence of full-scale operational testing."[9]

10. *The proposal calls for violation of the* ABM *Treaty—one of the most important arms control treaties ever signed.* In 1972 the United States and the USSR recognized that the construction of defenses would be destabilizing, causing an endless offensive and defensive arms race, and that preserving effective retaliatory capabilities was the best path to mutual security. SDI calls for violating an agreement that was a product of democratic debate and that the United States is legally bound to respect. It is therefore a legally indefensible policy.

11. *A system of national comprehensive defense for the United States would decouple its security from that of Western Europe.* It would end extended deterrence, allowing the United States, under its illusory defensive astrodome, to return to isolationism while leaving Western Europe to fend for itself. Moreover, if the Soviet Union developed defenses, the Soviets would use their conventional superiority to attack Western Europe without fear of unacceptable nuclear retaliation from any remaining nuclear states, such as France.

Critique of Retribution Policy

1. *Denuclearization—understood as the elimination of nuclear weapons of mass destruction—will increase the likelihood of war.* A policy of retribution calls for the substitution of accurate conventional weapons for nuclear forces. Without the fear of annihilation, the Soviet Union will have less to fear in launching an invasion of Eastern or Western Europe or risking an armed conflict with the United States. By lessening the horror of war, conventional weapons increase its likelihood. Thus, this policy violates the interpretation of the disaster-avoidance criterion that focuses on the probability of disaster.

2. *The devastation caused by modern conventional weapons, though not as great as that caused by nuclear weapons, will still be catastrophic.* One has only to recall the slaughter of World War I to realize the horror of conventional war. George Will sums up the lesson of that war: " 'Conventional forces.' The phrase has a soothing sound—until you remember what conventional forces did 70 years ago. They killed men one by one, but with a cumulative effect that was socially shattering. Nuclear weapons . . . are required today for the prevention of battles as ruinous

as the Somme."[10] Current and projected conventional weapons are much more powerful than those used in the first two world wars. A full-scale, global nonnuclear war between the United States and the Soviet Union would be catastrophic for both sides.

Moreover, if the Soviet Union had nuclear forces while we lacked them, there is no doubt that they would use them if they were losing a conventional conflict—or perhaps even if they were winning, in order to bring the war to a quicker termination (as we did in the war with Japan). The only way to prevent the horrors of a theoretically winnable conventional war is for each side to have the capacity to threaten to inflict the profoundly greater horrors of unwinnable nuclear war. Thus, making a mutual nuclear holocaust a possibility is the only way to make a Soviet–American war an improbability.

3. *A denuclearization of U.S. forces would uncouple the United States and Western Europe.* There would no longer be a nuclear umbrella under which the United States could extend deterrence to Western Europe. A nonnuclear United States would be tempted to retreat into neo-isolationism, seeking the protection of two oceans and leaving European security to the Europeans.

4. *To match the now superior Soviet conventional forces, the United States will have to reinstitute the draft.* There are two serious obstacles to this: (1) the supply of draft-age males is diminishing each year, and (2) there will be strong resistance to conscription. Matching Soviet conventional forces would, George Will warns, require permanent conscription of young men "on a scale that no democracy has been willing to suffer other than in wartime."[11] The funds required to substantially increase troop strength would place a burden on Western economies that they have hitherto shown no inclination to shoulder. The financial burden of large armies lies not only in the direct costs of paying for additional soldiers, but in the indirect costs of the lost contributions of these individuals to the civilian sector.

5. *A denuclearized* NATO *would in fact become too dependent upon a silver bullet.* It is not likely, given the demographics and decades of reluctance, that NATO will significantly increase its manpower. Inferiority in numbers and its forfeiture of the nuclear threat will force NATO to compensate by the use of emerging technologies. Security will be based on a small number of exceedingly complex, costly, and none-too-reliable weapons. No one has ever tried to fight a war with smart weapons. If they work, they are terrific. If they don't, you have disaster: the war will go awry very quickly. Keeping in mind what Clausewitz called *friction* and what we have more recently called Murphy's Law—the inherent tendency for things to go wrong—we should not count on technology to take the place of combatants. The very smartness of the

weapons may limit their flexibility. Moreover, for any smart solution, there is a smart counter.[12] Consequently, the feasibility of ET is very questionable.

6. *Automatic systems of troop and weapon management will transfer more and more control functions from human agents to automatic devices.* Mechanization and the use of military robots are part of the emerging technologies that are to compensate for Western manpower inferiority. Reliance on highly automated battle systems will prevent the political and supreme military command from sanctioning decisions. This could, in extreme cases, lead to an irreversible escalation of hostilities.[13] Taking the human being out of the loop will decrease, not increase, security.

7. *While the West ties its hands by adhering to rules of war that prohibit the use of indiscriminate weapons, the Soviet Union will exploit its capacity for terroristic coercion by using, or threatening to use, nuclear, chemical, and/or biological weapons.* If we allow unrealistic laws of war and abstract principles of justice to prevent us from using nuclear threats to deter Soviet aggression, we will be placed at a distinct disadvantage and suffer diminished security. To achieve its (now concealed) aggressive objectives and to conquer a denuclearized United States and Western Europe, it may not be necessary for the Soviet Union to use any of its weapons of horror. The Soviets need only engage in blackmail—that is, threaten to inflict indiscriminate destruction on free societies if they do not comply with Soviet demands. In other words, a retributive policy would face a distinct disadvantage vis-à-vis a ruthless, lawless, and amoral Soviet strategy.

8. *The view that finds moral salvation in new weapons mistakenly assumes that men have been indiscriminate in the conduct of war because they lacked the means to discriminate.*[14] The indiscriminate behavior of men at war does not reflect technological imperatives so much as the logic of war. War is by its very nature hell: once human beings enter this world, law and morality are necessarily silent. This applies to U.S. as well as Soviet commanders and combatants. War itself, not particular weapons, barbarizes human beings, turning previously civilized persons into mindless killers. War is a realm of excess in which anything goes. No technological fix can change this fact. Even discriminate or moderate means can be used in the pursuit of immoderate ends, as when a simple pistol is used to put bullets through the back of the necks of children. As long as there is war, there will be indiscriminate slaughter and atrocities.

9. *The retributive prohibition on directly attacking noncombatants can be reduced to moral absurdity.* It tells us, in effect, that an enemy who shelters his soldiers and weapons among unwilling civilians should not be attacked or even threatened with destruction, no matter how many lives could be saved by such attacks or threats to attack. What if the

noncombatant lives that could be saved by countervalue targeting substantially outnumber the lives that would be lost?[15] What if we could prevent attacks on our society (or bring a war to a close sooner)—thus saving millions of lives—by threatening to kill or actually killing thousands of noncombatants in Moscow whom Soviet leaders are using as shields? Retributive policy will not even allow us to *threaten* to attack population centers in which the Soviet leaders might shield themselves, even if such threats could prevent Soviet aggression from occurring in the first place.

There is moral incoherence here—a refusal to kill some innocents when in fact that is the only way to save more innocents. If innocent life is important and the only way to maximize its protection is to kill a smaller number of innocents, should we not choose to attack some population centers—or at least threaten to attack them—to achieve this end? Retributive policy appears to say no, requiring us to avoid all such attacks even if that means that more noncombatants will die than will be saved.

Critique of Rehabilitation Policy

1. *A policy of rehabilitation fails to recognize that the Soviet Union respects strength and exploits weakness.* This proposal plays into the hands of a Soviet strategy that seeks to disarm the West. In the absence of a nuclear threat, the Soviet Union has every reason to use aggressive military power to expand the Soviet empire and ultimately achieve the goal of world domination. The fruits of containment policy and the opportunity to get beyond it will be lost if we give up the deterrent strategy that has inhibited Soviet aggression for over forty years.

2. *The policy, in stressing cooperation with and acceptance of the Soviet Union, involves complicity with a criminal regime.* Our policy should not be governed by the temporary good will of Soviet leaders. Should we be economically aiding and culturally cooperating with a state that still systematically violates human rights? Is this not appeasement in the worst sense? The policy is therefore immoral: it contradicts the fundamental American values we supposedly are devising a defense policy to preserve.

3. *Civilian-based defense requires more discipline and patience than most citizens are capable of.* How long will people be able to refrain from violence when enemy forces arbitrarily arrest, jail, and torture citizens who resist enemy demands? It is probable that as abuses increase, anger will grow and haphazard or organized violence will be carried out by citizens. Moreover, such violence will provide justification for the oc-

cupier's acceleration of oppressive measures. The strategy of civilian-based defense—a whole community standing together, refusing to resort to force in the face of the abuse of their families, friends, and fellow citizens—is not feasible.

4. *Contact with disciplined invaders could in fact weaken the morale of the civilian population.* This will occur if (1) the invaders are convinced of the justice of their cause, or (2) significant incentives are provided for citizens to collaborate and supply information to the occupiers. A well-conditioned, successfully propagandized invasion force will not be susceptible to conversion techniques. Moreover, with the proper threats against resisters in the community—promises, for instance, to torture or kill members of their family unless they cooperate—the invaders might intimidate enough individuals to make the resistance unworkable. Threats to imprison or torture children unless the parents agree to the aggressor's demands will be enough to extinguish the resistance of most parents. With an enemy who is willing to resort to such ruthless methods, it will take superhuman commitment to maintain opposition to oppression. Most human beings simply will not continue to resist when confronted with threats to those they love, or in the face of physical threats (death or torture) to themselves.

5. *The policy will make it impossible for the nation practicing it to intervene to prevent or correct great injustices in other societies.* What if a newly aggressive Soviet Union uses its military power to subjugate a people not trained in the techniques of civilian-based defense, or even a nation trained in this strategy? We will have to sit helplessly as the Soviets impose their will on, or extract resources from, the defeated nation.

6. *The policy will eliminate deterrence forces in Western Europe while decoupling U.S. and West European security.* No longer will U.S. nuclear weapons exist on the continent to deter an invasion of Europe. We will be forced into being isolationists, no matter how much we might want to help an occupied Europe. We will no longer have a capacity to provide Western Europe with the retaliatory forces that make Soviet aggression too costly to consider. On the other hand, the Soviet Union will be able to use nuclear blackmail to achieve its aggressive objectives.

7. *The policy falsely assumes that a nuclear nation would not attack a nation that had renounced nuclear weapons.* If the nonnuclear nation refused to satisfy the demands of the nuclear nation, then to show that it means business the latter might engage in small, selective nuclear strikes. It should be remembered that the only use of nuclear weapons was against a nonnuclear power. The weapons were used allegedly to break the morale of the government and people of Japan—literally to shock the enemy into surrender.

If the Soviets became convinced that a confrontation between its troops and citizens trained in civilian-based defense might lead to their conversion or a loss of morale—to their nonviolent defeat—then they would seek some "nonconventional" method of defeating the unarmed resisters. Limited nuclear attacks—perhaps using enhanced radiation weapons that cause slow, agonizing death but minimal damage to the environment—might be a relatively cheap and efficient way to torture a people into submission, to break their morale without resorting to a costly use of troops. Small nuclear or chemical attacks could be gradually escalated after each refusal of the society to capitulate.

How long could the civilian population withstand limited but graduated nuclear and/or chemical attacks on their communities? After all, they would be trained to resist troops, not weapons that inflict an agonizing death. Thus, by a moderate use of neutron-type weapons, the Soviet Union could punish or terrify the noncooperative population of the United States, Western Europe, Japan, or any other denuclearized nation.

8. *Far from being a democratic defense of democracy, civilian-based defense will involve the violation of democratic principles.* To be effective, civilian-based defense would require universal training and participation. If even a small segment of the population engaged in sporadic violence or killed even a small percentage of the invading or occupying troops, the effect of nonviolence and the moral atmosphere that this strategy requires would be lost.

Universal participation would require compulsory training of citizens, a clear violation of democratic freedom. It would violate the rights of conscience of those who believe in martial values or who simply do not believe in compulsory training. To remove the physical possibility of violent resistance, moreover, the strategy would require the confiscation of all firearms, a clear violation of the Second Amendment to the U.S. Constitution.

Glossary

ABM (anti-ballistic missile): Defensive missile designed to intercept and destroy an incoming hostile missile.

ABM system: Anti-ballistic missile system; system for identifying, tracking, and intercepting offensive missiles. Contemporary research includes work on laser and particle beam weapons, smart bullets, and smart pebbles.

ABM Treaty: Signed in 1972. It prohibits the United States and the USSR from building *nationwide* ABM systems or their components. It allows ABM research but bans development, testing, and deployment of space-based systems.

Action policy: Defense policy a country actually plans to carry out, in contrast to declaratory policy.

Active defense: Protection of civilian and military targets through the use of defensive systems such as surface-to-air missiles, ABMs, and anti-aircraft guns. (*See also* Passive defense.)

Appeasement: Policy of being conciliatory in the face of unjustified demands or aggression.

Area defense: Defense covering a large area, such as a city.

Arms control: Any measure limiting or reducing forces, regulating armaments, and/or restricting the deployment of troops or weapons.

Bargaining chip: Actual or projected weapons system whose actual or threatened deployment is used to gain some concession in arms control negotiations.

Bus: Postboost vehicle on a MIRV-equipped ballistic missile. It carries low-thrust engines and control and guidance equipment for maneuvering after the initial boost in order to dispense multiple warheads on trajectories leading them to different targets. (*See* MIRV.)

Capability: Potential military power under a government's control. Although capability need not imply intent, it is so interpreted under worst-case analysis. (*See* Worst-case analysis.)

CEP (circular error probable): Accuracy of a missile, measured in terms of the radius of a circle within which 50 percent of the warheads aimed at the center will land.

Civil defense: Passive measures designed to minimize the effects of enemy attacks on all aspects of civilian life, particularly to protect the population and the production base. Civil defense includes fallout and blast shelters, crisis relocation plans, and emergency steps to repair and restore vital utilities and facilities.

Civilian-based defense (cbd): Defense by civilians (as opposed to soldiers) using civilian (nonviolent) means of struggle, such as widespread non-cooperation and massive public defiance.

Cold War: Intense post–World War II rivalry between the U.S. and the USSR in which war is an ever present possibility deliberately sought by neither side. It is the considered judgment of many politicians and political scientists that the Cold War is over.

Collateral damage: Incidental or accidental casualties and destruction of property that occur as a side-effect of military strikes against enemy forces or military resources.

Command/Control/Communication and Intelligence (C³I): Systems and procedures used to guarantee that the president and senior civilian and military officials remain in communication with U.S. armed forces and each other.

Consequentialism: Ethical viewpoint holding that the rightness of an act depends on its consequences. More specifically, it is the view that an action is right provided that it has good consequences or, on the whole, more good consequences than bad. Utilitarianism is a form of consequentialism.

Containment: U.S. policy toward the Soviet Union formulated by George Kennan in the late 1940s. The policy called for the U.S. to resist Soviet expansionism by means of steady counterpressure rather than to overthrow or "roll back" communism.

Conventional forces/weapons: Term usually applied to nonnuclear weapons—those which destroy or kill through explosive force, such as bullets, shrapnel, and incendiaries—but not to chemical or biological weapons.

Counterforce: Term used to describe attacks against enemy military targets either in retaliation or (preemptively) to remove the means of retaliation. Targets include ports, airfields, barracks, arms dumps, command and control centers, submarines, and hardened silos containing missiles.

Countermeasures: Measures taken by the offense to overcome aspects of a ballistic missile defense system.

Countervailing strategy: Strategy that aims to make clear to the Soviets that no course of aggression on any scale of attack and at any stage of conflict could lead to victory, however they may define victory.

Countervalue: Term for attacks on civilian targets, cities and industrial centers, which can be achieved with less accurate weapons than are required for counterforce targeting.

Coupling: Strategic language that refers to the idea that U.S. troops and European-based nuclear forces will act as an insurance policy against Soviet aggression in Europe. U.S. and Western European security are tied together, so that an attack on Western Europe is seen as a threat to the United States.

Credibility: Requirement of workable deterrence. The potential enemy must believe (or be unable to rule out) that a nation has the ability and the will to carry out its threats.

Crisis: Condition between peace and open conflict, usually characterized by rising tensions.

Crisis stability: Confidence shared by opponents that in a crisis neither side could gain a decisive advantage by using nuclear weapons first.

Cruise missile: Slow-flying (subsonic) pilotless aircraft equipped with its own guidance system. Usually flying at low altitude, it is capable of achieving high accuracy in striking a distant target.

Damage limitation: Refers to efforts to minimize the damage an adversary can inflict on one's civilian and/or military assets.

Decapitation: Targeting strategy designed to destroy the adversary's leadership and command structure with the purpose of impairing its retaliatory response.

Declaratory policy: Defense policy a country publicly states that it will carry out, in contrast to action policy.

Delivery system: Vehicle that delivers a warhead from its original site to its target; the means by which explosive devices are carried to the objects to be destroyed.

Denuclearization: Elimination of nuclear forces or substitution of conventional for nuclear weapons.

Deontological ethics: From *deon* (duty). This ethical viewpoint defines right action in terms of conformity to duty. One is expected to perform one's duty (e.g., to respect all persons), regardless of consequences.

Deployment: Putting weapons in place for military use.

Detente: General relaxation of Soviet–American tensions in the early 1970s. The term is also used to refer to any relaxation of the tensions between the two superpowers.

Deterrence: Prevention of proscribed action by the threat to inflict losses that exceed gains; the threat to deny the potential offender its objectives; or both.

DEW (directed energy weapons): Weapons that destroy their targets (e.g., ICBMs) by delivering energy (lasers, beams of atomic or subatomic particles, etc.) to them at nearly the speed of light.

Disarmament: Elimination of military forces or armaments, whether nuclear, biological, chemical, or conventional weapons.

Dual-capable system: Weapon or delivery system capable of carrying nuclear or conventional explosives.

Emerging technologies (ET): Highly advanced conventional weapons within a system managed by sophisticated computer systems. The new weapons include precision-guided munitions (PGM) and equally accurate missiles with extremely powerful conventional warheads.

EMP (electromagnetic pulse): Brief, intense burst of electrical and magnetic fields from an exploding nuclear weapon. It can destroy or impair the performance of electronic equipment, including communications technology, computer memories, and some missile guidance systems.

Escalation: Active (deliberate) or passive (unpremeditated) expansion of the level of violence of a war.

Escalation control: Ability to increase or decrease the level of violence in a war (especially nuclear conflict) through a developed C³I system.

Escalation dominance: Capacity of one side to dominate the other side at any level of nuclear exchange.

Escalation ladder: Steps (up or down) involving weapons or tactics: for example, from conventional weapons to battlefield nuclear forces, or from field warfare to bombardment of cities.

Existential deterrence: Strategy based on the assumption that the possession (or existence) of some retaliatory nuclear forces is sufficient to deter a nuclear attack.

Extended deterrence: Form of deterrence in which a nation attempts to prevent attacks on others, such as allies or clients, as well as on itself, usually but not necessarily through the threat of nuclear retaliation.

Fail-safe: Procedure that in theory prevents accidental or unintentional use of nuclear weapons. For instance, nuclear armed bombers on an attack mission do not proceed beyond a certain point unless they receive positive orders; if no orders are given, they return to base.

Fallout: Radioactive particles composed of contaminated debris from a nuclear explosion.

Firebreak: Barrier separating conventional from nuclear war.

First strike: Initial attack with strategic nuclear weapons. (*Cf.* First use.)

First-strike capability: Capacity to carry out a disarming first strike.

First-strike strategy: Intention to launch a first strike before absorbing an attack.

First use: Nonstrategic initial deployment of nuclear weapons—for example, the use by NATO of tactical nuclear weapons to stop a mass conventional attack on Western Europe by the Warsaw Pact.

Fission bomb: Nuclear bomb that detonates when atoms are split apart.

Flexible response (FR): Adopted by NATO in 1967 to replace the strategy of massive nuclear retaliation in the event of Soviet aggression with a strategy that allows for a number of options, including conventional and limited nuclear strikes.

Fusion bomb: Nuclear bomb that explodes when atomic nuclei are fused together.

Ground-launched cruise missile (GLCM): Cruise missile launched from a ground-based launcher. This missile was outlawed by the INF Treaty.

Ground zero: Point on the surface of the earth at or directly below a nuclear explosion.

Hardening: Protection with concrete, earth, and other materials to enable something to withstand the heat, radiation, and (especially) blast effects of a nuclear attack. The term is typically applied to missiles contained in underground concrete silos fitted with armored blast doors.

Hard target: Facility designed to resist attack—for example, buried deep in the ground and protected by thick layers of reinforced concrete and steel.

Hard-target kill capability: Ability to destroy "hardened" (fortified) targets, such as enemy missile silos.

ICBM (intercontinental ballistic missile): Ballistic missile with a range of approximately 3,500 miles or more. In other words, a rocket-propelled vehicle capable of delivering a nuclear warhead across intercontinental ranges. An ICBM may have a single warhead or multiple warheads, may be fixed or mobile (e.g., on tracks), and may be land- or sea-based. It consists of a booster, one or more reentry vehicles, possibly penetration aids, and, in the case of a MIRVed missile, a postboost vehicle. Once outside the atmosphere, an ICBM follows an elliptical ballistic trajectory. It can accelerate to about 15,000 miles per hour and can fly between two continents in about twenty-five minutes.

Intermediate Nuclear Forces (INF): Nuclear forces with a range between 300 and 3,000 miles.

Intermediate Nuclear Forces Treaty: Signed by the U.S. and the USSR in 1988. It outlaws land-based intermediate nuclear forces.

Jus ad bellum: Component of just war theory concerned with the justification for going to war and the conditions under which a war may legitimately be waged.

Jus in bello: Component of just war theory concerned with how a war is waged— the acts and methods that are and are not justifiable in wartime.

Kiloton (kt.): Equal to the energy of 1,000 tons of TNT.

Launch control center (LCC): Underground command posts used to launch land-based nuclear missiles.

Launch on warning (LOW): Condition under which bombers and missiles would be launched on receipt of early warning that an enemy has launched land-based missiles.

Launch under attack (LUA): Condition under which early-warning information on the launch of an opponent's missiles is confirmed and bombers and missiles are launched so that they will survive an attack.

Limited nuclear options (LNO): Strategy often associated with Secretary of Defense James Schlesinger, containing nuclear use options short of all-out nuclear retaliation. It refers to planning for nuclear attacks that are limited in number and types of targets.

MAD (mutual assured destruction): Capacity of both the United States and the USSR to inflict massive countervalue damage after suffering a full-scale nuclear attack from the other side.

Megaton (MT): Amount of energy that would be released by the explosion of 1,000 kilotons (one million tons) of TNT.

Midgetman missile: Small, single-warhead, mobile, land-based intercontinental ballistic missile under development by the United States.

Minuteman III missile: Major U.S. intercontinental ballistic missile, with a range of 7,020 miles and a payload consisting of three 160-kiloton independently targetable warheads.

MIRV (multiple independently targeted reentry vehicle): Ballistic missile payload consisting of two or more nuclear warheads, each of which can be assigned a separate target. Most modern ballistic missiles are MIRVed.

Modernization: Improvement of a weapon by modification of existing systems or by the creation of new systems. Improvements in the accuracy and mobilization of ICBMs would be an example.

MX missile: Originally called Missile Experimental (thus the *x*); now called the Peacekeeper. This land-based intercontinental ballistic missile with a capacity to deliver ten MIRVed warheads is highly accurate and has a range of 7,500 miles.

National Command Authority (NCA): Decision-making centers responsible for the authorization to use strategic weapons, including the president and the secretary of defense or their duly deputized stand-ins or successors. The chain of command runs from the president to the secretary of defense and through the Joint Chiefs of Staff to the commanders of the regional and specific commands.

National technical means (NTM): Methods of unilaterally verifying compliance with arms control agreements by the use of satellite surveillance, aircraft equipped with radar and other sensors, and sea- and ground-based systems for collecting the signals sent by missile test flights.

NATO (North Atlantic Treaty Organization): Alliance for defense against the Soviet Union, comprising Western European and North American countries, established in 1949. Members agree that an armed attack on one is to be regarded as an armed attack against all and is to be met by action, including the use of armed force "to restore and maintain the security of the North Atlantic area." The member countries are Belgium, Britain, Canada, Denmark, France, Greece, Iceland, Luxembourg, the Netherlands, Norway, Portugal, Spain, Turkey, the United States, and West Germany. France withdrew from the military organization in 1966.

Neutron bomb: Small fission bomb triggered by compression. Most of its energy is delivered in the form of high-speed neutrons, which are lethal to people but do little blast and heat damage, leaving property relatively unharmed.

NORAD (North American Aerospace Defense Command): Essential part of the U.S. C³I structure. Its operations include bomber detection and warning; ballistic missile and early warning system (BMEWS); detection of submarine-launched ballistic missiles; and space detection and tracking system (SADATS), which detects, identifies, and tracks all objects in space, noting their orbital characteristics so they can be targeted if necessary.

Nuclear proliferation: Acquisition of nuclear weapons by nations not previously possessing them.

Nuclear umbrella: Protection of Western Europe by U.S. nuclear forces deployed in Europe or based in the United States or aboard U.S. submarines. (*Cf.* Coupling; Extended deterrence.)

Nuclear winter: Controversial hypothesis that the dust and smoke from fires started by thousands (or even hundreds) of nuclear explosions could cause abnormally low temperatures worldwide for an extended period.

Nuclear yield: Energy released in the detonation of a nuclear weapon, measured in terms of kilotons or megatons of TNT.

On-site inspection: Method of verifying conformity to arms control agreements by examining suspected sites for weapons or weapons production.

Ontology: Theory of reality. For example, materialism is an ontology that holds that reality consists of units of matter/energy. An ontology can also include a theory of human nature.

Overkill: Destructive power in excess of what is adequate to destroy particular targets or groups of targets to achieve identified objectives; the ability destroy enemy targets more than once.

Overpressure: Pressure over normal atmospheric pressure which is 14.7 pounds per square inch. This is one effect of a nuclear blast.

Pacifism: Philosophy with a number of variants. Unqualified or pure pacifism is opposition to all war on the grounds that no war can be morally justified. Selective pacifism opposes a particular war on the grounds that it is immoral. Nuclear pacifism involves either opposition to all nuclear conflicts or opposition to all wars because any war could lead to a nuclear conflict (which is never morally justifiable).

PALS (permissive action links): Electronic devices incorporated into nuclear weapons that require use of a special code to arm and fire them.

Passive defense: Measures taken to enable a nation's population and/or military forces to survive an attack; protection of civil and military targets without the use of military forces. Population protection includes evacuation and shelters. Passive protection of military facilities includes hardening, dispersal, and camouflage.

Payload: Weapons and penetration aids carried by a delivery vehicle.

Presidential Directive 59: U.S. targeting doctrine formulated during the Carter administration. It emphasizes the destruction of Soviet military forces, the political leadership, and command and control facilities, as well as protection of our C^3I facilities and the ability of our nuclear forces to endure a protracted nuclear war.

Peaceful coexistence: Public Soviet position that asserts that war is not an appropriate form of East–West competition.

Precision-guided missile (PGM): Precision-guided munitions or precision-guided weapons (PGW). These conventional weapons of great accuracy home in on the target with terminal guidance. They are designed for warding off an attack and are especially effective against tanks. They can be connected to computers and aimed and fired by remote control.

Preemptive strike: Attack initiated in anticipation of an enemy's decision to resort to war, intended to limit the damage an enemy can inflict on one's forces and homeland.

Prevailing strategy (PVL): Doctrine that the most credible nuclear posture is one that convinces the Soviet Union that in a nuclear war the United States could achieve a significant victory. This strategy requires the capacity for escalation dominance and military superiority.

Preventive war: Unprovoked attack initiated on the assumption that war with the attacked nation is inevitable at some time in the future and can be fought more favorably now than later.

Protocol: Agreed addition or modification of a treaty.

Radiation sickness: Often the first sign of radiation exposure, caused by damage to the gastrointestinal tract. Such damage results, on average, from accumulated doses exceeding 150 roentgens.

Realism: School of political thought that holds that it is unrealistic to think that morality or laws of war will be respected by nations involved in war. In this view the only factor that governs behavior in war is national self-interest, specifically an interest in winning, using all means to achieve that end.

Reasonable sufficiency: Soviet military doctrine announced under Gorbachev, which calls for nuclear forces sufficient to absorb the worst possible nuclear attack and still retaliate, while not so great that they could threaten the security of the United States.

Reentry vehicle (RV): Part of a ballistic missile that carries the nuclear warhead and is designed to reenter the earth's atmosphere during the terminal phase of the missile's flight.

Rideout: Process of absorbing—or riding out—nuclear attack.

SAC (Strategic Air Command): Part of the U.S. Air Force concerned with strategic warfare, including bombers and ICBMs.

SALT (Strategic Arms Limitation Talks Treaty): Includes two treaties, both signed in 1972, that limited the number of Soviet and American ICBM and submarine-launched ballistic missile launchers; the other (never ratified by the U.S. Senate) limited missiles, bombers, and MIRV deployments.

Second strike: Retaliatory nuclear attack in response to a strategic nuclear strike by the adversary.

Second-strike capability: Capacity to carry out a nuclear attack against an opponent after suffering a first strike.

Silo: Underground emplacement housing a ballistic missile and its launch mechanism. They are hardened against blast and heat, and sometimes radioactivity, by thick reinforced concrete.

SIOP (single integrated operational plan): Detailed contingency plan for strategic retaliatory attacks in the event of nuclear war—in effect, the U.S. plan for fighting a nuclear war.

Spasm war: Presumes a preset plan that, once buttons are pressed, cannot be changed.

SS-18: Soviet ICBM. MIRVable, with eight to ten 600-kiloton warheads, this weapon is the world's largest ICBM, accurate enough to destroy silos and protected facilities such as major command headquarters.

START (Strategic Arms Reduction Talks): Series of Soviet–American negotiations initiated in 1982 in an attempt to reduce offensive strategic weapons.

Stealth: Family of technologies designed to reduce the probability that an aircraft will be detected by enemy sensors such as radar; also a strategic bomber utilizing such technologies.

Strategic: Applied to weapons, refers to those of long range, capable of reaching the homeland of the adversary, as contrasted with tactical weapons used on a battlefield. Strategic weapons include intercontinental forces such as ICBMs and long-range bombers.

Strategic Defense Initiative (SDI): Research, development, and testing program intended to create the means to intercept strategic ballistic missiles in all phases of flight.

Strategic delivery vehicle: Bomber or missile capable of delivering a nuclear (or other) warhead from one nation's homeland to another's.

Strategic nuclear weapons: Weapons based in the United States, the Soviet Union, or at sea and capable of striking targets in the adversary's homeland.

Strategic parity: Rough balance or equality between U.S. and Soviet strategic nuclear capabilities.

Strategic warning: Detection of actions that indicate that a nuclear attack could occur within days or hours: the movement of submarines from ports, the dispersing of aircraft, or the release of nuclear weapons from storage facilities.

Strategy: As applied to a nation, the art of developing and using political, economic, and military forces during peace or war to achieve national objectives. (*See* Tactics.)

Submarine-launched ballistic missiles (SLBM): Long-range ballistic missiles launched from submarines, the most mobile and least vulnerable leg of the strategic triad.

Superiority: Strategic doctrine calling for forces superior to those of an opponent.

Survivability: Ability of a nuclear arsenal to survive a nuclear attack and still retaliate.

Tactical: Relating to operations on the battlefield, as distinguished from strategic (long-range or intercontinental) operations.

Tactical forces: Forces designed for combat with opposing forces, rather than for reaching the rear echelons of the enemy's homeland.

Tactical nuclear weapons (TNW): Weapons designed for battlefield operations, including nuclear-tipped artillery shells. They have a range of less than 310 miles.

Tactical warning: Detection of a nuclear attack in progress—that is, after enemy weapons have been launched.

Tactics: Methods for employing military forces in combat, including the organization and maneuvering of units in relation to one another and the enemy.

Targeting: Selection of military targets and assignment of weapons to destroy them.

Teleological ethics: Viewpoint that judges the rightness of an action by its consequences and holds that we ought to act so as to promote the greatest balance of good consequences over bad ones. (*See* Utilitarianism.)

Theater: Large area in which a war is being fought (as contrasted to intercontinental war)—for example, the European theater and the Pacific theater of World War II.

Theater nuclear forces (TNF): Nuclear forces based in a region in which they would be used.

Thermonuclear weapon: Weapon in which part of the explosive energy results from thermonuclear fusion reactions. The term *thermonuclear* is used because it takes extreme heat to trigger the fusion explosion. The high temperatures required are obtained by means of a fission explosion. (*See* Fusion bomb.) The hydrogen bomb is a thermonuclear weapon.

Threat: Anticipated inventory of enemy weapons.

Throwweight: Deliverable payload of a missile, including nuclear warheads, decoys, and guidance systems.

TNT (trinitrotoluene): Common type of conventional chemical explosive.

TNT equivalence: Basic measure of explosive power equal to some weight (tons, thousand tons, million tons) of TNT.

Trajectory: Path followed by an object moving in space.

Triad: Three legs of intercontinental-range nuclear forces: bombers, land-based intercontinental ballistic missiles, and submarine-launched intercontinental ballistic missiles.

Trident: U.S. nuclear-powered submarine carrying intercontinental ballistic missiles. The submarine carries twenty-four missiles, each carrying up to fourteen warheads. The term is also used to refer to the missiles carried by this submarine.

Trident II (D5): Most advanced submarine-based ballistic missile in the U.S. arsenal, a long-range counterforce or hard-target weapon (applicable against missile silos, C^3I centers) for any target in the USSR. Each missile can carry nine to ten warheads of 475 to 600 kilotons or fifteen warheads of 150 kilotons.

Trip wire: Force that has as its basic task the triggering of a sizable commitment of supporting forces. For example, in the case of a Warsaw Pact attack, the presence of U.S. forces in Europe would guarantee U.S. involvement in the war.

Two-person rule: Procedure designed to prevent unauthorized use of nuclear weapons by making it impossible for such weapons to be armed and detonated without the consent of at least two persons.

Unilateral disarmament: Dismantling by one side of its military forces without any requirement that the other side reciprocate.

Utilitarianism: Ethical theory that judges the rightness of an action by its consequences. In its classical formulation, it is the doctrine that we should promote the greatest balance of pleasure over pain.

Verification: Process of confirming the degree to which the parties to an arms control or disarmament agreement are complying with its provisions.

Vulnerability: Susceptibility of a weapons system to enemy destruction.

War crimes: Violations of the laws or customs of war, including wanton destruction of cities, towns, or villages, or devastation not justified by military necessity.

War-fighting strategy: Plan for fighting, as opposed to merely deterring, war.

Warhead: Part of a missile, bomb, or other munition that contains the explosive or chemical or biological agent that is designed to do damage.

Warsaw Pact: Soviet-led military alliance comprising Eastern bloc countries (USSR, Bulgaria, Czechoslovakia, East Germany, Hungary, Poland, and Romania). The future of this organization is very much in doubt.

Worst-case analysis: Method requiring that we consider the most dangerous possible outcome of a situation and plan to counter it. Worst-case analysis requires us not only to attribute to the enemy the very worst intentions but to assume that the enemy will take high risks.

Yield: Total effective energy released in a nuclear explosion, usually measured and described in terms of an equivalent amount of TNT.

Notes

Introduction

1. George Kennan, "After the Cold War," *New York Times Magazine*, 6 February 1989, p. 38.

2. George Kennan, "Just Another Great Power," *New York Times*, 9 April 1989.

3. Graham Allison, "Testing Gorbachev," *Foreign Affairs* 67, no. 1 (Fall 1988): 31.

4. Ibid.

5. Ibid.

6. Robert Legvold, "Soviet Foreign Policy," *Foreign Affairs* 68, no. 1 (Special Issue: America and the World, 1988–1989): 83.

7. Ibid., pp. 84–86.

8. Ibid., p. 84.

9. Quoted ibid.

10. Stephen Meyer, "The Sources and Prospects of Gorbachev's New Political Thinking on Security," *International Security* 13, no. 2 (Fall 1988): 142.

11. Legvold, "Soviet Foreign Policy," p. 85.

12. David Holloway, "Gorbachev's New Thinking," *Foreign Affairs* 68, no. 1 (1988–89): 70–71.

13. William Odom, "Soviet Military Doctrine," *Foreign Affairs* 67, no. 2 (1988–89): 129.

14. Legvold, "Soviet Foreign Policy," p. 86.

15. Ibid., p. 86.

16. Seweryn Bialer, "Gorbachev and the Soviet Military," *U.S. News and World Report*, 13 March 1989, p. 40.

17. Meyer, "Sources and Prospects," 134.

18. Makhmut Gareyev, "The Revised Soviet Military Doctrine," *Bulletin of the Atomic Scientists* 44, no. 10 (December 1988): 30.

265

19. Meyer, "Sources and Prospects," p. 145.

20. Ibid., p. 150.

21. Legvold, "Soviet Foreign Policy," p. 91.

22. Mikhail Gorbachev, "The Problem of Mankind's Survival," speech to the United Nations, reported in *New York Times*, 8 December 1988.

23. Leon Gouré, "A 'New' Soviet Military Doctrine: Reality or Mirage?" *Strategic Review* 16, no. 3 (Summer 1988): 32.

24. H. Joachim Maitre, "Ask the Afghans," *Strategic Review* 17, no. 1 (Winter 1989): 6.

25. David J. Trachtenberg, "A Soviet Ruse," *New York Times*, 23 April 1989.

26. Jacques Chirac, "Soviet Change and Western Security," *Strategic Review* 17, no. 1 (Winter 1989): 13.

Chapter One

1. Although official U.S. policy appears to repudiate launch on warning, there is evidence of a gap between the official declared policy and the actual plans of those in charge of nuclear forces. See Gerald E. Marsh, "U.S. Missiles on Hair Trigger?" *Bulletin of the Atomic Scientists* 45, no. 4 (May 1989): 3. Despite Soviet assurances that they would never fire their strategic missiles first, there is reason to doubt that this is actual policy—mainly the vulnerability of Soviet land-based missiles (the bulk of its arsenal) to a first strike. See below for a discussion of the distinction between *declaratory* and *action* policy.

2. Fred Kaplan, *The Wizards of Armageddon* (New York: Touchstone, 1983), p. 319.

3. Paul H. Nitze, "Atoms, Strategy, and Policy," *Foreign Affairs* 34, no. 2 (January 1956): 187.

4. Lynn Davis, "Limited Nuclear Options: Deterrence and the New American Doctrine," *Adelphi Paper* 121 (Winter 1975–76): 5.

5. Michael Walzer, "Deterrence and Democracy," *New Republic*, 2 July 1984, p. 17.

6. Henry Stimson, "The Atomic Bomb and the Surrender of Japan," in Edwin Fogelman, ed., *Hiroshima: The Decision to Use the A-Bomb* (New York: Charles Scribner's Sons, 1964), p. 15.

7. Peter Pringle and William Arkin, *S.I.O.P.: The Secret U.S. Plan for Nuclear War* (New York: W. W. Norton, 1983), p. 45.

8. Ibid.; see also Desmond Ball, "Targeting for Strategic Deterrence," *Adelphi Paper* 185 (Summer 1983): 39.

9. Pringle and Arkin, *S.I.O.P.*, p. 52.

10. Sheila Tobias, Peter Goudinoff, Stephan Leader, and Shelah Leader, *The People's Guide to National Defense* (New York: William Morrow, 1982), pp. 236–85.

11. Freeman Dyson, *Weapons and Hope* (New York: Harper & Row, 1985), p. 229.

12. Solly Zuckerman, "Nuclear Fantasies," *New York Review of Books*, 14 June 1984, p. 7.

13. Walzer, "Deterrence and Democracy," pp. 16–17.

14. Dyson, *Weapons and Hope*, p. 9.

15. Jonathan Schell, *The Abolition* (New York: Alfred A. Knopf, 1984), p. 55.

16. Robert Dahl, *Controlling Nuclear Weapons: Democracy Versus Guardianship* (Syracuse, N.Y.: Syracuse University Press, 1985).

17. Ibid., p. 6.

18. Ibid., p. 25.

19. Ibid., p. 44.

20. Ibid., p. 25.

21. Ibid., p. 44.

22. Ibid., pp. 46–47.

23. Ibid., p. 47.

24. Ibid.

25. Ibid., p. 48.

26. Ibid., p. 50.

27. Alexander Hamilton, "The Federalist No. 51," in *The Federalist* (New York: Modern Library, n.d.), p. 337.

28. William Gay, "Nuclear Discourse and Linguistic Alienation," *Journal of Social Philosophy* 18, no. 2 (Summer 1987): 42–49.

29. General John T. Chain, "Strategic Fundamentals," *Air Force Magazine* 70, no. 7 (July 1987): 64.

Chapter Two

1. Michael Walzer, "Deterrence and Democracy," *New Republic*, 2 July 1984, p. 20.

2. Joseph S. Nye, Jr., *Nuclear Ethics* (New York: Free Press, 1986), p. 11.

3. Jeffrey Richelson, "Population Targeting and U.S. Strategic Doctrine," in Desmond Ball and Jeffrey Richelson, eds., *Strategic Nuclear Targeting* (Ithaca, N.Y.: Cornell University Press, 1986), p. 248.

4. Adam Roberts and Richard Guelff, eds., *Documents of the Laws of War* (Oxford: Clarendon Press, 1982), pp. 414–19.

5. John Griffin, "Nuclear Weapons and International Law," in Gwyn Prins, ed., *The Nuclear Crisis Reader* (New York: Vintage Books, 1984), p. 168.

6. Ibid., p. 165.

7. John Bosma, "Arms Control, SDI, and the Geneva Conventions," in Zbigniew Brzezinski, ed., *Promise or Peril: The Strategic Defense Initiative* (Washington, D.C.: Ethics and Public Policy Center, 1986), p. 342.

8. Robert Dahl, *Controlling Nuclear Weapons: Democracy Versus Guardianship* (Syracuse, N.Y.: Syracuse University Press, 1985), p. 88.

9. Ibid.

10. For a discussion of the role of the expert in democratic society, see Rosemarie Tong, *Ethics in Policy Analysis* (Englewood Cliffs, N.J.: Prentice-Hall, 1986), pp. 39–61.

11. Stephen Meyer, "The Sources and Prospects of Gorbachev's New Political Thinking on Security," *International Security* 13, no. 2 (Fall 1988): 154.

12. Phillip Petersen and Notra Trulock, "A 'New' Soviet Military Doctrine: Origins and Implications," *Strategic Review* 16, no. 3 (Summer 1988): 22.

13. Leon Gouré, "A 'New' Soviet Military Doctrine: Reality or Mirage?" *Strategic Review* 16, no. 3 (Summer 1988): 27.

14. Ibid., p. 28.

15. Honore M. Catudal, *Nuclear Deterrence: Does It Deter?* (London: Mansell, 1985), pp. 203–4.

16. Ibid., p. 202; see also David P. Barash, *The Arms Race and Nuclear War* (Belmont, Calif.: Wadsworth, 1987), p. 130.

17. Richard Pipes, "Soviet Strategic Doctrine," in P. Edward Haley, David M. Keithly, and Jack Merritt, eds., *Nuclear Strategy, Arms Control, and the Future* (Boulder, Colo.: Westview Press, 1985), p. 170; Barash, *Arms Race*, p. 129.

18. Barash, *Arms Race*, p. 138.

19. Marshal V. D. Sokolovsky, "The Nature of Modern War," in Haley, Keithly, and Merritt, *Nuclear Strategy*, p. 143.

20. Leonid Brezhnev, "Remarks on the Objectives of Soviet Nuclear Strategy," in Haley, Keithly, and Merritt, *Nuclear Strategy*, pp. 166–69.

21. Quoted in Sandra Sedacca, *Up in Arms: A Common Cause Guide to Understanding Nuclear Arms Policy* (Washington, D.C.: Common Cause, 1984), p. 111.

22. Ibid.

23. Ibid.

24. Mikhail Gorbachev, "Nuclear Disarmament by the Year 2000," in P. Edward Haley and Jack Merritt, eds., *Strategic Defense Initiative: Folly or Future?* (Boulder, Colo.: Westview Press, 1986), pp. 135–38.

25. Michael MccGwire, *Military Objectives in Soviet Foreign Policy* (Washington, D.C.: Brookings Institution, 1987), p. 29.

26. Raymond Garthoff, "Soviet Strategic Doctrine," in Haley, Keithly, and Merritt, *Nuclear Strategy*, p. 175.

27. Barash, *Arms Race*, p. 130.

28. Gene Sharp, *Making Europe Unconquerable: The Potential of Civilian-Based Deterrence and Defense* (Cambridge, Mass.: Ballinger, 1985), p. 8.

29. Barash, *Arms Race*, p. 130.

30. Henry Trofimenko, "Counterforce: Illusion or Panacea," *International Security* 5, no. 4 (Spring 1981): 28.

31. "U.S.–Soviet Nuclear Arms: 1985," *Defense Monitor* 14, no. 6 (1985): 1–5.

32. Douglas P. Lackey, *Moral Principles and Nuclear Weapons* (Totowa, N.J.: Rowman & Allanheld, 1984), pp. 125–28.

33. Nye, *Nuclear Ethics*, p. 64.

34. Lackey, *Moral Principles*, p. 127.

Chapter Three

1. Michael Walzer, *Just and Unjust Wars* (New York: Basic Books, 1977).

2. Ibid., p. 58.

3. A survey of the correction theories on which I base my exposition can

be found in Rudolph J. Gerber and Patrick D. McAnany, eds. *Contemporary Punishment: Views, Explanations, and Justifications* (Notre Dame, Ind.: University of Notre Dame Press, 1972).

Chapter Four

1. Y. Harkabi, *Nuclear War and Nuclear Peace*, trans. Y. Shenkman (Jerusalem: Israel Program for Scientific Translations, 1964), pp. 9–11.

2. Apocryphal quotation in Herman Kahn, *On Thermonuclear War* (Princeton: Princeton University Press, 1961), p. 17.

3. Office of Technology Assessment, *Strategic Defenses* (Princeton: Princeton University Press, 1986), p. 78.

4. David Fisher, *Morality and the Bomb: An Ethical Assessment of Deterrence* (London: Croom Helm, 1985), p. 63.

5. Robert McNamara, "The Military Role of Nuclear Weapons," in Charles W. Kegley, Jr., and Eugene R. Wittkopf, eds., *The Nuclear Reader: Strategy, Weapons, War* (New York: St. Martin's Press, 1985), p. 166.

6. Jonathan Schell, *The Fate of the Earth* (New York: Alfred A. Knopf, 1982), p. 196.

7. Ibid., p. 199.

8. David W. Ziegler, *War, Peace, and International Politics* (Boston: Little, Brown, 1981), pp. 227–29.

9. Ibid., p. 228.

10. Jonathan Schell, *The Abolition* (New York: Alfred A. Knopf, 1984), p. 55.

11. Patrick Morgan, *Deterrence: A Conceptual Analysis* (Beverly Hills, Calif.: Sage Publications, 1977), p. 109.

12. Ibid.

13. McGeorge Bundy, "Existential Deterrence and Its Consequences," in Douglas MacLean, ed., *The Security Gamble: Deterrence Dilemmas in the Nuclear Age* (Totowa, N.J.: Rowman & Allanheld, 1984), p. 9.

14. McGeorge Bundy, quoted in Ziegler, *War, Peace, and International Politics*, p. 229.

15. Leon Wieseltier, "When Deterrence Fails," *Foreign Affairs* 63, no. 4 (Spring 1985): 828.

16. Ibid., p. 831.

17. Ibid., p. 832.

18. Quoted in ibid., p. 837.

19. Donald Snow, *The Nuclear Future: Toward a Strategy of Uncertainty* (Montgomery: University of Alabama Press, 1983), pp. 137–38.

20. Peter Pringle and William Arkin, *S.I.O.P.: The Secret U.S. Plan for Nuclear War* (New York: W. W. Norton, 1983), p. 40.

21. Walter Slocombe, "The Countervailing Strategy," *International Security* 5, no. 4 (Spring 1981): 21.

22. Honore M. Catudal, *Nuclear Deterrence: Does It Deter?* (Bronx, N.Y.: Mansell, 1985), pp. 145–46.

23. Slocombe, "Countervailing Strategy," p. 20.

24. Ibid.

25. Ibid.

26. Ibid.

27. Ibid., p. 23.

28. Office of Technology Assessment, *Strategic Defenses*, p. 77.

29. Slocombe, "Countervailing Strategy," p. 21.

30. Ian Clark, *Limited Nuclear War* (Princeton: Princeton University Press, 1982), p. 195.

31. Office of Technology Assessment, "Strategic Defenses," p. 89; Colin S. Gray, "Nuclear Strategy: The Case for a Theory of Victory," in Steven E. Miller, ed., *Strategy and Nuclear Deterrence* (Princeton: Princeton University Press, 1984), pp. 54–56; see also Gray's, "Victory Is Possible," *Foreign Policy* 39, no. 2 (Summer 1980): 19.

32. Colin S. Gray, "Presidential Directive 59: Flawed but Useful," in Herbert Levine and David Carlton, eds., *The Nuclear Arms Race Debated* (New York: McGraw-Hill, 1986), p. 270.

33. For a concept of success see Colin S. Gray, "Victory Is Possible," pp. 14–27. See also Gray, "Nuclear Strategy: The Case for Victory," p. 51.

34. Gray, "Victory Is Possible," p. 27.

35. Ibid., pp. 20–21.

36. Gray, "Nuclear Strategy: The Case for Victory," p. 53.

37. Ibid., p. 36.

38. Ibid., p. 37.

39. Ibid.

40. Colin S. Gray, "Targeting Problems for Central War," in Desmond Ball and Jeffrey Richelson, eds., *Strategic Nuclear Targeting* (Ithaca, N.Y.: Cornell University Press, 1986), p. 174.

41. Ibid.

42. Paul H. Nitze, "Atoms, Strategy, and Policy," *Foreign Affairs* 34, no. 2 (January 1956): 189.

43. Ibid., p. 191.

44. According to an unclassified report of the Senate Armed Services Committee, there were 151 "serious alarms" between 1 January 1979 and 30 June 1980; David P. Barash, *The Arms Race and Nuclear War* (Belmont, Calif.: Wadsworth, 1987), p. 175.

45. Pringle and Arkin, *S.I.O.P.*, pp. 154–55; see also "Who Could Start a Nuclear War?" *The Defense Monitor* 14, no. 3 (1985): 4.

46. Pringle and Arkin, *S.I.O.P.*, pp. 154–55; see also "Who Could Start a Nuclear War?" p. 4.

47. Quoted in Pringle and Arkin, *S.I.O.P.*, pp. 154–55; see also "Who Could Start a Nuclear War?" p. 4.

48. Pringle and Arkin, *S.I.O.P.*, pp. 154–55; see also "Who Could Start a Nuclear War?" p. 4.

49. "Who Could Start a Nuclear War?" p. 4.

50. Paul Bracken, *The Command and Control of Nuclear Forces* (New Haven: Yale University Press, 1983), p. 70.

51. Michael Stephenson and John Weal, *Nuclear Dictionary* (Essex: Long-

man Group, 1985), p. 123; "Who Could Start a Nuclear War?" pp. 4–5; *S.I.O.P.*, pp. 164–67.

52. Pringle and Arkin, *S.I.O.P.*, p. 167; see also "Who Could Start a Nuclear War?" p. 5.

53. Pringle and Arkin, *S.I.O.P.*, pp. 160–61; see also "Who Could Start a Nuclear War?" p. 6.

54. Pringle and Arkin, *S.I.O.P.*, p. 161.

55. Richard Ned Lebow, *Nuclear Crisis Management* (Ithaca, N.Y.: Cornell University Press, 1987), p. 88.

56. Ibid.

57. Pringle and Arkin, "Who Could Start a Nuclear War?" p. 7.

58. Ibid., p. 4.

59. Ibid., p. 6.

60. Bruce G. Blair, *Strategic Command and Control: Redefining the Nuclear Threat* (Washington, D.C.: Brookings Institution, 1985), p. 282.

61. For a discussion of the Hotline and the other measures listed, see William Ury, *Beyond the Hot Line* (Boston: Houghton Mifflin, 1985), pp. 51–54.

62. "U.S., Soviets Will Establish Centers to Reduce the Risk of Nuclear Conflict," *Minneapolis Star and Tribune*, 6 May 1987.

63. Francis X. Clines, "U.S. and Soviets Sign Pact to Reduce Risk of War," *New York Times*, 13 June 1989.

64. Ury, *Beyond the Hot Line*, pp. 64–67.

65. Ibid., pp. 68–69.

Chapter Five

1. David P. Barash, *The Arms Race and Nuclear War* (Belmont, Calif.: Wadsworth, 1987), pp. 142–44.

2. Ronald Reagan, "Address to the Nation on the Strategic Defense Initiative," in P. Edward Haley and Jack Merritt, eds., *Strategic Defense Initiative: Folly or Future?* (Boulder, Colo.: Westview Press, 1986), p. 24.

3. For example, Lt. Gen. James Abrahamson, director of the Strategic Defense Organization, describes SDI as satisfying the deterrence objective of creating uncertainty in the mind of Soviet targeters. See Hans Binnendijk, ed., *Strategic Defense in the Twenty-First Century* (Washington, D.C.: Foreign Service Institute of the Department of State, 1986), p. 5.

4. Robert McNamara, *Blundering Into Disaster* (New York: Pantheon Books, 1986), p. 92.

5. See Ben Bova, *Assured Survival* (Boston: Houghton Mifflin, 1984).

6. Reagan made this offer shortly after his 1983 address on SDI.

7. Colin Gray, "A Case for Strategic Defense," in Haley and Merritt, *Strategic Defense Initiative*, p. 82.

8. Office of Technology Assessment, *Strategic Defenses* (Princeton: Princeton University Press, 1986), p. 20.

9. Reagan, "Address," p. 24.

10. Nikolai Talensky, "Missile Defense: A Response to Aggression," in

Zbigniew Brzezinski, ed., *Promise or Peril: The Strategic Defense Initiative* (Washington, D.C.: Ethics and Public Policy Center, 1986), p. 214.

11. McNamara, *Blundering Into Disaster,* p. 123.

12. John Guthrie, "Midgetman Missile," *International Combat Arms,* March 1986, pp. 22–28.

13. Quoted in Michael Gordon, "Reagan's Missile Offer Sets Off Shifting Debate," *New York Times,* 24 October 1986.

14. Ibid.

15. Keith B. Payne and Colin S. Gray, "Nuclear Policy and the Defensive Transition," *Foreign Affairs* 62, no. 4 (Spring 1984): 824.

16. Anthony Kenny, *The Logic of Deterrence* (Chicago: University of Chicago Press, 1985), p. 71.

17. Office of Technology Assessment, *Strategic Defenses,* p. 69.

18. Payne and Gray, "Nuclear Policy," p. 839.

19. Ibid., p. 838.

20. Ibid.

21. Paul Nitze, "On the Road to a More Stable Peace," in Haley and Merritt, *Strategic Defense Initiative,* p. 38.

22. Richard Lipton, "Comments on the Strategic Defense Initiative," statement before Subcommittee on Strategic and Theater Nuclear Forces of Committee on Armed Services, U.S. Senate, Ninety-Ninth Congress, 30 October 1985 (Washington, D.C.: U.S. Government Printing Office, 1985), p. 56.

23. Michael Altfeld, "Strategic Defense and the 'Cost-Exchange Ratio,'" *Strategic Review* 14, no. 4 (Fall 1986): 23.

24. Lt. Gen. James Abrahamson, statement before Subcommittee on Strategic and Theater Nuclear Forces, p. 31.

25. Altfeld, "Strategic Defense," p. 24.

26. Alexei N. Kosygin, "Missile Defense: For Saving Lives," in Brzezinski, *Promise or Peril,* p. 219.

27. For a discussion of the properties of the phases, see Office of Technology Assessment, *Strategic Defenses,* pp. 141–45.

28. Ibid., p. 144.

29. Ibid.

30. Ibid.

31. Ibid., p. 145.

32. Ibid., pp. 146–94.

33. Ibid.

34. Quoted in Matthew Bunn, "Abrahamson Proposes 'Brilliant Pebbles' Space Defense," *Arms Control Today* 19, no. 3 (April 1989): 26.

35. Abrahamson, statement before Subcommittee on Strategic and Theater Nuclear Forces, p. 38.

36. Quoted by Kenneth Adelman, "Setting the Record Straight," in Brzezinski, *Promise or Peril,* p. 200.

37. Ibid.

38. Quoted in Binnendijk, *Strategic Defense in the Twenty-First Century,* p. 9.

39. Barash, *Arms Race,* p. 140.

40. Ibid.

41. Ibid., p. 136.

42. Ibid.

43. Ibid.

44. Freeman Dyson, *Weapons and Hope* (New York: Harper & Row, 1985), p. 85.

45. Ibid., p. 90.

46. Frederick P. Brooks, professor of computer science, statement before Subcommittee on Strategic and Theater Nuclear Forces, p. 55.

47. Boyce Rensberger, "Computer Bugs Seen as Fatal Flaw in 'Star Wars,'" statement, ibid., p. 67.

48. Lipton, "Comments on the Strategic Defense Initiative," ibid., p. 57.

49. Brooks, statement, ibid., p. 55.

50. Quoted in the *Christian Science Monitor,* 23 October 1986.

51. "The ABM Treaty," in Brzezinski, *Promise or Peril,* p. 443.

52. Ibid., p. 444.

53. Ibid., p. 446.

54. Ibid., p. 444.

55. For a good summary of the debate, see "Constitutional Drama: Washington's Wrangle Over the Meaning of the ABM Treaty," *Christian Science Monitor,* 20 May 1987.

56. Ibid.

57. Dan Quayle, "Beyond SALT: Arms Control Built Upon Defenses," *Strategic Review* 14, no. 3 (Summer 1986): 10.

58. Ibid.

59. Ibid., p. 11.

60. Quoted ibid.

61. Ibid.

62. John Bosma, "Arms Control, SDI, and the Geneva Conventions," in Brzezinski, *Promise or Peril,* p. 342.

63. Ibid.

64. Ibid., p. 343.

65. Ibid., p. 342.

66. Ibid., p. 346.

67. Ibid., p. 347.

68. Ibid., p. 349.

69. Ibid.

70. Robert Jastrow, "Missile Defense: Threat and Response," ibid., p. 147.

71. Bosma, "Arms Control, SDI, and Geneva Conventions," p. 363.

72. John W. Coffey, "SDI Makes Moral Sense, Too," *Los Angeles Times,* 25 February 1987.

73. Ibid.

74. Ibid.

75. Arnold Kanter, "An Alliance Perspective," in Brzezinski, *Promise or Peril,* p. 287.

76. Ibid., p. 290.
77. Manfred Wörner, "A Missile Defense for NATO Europe," in Brzezinski, *Promise or Peril*, p. 313.
78. Ibid., p. 314.
79. Ibid., p. 315.

Chapter Six

1. "1946 Judgment of the International Military Tribunal at Nuremberg," in Adam Roberts and Richard Guelff, eds., *Documents of the Laws of War* (Oxford: Clarendon Press, 1982), p. 155.
2. "Charter of the United Nations, 1945," in Gerard J. Mangone, ed., *The Elements of International Law* (Homewood, Calif.: Dorsey Press, 1967), p. 440.
3. Ibid., p. 444.
4. "1868 St. Petersburg Declaration Renouncing the Use, in Time of War, of Explosive Projectiles Under 400 grammes Weight," in Roberts and Guelff, *Documents of the Laws of War*, p. 31.
5. "The 1907 Hague Convention IV Respecting the Laws and Customs of War on Land," ibid., p. 53.
6. David P. Barash, *The Arms Race and Nuclear War* (Belmont, Calif.: Wadsworth, 1987), p. 314.
7. Roberts and Guelff, *Documents of the Laws of War*, pp. 437–38.
8. Jeffrey Richelson, "Population Targeting and U.S. Strategic Doctrine," in Desmond Ball and Jeffrey Richelson, eds., *Strategic Nuclear Targeting* (Ithaca, N.Y.: Cornell University Press, 1986), p. 248.
9. Michael Walzer, *Just and Unjust Wars* (New York: Basic Books, 1977), p. 308.
10. George H. Quester, "Substituting Conventional for Nuclear Weapons: Some Problems and Some Possibilities," in Russell Hardin et al., eds., *Nuclear Deterrence: Ethics and Strategy* (Chicago: University of Chicago Press, 1985), p. 246.
11. For a good discussion of the requirements of retribution, see C. S. Lewis, "The Humanitarian Theory of Punishment," in Rudolph J. Gerber and Patrick D. McAnany, eds., *Contemporary Punishment: Views, Explanations, and Justifications* (Notre Dame, Ind.: University of Notre Dame Press, 1972), pp. 194–99.
12. George Mavrodes, "Conventions and the Morality of War," in James Sterba, ed., *Morality in Practice* (Belmont, Calif.: Wadsworth, 1984), pp. 302–11.
13. Paul Ramsey, "The Case for Making 'Just War' Possible," in John Bennet, ed., *Nuclear Weapons and the Conflict of Conscience* (London: Butterworth Press, 1962), p. 142. See also David Lewis, "Finite Deterrence," working paper (Baltimore: Maryland Center for Philosophy and Public Policy, 1987), p. 38.
14. David Fisher, *Morality and the Bomb: An Ethical Assessment of Deterrence* (London: Croom Helm, 1985), p. 28.
15. This is the justification for strategic bombing. The idea is that we

can shorten the war and terminate aggression by attacking the industrial means of making war (workers as well as factories) and the will of the people (i.e., the civilian population) to resist. Giulio Douhet in *Command of the Air* (New York: Coward-McCann, 1942) gives a representative argument for this strategy of population attacks.

16. Desmond Ball, "The Development of the S.I.O.P., 1960–1983," in Ball and Richelson, *Strategic Nuclear Targeting*, p. 82.

17. Elaine Scarry, *The Body in Pain: The Making and Unmaking of the World* (New York: Oxford University Press, 1985), p. 153.

18. Quoted in Fisher, *Morality and the Bomb*, p. 29.

19. James Turner Johnson, *Can Modern War Be Just?* (New Haven: Yale University Press, 1984), pp. 145–46.

20. Bruce Russett, *The Prisoners of Insecurity* (New York: W. H. Freeman, 1983), p. 150.

21. Bruce Russett, "Counter-combatant Deterrence: A Proposal," *Survival* 16, no. 3 (Autumn 1974): 140.

22. Quoted in Ian Clark, *Limited Nuclear War* (Princeton: Princeton University Press, 1982), p. 227.

23. Bernard Brodie, *Strategy in the Missile Age* (Princeton: Princeton University Press, 1959), p. 403.

24. Caspar Weinberger, "U.S. Defense Strategy," *Foreign Affairs* 64, no. 4 (Spring 1984): 680.

25. Johnson, *Can Modern War Be Just?* p. 47.

26. Ibid., p. 116.

27. Ibid.

28. "Incredible Bungling of the Neutron Bomb," editorial, *Minneapolis Tribune*, 13 August 1981.

29. Johnson, *Can Modern War Be Just?* p. 81.

30. Ibid.

31. "1907 Hague Convention," sec. II, chap. I, p. 52.

32. Martin Dunn, "What Are the Effects of the Neutron Bomb?" *Minneapolis Tribune*, 10 March 1982.

33. Brian Beckett, *Weapons of the Future* (London: Orbis, 1982), p. 99.

34. William Daugherty, Barbara Levi, and Frank von Hippel, "The Consequences of a 'Limited' Nuclear Attack on the United States," *International Security* 10, no. 4 (Spring 1986): 42.

35. Desmond Ball, "Targeting for Strategic Deterrence," *Adelphi Paper* 185 (Summer 1983): 38.

36. Theodore B. Taylor, "Third-Generation Nuclear Weapons," *Scientific American* 256 (April 1987): 30–39. For a brief summary of Taylor's views, see "A Third Generation of Nukes," *Time*, 25 May 1987, p. 36.

37. Quoted in "Third Generation of Nukes," p. 36.

38. Albert Wohlstetter, "Bishops, Statesmen, and Other Strategists on the Bombing of the Innocents," in Charles W. Kegley, Jr., and Eugene R. Wittkopf, *The Nuclear Reader: Strategy, Weapons, War* (New York: St. Martin's Press, 1985), p. 65.

39. Gen. Sir Hugh Beach, "On Improving NATO Strategy," in Andrew

Pierre, ed., *The Conventional Defense of Europe: New Technologies and Strategies* (New York: Council on Foreign Relations, 1986), p. 163.

40. Jon Connell, *The New Maginot Line* (New York: Arbor House, 1986), p. 6.

41. Elizabeth Pond, "Beyond the 'Bean Count' of Conventional Forces," *Christian Science Monitor*, 5 November 1986.

42. Carl von Clausewitz, *On War* (New York: Penguin Books, 1983), p. 114.

43. Quoted in Elizabeth Pond, "Beyond the 'Bean Count' of Conventional Forces."

44. Joshua M. Epstein, "NATO Strategy for the 1990's," statement prepared for the Senate Foreign Relations Committee, U.S. Senate, Ninety-Ninth Congress, 3 October 1985 (Washington, D.C.: U.S. Government Printing Office, 1985), p. 36.

45. Ibid.; see also Joshua Epstein, "NATO Can Hold Its Own," *New York Times*, 14 December 1986.

46. John Mearsheimer, "NATO's Deterrent Posture," statement prepared for the Senate Foreign Relations Committee, U.S. Senate, Ninety-Ninth Congress, 3 October 1985 (Washington, D.C.: U.S. Government Printing Office, 1985), p. 122.

47. Andreas von Bulow, "Defensive Entanglement: An Alternative Strategy for NATO," in Pierre, *Conventional Defense of Europe*, p. 123.

48. Mearsheimer, "NATO's Deterrent Posture," p. 125.

49. Connell, *New Maginot Line*, p. 111.

50. Richard D. DeLauer, "Emerging Technologies and Their Impact on the Conventional Deterrent," in Pierre, *Conventional Defense of Europe*, p. 50.

51. Beach, "On Improving NATO Strategy," p. 169.

52. Quoted in Stephen Budiansky, "One Shot, One Kill: A New Era of 'Smart' Weapons," *U.S. News and World Report*, 16 March 1987, p. 28.

53. Ibid., p. 29.

54. Ibid., p. 31.

55. Quoted in von Bulow, "Defensive Entanglement," p. 128.

56. Budiansky, "One Shot, One Kill," p. 31; see also Stephen Budiansky, "The Russians Aren't Coming," *U.S. News and World Report*, 27 November 1989, pp. 47–54.

57. Ibid.; see also Andrew Cockburn, *The Threat: Inside the Soviet Military Machine* (New York: Random House, 1983), p. 209; Mearsheimer, "NATO's Deterrent Posture," pp. 122–23.

58. Mearsheimer, "NATO's Deterrent Posture," p. 124.

59. Stephen J. Cimbala, "Soviet 'Blitzkrieg' in Europe: The Abiding Nuclear Dimension," *Strategic Review* 14, no. 3 (Summer 1986): 71.

60. Ibid.

61. James Dunnigan, *How to Make War* (New York: William Morrow, 1982), p. 251.

62. Mearsheimer, "NATO's Deterrent Posture," p. 124.

63. Cited in "Soviet 'Blitzkrieg,' " Cimbala, p. 72.

64. Ibid.

65. Ibid.

66. Mearsheimer, "NATO's Deterrent Posture," p. 124.

67. Von Bulow, "Defensive Entanglement," p. 120.

68. Quoted in Cockburn, *The Threat*, p. 202.

69. Denis Healey, "A Labor Britain, NATO, and the Bomb," *Foreign Affairs* 65, no. 4 (Spring 1987): 724.

70. Mearsheimer, "NATO's Deterrent Posture," p. 125; Cockburn, *The Threat*, p. 192; see also Epstein, "NATO Can Hold Its Own."

71. Mearsheimer, "NATO's Deterrent Posture," p. 123.

72. Mearsheimer, "NATO's Deterrent Posture," p. 122.

73. Ibid.

74. Cimbala, "Soviet 'Blitzkrieg,'" p. 70.

75. François L. Heisbourg, "Conventional Defense: An Alternative Strategy for NATO," in Pierre, *Conventional Defense of Europe*, p. 89.

76. Quoted in Healey, "Labor Britain," p. 727.

77. Ibid.

78. Beach, "On Improving NATO Strategy," p. 73.

79. Von Bulow, "Defensive Entanglement," p. 132.

80. Ibid.

81. Laurence Martin, *Before the Day After: Can NATO Defend Europe?* (London: Newnes Books, 1985), p. 117.

82. Budiansky, "One Shot, One Kill," p. 33.

83. Cimbala, "Soviet 'Blitzkrieg,'" p. 72.

84. Von Bulow, "Defensive Entanglement," p. 120.

85. Ibid., p. 121.

86. Cimbala, "Soviet 'Blitzkrieg,'" p. 72.

87. Johnson, *Can Modern War Be Just?* p. 126.

88. Quester, "Substituting Conventional for Nuclear Weapons," p. 260.

89. Ibid., p. 264.

90. R. A. Mason, "The Non Nuclear Alternative," paper presented at the United States Air Force War College Nuclear Strategy Symposium, Maxwell Air Force Base, Alabama, 12 September 1987.

91. Von Bulow, "Defensive Entanglement," p. 132.

92. Quester, "Substituting Conventional for Nuclear Weapons," p. 162.

93. Colin S. Gray, "Nuclear Strategy: The Case for a Theory of Victory," in Steven E. Miller, ed., *Strategy and Nuclear Deterrence* (Princeton: Princeton University Press, 1984), p. 36.

94. Ibid.

95. Carl Builder, "The Prospects and Implications of Non-nuclear Means for Strategic Conflict," *Adelphi Paper* 200 (Summer 1985): 2.

96. Quoted ibid.

97. Thomas Brown, Steve Head, David McGarvy, Arthur Steiner, and Albert Wohlstetter, "The Political–Military Significance of Continuous Terminal Homing," *Background Paper* 31 (St. Paul de Vence, France: European–American Institute for Security Workshop on Improved Technologies in a Changing NATO Strategy, 1976), p. 3.

98. Russett, "Counter-combatant Deterrence," p. 138.

99. Ibid., p. 132.
100. Builder, "Prospects and Implications of Non-nuclear Means," p. 18.
101. Honore M. Catudal, *Soviet Nuclear Strategy from Stalin to Gorbachev: A Revolution in Soviet Military and Political Thinking* (Atlantic Highlands, N.J.: Humanities Press International, 1988), p. 115.

Chapter Seven

1. Mark Sommer, *Beyond the Bomb: Living Without Nuclear Weapons* (Boston: Expro Press, 1985), p. 114.
2. Ibid., p. 140.
3. Ibid., p. 36.
4. Richard Barnet, "Real Security: An Alternative Foreign Policy," in Paul Joseph and Simon Rosenblum, eds., *Search for Sanity: The Politics of Nuclear Weapons and Disarmament* (Boston: South End Press, 1984), pp. 561–75.
5. Daniel Axelrod and Michio Kaku, *To Win a Nuclear War* (Boston: South End Press, 1986), p. 5.
6. Gene Sharp, *Making Europe Unconquerable: The Potential of Civilian-Based Deterrence and Defense* (Cambridge, Mass.: Ballinger, 1985), p. 102.
7. Ibid., p. 103.
8. Ibid., p. 104.
9. Ibid., p. 105.
10. For example, see Mikhail Gorbachev, "Nuclear Disarmament by the Year 2000," in P. Edward Haley and Jack Merritt, eds., *Strategic Defense Initiative: Folly or Future?* (Boulder, Colo.: Westview Press, 1986), pp. 135–38.
11. Sommer, *Beyond the Bomb*, p. 64.
12. Ibid., p. 29.
13. Gene Sharp, *National Security Through Civilian-Based Defense* (Omaha, Nebr.: Association for Transarmament Studies, 1985), p. 47.
14. Gene Sharp, *Making Europe Unconquerable*, p. 103.
15. Gene Sharp, "National Defense Without Armaments," in Charles Betz and Theodore Herman, eds., *Peace and War* (San Francisco: W. H. Freeman, 1973), p. 351.
16. Ibid.
17. Sharp, "National Defense Without Armaments," pp. 352–56; *Making Europe Unconquerable*, p. 193.
18. Sharp, *Making Europe Unconquerable*, p. 193.
19. Sommer, *Beyond the Bomb*, p. 69.
20. Sharp, *Making Europe Unconquerable*, p. 193.
21. Schelling quoted in *Beyond the Bomb*, Sommer, p. 67.
22. Sharp quoted in ibid., p. 72.
23. Ibid., p. 70.
24. Sharp, *National Security Through Civilian-Based Defense*, p. 48.
25. Sharp, *Making Europe Unconquerable*, p. 50.
26. Sharp, *National Security Through Civilian-Based Defense*, p. 23.
27. Ibid., p. 51.

28. Gene Sharp, *The Politics of Nonviolent Action*, part 1: *Power and Struggle* (Boston: Porter Sargent, 1973), p. 69.

29. Ibid.

30. Ibid.

31. Gene Sharp, *The Politics of Nonviolent Action*, part 2: *The Methods of Nonviolent Action* (Boston: Porter Sargent, 1973), p. 423; Norman Freund, "Nonviolent National Defense," *Journal of Social Philosophy* 13, no. 2 (May 1982): 15.

32. Freund, "Nonviolent National Defense," p. 12.

33. Sommer, *Beyond the Bomb*, p. 6.

34. Sharp, *Making Europe Unconquerable*, p. 30.

35. Ibid., p. 110.

36. Ibid., p. 113.

37. Ibid., p. 116.

38. Ibid., p. 117.

39. Ibid., p. 119.

40. Ibid.

41. Ibid., p. 114.

42. Sharp, *National Security Through Civilian-Based Defense*, p. 27.

43. Sharp, *Making Europe Unconquerable*, p. 120.

44. Ibid., p. 114.

45. Ibid.

46. Ibid., p. 115.

47. Ibid.

48. Ibid., p. 116.

49. Ibid.

50. Ibid., p. 115.

51. Ibid.

52. Ibid., p. 118.

53. Ibid.

54. Ibid., p. 129.

55. Ibid., p. 128.

56. Sharp, "Philippines Taught Us Lessons of Nonviolence," *Los Angeles Times*, 4 April 1986.

57. Sharp, *Making Europe Unconquerable*, p. 130.

58. Freund, "Nonviolent National Defense," p. 14.

59. Sharp, *Making Europe Unconquerable*, p. 130.

60. Ibid., p. 131.

61. Ibid.

62. Quoted in Sommer, *Beyond the Bomb*, p. 71.

63. Sharp, *Making Europe Unconquerable*, p. 131.

64. Ibid., p. 124; see also Sharp, *The Politics of Nonviolent Action*, part 3: *The Dynamics of Nonviolent Action* (Boston: Porter Sargent, 1973), pp. 705–67.

65. Sharp, *The Dynamics of Nonviolent Action*, p. 706.

66. Ibid., p. 707.

67. Freund, "Nonviolent National Defense," p. 16.

68. Quoted in Sharp, *The Dynamics of Nonviolent Action*, p. 707.

69. Ibid.

70. Freund, "Nonviolent National Defense," p. 14.

71. Ibid.

72. Sharp, *Making Europe Unconquerable*, p. 167.

73. Jessie Hughan and Cecil Hinshaw, "Toward a Nonviolent National Defense," in Mulford Sibley, ed., *The Quiet Battle* (Boston: Beacon Press, 1963), p. 342.

74. Sharp, *Making Europe Unconquerable*, p. 94.

75. Quoted in Andrew Cockburn, *The Threat: Inside the Soviet Military Machine* (New York: Random House, 1983), p. 132.

76. Sharp, *Making Europe Unconquerable*, p. 94.

77. Ibid., p. 167.

78. Ibid.

79. Paul Quinn-Judge, "Soviet Soldiers Are Tongue-tied," *Christian Science Monitor*, 13 March 1987.

80. Ibid.

81. Cockburn, *The Threat*, pp. 132–33.

82. Sharp, *The Dynamics of Nonviolent Action*, p. 731.

83. Ibid., p. 733.

84. Freund, "Nonviolent National Defense," p. 16.

85. Sharp, *The Dynamics of Nonviolent Action*, p. 733.

86. Quoted in ibid., p. 738.

87. Sharp, *Power and Struggle*, pp. 88–89; *The Dynamics of Nonviolent Action*, p. 735.

88. Sharp, *The Dynamics of Nonviolent Action*, p. 741.

89. Freund, "Nonviolent National Defense," p. 16.

90. Sharp, *The Dynamics of Nonviolent Action*, pp. 744–55.

91. Freund, "Nonviolent National Defense," p. 16.

92. Sharp, *The Dynamics of Nonviolent Action*, p. 743.

93. Ibid., p. 741.

94. Ibid., p. 754.

95. Sharp, *Making Europe Unconquerable*, p. 152.

96. Sharp, "National Defense Without Armaments," p. 357.

97. Sharp, *Making Europe Unconquerable*, p. 163.

98. Ibid., p. 167.

99. Sommer, *Beyond the Bomb*, p. 91.

100. Sharp, *National Security Through Civilian-Based Defense*, p. 23.

101. Ibid.

102. Sharp, *Making Europe Unconquerable*, p. 175.

103. Sharp, *National Security Through Civilian-Based Defense*, p. 22.

104. Sharp, "National Defense Without Armaments," p. 357; Freund, "Nonviolent National Defense," p. 13.

105. Sharp, "National Defense Without Armaments," p. 357.

106. Ibid.

107. Freund, "Nonviolent National Defense," p. 13.

108. Ibid.

109. Sommer, *Beyond the Bomb*, pp. 97–99.

110. Ibid., p. 77.

111. Adam Roberts, "Civilian Defense Strategy," in Adam Roberts, ed., *Civilian Resistance as a National Defense* (Baltimore: Penguin Books, 1967), p. 253.

112. Sharp, *National Security Through Civilian-Based Defense*, p. 25.

Chapter Eight

1. Gene Sharp, *Making Europe Unconquerable: The Potential of Civilian-Based Deterrence and Defense* (Cambridge, Mass.: Ballinger, 1985), p. 105.

2. Charles Osgood, *An Alternative to War and Surrender* (Champaign: University of Illinois Press, 1962).

3. Ibid., p. 34.

4. Henry Kissinger, "Should We Try to Defend Against Russia's Missiles?" *Washington Post*, 23 September 1984.

5. Anders Boserup, "A Way to Undermine Hostility," *Bulletin of the Atomic Scientists* 44, no. 7 (September 1988): 18.

6. Ibid.

7. Hal Harvey, "Defense Without Aggression," *Bulletin of the Atomic Scientists* 44, no. 7 (September 1988): 12.

8. Stephen Flanagan, "Nonoffensive Defense Is Overrated," *Bulletin of the Atomic Scientists* 44, no. 7 (September 1988): 47.

9. Ibid.

10. Boserup, "Way to Undermine Hostilities,"

11. Ibid., p. 19.

Conclusion

1. Robert Dahl, *Controlling Nuclear Weapons: Democracy Versus Guardianship* (Syracuse, N.Y.: Syracuse University Press, 1985), p. 3.

2. Ibid., p. 5.

3. Quoted in Jay Rosen, "Phantom Public Haunts Nuclear Age," *Bulletin of the Atomic Scientists* 45, no. 5 (June 1989): 16.

4. Ibid., p. 18.

5. Ibid.

6. Ibid.

7. Ibid.

8. Quoted in Joseph S. Nye, Graham Allison, and Albert Carnesale, eds., *Fateful Visions: Avoiding Nuclear Catastrophe* (Cambridge, Mass.: Ballinger, 1988), p. 197.

Appendix

1. See Charles Kegley, Jr., and Eugene R. Wittkopf, "Strategy, Weapons, and War in the Nuclear Age," in Charles W. Kegley, Jr., and Eugene R.

Wittkopf, eds., *The Nuclear Reader: Strategy, Weapons, War* (New York: St. Martin's Press, 1985), pp. 3–7.

2. References have been given in previous chapters. For a good treatment, see John Dewar, Abdul Paliwala, Sol Picciotto, and Matthias Ruete, eds., *Nuclear Weapons, the Peace Movement, and the Law* (New York: Macmillan, 1984).

3. This criticism is developed in detail in Morton H. Halperin, *Nuclear Fallacy: Dispelling the Myth of Nuclear Strategy* (Cambridge, Mass.: Ballinger, 1987).

4. Robert Bowman, "No to Star Wars," in Craig Snyder, ed., *The Strategic Defense Debate* (Philadelphia: University of Pennsylvania Press, 1986), pp. 183–92.

5. R. Sagdeyev, Ye. Velikov, and A. Kokoshin, quoted in Leon Gouré, "The Soviet Strategic Review," *Strategic Review* 15, no. 2 (Spring 1987): 85–87.

6. Jonathan Jacky, "The 'Star Wars' Defense Won't Compute," *The Atlantic*, June 1985, p. 18.

7. Greg Nelson and David Redell, "The Star Wars Computer System," statement before the Subcommittee on Strategic and Theater Nuclear Forces of the Committee on Armed Services, U.S. Senate, Ninety-Ninth Congress, 3, 5 December 1985 (Washington, D.C.: U.S. Government Printing Office, 1985), p. 361.

8. Union of Concerned Scientists, "Star Wars: A Critique," in Kegley and Wittkopf, *Nuclear Reader*, p. 230.

9. Nelson and Redell, "Star Wars Computer System," p. 361.

10. George Will, "Elimination of Nuclear Weapons Is a Mistake," *Washington Post*, 28 June 1986.

11. Ibid.

12. Stephen Budiansky, "One Shot, One Kill: A New Era of 'Smart' Weapons," *U.S. News and World Report*, 16 March 1987, p. 33.

13. Vitaly Shabanov, "Deadlier Conventional War," *Strategic Review* 15, no. 1 (Winter 1987): 89.

14. Robert Tucker, "The Nuclear Debate," *Foreign Affairs* 63, no. 1 (Fall 1984): 17.

15. David Lewis, "Finite Deterrence," working paper (Baltimore: Maryland Center for Philosophy and Public Policy, 1987), p. 34.

Bibliography

Abrahamson, James. "The New Strategic Defense Debate." In Hans Binnen-
dijk, ed., *Strategic Defense in the Twenty-First Century*, pp. 1–9. Washington,
D.C.: Department of State, 1986.
———. Testimony on strategic defense before the Subcommittee on Strategic
and Theater Nuclear Forces of the Committee on Armed Services, U.S.
Senate, Ninety-Ninth Congress. 30 October 1985. Pp. 1–68.
Adelman, Kenneth. "Setting the Record Straight." In Zbigniew Brzezinski,
ed., *Promise or Peril: The Strategic Defense Initiative*. Washington, D.C.:
Ethics and Public Policy Center, 1986.
Allison, Graham. "Testing Gorbachev." *Foreign Affairs* 67, no. 1 (Fall 1988): 18–
32.
Allison, Graham; Carnesale, Albert; and Nye, Joseph, Jr., eds. *Hawks, Doves,
and Owls: An Agenda for Avoiding Nuclear War*. New York: W. W. Norton,
1985.
Altfeld, Michael. "Strategic Defense and the 'Cost-Exchange Ratio.'" *Strategic
Review* 14, no. 4 (Fall 1986): 21–26.
Arkin, William, and Fieldhouse, Richard. *Nuclear Battlefields: Global Links in the
Arms Race*. Cambridge, Mass.: Ballinger, 1985.
Axelrod, Daniel, and Kaku, Michio. *To Win a Nuclear War*. Boston: South End
Press, 1986.
Ball, Desmond. "Targeting for Strategic Deterrence." *Adelphi Paper* 185 (Sum-
mer 1983): 1–46.
Ball, Desmond, and Richelson, Jeffrey, eds. *Strategic Nuclear Targeting*. Ithaca,
N.Y.: Cornell University Press, 1986.
Barash, David P. *The Arms Race and Nuclear War*. Belmont, Calif.: Wadsworth,
1987.
Barnet, Richard. "Real Security: An Alternative Foreign Policy." In Paul Joseph

and Simon Rosenblum, eds., *Search for Sanity: The Politics of Nuclear Weapons and Disarmament*, pp. 561–75. Boston: South End Press, 1984.

Beach, Sir Hugh. "On Improving NATO Strategy." In Andrew Pierre, ed., *The Conventional Defense of Europe: New Technologies and Strategies*, pp. 152–85. New York: Council on Foreign Relations, 1986.

Beckett, Brian. *Weapons of the Future*. London: Orbis, 1982.

Bialer, Seweryn. "Gorbachev and the Soviet Military." *U.S. News and World Report*, 13 March 1989, pp. 40–42.

Binnendijk, Hans, ed. *Strategic Defense in the Twenty-First Century*. Washington, D.C.: Foreign Service Institute of the Department of State, 1986.

Blair, Bruce G. *Strategic Command and Control: Redefining the Nuclear Threat*. Washington, D.C.: Brookings Institution, 1985.

Blair, David. *First and Final War*. Oxford: Oxford University Press, 1986.

Blechman, Barry, ed. *Preventing Nuclear War: A Realistic Approach*. Bloomington: Indiana University Press, 1985.

Bok, Sissela. *A Strategy for Peace: Human Values and the Threat of War*. New York: Pantheon Books, 1989.

Boserup, Anders. "A Way to Undermine Hostility." *Bulletin of the Atomic Scientists* 44, no. 7 (September 1988): 16–19.

Bosma, John. "Arms Control, SDI, and the Geneva Conventions." In Zbigniew Brzezinski, ed., *Promise or Peril: The Strategic Defense Initiative*, pp. 339–63. Washington, D.C.: Ethics and Public Policy Center, 1986.

Bova, Ben. *Assured Survival*. Boston: Houghton Mifflin, 1984.

Bowman, Robert. "No to Star Wars." In Craig Snyder, ed., *The Strategic Defense Debate*, pp. 183–92. Philadelphia: University of Pennsylvania Press, 1986.

Bracken, Paul. *The Command and Control of Nuclear Forces*. New Haven: Yale University Press, 1983.

Brezhnev, Leonid. "Remarks on the Objectives of Soviet Nuclear Strategy." In P. Edward Haley, David M. Keithly, and Jack Merritt, eds., *Nuclear Strategy, Arms Control, and the Future*. Boulder, Colo.: Westview Press, 1985.

Brodie, Bernard. *Strategy in the Missile Age*. Princeton: Princeton University Press, 1959.

Brooks, Frederick. Statement before Subcommittee on Strategic and Theater Nuclear Forces of Committee on Armed Services, U.S. Senate, Ninety-Ninth Congress, 30 October 1985. Washington, D.C.: U.S. Government Printing Office, 1985.

Brown, Thomas; Head, Steve; McGarvy, David; Steiner, Arthur; Wohlstetter, Albert. "The Political-Military Significance of Continuous Terminal Homing." *Background Paper* 31. St. Paul de Vence, France: European–American Institute for Security, Workshop on Improved Technologies in a Changing NATO Strategy, 1976.

Budiansky, Stephen. "One Shot, One Kill: A New Era of 'Smart' Weapons." *U.S. News and World Report* (10 March 1987): 28–35.

———. "The Russians Aren't Coming." *U.S. News and World Report* (27 November 1989): 47–54.

Builder, Carl. "The Prospects and Implications of Non-nuclear Means for Strategic Conflict." *Adelphi Paper* 200 (Spring 1985): 1–35.

————. "Strategic Conflict Without Nuclear Weapons." Report prepared for the Ford Foundation. Santa Monica, Calif.: Rand, 1983.

Bulow, Andreas von. "Defensive Entanglement: An Alternative Strategy for NATO." In Andrew Pierre, ed., *The Conventional Defense of Europe: New Technologies and Strategies*, pp. 112–51. New York: Council on Foreign Relations, 1986.

Bundy, McGeorge. *Danger and Survival: Choices About the Bomb in the First Fifty Years*. New York: Random House, 1988.

————. "Existential Deterrence and Its Consequences." In Douglas MacLean, ed., *The Security Gamble: Deterrence Dilemmas in the Nuclear Age*, pp. 3–13. Totowa, N.J.: Rowman & Allanheld, 1984.

Bunn, Matthew. "Abrahamson Proposes 'Brilliant Pebbles' Space Defense." *Arms Control Today* 19, no. 3 (April 1989): 26–27.

Carter, Ashton; Steinbruner, John; and Zraker, Charles; eds. *Managing Nuclear Operations*. Washington, D.C.: Brookings Institution, 1987.

Catudal, Honore M. *Nuclear Deterrence: Does It Deter?* Bronx, N.Y.: Mansell, 1985.

————. *Soviet Nuclear Strategy from Stalin to Gorbachev: A Revolution in Soviet Military and Political Thinking*. Atlantic Highlands, N.J.: Humanities Press International, 1988.

Chain, General John T. "Strategic Fundamentals." *Air Force Magazine* 70, no. 7 (July 1987): 62–66.

Chirac, Jacques. "Soviet Change and Western Security." *Strategic Review* 17, no. 1 (Winter 1989): 9–15.

Christian Science Monitor. "Constitutional Drama: Washington's Wrangle Over the Meaning of the ABM Treaty." *Christian Science Monitor*, 20 May 1987.

Cimbala, Stephen J. "Soviet 'Blitzkrieg' in Europe: The Abiding Nuclear Dimension." *Strategic Review* 14, no. 3 (Summer 1986): 67–75.

Clark, Ian. *Limited Nuclear War*. Princeton: Princeton University Press, 1982.

————. *Nuclear Past, Nuclear Present: Hiroshima, Nagasaki, and Contemporary Strategy*. Boulder, Colo.: Westview Press, 1985.

Clausewitz, Carl von. *On War*. New York: Penguin Books, 1983.

Clines, Francis X. "U.S. and Soviets Sign Pact to Reduce Risk of War." *New York Times*, 13 June 1989.

Cockburn, Andrew. *The Threat: Inside the Soviet Military Machine*. New York: Random House, 1983.

Coffey, John W. "SDI Makes Moral Sense, Too." *Los Angeles Times*, 25 February 1987.

Cohen, Avner, and Lee, Steven, eds. *Nuclear Weapons and the Future of Humanity*. Totowa, N.J.: Rowman & Allanheld, 1986.

Connell, Jon. *The New Maginot Line*. New York: Arbor House, 1986.

Dahl, Robert. *Controlling Nuclear Weapons: Democracy Versus Guardianship*. Syracuse, N.Y.: Syracuse University Press, 1985.

Daugherty, William; Levi, Barbara; and Von Hippel, Frank. "The Consequences of 'Limited' Nuclear Attacks on the United States." *International Security* 10, no. 4 (Spring 1986): 3–45.

Davis, Lynn. "Limited Nuclear Options: Deterrence and the New American Doctrine," *Adelphi Paper* 121 (Winter 1975–76): 1–22.

Delauer, Richard D. "Emerging Technologies and Their Impact on the Conventional Deterrent." In Andrew Pierre, ed., *The Conventional Defense of Europe: New Technologies and Strategies*, pp. 40–70. New York: Council on Foreign Relations, 1986.

Dewar, John; Paliwala, Abdul; Picciotto, Sol; and Ruete, Matthias; eds. *Nuclear Weapons, the Peace Movement, and the Law*. New York: Macmillan, 1984.

Douhet, Giulio. *Command of the Air*. New York: Coward-McCann, 1942.

Dunn, Martin. "What Are the Effects of the Neutron Bomb?" *Minneapolis Tribune*, 10 March 1982.

Dunnigan, James. *How to Make War*. New York: William Morrow, 1982.

Dyson, Freeman. *Weapons and Hope*. New York: Harper & Row, 1985.

Epstein, Joshua M. "NATO Can Hold Its Own." *New York Times*, 14 December 1986.

———. "NATO Strategy for the 1990's." Statement prepared for the Senate Foreign Relations Committee, 3 October 1985. Washington, D.C.: U.S. Government Printing Office, 1985.

Finnis, John; Boyle, Joseph; and Grisez, Germain. *Nuclear Deterrence, Morality, and Realism*. Oxford: Clarendon Press, 1987.

Fisher, David. *Morality and the Bomb: An Ethical Assessment of Deterrence*. London: Croom Helm, 1985.

Flanagan, Stephen. "Nonoffensive Defense Is Overrated." *Bulletin of the Atomic Scientists* 44, no. 7 (September 1988): 46–48.

Frankel, Ellen; Miller, Fred; Paul, Jeffrey; and Ahrens, John; eds. *Nuclear Rights/Nuclear Wrongs*. Oxford: Basil Blackwell, 1986.

Freedman, Lawrence. *The Evolution of Nuclear Strategy*. New York: St. Martin's Press, 1983.

Freund, Norman. "Nonviolent National Defense." *Journal of Social Philosophy* 13, no. 2 (May 1982): 12–18.

Friedman, Richard S. *Advanced Technology Warfare*. New York: New Harmony Books. 1985.

Gareyev, Makhmut. "The Revised Soviet Military Doctrine." *Bulletin of the Atomic Scientists* 44, no. 10 (December 1988): 30–34.

Garthoff, Raymond. "Soviet Strategic Doctrine." In P. Edward Haley, David M. Keithly, and Jack Merritt, eds., *Nuclear Strategy, Arms Control, and the Future*, pp. 169–79. Boulder, Colo.: Westview Press, 1985.

Gay, William. "Nuclear Discourse and Linguistic Alienation." *Journal of Social Philosophy* 18 no. 2 (Summer 1987): 42–49.

Gerber, Rudolph J., and McAnany, Patrick D., eds. *Contemporary Punishment: Views, Explanations, and Justifications*. Notre Dame, Ind.: University of Notre Dame Press, 1972.

Goodwin, Peter. *Nuclear War: The Facts on Our Survival*. New York: Rutledge Press, 1981.

Gorbachev, Mikhail. "Nuclear Disarmament by the Year 2000." In P. Edward Haley and Jack Merritt, eds., *Strategic Defense Initiative: Folly or Future?* pp. 135–38. Boulder, Colo.: Westview Press, 1986.

———. "The Problem of Mankind's Survival." Speech to the United Nations. *New York Times*, 8 December 1988.

Gordon, Michael. "Reagan's Missile Offer Sets Off Shifting Debate." *New York Times*, 24 October 1986.

Gottfried, Kurt, and Blair, Bruce. *Crisis Stability and Nuclear War.* New York: Oxford University Press, 1988.

Gouré, Leon. "A 'New' Soviet Military Doctrine: Reality or Mirage?" *Strategic Review* 16, no. 3 (Summer 1988): 25–33.

Gray, Colin S. "A Case for Strategic Defense." In P. Edward Haley and Jack Merritt, eds., *Strategic Defense Initiative: Folly or Future?* pp. 81–87. Boulder, Colo.: Westview Press, 1986.

———. "Nuclear Strategy: The Case for a Theory of Victory." In Steven E. Miller, ed., *Strategy and Nuclear Deterrence*, pp. 23–56. Princeton: Princeton University Press, 1984.

———. *Nuclear Strategy and National Style.* Lanham, Md.: Hamilton Press, 1986.

———. "Presidential Directive 59: Flawed but Useful." In Herbert Levine and David Carlton, eds., *The Nuclear Arms Race Debated*, pp. 267–75. New York: McGraw-Hill, 1986.

———. "Targeting Problems for Central War." In Desmond Ball and Jeffrey Richelson, eds., *Strategic Nuclear Targeting*, pp. 171–93. Ithaca, N.Y.: Cornell University Press, 1986.

———. "Victory Is Possible." *Foreign Policy* 39, no. 2 (Summer 1980): 14–27.

Gregg, Richard G. *The Power of Nonviolence.* New York: Schocken Books, 1966.

Griffin, John. "Nuclear Weapons and International Law." In Gwyn Prins, ed., *The Nuclear Crisis Reader*, pp. 154–71. New York: Vintage Books, 1984.

Guthrie, John. "Midgetman Missile." *International Combat Arms*, March 1986, pp. 22–28.

Halperin, Morton. *The Nuclear Fallacy: Dispelling the Myth of Nuclear Strategy.* Cambridge, Mass.: Ballinger, 1987.

Hamilton, Alexander. "The Federalist No. 51." In *The Federalist*. New York: Modern Library, n.d.

Harkabi, Y. *Nuclear War and Nuclear Peace*, trans. Y. Shenkman. Jerusalem: Israel Program for Scientific Translations, 1964.

Harvey, Hal. "Defense Without Aggression." *Bulletin of the Atomic Scientists* 44, no. 7 (September 1988): 12–15.

Healey, Denis. "A Labor Britain, NATO, and the Bomb." *Foreign Affairs* 65, no. 4 (Spring 1987): 716–29.

Heisbourg, François L. "Conventional Defense: An Alternative Strategy for NATO." In Andrew Pierre, ed., *The Conventional Defense of Europe: New Technologies and Strategy*, pp. 71–111. New York: Council on Foreign Relations, 1986.

Holloway, David. "Gorbachev's New Thinking." *Foreign Affairs* 68, no. 1 (1988–89): 66–81.

Hughan, Jessie, and Hinshaw, Cecil. "Toward a Nonviolent National Defense." In Mulford Sibley, ed., *The Quiet Battle*, pp. 316–56. Boston: Beacon Press, 1963.

Jacky, Jonathan. "The 'Star Wars' Defense Won't Compute." *The Atlantic*, June 1985.

Jastrow, Robert. "Missile Defense: Threat and Response." In Zbigniew Brzezinski, ed., *Promise or Peril: The Strategic Defense Initiative*, pp. 143–64.
Washington, D.C.: Ethics and Public Policy Center, 1986.

Johnson, James Turner. *Can Modern War Be Just?* New Haven: Yale University
Press, 1984.

Kahn, Herman. *On Thermonuclear War*. Princeton: Princeton University Press,
1961.

Kanter, Arnold. "An Alliance Perspective." In Zbigniew Brzezinski, *Promise or
Peril: The Strategic Defense Initiative*, pp. 283–306. Washington, D.C.:
Ethics and Public Policy Center, 1986.

Kavka, Gregory S. "Nuclear Deterrence: Some Moral Perplexities." In James
Sterba, ed., *The Ethics of War and Nuclear Deterrence*, pp. 127–38. Belmont,
Calif.: Wadsworth, 1985.

———. "Nuclear Weapons and World Government." *The Monist* 70, no. 3
(Special Issue: The Ethics of Nuclear Warfare, July 1987): 298–315.

Kegley, Charles W., Jr., and Wittkopf, Eugene R. "Strategy, Weapons and War
in the Nuclear Age." In Charles W. Kegley, Jr., and Eugene R. Wittkopf,
eds., *The Nuclear Reader: Strategy, Weapons, War*, pp. 3–7. New York: St.
Martin's Press, 1985.

Kennan, George. "After the Cold War." *New York Times Magazine*, 5 February
1989, pp. 32–33, 38, 58, 64–65.

———. "Just Another Great Power." *New York Times*, 9 April 1989.

Kenny, Anthony. *The Logic of Deterrence*. Chicago: University of Chicago Press, 1985.

Kissinger, Henry. "Should We Try to Defend Against Russia's Missiles?" *Washington Post*, 23 September 1984.

Kolkowicz, Roman, ed. *The Logic of Nuclear Terror*. Boston: Allen and Unwin,
1987.

Kosygin, Alexei N. "Missile Defense: For Saving Lives." In Zbigniew Brzezinski, ed., *Promise or Peril: The Strategic Defense Initiative*, pp. 209–19.
Washington, D.C.: Ethics and Public Policy Center, 1986.

Kull, Steven. *Minds at War: Nuclear Reality and the Inner Conflicts of the Defense
Policymakers*. New York: Basic Books, 1988.

Lackey, Douglas. *Moral Principles and Nuclear Weapons*. Totowa, N.J.: Rowman
& Allanheld, 1984.

———, ed. *Ethics and Strategic Defense*. Belmont, Calif.: Wadsworth, 1988.

———. *The Ethics of War and Peace*. Englewood Cliffs, N.J.: Prentice-Hall, 1989.

Lebow, Richard Ned. *Nuclear Crisis Management*. Ithaca, N.Y.: Cornell University Press, 1987.

Legvold, Robert. "The Revolution in Soviet Foreign Policy." *Foreign Affairs* 68,
no. 1 (Special Issue: America and the World, 1988–89): 82–98.

Lewis, C. S. "The Humanitarian Theory of Punishment." In Rudolph J.
Gerber and Patrick D. McAnany, *Contemporary Punishment: Views, Expla-
nations, and Justifications*, pp. 194–99. Notre Dame, Ind.: University of
Notre Dame Press, 1962.

Lewis, David. "Finite Deterrence." Working Paper. Baltimore: Maryland Center for Philosophy and Public Policy, 1987.

Lifton, Robert J. "Is Hiroshima Our Text?" In Robert J. Lifton, ed., *Indefensible
Weapons*, pp. 38–47. New York: Basic Books, 1982.

Lipton, Richard. "Comments on the Strategic Defense Initiative," statement before Subcommittee on Strategic and Theater Forces of Committee on Armed Services, U.S. Senate, Ninety-Ninth Congress, 30 October 1985. Washington, D.C.: U.S. Government Printing Office, 1985.

MccGwire, Michael. *Military Objectives in Soviet Foreign Policy.* Washington, D.C.: Brookings Institution, 1987.

McNamara, Robert. *Blundering Into Disaster.* New York: Pantheon Books, 1986.

———. "The Military Role of Nuclear Weapons." In Charles W. Kegley, Jr., and Eugene R. Wittkopf, eds., *The Nuclear Reader: Strategy, Weapons, War,* pp. 153–67. New York: St. Martin's Press, 1985.

Maitre, H. Joachim. "Ask the Afghans." *Strategic Review* 17, no. 1 (Winter 1989): 7–8.

Mangone, Gerald J., ed. *The Elements of International Law.* Homewood, Calif.: Dorsey Press, 1967.

Marsh, Gerald E. "U.S. Missiles on Hair Trigger?" *Bulletin of the Atomic Scientists* 45, no. 4 (May 1989): 3.

Martin, Laurence. *Before the Day After: Can NATO Defend Europe?* London: Newnes Books, 1985.

Mason, R. A. "The Non Nuclear Alternative." Paper presented at the United States Air Force War College Nuclear Strategy Symposium, Maxwell Air Force Base, Alabama, 12 September 1987.

Mavrodes, George. "Conventions and the Morality of War." In James Sterba, ed., *Morality in Practice,* pp. 302–11. Belmont, Calif.: Wadsworth, 1984.

Mearsheimer, John. "NATO's Deterrent Posture." Statement prepared for the Senate Foreign Relations Committee, U.S. Senate, Ninety-Ninth Congress, 3 October 1985. Washington, D.C.: U.S. Government Printing Office, 1985.

Meyer, Stephen. "The Sources and Prospects of Gorbachev's New Political Thinking on Security." *International Security* 13, no. 2 (Fall 1988): 124–63.

Morgan, Patrick. *Deterrence: A Conceptual Analysis.* Beverly Hills, Calif.: Sage Publications, 1977.

Nelson, Greg, and Redell, David. "The Star Wars Computer System." Statement before the Subcommittee on Strategic and Theater Nuclear Forces of the Committee on Armed Services, U.S. Senate, Ninety-Ninth Congress, 3–5 December 1985. Washington, D.C.: U.S. Government Printing Office, 1985.

Newhouse, John. *War and Peace in the Nuclear Age.* New York: Alfred A. Knopf, 1989.

Nitze, Paul. "Atoms, Strategy, and Policy." *Foreign Affairs* 34, no. 2 (January 1956): 187–98.

———. "On the Road to a More Stable Peace." In P. Edward Haley and Jack Merritt, eds., *Strategic Defense Initiative: Folly or Future?* pp. 37–41. Boulder, Colo.: Westview Press, 1986.

Nye, Joseph S., Jr. *Nuclear Ethics.* New York: Free Press, 1986.

Nye, Joseph S.; Allison, Graham; Carnesale, Albert; eds. *Fateful Visions: Avoiding Nuclear Catastrophe.* Cambridge, Mass.: Ballinger, 1988.

Odom, William. "Soviet Military Doctrine." *Foreign Affairs* 67, no. 2 (Winter 1988–89): 114–34.

Office of Technology Assessment. *The Effects of Nuclear War.* Washington, D.C.:
    Washington Office of Technology Assessment, 1980.
————. *Strategic Defenses.* Princeton: Princeton University Press, 1986.
Osgood, Charles. 1962. *An Alternative to War and Surrender.* Champaign: Univer-
    sity of Illinois Press, 1962.
Payne, Keith, and Gray, Colin S. "Nuclear Policy and the Defensive Transi-
    tion." *Foreign Affairs* 62, no. 4 (Spring 1984).
Petersen, Phillip, and Trulock, Notra. "A 'New' Soviet Military Doctrine:
    Origins and Implications." *Strategic Review* 16, no. 3 (Summer 1988): 9–
    24.
Pipes, Richard. "Soviet Strategic Doctrine." In P. Edward Haley, David M.
    Keithly, and Jack Merritt, eds., *Nuclear Strategy, Arms Control, and the
    Future*, pp. 169–79. Boulder, Colo.: Westview Press, 1985.
Pond, Elizabeth. "Beyond the 'Bean Count' of Conventional Forces." *Christian
    Science Monitor*, 5 November 1986.
Pringle, Peter, and Arkin, William. *S.I.O.P.: The Secret U.S. Plan for Nuclear War.*
    New York: W. W. Norton, 1983.
Quayle, Dan. "Beyond SALT: Arms Control Built Upon Defenses." *Strategic
    Review* 14, no. 3 (Summer 1986): 9–16.
Quester, George. "Substituting Conventional for Nuclear Weapons: Some
    Problems and Some Possibilities." In Russell Hardin, John Mearsheimer,
    Gerald Dworkin, and Robert Goodin, eds., *Nuclear Deterrence: Ethics and
    Strategy*, pp. 245–66. Chicago: University of Chicago Press, 1985.
Quinn-Judge, Paul. "Soviet Soldiers Are Tongue-tied." *Christian Science Moni-
    tor*, 13 March 1987.
Ramberg, Bennet. "Targeting Nuclear Energy." In Desmond Ball and Jeffrey
    Richelson, eds., *Strategic Nuclear Targeting*, pp. 250–66. Ithaca, N.Y.:
    Cornell University Press, 1986.
Ramsey, Paul. "The Case for Making 'Just War' Possible." In John Bennet, ed.,
    Nuclear Weapons and the Conflict of Conscience, pp. 31–152. London: Butter-
    worth Press, 1962.
Reagan, Ronald. "Address to the Nation on the Strategic Defense Initiative." In
    P. Edward Haley and Jack Merritt, eds., *Strategic Defense Initiative: Folly or
    Future?* pp. 23–24. Boulder, Colo.: Westview Press, 1986.
Rensberger, Boyce. "Computer Bugs Seen as Fatal Flaw in 'Star Wars,' " state-
    ment before Subcommittee on Strategic and Theater Nuclear Forces of
    Committee on Armed Services, U.S. Senate, Ninety-Ninth Congress, 30
    October 1985. Washington, D.C.: U.S. Government Printing Office, 1985.
Reule, Fred, ed. *Dynamic Stability.* Montgomery, Ala.: Air University Press,
    1987.
Richelson, Jeffrey. "Population Targeting and U.S. Strategic Doctrine." In
    Desmond Ball and Jeffrey Richelson, eds., *Strategic Nuclear Targeting*,
    pp. 234–48. Ithaca, N.Y.: Cornell University Press, 1986.
Roberts, Adam. "Civilian Defense Strategy." In Adam Roberts, ed., *Civilian Re-
    sistance as a National Defense*, pp. 249–94. Baltimore: Penguin Books, 1967.
Roberts, Adam, and Guelff, Richard, eds. *Documents of the Laws of War.* Oxford:
    Clarendon Press, 1982.

Rosen, Jay. "Phantom Public Haunts Nuclear Age." *Bulletin of the Atomic Scientists* 6, no. 5 (June 1989): 16–19.

Russett, Bruce. "Counter-Combatant Deterrence: A Proposal." *Survival* 16, no. 3 (Autumn 1974): 31–38.

———. *The Prisoners of Insecurity.* New York: W. H. Freeman, 1984.

Scarry, Elaine. *The Body in Pain: The Making and Unmaking of the World.* New York: Oxford University Press, 1985.

Schell, Jonathan. *The Abolition.* New York: Alfred A. Knopf, 1984.

———. *The Fate of the Earth.* New York: Alfred A. Knopf, 1982.

Schroeer, Dietrich. *Science, Technology and the Nuclear Arms Race.* New York: John Wiley and Sons, 1984.

Sedacca, Sandra. *Up in Arms: A Common Cause Guide to Understanding Nuclear Arms Policy.* Washington, D.C.: Common Cause, 1984.

Shabanov, Vitaly. "Deadlier Conventional War." *Strategic Review* 15, no. 1 (Winter 1989): 87–89.

Sharp, Gene. *Making Europe Unconquerable: The Potential of Civilian-Based Deterrence and Defense.* Cambridge, Mass.: Ballinger, 1985.

———. National Defense Without Armaments." In Charles Betz and Theodore Herman, eds., *Peace and War,* pp. 349–67. San Francisco: W. H. Freeman, 1973.

———. *National Security Through Civilian-Based Defense.* Omaha, Nebr.: Association for Transarmament Studies, 1985.

———. "Philippines Taught Us Lessons of Nonviolence." *Los Angeles Times,* 4 April 1986.

———. *The Politics of Nonviolent Action.* 3 parts. Boston: Porter Sargent, 1973.

Slocombe, Walter. "The Countervailing Strategy." *International Security* 5, no. 4 (Spring 1981): 20–27.

Snow, Donald. *The Nuclear Future: Toward a Strategy of Uncertainty.* Montgomery: University of Alabama Press, 1983.

Sokolovsky, Marshal V. D. "The Nature of Modern War." In P. Edward Haley, David M. Keithly, and Jack Merritt, eds., *Nuclear Strategy, Arms Control and the Future,* pp. 138–46. Boulder, Colo.: Westview Press, 1985.

Sommer, Mark. *Beyond the Bomb: Living Without Nuclear Weapons.* Boston: Expro Press, 1985.

Stimson, Henry. "The Atomic Bomb and the Surrender of Japan." In Edwin Fogelman, ed., *Hiroshima: The Decision to Use the A-Bomb,* pp. 12–24. New York: Charles Scribner's Sons, 1964.

Talensky, Nikolai. "Missile Defense: A Response to Aggression." In Zbigniew Brzezinski, ed., *Promise or Peril: The Strategic Defense Initiative,* pp. 211–19. Washington, D.C.: Ethics and Public Policy Center, 1986.

Taylor, Theodore B. "Third-Generation Nuclear Weapons." *Scientific American* 256 (April 1987): 30–39.

Tobias, Sheila; Goudinoff, Peter; Leader, Stephan; and Leader, Shelah. *The People's Guide to National Defense.* New York: William Morrow, 1982.

Tong, Rosemarie. *Ethics in Policy Analysis.* Englewood Cliffs, N.J.: Prentice-Hall, 1986.

Trachtenberg, David. "A Soviet Ruse." *New York Times,* 23 April 1989.

Trofimenko, Henry. "Counterforce: Illusion or Panacea." *International Security* 5, no. 4 (Spring 1981): 28–48.

Tucker, Robert. "The Nuclear Debate." *Foreign Affairs* 63, no. 1 (Fall 1984): 1–33.

Union of Concerned Scientists. "Star Wars: A Critique." In Charles W. Kegley, Jr., and Eugene R. Wittkopf, eds., *The Nuclear Reader: Strategy, Weapons, War.* New York: St. Martin's Press, 1985.

Ury, William. *Beyond the Hot Line.* Boston: Houghton Mifflin, 1985.

Walzer, Michael. "Deterrence and Democracy." *New Republic,* 2 July 1984, pp. 16–21.

———. *Just and Unjust Wars.* New York: Basic Books, 1977.

Weinberger, Caspar. "U.S. Defense Strategy." *Foreign Affairs* 64, no. 4 (Spring 1986).

Wieseltier, Leon. "When Deterrence Fails." *Foreign Affairs* 63, no. 4 (Spring 1985): 827–47.

Will, George. "Elimination of Nuclear Weapons Is a Mistake." *Washington Post,* 28 June 1986.

Wohlstetter, Albert. "Bishops, Statesmen, and Other Strategists on the Bombing of Innocents." In Charles W. Kegley, Jr., and Eugene R. Wittkopf, eds., *The Nuclear Reader: Strategy, Weapons, War,* pp. 58–76. New York: St. Martin's Press, 1985.

Woolsey, James R. *Nuclear Arms: Ethics, Strategy, Politics.* San Francisco: Institute for Contemporary Studies, 1984.

Wörner, Manfred. "A Missile Defense for NATO Europe." In Zbigniew Brzezinski, ed., *Promise or Peril: The Strategic Defense Initiative.* Washington, D.C.: Ethics and Public Policy Center, 1986.

Ziegler, David. *War, Peace and International Politics.* Boston: Little, Brown, 1981.

Zuckerman, Solly. "Nuclear Fantasies." *New York Review of Books,* 14 June 1984.

———. *Nuclear Illusions and Reality.* New York: Vintage Books, 1982.

Index

ABM Treaty, 51, 80; and strategic defense, 130–134
Abrahamson, James, 120, 125, 126
Action policy, 15–18, 125, 187
Affordability, of policy proposal: costs and benefits, 45–47; economic conversion, 46–47; effects on Soviet economy, 46
Allison, Graham, 3, 4
Altfeld, Michael, 121
Arms control, 118–119; and strategic defense, 132–134

Ball, Desmond, 167
Blair, Bruce, 117
Boserup, Anders, 231
Bosma, John, 132–134, 175, 176
Bracken, Paul, 100
Builder, Carl, 188
Bundy, McGeorge, 80, 81

Chain, Gen. John T., 29
Chirac, Jacques, 8
Cimbala, Stephen, 175, 177
Civil defense, 127–128, 195, 196, 226, 227
Civilian based defense, 199–216, 226, 227
Coffey, John, 134
Cold War, xiii, xv, 3, 12, 98, 199
Containment, 3
Criminal correction models, 62–64; deter-

rence, 55–57; social defense, 59–60; rehabilitation, 61–62; retribution, 60–61
Crisis control measures, 104–108
Crisis instability, 36, 37, 47, 77, 115
Crisis stability, 36, 72, 81, 115, 116, 186, 187
C³I (Crisis, Control, Communications, and Intelligence), 87, 93, 96, 98, 159, 230, 236

Dahl, Robert, 23–27, 45, 233
Damage limitation, 17, 49, 94, 187
De-escalation, 85, 90
Deontological ethics, 37–38, 111, 152, 209, 216. *See also* Morality
Deterrence-only, 73–83. *See also* Deterrence policy, existential *and* as mutual assured destruction
Deterrence-plus, 83–93, 140. *See also* Deterrence policy, as countervailing strategy *and* as prevailing strategy
Deterrence policy: communication and, 67; as countervailing strategy, 87–91, 228, 229, 241–244; credibility of, 67–68; criticism of, 239–244; as domestic theory, 58–59; existential, 36, 80–83, 227, 228, 230; extended, 13–14, 73; finite, 76; intrawar, 86, 89, 91, 93; and will,

293

Deterrence policy (*cont.*)
67–68; as mutual assured destruction, 16, 17, 74–80, 239–241; and
power, 67–68; premises of, 66; as
prevailing strategy, 91–98; prewar,
86, 89; rationality and, 69; requirements of, 67–69
Disaster avoidance: interpreted in terms of
magnitude, 54; interpreted in
terms of probability of failure, 54–
55
Domestic analogy, xiv, 57–65; criticisms
of, 57, 235–238; and nuclear deterrence, 69–73; and rehabilitation,
193–224; and retribution, 147–148;
and social defense, 110–112; value
of, 57, 235, 238
Dyson, Freeman, 20, 22, 23, 128

Einstein, Albert, 126, 236
Emerging technologies, 170–173, 178
Enhanced deterrence. *See* Deterrence-
plus
Escalation control, 90, 155, 163, 164, 168
Escalation dominance, 92–93

Feasibility: operation, 44; scientific, 43–
44; technical, 44–45
First strike, 17, 19, 35, 47, 76, 82, 109,
114, 115, 117, 159, 229
First use, 4, 11, 41, 49, 144, 170, 231
Fisher, David, 150
Flexible response, 41, 163, 170, 210

Gareyev, Mikhmut, 6
Garthoff, Raymond, 52
Geneva Conventions, 42, 43, 133, 142
Glasnost, 13, 22, 27, 95, 154, 159
Gorbachev, Mikhail, 6, 7, 175
Gouré, Leon, 7, 49
Gray, Colin, 93, 95, 96, 97, 112, 114
Guardianship, 21–22, 23, 33

Hague Conventions, 42, 142, 166
Hamilton, Alexander, 27

Ikle, Fred, 184
Immunity of noncombatants, 132, 133,
134, 144, 149, 154, 156, 164, 165
Inadvertent nuclear war, xiv, 11, 98, 129,
194

Instrumental coherence, 35–37
Intermediate nuclear forces, 5, 179, 180

Johnson, James Turner, 155, 165, 166, 180
Just war tradition, 134, 141–147

Kant, Immanuel, 38, 115, 157, 192, 209,
216
Kennan, George, 3, 4, 208
Kissinger, Henry, 229

Launch on warning, 11, 115, 117, 234, 266
n.1
Law and nuclear policy, 40–43
Laws of war: rationale for, 142–144; and
strategic defense, 132
Lebow, Richard Ned, 102
Legvold, Robert, 4, 5, 6
LeMay, Curtis, 19, 20
Linguistic alienation, 28–29

McNamara, Robert, 74, 75, 110, 227, 229
Marxism-Leninism, 7, 50, 52
Mavrodes, George, 149
Mearsheimer, John, 175, 176
Meyer, Stephen, 48
Mill, John Stuart, 39
Modernization, 83
Morality, xvi, xvii, 34, 55, 56; deontologi-
cal view of, 37–38; and guardian-
ship thesis, 23–24; teleological
view of, 39–40
Morgan, Patrick, 77

NATO, 4, 7, 41, 105, 166, 180, 187, 231;
and emerging technologies, 170–
173; and strategic defense, 135–
137
Neutron bomb, 165–168
New Soviet thinking, xiv, 4–8, 28, 30, 33,
144, 194, 200, 235; on defensive
defense, 6, 7, 48, 137, 197; and
policy evaluation, 51; on reasonable sufficiency, 51; on war prevention, 6
Nitze, Paul, 16, 96, 97, 119
Nonnuclear weapons, as substitute for nuclear weapons, 169–184
Nonprovocative defense, 6, 229–331
Nuclear coercion, 13, 76, 199
Nuclear defense policy, xvi; as action pol-

icy, 15–18, 125, 187; as declaratory
policy, 15–18, 37, 81, 125, 158;
checks and balances on, 27; democracy and, 12, 18–31, 21, 22–
28, 45; forces of, 14–15; and individual freedom, 12, 13; fundamental question of, 9–10, 13; and
morality, 23–24; primary objective
of, 12–14; and risk assessment, 26,
27, 53–55; secrecy and, 15, 16, 18,
19; strategy of, 14
Nye, Joseph, 34

Osgood, Charles, 227–228

Pacifists, 143, 146
Perestroika, 7, 13, 22, 46, 175
Plato, 23, 27
Policy impoverishment, 28–29
Preemption, 49, 87, 98, 118, 159, 194
Presidential Directive, 159, 90–91
Prevention of nuclear war: and negative
control of nuclear weapons, 102–
104; through permissive action
links, 99–101; and positive control
of nuclear weapons, 103–104;
through two-person rule, 99
Principle of culpability: application to military policy, 148–150; definition of,
148
Principle of proportionality: application to
military policy, 161–163; definition
of, 148
Pure deterrence. *See* Deterrence-only

Quester, George, 181

Ramsey, Paul, 150
Reagan, Ronald, 30, 109–110, 114, 228
Realists, 143, 146
Rehabilitation policy, 11–12, 61–62, 63,
64, 191–224; criticisms of, 250–
252; and accommodation, 213–
215; and civilian-based defense,
199–216; and conversion, 209–213;
and corrective measures, 198–208;
and nonviolent coercion, 215–216;
and preventive measures, 192–198;
and transarmament, 199
Retribution policy, 11, 60–61, 63, 64,
147–190; criticisms of, 247–250;

and just war tradition, 141–148;
and principle of culpability, 148–
150; and principle of proportionality, 161–163
Rommel, Erwin, 143
Russett, Bruce, 158–160, 185

Scarry, Elaine, 152–153
Schell, Jonathan, 23, 74, 75, 77
Schlesinger, James, 86, 163
Sharp, Gene, 199–216, 226
Slocombe, Walter, 87, 88
Social defense policy, 59–60, 61, 109–139;
ambiguity of, 112–119; and active
defense, 122–126; and passive de-
fense, 126–128; criticisms of, 244–
247
Soviet nuclear policy, xv; as purely defen-
sive, 50–53, 118, 137; as victory
strategy, 48–50
Soviet nuclear threat, xiii, xiv, 10, 11, 12
Strategic defense initiative (SDI, Star
Wars), 11, 18, 30, 43, 64, 109–139.
See also Social defense policy

Targeting strategy: countercombatant,
159–160; counterforce, 52, 75, 80,
94, 146, 188, 230; countervalue,
75, 80, 184; decapitation, 96, 155;
flexible, 90–91; focused on Soviet
state, 94–97
Teleological ethics, 39–40
Third-generation nuclear weapons, 168–
169

Unacceptable damage, 75
Unauthorized use of nuclear weapons, 98–
90
Unilateral disarmament, 186, 194, 195,
196, 198, 210
Utilitarianism, 39–40, 66, 111, 192

Walzer, Michael, 18, 19, 33, 57, 146
Warsaw Treaty Organization, 52, 170, 211
Weinberger, Caspar, 164
Wieseltier, Leon, 83–84
World government, 231–232
Worst case analysis, 170, 171

Zuckerman, Solly, 20

44.95